NONVIOLENCE

Social and Psychological Issues

V.K. Kool
State University
of New York
Utica, NY

UNIVERSITY
PRESS OF
AMERICA

Lanham • New York • London

Library of Congress Cataloging-in-Publication Data

Nonviolence : social and psychological issues /
[edited by] V.K. Kool.
p.   cm.
Includes bibliographical references.
1. Nonviolence—Congresses. 2. Peace—Congresses.
I. Kool, Vinod K.
HM278.N673   1993   303.6'1—dc20   93–25515 CIP

ISBN 0–8191–9231–7 (cloth : alk. paper)
ISBN 0–8191–9232–5 (pbk. : alk. paper)

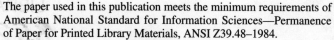

This book is dedicated to:

My parents, who taught me
    justice and compassion,
Professor Kenneth Boulding, who inspired me
    to work on nonviolence,
My mentors, Professor Michael Posner
    and Professor Hari Asthana,
My wife and two sons,
My brothers and sister,
And all my students, with whom I
    share knowledge

Contents

Preface

The subject of nonviolence has a legitimate place in the field of psychology. However, it is very disheartening to note that the textbook writers in the field of social psychology have virtually overlooked the topics of nonviolence and peace and have instead simply focused on the issues of aggression and violence. Recent books on applied social psychology devote space to new fields like law, health, environment, religion, etc., but ignore reference to nonviolence. Consequently, this book intends to fill the gap existing in the psychological literature.

The impetus to the understanding of psychology of nonviolence emerged from social sciences like political science, sociology, history, etc., a development which has contributed to its multidimensional growth--from broad areas like international relations to narrow areas like cognitive schema of nonviolent individuals. The members of the American Psychological Association realized in 1990, albeit very late, that it was time to establish a division of Peace Psychology, and that they can no longer afford to ignore policy issues on peace and nonviolence.

This book is an outcome of a symposium on nonviolence conducted at the SUNY Institute during the summer, 1992. Although not declared as an official celebration for the Silver Jubilee of the Institute, the event was deliberately kept close to the end of the celebration. We were delighted to have Professor Kenneth Boulding deliver the key-note address, *Nonviolence in the 21st Century*, on May 21, 1992, and provide a chapter for this book shortly before his death. Although the community of scholars and activists will remember him as one of the giants in the field who left a permanent mark on all of us, his presence on all three days of the symposium was a rare experience of inspiration to the delegates. We will miss the scholarly guidance of this great man who blended his academic life with concerns for people in every corner of the world. I agree with Professor Olson's comment that he was "half Milton Friedman and half Mahatma Gandhi" (New York Times, March 20, 1993).

The contributors in this book represent several domains of psychology of nonviolence--from international relations to psychometric and laboratory studies--with the overall effort to offer an empirical base for the psychology of nonviolence. The reader will notice that the chapters cover a wide range of topics: theoretical approaches (Kool), developmental changes (McConnell, et. al.), measurement (Sen), global and community issues (Schwebel, Wessells, Wagner, and Nagata), feminist debates (Woehrle), rules of war (Mann), myths (Britton), overview and taxonomy (Blumberg), and conceptual issues (Harris, Presbey, and Joseph). Additionally, the reader will find stimulating ideas on the social and psychological issues concerning training in and education of nonviolence (see chapters contributed by Herman, Coy, Wronka, and Johnson).

It has been generally observed that maintaining a unified theme and direction in any edited book is a difficult task. My feelings were not different but the experience of sharing our work and the coordination which ultimately led to the production of this book have been a great personal experience for me. I think that the reviewers, who have very kindly helped me in judging the quality of the manuscripts, will appreciate the improvements that were made as a result of their critical comments.

I express my gratitude to President Dr. Peter Cayan and Vice President Dr. Shirley Van Marter of our Institute for encouraging me to host the symposium and providing material support for the event. The College Foundation managed the symposium under the able guidance of Mr. Milton Smith. Help received from Ms. Dawn Farry (popularly called "Mom" by the delegates at the symposium), Mr. Michael DeCicco, Ms. Adrianne Hessler, Mr. Jay Bramer and Ms. Elizabeth Elle was appreciated by all of us. I would like to express my thanks to my colleagues at the Psychology Department, the School of Arts and Sciences, and the Institute of Technology, and to the delegates, including Dr. David Hanson (SUNY at Potsdam) and Dr. Louis Kriesberg (Syracuse University), for introducing the speakers and helping me manage the symposium. Support received from Ms. Margerie Campbell, Ms. Dawn Kloczkowski and Mr. Bob Stabler was greatly appreciated in organizing the symposium and preparing material for the book. Ms. Lori Munger worked extremely hard to meet the deadline for delivering the manuscript to the publisher. I appreciate her dedication.

April 30, 1993

V.K. Kool
SUNY, Utica, New York

CHAPTER 1

Toward a Theory of the Psychology of Nonviolence

V. K. Kool

Psychologists prefer to use the word "aggression" over "violence" because aggression is usually described in the context of individual behavior, whereas violence is commonly used in an institutional or a group context. This difference in the approach, according to Groebel and Hinde (1989), leads to a failure of significant contributions so far to our understanding of major policy issues. According to Siann (1988), prominent researchers in the field of human aggression avoid using the word "violence" in their books. As a result, leading psychologists have played only a minor role on a vital social problem like violence. In this chapter I will show how the gap between the use of terms like violence and aggression becomes less significant when we view these concepts from a new perspective, that is, the psychology of nonviolence.

Psychologists have also neglected their rich heritage in the field of nonviolence, an area in which they could have contributed very significantly. For instance, the work of William James on memory and emotion was explored in depth by psychologists, but his contribution in the field of nonviolence remained unknown. Despite current ignorance about his work, according to Professor Lynd (1966) of Yale University, the contribution of William James in the area of nonviolence was second only to Thoreau's.

In his famous essay, "The Moral Equivalent of War," William James (1966; first published in 1910) emphasized that people in the helping professions, for example, physicians, promote positive values of our society. In his book, "Talks to Teachers," he wrote, "The expression itself comes back to us ..." (p. 41, 1958), and this statement supported his notion that behavioral expression of people in the helping professions served as a model to mirror the values of a society.

If we look at the history of psychology during the past 50 years, we find that two categories of experimental psychologists made an attempt to analyze nonviolence. In the first category are included those who were mainly concerned with laboratory research on animals and/or human beings. Tolman (1942) worked in the area of learning and cognition but at the same time, as an activist, addressed issues concerning peace. Although his laboratory work did not show how the research was related to war, he published the book, "Drives Toward War" (1942). The experimental psychologists in the second category were more enthusiastic about addressing the issues of violence and offered practical solutions. Osgood's GRIT model (1962) serves as a good example of this category of scholars. In short, while some experimental psychologists have been engaged in the study of nonviolence, the growth of the psychology of nonviolence has remained a very piecemeal exercise in the history of experimental psychology.

Among those psychologists who pursued nonexperimental approaches to study nonviolence, three groups of psychologists figure prominently. In the first category were humanistic psychologists like Maslow (1954) and May (1972) who investigated the personality patterns of nonviolent individuals with their "soft boiled" approach. Obviously, in the emerging tradition of "hard boiled" psychology, they constituted a very weak influence and could not convince psychologists that there was a serious need for research in this area.

The second group consisted of those who pursued a psychoanalytic approach. Erikson's work (1958, 1969) represents the best example in this category. He analyzed the behavior patterns of Gandhi and King based on their childhood experiences and development of identity.

Lastly, the cognitive approaches emerged out of the limitations of other approaches. Kohlberg's (1976) analysis of moral judgment and postulation of higher stages of moral development was perhaps the best background work for the growth of the psychology of nonviolence. Although his elaborate method of analysis was not acceptable to many researchers, it gave impetus to cross-cultural research as well as to a need for applying a refined method to study moral judgments and the behavior of individuals.

A difficult and multidimensional concept like nonviolence is not easy to define. Sharp (1979) defined nonviolence as "...noninjury in thought, word, and deed to all forms of life" (p. 134). This definition represents an ideal view of nonviolence. In a typical sense, individuals belonging to Buddhist and Quaker groups seem to represent an ideal view of nonviolence. Nonacceptance of force, the use of compassion and tolerance against their opponents, and respect for all forms of life highlight their behavior and attitudes. Such individuals are said to follow *principled* nonviolence.

On the other hand, we also find individuals who do not necessarily adopt principled forms of nonviolence but practice it with some degree of imperfection and inconsistency. Individuals in this category do not adopt nonviolence as a precondition or corollary but use it as a *technique* to resolve conflicts. According to Sharp (1979, p. 276), such individuals, as a matter of their training and experience, use noncooperation, civil disobedience, self punishment, etc., to demonstrate that nonviolence is a better alternative than violence and that the society will not interpret their behavior as cowardice. In some situations, seemingly nonviolent individuals may use violence if such an action is considered appropriate by them.

In a typical psychological sense, it is easier to understand nonviolent individuals in their principled form than those who use nonviolence as a technique. According to Flanagan (1991), the *tzaddik* of Judaism and the Buddhists try always to do what is right and remain ethically exemplary, for example, using great compassion, humility, and so on. They show "... a set of excellences, or a worthy personality type ..." (p. 4). As a consequence, they are seen as saints who are "guided by a unitary moral principle--a general-purpose moral algorithm suitable for solving all moral problems in all domains" (p. 6). Unfortunately, when we study the lives of Gandhi, King and others, their expressions do not seem to conform to a unitary moral principle. For instance, the way Gandhi treated his wife, Kasturba, has been widely criticized (Howard, 1990). In short, saints also show ordinary human flaws but they are more easily understood when they maintain a general purpose moral principle.

The study of the psychology of nonviolence becomes an interesting topic as we observe that the components of a nonviolent personalty do not interact consistently to predict nonviolent behavior. Cultural and situational variations contribute to the differences in beliefs and expressions of nonviolent behavior. It is contended here that the psychology of nonviolence can be a subject of research in much the same way as psychologists studied successfully the concept of love--another multidimensional concept involving several sets of psychological structures. Although it is not easy to define love, several psychologists have attempted to describe its nature in the form of combinations of psychological characteristics. Sternberg (1986) found that the varying combinations of passion, intimacy and commitment, though each one independently did not constitute love, at their combined high and low levels reflected different forms of love. Using a similar model, it is not difficult to understand the concept of nonviolence as reflected in the nature of interrelationships of (1) aggression, (2) moral concerns and (3) power (see Figure 1).

Aggression

Aggression, according to Geen (1990), is "the delivery of noxious stimulation to another person with the intent of harming that person, and in the expectation that the aversive stimulus will reach its destination" (p. 28). Intention to harm another individual is the key element in any form of aggressive behavior. Because it is not easy to study intention in controlled conditions, psychologists have remained unclear in uniformly describing various motives in different forms of aggressive behavior.

Certain acts like war are categorized, and they are referred to as *acts of violence*. While performing such acts, the aggressor uses method(s), usually with some sort of social approval or a standard practice, of dealing with other people to achieve a desired outcome. On the other hand, *a violent act*, like kicking a chair, needs to be judged exclusively from the intention of an individual. Such acts may be purely descriptive and can be performed without violence on other individuals. One may say that acts that are not acts of violence and yet can be performed violently constitute violent acts. Such acts represent intrinsically preferred

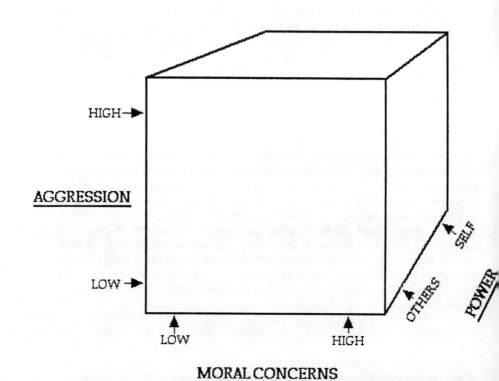

FIG. 1. A THREE DIMENSIONAL VIEW OF NONVIOLENCE

orientation, say values or learning, which exhibit the intentions of an individual. It should be noted here that the difference between a violent act and an act of violence is not merely semantic but represents the difference between the conceptualized categories with perceived social norms and sanctions and those not necessarily categorized but are intrinsic orientations or intentions of an individual. The aforesaid classification of aggressive behavior has a cognitive basis which may be also illustrated in a historical context. For example, when we say, "colored people" it implies degradation and is offensive, but the expression "people of color" does not generate a similar negative attitude. Analysis of acts of violence and violent acts show how violence is represented in our cognitive system.

Let's now translate the above classification in the context of nonviolent behavior. Acts of nonviolence, being categorical in nature, refer to those acts which are knowingly and willfully used to *substitute* for violence. Such acts are designed to communicate that an alternative to violence exists and that a goal can be achieved without inflicting injury. In this sense, nonviolent behavior refers to adoption of a method to achieve a goal without doing any harm to the adversary. Techniques of nonviolence like sit-ins and obstruction are typical forms of nonviolent behavior. On the other hand, acts that are not "acts of nonviolence" may still be called "nonviolent acts." When I asked students in my aggression and nonviolence course and those in social psychology to cite an example of a nonviolent act, they were unable to provide an example of a nonviolent act. On the other hand, they did understand that, as in a violent act, the nonviolent act would also involve an intrinsic orientation to produce an act but, or course, without violence. I wondered why the students failed to illustrate nonviolent acts, but they had no trouble explaining acts of violence, violent acts, or acts of nonviolence (see Table 1).

TABLE 1

Agreement levels on acts of violence and nonviolence, a violent act and a nonviolent act.

Act of violence	Act of nonviolence
war: 100% agreement	sit-in: 100% agreement
Violent act	Nonviolence act
kicking a chair: 100% agreement	caring for animals: 30% agreement

----

The problem in conceiving nonviolent acts as an exclusive category is that it is not highly salient to most individuals compared to acts of violence, violent acts and acts of nonviolence, for they all require deviation from normative patterns of behavior. War, kicking a chair, and sit-in--each illustrating these latter categories-- are uncommon events which involve distinct efforts on the part of individuals. Nonviolent acts are less salient because they are normative patterns of our behavior

(Kool, 1992a). Nurturing young children and caring for very old people are socially desired activities in which most of us are engaged. Such patterns of behavior become salient only upon the breakdown of norms. In other words, success in nurturing young children is not described as a nonviolent act but failure to do so constitutes a violent act. When parents abuse their children physically, we call them violent parents, but if they take care of them as usually we rarely describe their acts as nonviolent acts!

As described in the beginning of this chapter, William James (1966) presented a classic work on nonviolence. He expressed the need to highlight the role of priests and medical people because their work would actively demonstrate the futility of violence. In essence, he was emphasizing that if qualities and behavior associated with the role of helping professionals are not highlighted in a community, components of nonviolent acts will appear less salient.

The debate between those who hold a genetic view of aggression and those who regard it as some form of learned behavior is very well known, but very few people will disagree that aggression has survival value. All those who believe in violence and those who do not may use violence in a given situation. Gandhi did not rule out violence completely and believed that his principle of nonviolence was not the creed of a coward but that of a strong human being who could look into the eyes of his adversary and make him/her understand that an alternative to violence is a superior method to solve a conflict (Iyer, 1983).

All human beings, violent or nonviolent, meet their survival problems with a mixture of force: minimal in some cases, intermediary in most cases, and maximum in the remaining cases. Behavior of violent and nonviolent individuals, therefore, may be represented on a continuum (see Figure 1), a viewpoint we reinforced while developing a forced-choice test of nonviolence, popularly known as the NVT (Kool and Sen, 1984). In this test a subject is presented with several subtly contrasting pairs in which endorsement of one is postulated to indicate nonviolent orientation while the other represents violent orientation. This test is designed to show that the violent individual readily injures others, takes revenge, and flares up with instigation in sharp contrast to nonviolent individuals who adopt a rational approach. Lack of self-control is the essence of a violent individual's behavior in contrast to self-control or withdrawal by a nonviolent individual under similar conditions. Here is an item of the NVT for the purpose of illustration:

> #1.   A car driving through a parking lot splashes water on you. You feel like
>   a.   making him (the driver) apologize and pay for the damages.
>   b.   telling him to be more careful in the future.

Other items of the NVT refer to various situations involving a variety of psychological components commonly associated with nonviolent behavior: self-control, anti-punitiveness, forbearance, and inequality of justice. Factor analysis of the NVT scale items lends support to the existence of such factors (Kool and Keyes,

1990). The NVT showed a very strong negative correlation (-.44) with the Buss-Durkee scale of aggression on the samples used in the USA and abroad. In a recent study Kool and Keyes (1990) found the following significant negative correlations between the NVT and the subscales of Buss-Durkee: assault (-.51), indirect aggression (-.23), irritability (-.30), negativism (-.34), verbal aggression (-.28), resentment (-.30), and suspicion (-.43).

A psychological theory explaining the behavior of violent and nonviolent individuals should allow predictions regarding their behavior in various situations. It is proposed here that the expression of violent or nonviolent behavior involves awareness of the consequences of behavior. In his model of aggression and nonaggression, Goldstein (1986) proposed the significance of long term and situational factors in shaping the behavior of individuals. In the first category he included the long term factors which are norm-based, refer to the beliefs of individuals, and develop on the basis of selective reinforcements in society. A typical example of a long term factor facilitating aggressive behavior is war. However, the same individual also learns not to aggress in a church which is an example of long term nonaggressive behavior. The implication of Goldstein's model for our purpose is that if an individual refuses to aggress both in a church and in a war, he will be at the lowest end of the continuum in Figure 1.

In the second category Goldstein included situational factors associated with aggression and nonaggression. According to him, the presence of weapons increases the probability of aggression, while the presence of police officers reduces the probability of aggression. In her study Sen (1981) reported that the violent subjects, that is, those scoring low on the NVT, were more aggressive upon being annoyed than those in the nonviolent group, that is, those scoring high on the NVT (For details, see Sen's chapter in this book). The idea presented here is that while psychologists may continue to debate on the use of different words like "nonaggression," "nonviolence," "peace," or "Ahimsa," it is possible to grade human aggression on a continuum, and that it is possible to manipulate situational and long term factors to determine the nature and extent of nonaggressive behavior of individuals in an empirical setting.

In the foregoing discussion on the relationship between aggression and the psychology of nonviolence, I made an attempt to explain the difference between categorized acts, that is, acts of violence/nonviolence, and non-categorized acts, that is, violent/nonviolent acts, and showed how they are differently represented in the structures of our knowledge. It is this knowledge that shapes the promotion of or alternatives to violence. Second, I believe that the psychology of nonviolence cannot develop by denying the survival value of aggression. Generally speaking, all forms of aggressive behavior may be represented on a continuum. Finally, I propose that all communities need to emphasize those cues that are salient in the acts of nonviolence and nonviolent acts, a generic idea William James presented in his essay, "The Moral Equivalent of War."

Moral dimensions of nonviolence

Prevention of violence often calls for moral concerns which may be due to social concerns or self-worth or a combination of both. It grows out of interaction with the members of a society. Although psychologists have reported the stages of moral development of individuals, recent developments in moral psychology show that both personality psychologists and social psychologists need to integrate their efforts. An individual may have several virtues but they may not be useful for social purposes. Refusing to participate in a war may be considered a personal virtue, but what if it brings defeat, death and humiliation to the members of the group?

The psychology of nonviolence is essentially based on the components of moral personality. The moral concerns of individuals are mediated by a complex set of psychological dispositions. It is not easy to find an ethic guided by a single principle which integrates the social and individual good. And yet we tend to look at the common components of a moral personality in the form of maturity in resolving conflicts within and without the framework of social norms, something of a personal ethic over and above the commonly accepted modes of behavior in many situations (Flanagan, 1991). At this point, moral psychology as an area of empirical research becomes an uphill task for a psychologist who may discover that moral judgments, moral behavior and moral feelings may not necessarily lead to the same conclusions.

Moral judgment and behavior are supposed to be governed by the moral rules which are based on moral reasoning. At least this is the stand most psychologists have taken to form an empirical base of psychological research. For example, beginning with the studies by Piaget (1932), psychologists have argued that a pattern of rules develops in the moral reasoning of all children and that these rules become more harmonious, autonomous and independent with change in age and social interaction.

I believe that five major trends in the growth of moral psychology may help us in the understanding of behavior and judgments of nonviolent individuals.

Piaget's contribution

First, Piaget (1932) focused on the rules children follow in their interaction with other people and his studies led him to conclude that, as compared to the first stage of moral development in which rules are considered as unchanging properties of the world, the second stage shows awareness of children in judging an actor's intentions. As described earlier, intention is a key element in judging aggressive behavior because even young children use a wide variety of cues to judge the intention of an aggressor. Nelson (1980) reported that kindergarten children used facial expression of the transgressors to judge the intentions involved in a harmful act. When a mother is dusting a doll, a three-year-old child may misunderstand her mother's behavior as punishment to the doll for not being clean. The child is likely to say, "Mom, don't beat her. She can't take a bath." Every child, then, becomes a nonviolent individual as soon as s/he develops awareness of intentions and rules involved in an act.

Piaget made two major contributions in the field of moral psychology. First, development of rules helps a child make a conceptual adjustment to the environment. His observation of children's behavior led him to postulate that children have a system of mental structures which evolve in a series of developmental stages. Second, he provided an empirical, albeit nonexperimental, base for the study of intentions which had no place in the rigorous behavioristic psychology. Although Piaget's theory faded in the 1960s and 1970s owing to its failure to identify the age levels involved in the judgement of intentionality, it has returned to show us once again that rules are the essence of morality and to emphasize that the moral interpretation of events in a child's mind is "bathed in rules." Recent research using simulation techniques to investigate how individuals use moral rules proves that Piaget was several decades ahead of his time.

Kohlberg's stages of moral development

The second major impact for the understanding of moral judgments and behavior was made by Kohlberg (1976) who believed that a moral person is one who reasons with, and acts on the basis of, principles of justice and fairness. Using imaginary cases like the Heinz dilemma in which Heinz's wife is dying but the pharmacist would not lower the cost of a drug, Kohlberg cited moral development at three levels, preconventional, conventional, and postconventional, explaining how each one of the two stages at a level is characterized by a shift from external to internal control of behavior. Although the stage 6 at level III represents the highest growth of moral development, it has remained an elusive, ideal stage in Kohlberg's system because no case has been found in this category. The stage 5 at level III characterizes the next highest level of moral development in which fewer than 10 percent of the individuals entered only after about 20 years of age (Colby, et al., 1983). I wonder at this point what would be the nature of aggression of those individuals who belong to this category.

There are two examples for moral reasoning at each stage in the Kolhbergian system: one that supports Heinz's theft of the drug and the other that he should not do it at all. I believe that subjects who adhere to nonviolence in its principles form and reach the Stage 5 are not likely to use violence to steal the drug. On the other hand, those who will endorse stealing the drug and are at the Stage 5 may use aggression directed either at the pharmacist in a controlled form or upon themselves in the form of hunger strike or other self-punishment methods. In any case, no one in the Stage 5 is expected to endorse heightened aggression because it may save Heinz's wife but may cost the life of the pharmacist.

It is reasonable to argue here that there is no such thing as an overall moral personality, because all individuals, highly moral or ordinary, do not have similar experiences or socio-moral environments. Parents tell us not to steal but they do not normally teach us what to do in a Heinz type of situation, that is, how to get medicine for a sick wife at a time when one can't pay for it. In short, confronting individuals with moral problems may not be the only diagnostic test of moral personality because adhering to a single set of virtues is not the only way to describe a moral person. The relationship of nonviolence and morality, then, becomes a matter of one's cultural learning and a compromise between one's personal ideal and his/her social ideal. At an advanced stage of moral development, people often think what is right for them may not be right for the community. Many pacifists during World War II debated if any war could be called a "just war" and reluctantly participated in it. They were, I am sure, in the Stage 5 of Kohlberg's analysis and believed that Hitler's genocide was impossible to stop without war, although personally they remained opposed to war.

Like Piaget, Kohlberg believed that a child does not passively learn moral rules but tends to restructure them in terms of his/her experiences. However, he differed from Piaget in the sense that an individual's moral development is not a matter of two stages but rather it is a long, continued and complex process which expresses itself in several stages. Describing moral development is like teaching rules of grammar. After learning the rules of a language, an individual can construct simple sentences. However, s/he will comprehend the deeper levels of the language only when s/he can express the same idea in different sentences. I believe that the interaction of moral judgments and nonviolence refers to a similar type of deep structure to embody alternatives to violence.

Recently, Flanagan (1991) argued that the presence of only six categories in Kohlberg's theory do not provide enough space for explaining moral development. Patterns of moral reasoning and the behavior of Gandhi, King, Muste, Tutu and several others during this century alone will need a variety of moral categories to mirror the relationship between nonviolence and moral development.

Gilligan: Caring and justice perspectives

The third major contributor in the relationship between nonviolence and moral judgment and behavior is Carol Gilligan (1982) who, by pointing out the flaws in Kohlberg's analysis, like the lack of female samples, proceeded to show that moral reasoning alone is not enough to understand moral development. Instead of focusing on the justice perspective, she argued for a caring perspective that sees people in terms of their connectedness and concern for others. For her, moral requirements were not merely confined to fairness and justice but emerged from the particular needs of people with whom we connect. She produced empirical data to show that women, more than men, orient to ethics of care which make them function "in a different voice". According to Flanagan (1991), Gilligan created two moral psychologies--one for men and the other for women.

The main argument for offering a hypothesis of two distinct voices is that all children experience inequality and attachment during the course of development. In a neo-Freudian account, Gilligan highlighted the role of powerlessness and inequality at the one end, and attachment, at the other end, a situation which prepared the groundwork for two moral versions--of justice and care. As children get older, they tend to develop a self concept which is reinforced by their gender roles. Because in most cases the mother is the caregiver in the family, girls, more intensely than boys, learn to value empathy, connectedness and interpersonal communication.

Gilligan believes that the two ethics--of justice and caring--are competing in nature and tend to divide an individual much like a vase-face illusion. Faced with a moral dilemma, says Gilligan, an individual will oscillate between issues of justice and care orientations. Is there a way to unify the two perspectives? As far as Gilligan is concerned the answer is negative. When she started her work by asking the question, "What does morality mean to you?" and found that the males and females differed in their orientations, she concluded that a new dimension of psychology in relation to ethics was discovered (Flanagan, 1991). Avenues of the relationship between the psychology of nonviolence and morality will show that although Gilligan established a landmark for the psychology of nonviolence by concentrating on the justice and care dichotomy, her focus grew unidimensional in an effort to reify the gender differences.

I recall here a factual event dramatized in the movie, *Gandhi*. When Gandhi was charged for instigating the people of India to overthrow British rule and was brought into the court room, the British judge stood up to show his respect, categorically stated that the charge against Gandhi was beyond consideration in any court in the world, and yet, followed faithfully the rule of law by sending Gandhi to prison for several years. The judge had no doubt experienced the difficulty in focusing on care and justice perspectives in this case, but in the end showed moral responsiveness by integrating both the justice and care perspectives.

The psychology of nonviolence need not be built on extraordinary personalities. I recall here another incident to show how ordinary people integrate justice and caring in their lives. One day the clerk in my office lost an expensive gadget, for which the administration ordered him to compensate. It was beyond his means to replace the material or raise the money. The chairman of the department, who was new to the place, paid all the money from his personal funds but made the clerk pay a very small amount. When I asked the chairman why did he not pay all the money to take full credit for his philanthropic act, he said in all humility that he wanted the clerk to feel responsible for the negligence. He cared, but justice was served within the means of the clerk! In short, when people experience a dilemma caused by fluctuating care and justice perspectives, they tend to remember their childhood experiences, take clues from their holy and other important books, emulate their role models, and integrate these experiences with their own to sharpen the level of their moral judgment. Critical studies show that an individual faced with a dilemma tends to integrate the two perspectives. (Brown, 1987; Flanagan, 1991).

Erikson's work

Using a psychoanalytic model, Erikson (1958, 1969) presented a unique analysis for understanding the behavior of nonviolent individuals. His psychobiographical studies of Gandhi and King, with a focus on the development of identity, constituted the fourth major force in the psychology of nonviolence. so intense did he become in his analysis of one episode (the Ahmedabad event) that he could not help writing at the end of his book, *Gandhi's truth* (1969): "... I sensed an affinity between Gandhi's truth and the insights of modern psychology" (p. 440).

For Erikson, identity without affiliation had no meaning. He believed that identity is a "process located in the core of the individual and yet also in the core of his communal culture, a process which establishes, in fact, the identity of those two identities" (p. 266). Those who adhere to nonviolence understand the identity struggle of their own as well as of the members of the community they belong to in a very personal and representative way. Erikson also believed that nonviolence in any form will be successful only when moral considerations will be replaced by ethical consideration. "Ethics," wrote Erikson, "is marked by an insightful assent to human values, whereas moralism is blind obedience; ... ethics is transmitted with informed persuasion ..." (p. 251). In short, the psychology of nonviolence will grow with the understanding of how people solve different moral problems in different ways. An ethic of care will be difficult to understand without understanding the diverse conditions of fairness and justice. We cannot teach children justice in one context and caring in a totally different context.

Given the scenario that people learn the components of justice and caring in different ways, it is argued that the saliencies that describe the range of nonviolent behavior can be represented in a 2 x 2 matrix (see Figure 2) in the following four combinations:

(1)   those who are high on issues of justice as well as caring are likely to consider what is most fair and compassionate in a situation,

(2)   those who are high on justice but low on caring are likely to follow rules,

(3)   those who are low on justice but high on caring are likely to show supreme compassion, and

(4)   those who are low on both justice and caring are likely to be Machiavellian in their style, showing what is "good" must be implemented with or without care.

When issues of justice and caring become equally important at the same time, the two perspectives fluctuate in the mind of a nonviolent individual to give him/her the experience of "spiritual" schizophrenia. In this state s/he shows awareness of a problem, evaluates the consequences of a decision, and finally, chooses a path that is best in a given situation.

JUSTICE

	HIGH	LOW
HIGH	WHAT IS MOST FAIR AND COMPASSIONATE	SUPREME COMPASSION
CARING		
LOW	FOLLOW RULES: EQUITY/EQUALITY	WHAT IS GOOD IS WHAT WORKS

FIG.2. A 2 x 2 MATRIX FOR MORAL ORIENTATIONS

I do not claim that the above dichotomies will encompass all that is salient in nonviolent personalities, but there seems to be an inherent claim in this approach to begin with an empirical base for the psychology of nonviolence by integrating the frontiers of moral and ethical sides of human judgement, feelings and behavior in searching the alternatives to violence. For a practical psychologist like Gandhi, nonviolence was *experiments with truth* and if the same truth was not tested again and again, it lost the virtue of being a truth. For a modern empirical psychologist, this truth consists of exploring what makes justice and caring considerations integrate to avoid violence, how an individual processes rules to understand fairness, and what happens to his cognitions when s/he seeks better methods to resolve conflicts. To the extent that the above mentioned four typologies help in understanding the broad nature of the psychology of nonviolence, it seems to be a reasonable headstart.

Rest: The Defining Issues Test

The fifth significant support in the growth of the psychology of nonviolence may be found in the work of James Rest (1979) who was more concerned with the methodological issues than on refining the conceptual framework. Borrowing from the work of Piaget and Kohlberg, he constructed a test, The Defining Issues Test

(DIT), in which subjects are given several moral dilemmas and are asked what an actor should do in a given situation. Unlike Piaget and Kohlberg, he was not concerned with stages of moral development but believed that individuals could operate at several stages at a time. For instance, he found that with increasing age and education, people more often preferred higher concepts of justice, but these same people might use lower concepts of justice on several dilemmas. A very useful development in the DIT has been the creation of a "Utilizer" (U) dimension which is computed on the basis of correspondence between action choices of subjects and their concepts of justice. Whereas issues of justice constitute the principled (P) dimension of DIT, the U dimension is a moderator variable which gave insights in how subjects put their moral judgments into action (Kool and Keyes, 1990).

The P and U scores of 57 subjects were correlated with the NVT in a study by Kool and Keyes (1990). As expected, the correlations (.20 for P; .20 for U) were positive but insignificant. Even the correlation between P and U dimensions was not high (.33) It should be noted here that nonviolence is a wider concept than one's knowledge of issues of justice as measured by the DIT. Because people with nonviolent orientations weigh humanitarian concerns like compassion, forgiveness, and anti-punitiveness in addition to issues of justice, they may ignore their concern for justice in favor of humanitarian concerns. Similarly, P and I dimensions may not show a strong relationship if the subjects show a wide gap between knowledge of issues of justice and its usefulness. In other words, "knowledge of moral issues and use of moral concepts may have related but different bases, but an individual may be guided by various social, religious and humanitarian considerations when deciding what is the most appropriate thing to do in a situation" (Kool and Keyes, 1990, p. 31).

I will now focus very briefly on two other significant developments in social psychology which have enriched the psychology of nonviolence. Recent work on two kinds of fairness, distributive and procedural (Deutsch, 1985), has provided insights into how we base our decisions in terms of equity (proportionately) and equality and whether the procedures used to determine who is guilty are fair. Empirical research shows that women prefer equality to equity, whereas men prefer equal ratios of outputs to inputs.

Arising from the above analysis of justice is the concept of moral exclusion (Staub, 1990) which refers to viewing individuals or groups as outside the boundary of the rules of justice (Oskamp, 1990). When people are viewed outside one's moral boundaries, it becomes easy to harm others. Perpetrators of violence who view members of other groups as unconnected tend to perceive their own group as moral (Deutsch, 1973).

The problem associated with moral exclusion is that we do not know whom we include and whom we don't. Should we include all forms of life? Should we include our own pet but not other animals? Should we include trees and all the environment? Drawing an appropriate boundary is not easy unless we confine to members of the same species. The implications of moral exclusion to the psychology of nonviolence are vital. Nagata's chapter in this book will focus on this issue in general and Japanese internment during WW II in particular. For a detailed discussion on moral exclusion the reader is also referred to her chapter in this book. Information processing approaches to study moral judgments involve investigating how people make moral decisions. Our judgment of a morally right or wrong act is based on whether the moral rule has been obeyed or not. Schultz and Schleifer (1983), Shaver (1985) and others have adopted simulation methods to explain how people arrive at their moral judgments. The application of this approach to study the psychology of nonviolence is very limited because such model's fail to explain (a) developmental changes in moral judgments, and (b) whether a moral judgment is based on mental representation of knowledge or to the obligation to obey (Darley and Shultz, 1990).

To sum up, moral concerns form the core of the study of psychology of nonviolence. As in the analysis of aggression, intentionality plays a very important role in the understanding of moral behavior. The psychology of nonviolence has moved a long way claiming its legitimacy with the early studies of Piaget who began by explaining the significance of intentions in a child's moral development, and this pioneering work was followed by Kohlberg who traced it in several stages, Gilligan by adding a caring perspective, Rest by separating principle and utilizer components, and Erikson by offering the role of identity and childhood experiences. Based on the above discussion we may conclude that nonviolent individuals do not approach various components like justice or caring, moral principle or its utilization, and aggression or nonaggression as isolated parts but tend to view them as a Gestalt, a configuration in which the best of their intentions and conduct mirrors the components of social harmony and welfare. While such individuals appear to be god-like, they may still show the flaws of an ordinary human being.

Power and nonviolence

Power is a very complex phenomenon which is generally defined as the capacity to influence the behavior of others. Violence is a handy tool to influence others by controlling their behavior. Since the Victorian era, pacifists have held the position that power leads to domination and violence.

Sociologists like Gene Sharp (9173), who have written extensively on nonviolence, believe that power may be viewed from two different angles. An individual may regard himself/herself as dependent upon the good will of those in the hierarchical system. In the other sense, power may be viewed as a hierarchical system dependent upon the good will of people. This latter notion of power is pluralistic and hence useful for the psychology of nonviolence.

Another prominent social scientist, Kenneth Boulding (1989), has distinguished three "faces of power": (a) coercive or threat power, (b) economic power which comes out of material wealth and production, and (c) integrative power. It is with the third face of power that we learn how nonviolent actions provide an alternative to violence. This power is derived from the trust and good will of the followers who give it to the powerful. In a separate chapter in this book, Boulding has elaborated his concept of integrative power in the context of social, historical and political factors.

Perhaps the most in-depth psychological analysis of power in the past two decades has been offered by Rollo May (1972) who, like Boulding, uses the term integrative power but preferred to confine his analysis to the humanistic level and did not extend it to the level of community action. He classified five kinds of power. First, exploitative power, which subjects people to abuse of all kinds, (e.g., slavery), and it manifests itself with force. Second, manipulative power is reflected in the passion to control others in various ways. Third, competitive power is the power to go up against the opponents who go down. Achievement motivation (McClleland, 1961) is a good example to illustrate this type of power. Fourth, nutrient power reflects in one's care for others, for example, parents care for their children. And fifth, integrative power which is "power *with* the other" (p. 109).

May (1972) concluded that all individuals tend to use different kinds of power in various combinations but those who adhere to nonviolence use integrative power as the core of their life style. He related the essence of this power to Hegel's dialectic of thesis, antithesis, and synthesis. A corollary to this type of analysis is that if there is a body, there will be an anti-body, and growth will result from the attraction or repulsion of these two bodies into a new system. Thus, if a moral viewpoint is challenged by another moral viewpoint, the result will be a new synthesis, a new ethic embodying a higher moral principle. The notion of power in the minds of nonviolent individuals lies in their efforts to align themselves to the goodness of their community, a process which leads them to self-cultivation and self-perfection. They are comfortable with criticism or even hatred because they tend to look beyond the existing social order and do not play by the conventional rules. In doing so, they never manipulate others because they do not promote their personal interests.

According to Hagberg (1984), a clergyman may feel threatened by the power of nonviolent individuals. Generally speaking, the leadership of a clergyman is based on seeking support from others and to develop unconditional respect for their religious organization. In sharp contrast, nonviolent individuals pursue ethics which are not bound by any system of given rules. At a personal level, they have fewer regrets in life because they are always ready to test new ideas as compared to a clergyman who rarely changes his views. Hagberg analyzed several paradoxes in the reasoning of nonviolent individuals: "The more we know the less we know"; "commitment means detachment"; and so on (p. 134).

May (1972) believed that there are three conditions that set the stage for the relationship between nonviolence and power:

1.   Nonviolent individuals will always be ready to become aware of a problem.
2.   They will not hesitate to take blame and responsibility.
3.   Their attempt will be to help the community, not themselves.

In short, nonviolent individuals do not *seek* power but power *ascends* to them when they make an effort to achieve social harmony by offering a mature moral conduct. This type of power is unique because it operates on the conscience of the perpetrators of violence and weakens their moral defenses. The methods of nonviolent action as used by Gandhi and King were real life experiments which laid the foundation for the psychology of nonviolence.

Given the above relationship of power and nonviolence, I conducted a study with Keyes to investigate power orientations of the individuals in relations to their scores on the NVT (Kool and Keyes , 1990). A popular test (Christie, 1970), the Machiavellianism V Scale (Mach), which measures subjects' beliefs regarding the use of manipulation, deceit and flattery as interpersonal tactics and their beliefs concerning the moral qualities of other people, was used to study the relationship with the NVT. A strong negative correlation ($r = .44$, $p < .01$) was obtained between the NVT and the Mach scores. These results were similar to another study conducted in India by Hasan and Khan (1983) to investigate the relationship between Mach and Gandhian ideology. A few other significant correlations between the NVT and the Mach subscales were: Deceit (-.31), Flattery (-.32), Cynicism (-.43), Mach tactics (-.38), and Mach views (-.42). The overall results of this study indicated that people with higher nonviolent orientations do not manipulate others and refrain from using deceit and flattery in their interpersonal relationships. In short, those who score high on our NVT do not use Mach methods for their self-enhancement, they show willingness to share blame (Baumgardner, 1990), and present a set of positive values (Mayton, 1992).

Interrelationship between aggression, moral and power components, and the psychology of nonviolence

The "genes" of psychology of nonviolence are formed by moral components which determine the features of aggression and power, and the operation of these genes is controlled by intentions. The significant role of intentions in moral responsiveness of individuals is important in understanding the structure of human cognition. Developments in the field of psychology of nonviolence will be a major step in this direction.

It is suggested here that the psychology of nonviolence should focus on how the frontiers of human cognition develop in relating aggression to issues of power and moral concerns (see Figure 3). Use of power for one's own benefit and for social harmony alone makes a lot of difference in judging the aggressive behavior of individuals. It is this knowledge that helps people perceive the difference between a conman and a saint, a Hitler and a Martin Luther King. However, one may argue here that Hitler had also championed social harmony by building Germany as a better racial society. Our contention is that the issues of morality in the domain of justice, coupled with those of caring, are important in understanding nonviolent behavior. If the supporters of Hitler argue that justice in the form of freedom from economic oppression was the goal of Germans, then we say that the lack of caring and the

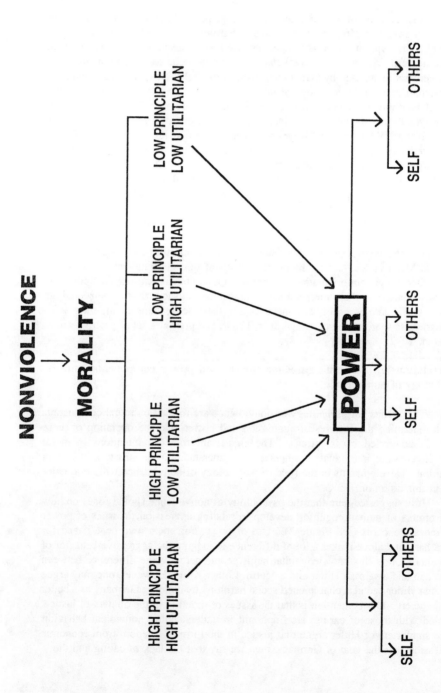

FIG. 3. INTERRELATIONSHIP BETWEEN NONVIOLENCE, POWER AND MORAL CONCERNS

ensuing violence unparalled in history was an antithesis which enriched the subject matter of the *psychology of violence,* not the *psychology of nonviolence.*

Recent research work in cognition on how people form categories by perceiving and recalling events has come to be known as the study of schemas. These dynamic mental categories help us to remember new information and to expect it when appropriately primed by a cue. Schemas have been widely studied in the context of person, self, events and roles. Josephson (1987) conducted an interesting study to show how subjects who were exposed to violent and nonviolent programs recalled the events differently when the instrument for priming the subjects' recall of the story was present or absent. The study also concluded that subjects who were rated very aggressive by their teachers were the ones who recalled the aggressive scripts most. If a cue could prime the schema related to aggression of boys in the study of Josephson, it is also possible that similar cues--not studied by Josephson-- may also prime the schema related to nonviolence.

We wondered if schemas for the roles of people exist vis-a vis their moral and power orientations. In a study (Kool, 1992), I asked 29 subjects to classify a typical saint, monarch, clergy, businessman, social worker, conman, and mafia leader on the basis of (1) high (H) or low (L) use of principled (P) or utilizer (U) moral components, and (2) use of power for personal benefit (self, S) or for the community (others, O). The study was designed to investigate how moral and power components were used in the judgment of aggression levels of individuals affiliated to a category (see Table 2).

Two important facts emerge from the study. First, the two extremes, LP/LU, S & O and HP/HU, S & O consisting of a mafia leader and a saint represent the highest and the lowest dimension of human aggression. This finding clearly shows that the interrelationship between power, moral concerns, and aggression is perceived, categorized and retrieved by people while making their judgments to describe broad social groups and roles (see Figure 3). Based on the findings reported in this chapter, it is proposed that nonviolent individuals will occupy the lowest right corner in Figure 1: high moral concerns, other-oriented power and low aggression.

Table 2
Categorization of individuals based on their power and moral orientations

Category	Example	Ss agreed/disagreed
LP/LU, S & O	Mafia leader	26/3
LP/LU, S	Conman	28/1
LP/HU, S	Businessman	21/8
LP/HU, O	Social worker	25/4
HP/LU, S	Monarch	20/9
HP/LU, S & O	Clergy	25/4
HP/HU, S & O	Saint	29/0

Second and significantly, perceiving and judging behavior in the typical categories may result in frequent misattribution when the behavior of an individual does not represent the features of a domain which has been commonly used in classifying his other behavior. For instance, a businessman who claims to be highly moral and ethical will have a harder time convincing others regarding his views than a clergyman who is expected to deliver a sermon every Sunday in his church. In other words, adopting nonviolent forms of behavior *against* the categorically perceived roles is likely to generate false attributions, a problem which we often face in our daily lives. When a very rich man with a flourishing logging business advocates protection of the environment and saving the forests, people may react by saying, "Now that this businessman has earned a lot of money, he is trying to project himself as a holy cow."

I will now return to the earlier analysis of *nonviolent act vs. act of nonviolence*. If a clergyman and the above described businessman participate in a sit-in to stop deforestation, people will perceive consistency in the behavior of a clergyman, as against the businessman, because the intentions of a clergyman are generalized in both forms of behavior--categorized (act of nonviolence) or noncategorized (individual orientation). On the other hand, the businessman, no matter how serious his intentions are in protecting the environment, will face misattribution, that is, his act of nonviolence--sit-in in this case--will not match his individual orientation in the past. As I mentioned before, saints blend their moral conduct with a social purpose such that they tend to minimize the gap between their personal and social lives, and between their nonviolent acts and acts of nonviolence. The broad spectrum of intentions in them represents a unity of purpose which reduces the perception of distance between categorized and noncategorized acts. If caring for other people's children--a personal orientation--is a nonviolent act and participating in a sit-in to stop child abuse is an act of nonviolence, then Gandhi is said to have removed the toughest barriers in the human cognition reifying *nonviolent acts* and *act of nonviolence* by declaring that he had no right to give anything more to his children that he would not give to other children. To him, his own children were a biological reality for whom he had a personal obligation, but he blended his personal and social intentions into a unified purpose to promote the highest ethic of justice and caring for all children. The psychology of nonviolence, then, helps to integrate moral cognitions, moral reasoning and moral behavior, a meeting ground which Kohlberg failed to measure in his work.

In short, a researcher in the field of psychology of nonviolence needs to focus on the components which divide and harmonize the structures in human cognition, what primes a nonviolent script, and how to retrieve it. Critics may argue that this approach may help us understand the thinness of the psychology of nonviolence like that of studying the formation of a bubble in several patterns of waves in a stream. True, but it will not be an unhealthy trend at all in the growth of the psychology of nonviolence.

The thickness of the psychology of nonviolence will emerge from the current studies on efficacy which help us understand how people believe that one could perform the behavior to accomplish one's goals (Bandura, 1977). Nonviolent individuals know how to blend their personal and social orientations into social harmony and action. When an act becomes salient to an individual s/he feels a sense of personal capability with a belief that the mission is attainable. Fiske (1987) has reported that antinuclear activists report frequently thinking about the issue. Such an orientation "apparently creates detailed and concrete images of nuclear war" in the minds of activists (p. 213). Efficacy grows out of one's frequent encounters with and prolonged deliberations on an issue. When an individual's beliefs translate into behavior, the gap between perception, judgment and feeling aspects of moral concerns reduces. Perhaps a generalized spectrum of efficacies may be helpful in depicting a nonviolent personality. However, as I mentioned before, the psychology of nonviolence need not be focused on saints alone, for a single episode of efficacy in an individual may explain how the seeds of nonviolence germinate in the behaviors of an ordinary individual or a saint. The truth is that most saints also proceed to saintliness with a major encounter in their lives which develops a sense of efficacy in them. For an ordinary person like Rosa Parks, the journey to nonviolence began with the denial of a seat in a bus in Alabama; for *Mahatma* (the great soul) Gandhi, the journey to nonviolence began with the denial of travel in a first class coach in a train in South Africa.

Let me conclude this chapter with three major comments. First, the legitimacy of the psychology of nonviolence is as real as the existence of psychology of violence. The founding father of modern American psychology, William James, provided the ingredients of the psychology of nonviolence but psychologists ignored them for a long time. It should be also borne in mind that the nature of the psychology of nonviolence should not be misconstrued as an inverted mirror image of the psychology of violence. Just as truce does not mean the end of all war, keeping peace does not mean making peace. The sources for promoting violence and nonviolence have different roots and conditions.

Second, the psychology of nonviolence will develop out of the interrelationships with several psychological structures. As proposed in this chapter, at the minimum, the psychology of nonviolence needs aggression, power and moral concerns as the core components of psychological significance to build an acceptable theory. And third, the focus on the study of cognitive structures involved in the study of the psychology of nonviolence should be sharpened, for without this focus it will remain a black box. While studies on priming and efficacy of behavior will provide a great help in explaining the frontiers of nonviolent behavior, other approaches, as discussed in this chapter, are also helpful. Three years before his death, Skinner (1987) published an article in which he made an attempt to explain the behavior of Gandhi with the help of his popular theory of reinforcement. I find now that from Skinner, a hard boiled psychologist, to May and Maslow, both soft boiled psychologists, and from William James to information processing in moral reasoning, there has been a direct or indirect, passive or active interest to develop and understand the psychology of nonviolence which, unfortunately, has not grown to any significant proportion as compared to the psychology of violence. The proposed metatheoretical analysis of the psychology of nonviolence is expected to help us investigate the psychological structures that are vital for our understanding of nonviolent behavior.

Postscript

1.   Tedeschi (personal communication, April 12, 1993) believes that "aggression" should be replaced by "coercion" in Figure 1. According to him, "coercive actions are guided by expectations about the immediate outcomes they produce, such as compliance or signs of suffering by the target person." The advantage in using the word "coercion" is that it takes into account intentions and "incorporates the causal process resulting in harm-doing." If acts of nonviolence (e.g., sit-ins), are perceived as "harm to others" in a given situation, "coercion" may replace "aggression" in Figure 1; otherwise, aggression is used here in a generic sense. On the other hand, most nonviolent individuals may find neither "aggression" nor "coercion" suitable to describe their intentions. They are likely to prefer the word "persuasion" because they intend to solve a conflict without "harm to others."

2.   Wessells (personal communication, April 26, 1993) believes that nonviolence involves "not only love and ahimsa but also of active resistance, which ... can be quite coercive and confrontational. Resistance involves dissent, moral shaming, large-scale organization, and a refusal to fight back through physical violence." I agree with him. The core of a nonviolent personality consists of (1) using minimum physical or other types of aggression; (2) applying practical moral considerations (e.g., minimum moral shaming) in the absence of a principled form of nonviolence; and (3) refusing to use power for self-enhancement. It seems to me that the three components in Figure 1 account for the behaviors of not only those who believe in nonviolence in its principled form but also those who use nonviolence as a technique to solve a conflict. The reader will notice that I have not made any attempt to answer some specific issues in the social psychology of nonviolence (e.g., active resistance, individual and collective orientations as related to nonviolence, etc.). The theoretical analyses presented in this chapter will raise a number of these issues in future research on the psychology of nonviolence.

REFERENCES

Baumgardner, S.R. (1990). Attributions of cause, responsibility and blame among violent and nonviolent individuals. In V.K. Kool (Ed.), Perspectives on nonviolence. New York: Springer-Verlag.

Bandura, A. (1977). Self-efficacy: toward a unifying theory of behavior change. Psychological Review, 84, 199-215.

Boulding, K.E. (1989). Three faces of power. Newbury Park, CA: Sage.

Brown, L. (1987). A guide to reading narratives of moral conflict and choice for self and moral voice. School of Education, Harvard University Report.

Buss, A.H. & Durkee, A. (1957). An inventory for assessing different kinds of hostility. Journal of Consulting Psychology, 21 (4), 343-349.

Christie, R. (1970). Scale construction. In R. Christie & F.L. Geis (Eds.) Studies in Machiavellianism. New York: Academic Press.

Colby, A., et al. (1983). A longitudinal study of moral judgment. Monographs for the society for research in child development, 201.

Darley, J.M. & Shultz, T.R. (1990). Moral rules: Their content and acquisition. In M.R. Rosenzweig & L.W. Porter (Eds.), Annual Review of Psychology, 41, 525-556.

Deutsch, M. (1973). The resolution of conflict: constructive and destructive processes. New Haven: CT: Yale University Press.

Deutsch, M. (1985). Distributive justice: A social psychological perspective. New Haven, CT: Yale University Press.

Erikson, E. (1958). Young man Luther. New York: Norton.

Erikson, E. (1969). Gandhi's truth, New York: Norton.

Fiske, S.T. (1987). People's reaction to nuclear war: implications for psychologists. American Psychologist, 42, 207-217.

Flanagan, O. (1991). Varieties of moral personality. Cambridge, MA: Harvard University Press.

Gandhi, M.K. (1948). The story of my experiments with truth. (Translated). Ahmedabad, India: Navjivan.

Geen, R.G. (1990). Human aggression. Pacific Grove, CA: Brooks/Cole.

Gilligan, C. (1982). In a different voice. Cambridge, MA: Harvard University Press.

Goldstein, J. (1986). Aggression and crimes of violence. New York: Oxford University Press.

Groebel, J. & Hinde, R. (Eds.) (1989). Aggression and war. New York: Cambridge University Press.

Hagberg, J. (1984). Real power. Minneapolis: Winston Press.

Hasan, Q. & Khan, S.R. (1983). A study toward validation of the scale measuring Gandhian (nonviolent) personality. Psychological Studies, 28, 74-77.

Howard, R.W. (1990). Mohandas K. Gandhi: Nonviolence, principles, and the Chamber-Pots. In V.K. Kool (Ed.), Perspectives on nonviolence. New York: Springer-Verlag.

Iyer, R. (1983). The moral and political thought of Mahatma Gandhi. New York: Concord Grove Press.

James, W. (1958). Talks to teachers. New York: Norton.

James, W. (1966). The moral equivalent of war. In S. Lynd (Ed.), Nonviolence in America. New York: The Bobbs-Merrill Company.

Josephson, W.L. (1987). Television violence and children's aggression: Testing the priming, social script, and disinhibiting predictions. Journal of Personality and Social Psychology, 53, 882-90.

Kagan, J. (1987). Introduction. In J. Kagan and S. Lamb (Eds.), The emergence of morality in young children. Chicago: The University of Chicago Press.

Kohlberg, L. (1976). Moral stages and moralization: The cognitive-development approach. In T. Lockina (Eds.), Moral development and behavior. New York: Holt, Rinehart & Winston.

Kool, V.K. (Ed.) (1990). Perspectives on nonviolence. New York: Springer-Verlag.

Kool, V.K. (1991). The Social Psychology of Nonviolence (Symposium). Annual Convention of the American Psychological Association, San Francisco.

Kool, V.K. (1992). Occupations and cognitive schemas. Unpublished study.

Kool, V.K. (1992a). Nonviolence and the mainstream psychology (Symposium). Annual Convention of the American Psychological Association, Washington, D.C.

Kool, V.K. & Keyes, M.L. (1990). Explorations in the nonviolent personality. In V.K. Kool (Ed.), Perspectives on nonviolence. New York: Springer-Verlag.

Kool, V.K. & Sen, M. (1984). The nonviolence test. In D.M. Pestonjee (Ed.) Second handbook of psychological and sociological instruments (pp. 48-54). Ahmedabad: Indian Institute of Management.

Lynd, S. (1966). Nonviolence in America: A documentary history. New York: The Bobbs-Merrill Company.

McClleland, D.C. (1961). The achieving society. New York: Appleton-Century-Crofts.

Maslow, A.H. (1954). Motivation and personality. New York: Harper.

May, R. (1972). Power and innocence. New York: Norton.

Mayton, D. (1992). Nonviolence and mainstream psychology (Symposium). Annual Convention of the American Psychological Association, Washington, D.C.

Nelson, S.A. (1980). Factors influencing young children's use of motives and outcomes as moral criteria. Child Development, 51, 823-829.

Oskamp, S. (1990). The editor's page. Journal of Social Issues, 46.

Osgood, C.E. (1962). An alternative to war or surrender. Urbana: The University of Illinois Press.

Piaget, J. (1932). The moral judgment of the child. New York: The Free Press.

Rest, J. (1979). Development in judging moral issues. Minneapolis, MN: University of Minnesota Press.

Schultz, T.R. and Schleifer, M. (1987). Towards a refinement of attribution concepts. In Jaspers, et. al., (Eds.). Attribution theory and research: conceptual, developmental and social dimensions. London: Academic Press.

Sen, M. (1981). Reduction of aggression in violent and nonviolent individuals. Unpublished doctoral dissertation, University of Bombay, Bombay, India.

Sharp, G. (1973). The politics of nonviolent action. Boston, MA: Porter Sargent.

Sharp, G. (1979). Gandhi as a political strategist. Boston, MA: Porter Sargent.

Shaver, K. (1985). The attribution of blame. New York: Springer-Verlag.

Siann, G. (1988). Accounting for aggression. Boston, MA: Allen & Unwin.

Skinner, B.F. (1987). Whatever happened to psychology as the science of behavior? American Psychologist, 42-8, 780-786.

Staub, E. (1990). Moral exclusion, personal goal theory, and extreme destructiveness. Journal of Social Issues, 46 (1), 47-64.

Sternberg, R. (1986). A triangular theory of love. Psychological Review, 93, 119-135.

Tolman, C.E. (1942). Drives toward war. New York: Appleton-Century.

CHAPTER 2

Psychological Obstacles to Peace

Michael G. Wessells

Events of the past several years have opened striking new opportunities for building peace and nonviolence. Having freed the world from the shackles of East-West enmity, the ending of the Cold War has decreased the immediate threat of World War III, allowed significant cuts in nuclear arsenals and military forces, and lifted hopes for achieving security through means other than mutual nuclear terror.

Unfortunately, there are many grim reminders that peace is not at hand--the Gulf War, the rage and looting in Los Angeles, the threat of loose nukes in the CIS, and the ethnic and nationalistic violence between Serbs and Croats, Armenians and Azerbaijainis, and Arabs and Jews, to name only a few. In addition, major players in the global arena, particularly the U.S., are not taking full advantage of this extraordinary set of opportunities. For the first time in over forty-five years, the U.S. has the opportunity to develop new approaches to security that emphasize nonviolent methods over the militaristic approaches of the past and that broaden concepts of security to accommodate the full range of interconnected security problems such as nuclear proliferation, virulent nationalism, ecological destruction, community violence, poverty, overpopulation, economic inequities, and social injustices. But this broadening has not occurred, bold new visions of peace have not been generated, and nations such as the U.S. are failing to take the lead in constructing a peaceful, nonviolent world.

If the opportunities for peacemaking are so abundant, why is it so difficult to take advantage of them? No doubt bureaucratic inertia and the complexity of the world situation are partly to blame. But beyond these obvious factors lies the more subtle, compelling truth that movement toward real security is hampered by the continuation of the war system, which embodies and nourishes a system of interlocking political, economic, social, and psychological obstacles to peace. Creating a nonviolent world requires not only a vision of peace but also the deliberate construction of strategies for overcoming the obstacles that block movement toward the achievement of this vision.

An essential first step is to bring the obstacles to light where they can be

PSYCHOLOGICAL BARRIERS TO PEACE

TABLE 1
A selective list of cognitive, affective, and social obstacles to peace. Although listed separately, these processes interact extensively in natural settings.

COGNITIVE	AFFECTIVE	SOCIAL
stereotypic distortion	hostility	us-them differentiation
enemy imaging	distrust	groupthink
attribution biases	existential fears	mirror imaging & propaganda
selective attention & memory	dehumanization & moral exclusion	blaming & scapegoating
biased heuristics & judgments	hardening of negative attitudes	malignant spiral processes
ideological rigidity	macho pride	self-fulfilling prophecy
unchallenged assumptions & contradictions	desire for power	problems communicating & negotiating
sanitization	denial	superpatriotism & virulent nationalism
rationalization	hopelessness	excessive obedience & conformity
compartmentalized thinking	psychic numbing	militarism & normalization, legitimation of violence

examined consciously and dealt with as they apply in diverse situations around the world. This chapter identifies some of the main psychological obstacles that constitute the human factor which must be dealt with in moving toward a nonviolent world. In analyzing these obstacles, it is important to note that international conflicts are not strictly psychological--reality does include severe conflicts of interest and tyrants willing to inflame and exploit them. Moreover, international conflicts are multidimensional, and the psychological dimension is only part of a much broader picture.

Analysis of the psychological obstacles to peace is best done within a diagnostic framework that includes cognitive, affective, and social categories, some elements of which are shown in Table 1. To add flesh to this framework and to show how psychological obstacles to peace interact in natural contexts, it is useful to examine a real-world case study. The recently ended Cold War is a particularly interesting case because it was a defining epoch in world history, because it stimulated much of the policy relevant psychological research in the U.S., and because it was animated by a wide array of psychological processes that generalize to many different conflicts. Furthermore, a post mortem examination will reveal that the Cold War left a powerful psychological residue which continues to shape U.S. security policy. The analysis that follows will necessarily be brief, nonexhaustive, and centered on the U.S.

Cognitive Obstacles

A major theme in contemporary research on cognition is that perception and thinking are not passive, data-driven processes--the pickup and processing of information is guided also by mental schemata, which are organized frameworks of knowledge, beliefs, and expectations (Anderson, 1985; Rumelhart, 1977; Schank and Abelson, 1977; Wessells, 1982). Although schemata are useful in simplifying complex data and in constructing a coherent picture of the world, significant hazards arise when they are used uncritically and dogmatically.

In the West, the Cold War was widely depicted as an heroic struggle of Good versus Evil, with the forces of freedom and democracy pitted against those of communism and godless atheism. As White (1984, 1991) points out, the mental schema of the Good Guys against the Bad Guys became deeply entrenched, and it served as the cognitive backbone of the exaggerated enemy images of the Soviet Union. This cognitive schema had a number of harmful effects, not the least of which was stereotypic distortion. Manichean simplicity obscured the rich diversity within the Soviet Union and between the nations of the communist world, portraying communism as a colorless, corrupt monolith. The schema colored perceptions of Third World countries, which were judged, often in the most superficial manner, as either free or communist, hence, friend or enemy. The costs of this simplistic approach became apparent in damaged relations with many developing nations, unnecessary and counterproductive wars, weapons proliferation, and disclosures about the corruption of U.S.-supported regimes.

The Good Guys-Bad Guys schema created a host of misperceptions, including strong tendencies to attribute negative motives to the Soviets. Indeed, early studies by Oskamp (1965, 1968) and more recent studies by Sande et al. (1989) showed that when American students judged the probable motives behind the same actions performed by either the U.S. or the Soviet Union, negative motives were imputed more frequently to the Soviets. In policy circles, attribution biases showed up regularly in beliefs that the Soviets sought arms control treaties only to weaken the U.S., in doubts that the Soviets will obey the treaties they enter (the *New York Times* pointed out that in 1963 opponents to the partial test ban treaty which limited atmospheric nuclear testing said that the Soviets would evade the ban by testing behind the moon or in outer space (Larson, 1991)), and in overestimation of the amount of centralized, internal planning of the Soviets' actions (Jervis, 1976). These biases had a powerful corrosive effect on efforts to achieve peace through negotiation (Pruitt, 1965).

Functioning as a lens that filtered or at least colored incoming information, the Good Guys-Bad Guys schema also encouraged selective attention and memory. For example, Silverstein and Flamenbaum (1989; see also Silverstein, 1989, 1992) reported that students who read a description of actions supposedly undertaken by the Soviet Union were more likely to remember aggressive actions than were students who read the same description, but this time with the actions undertaken by Australia, an ally. By guiding the pickup and retention of primarily confirmatory information, the schema becomes self-sustaining, preventing the consideration of information regarding the positive qualities of the Soviets. This circular process served to rigidify both the negative beliefs about the Soviets and to strengthen belief in the ideology of Western moral superiority (Pruitt, 1965).

Cognitive biases were also evident in the use of heuristics or mental rules of thumb such as reasoning by analogy. While the use of historical analogy is not itself problematic, it becomes so when pursued uncritically. For example, research by Neustadt and May (1986) and by Khong (1991) indicates that the fateful decisions of the Johnson administration to escalate U.S. involvement in Vietnam stemmed from the rigid belief of key leaders such as Johnson, Dean Rusk, and Robert McNamara that the U.S. situation in Vietnam in the mid-1960s was analogous to the situation in Korea immediately preceding the outbreak of the Korean War. Disputing this Korean analogy, Undersecretary of State George Ball wrote a long memorandum in 1964, pointing out that in Korea, unlike Vietnam, there had been a clear U.N. mandate, the presence of over 50,000 international troops, a stable government, and a massive enemy invasion that provided an unimpeachable political and legal base for counteraction. Unfortunately, the leaders overlooked these differences and rejected Ball's argument that the U.S. situation actually had stronger parallels with the disastrous situation faced by the French in Vietnam in 1954. As a result, the U.S. plunged into a catastrophic, unwinnable war that stands as poignant reminder of the price of faulty reasoning by analogy and of the misappropriation of history.

Affective Obstacles

Turning next to the emotional, affective processes, which interact continually with cognitive processes, the Cold War is a monumental case study of the pernicious effects of hostility, fear, and distrust. Those who lived through the era of duck-and-cover drills, the Soviet invasions of Hungary, Czechoslovakia, and Afghanistan, the downing of KAL flight 003, etc. are quite familiar with the waves of rage and anger that swept over the U.S., increasing tensions and cementing the enemy schema discussed earlier. As one index of the extent to which distrust built up, a 1984 Public Agenda Survey reported that 90% of the respondents agreed with the statement "During the 1970s, when we were trying to improve relations, the Soviets secretly built up their military strength" (Yankelovich and Doble, 1986).

Ralph White (1984, 1991) has made a compelling case that intense fear was the primary factor that drove the superpowers toward the brink of war by motivating or encouraging misperceptions and misguided actions on both sides. These fears were not simply fears of being eclipsed by the other--they were survival fears, which for the Soviets were rooted in encirclement by enemies, in the dispatch of U.S. troops to fight against the Reds during the Bolshevik Revolution, and in the historical trauma of repeated invasions from the West, the most recent of which had killed 20 million Soviets. On the U.S. side, survival fears were intimately intertwined with the strong beliefs that the other was implacably aggressive. For 45 years, fear of Soviet expansion virtually scripted U.S. foreign policy, and a 1982 poll by the *Los Angeles Times* indicated that 63% of the respondents believed that the Soviet Union would start a nuclear war. It was fear that entrapped both superpowers in a fragile balance of nuclear terror.

Fear was amplified by the dehumanizing rhetoric and images that were widely circulated by leaders and the media. President Reagan's dehumanizing statements toward the Soviet Union did not fall on deaf ears, as in 1984, over half of Americans agreed that the Soviet Union is an "evil empire" (Yankelovich Group, 1988; cited in Yatani & Bramel, 1989). Meanwhile, popular films such as *Rocky, Rambo,* and *Amerika* drove home the message that the Soviets are inhumane, evil, and utterly bereft of humane qualities. This stripping away of human qualities heightened popular fears, prepared the way for killing Soviets if it came to that, and provided a convenient justification for U.S. aggression on the grounds that it was necessary to achieve the broader good of halting the communist monster. Moreover, it strengthened the enemy schema which confirmed and consolidated negative beliefs, hardening the negative attitudes toward the Soviets.

Although self-protection was consistently held up as the stated motive for U.S. participation in the arms race, macho pride and desire for power, the psychological allies of nationalism, also animated the arms buildup (Frank, 1987; White, 1984). In 1976, a Gallup poll showed that 52% of Americans agreed that "The U.S. should maintain its dominant position as the world's most powerful nation at all costs, even going to the brink of war if necessary." Among American leaders, these macho tendencies have surfaced in atomic bullying by a number of U.S. Presidents (Kaku

& Axelrod, 1987), in the "we will be second to none" attitude, and in statements made behind closed doors by Presidents such as Lyndon Johnson, who said following the 1964 bomber raids on vietcong PT boats and oil depots, "I didn't just screw Ho Chi Minh; I cut his pecker off" (Halberstam, 1972, p. 414). As Richard Barnet (1972) has pointed out, "glory, machismo, and the excitement of winning" (p. 237) are the primary goals of national security managers.

Of course, machismo is only part of the affective picture, as worries about the nuclear threat became widespread, particularly during the early 1980s (for reviews, see Schatz & Fiske, 1992; Solantaus, 1991). Furthermore, as superpower arsenals grew to include over 50,000 nuclear weapons and as East-West tensions mounted in the early 1980s, there was broad (nearly 80%) support for a nuclear freeze. Nonetheless, sustained public action to halt the arms race was not as extensive as one might have expected in light of the profundity of the threat. Many continued to see nuclear war as a relatively remote threat (Schuman, Ludwig, and Krosnick, 1986), and there were pervasive pressures to accept the nuclear status quo. However, affective barriers to action were also at work. Although Lifton (1979, 1982) diagnosed the problem in terms of psychic numbing, Schwebel (1990) and others (Smith, 1986; Locatelli & Holt, 1986) pointed out that processes such as denial may have been less influential than suppression, the deliberate pushing out of one's mind that which is uncomfortable but cannot be changed. In addition, widespread feelings of political inefficacy in responding to the nuclear threat may have combined with the feelings of hopelessness and futurelessness reported to produce excessive passivity. (Christie & Murphy, in press; Diamond and Bachman, 1986; Escalona, 1982; Goldberg et al., 1985; Nelson, 1985; Newcomb, 1986; Schwebel, 1982).

At the same time, the processes of rationalization and sanitization were used widely to adjust emotionally to life under the nuclear sword of Damocles. These were most apparent in the arcane technical vocabulary of the nuclear planners and the euphemisms of leaders (Cohn, 1987). Civilian death and suffering was intellectualized as "collateral damage," the targeting of cities was labeled "countervalue targeting," and the powerful MX missile, which carried ten devastating bombs and had destabilizing first-strike capabilities, was cozily referred to as "peacekeeper." In retrospect, it is apparent that linguistic abstractions became tools of self-delusion on a grand scale.

Social Obstacles

These cognitive and affective obstacles operated at many different levels and were woven into the fabric of national social systems that institutionalized the Black-White view of the world and the military approach to achieving security. As Bronfenbrenner (1961) reported, both sides cultivated enemy images of the other and used propaganda to cement those images in the civilian population. This enabled each side to use the other as a scapegoat, blaming it for global tensions and using the threat of the other as a justification for building new weapons. As a result, the superpowers became locked in what Deutsch (1983) aptly called a "malignant spiral process of hostile interaction," an upwardly escalating dynamic of conflict marked by excessive competition, runaway misperceptions, and high levels of rigidity. The sad irony is that although there were real conflicts of interest dividing the U.S. and the Soviet Union, the superpower confrontation often had the character of a self-fulfilling prophecy. In the late 1950s, for example, the CIA estimated that the Soviets had 200 missiles, triggering fears of a "missile gap" and motivating the rapid buildup of U.S. ICBM forces. Subsequently, it turned out that the Soviets had possessed only four missiles, while the U.S. had 40 (Kaku & Axelrod, 1987).

Throughout the Cold War, the U.S. relied excessively on worst-case thinking, arguing that it is imperative to develop a particular weapon system or force because if we do not, the Russians will. Operating on both sides, a dynamic of continuous weapons escalation was created in which each side, fearing the other would build weapons that would tilt the balance of power, felt compelled to build more and more weapons and to constantly seek to develop new kinds of weapons. Hans Bethe, one of the architects of the hydrogen bomb, commented sadly that if the U.S. had not built the hydrogen bomb, perhaps the Soviets would not have built it (Bernstein, 1981). It was as if both sides became more invested in maintaining their illusions than in providing real security, not unlike the man in the Woody Allen joke who runs into the doctor's office exclaiming "Doctor, you've got to help my brother--he thinks he's a chicken." Nonplussed, the doctor replied "That's ridiculous-just tell your brother he's not a chicken." But the man replied "I can't--I need the eggs."

Considered piecemeal, these obstacles are formidable. But their impact was magnified many times over by their institutionalization and their integration into a complex social system that nourished militaristic values and that normalized and legitimated violence. The systemic nature of the superpower conflict is apparent in the sprawling military industrial complex, which was explicitly constructed to resist the Communist enemy and which offered huge profits and minimal financial risks to attract top individual talent as well as the involvement of the largest, most technically advanced defense contractors. Working within the national security establishment, the same processes of bureaucratization, obedience, and conformity that had been exploited by Hitler were used to keep workers task oriented, to quiet moral qualms about creating weapons of mass destruction, and to silence whistleblowers (Lifton, 1986; Lifton and Markusen, 1990).

The systemic nature of the conflict is also apparent in the mass media images used to stir the fires of patriotism and to inculcate fears of the other at an early age (Hesse & Mack, 1991). Powerful legitimation of the system came from the rhetoric of leaders who pointed repeatedly to the necessity of using military means of resisting communism, to the importance of making sacrifices in order to protect one's country, and to the moral superiority of the forces of freedom.

Having focused thus far on the superpower rivalry, it is worth noting that these diverse obstacles have not been put to rest by the end of the Cold War. The Gulf War, for example, illustrated the powerful role of superpatriotism, enemy imaging of the Arabs, machismo (Admiral LaRoque of the Center for Defense Information compared our use of excessive force against Iraq to using a sledgehammer to kill a cockroach), and sanitization (the media mentioned collateral damage but few showed pictures of thousands of children dying each week of chronic diarrhea due to bombing of electric water purification plants). Moreover, in ethnic clashes such as those in former Yugoslavia, enemy imaging and existential fears continue to spark violence. And in underdeveloped nations, fears of powerful neighbors and the quest for power and prestige make for a thriving arms bazaar and continuing nuclear proliferation. Thus the obstacles discussed above are by no means particular to the Cold War.

The Psychological Legacy and Its Policy Implications

Although the Cold War has ended, its effects have not. In the same way that early atmospheric nuclear tests left extensive radioactive fallout that persisted for many years, so too has the Cold War left extensive psychological fallout which embodies some of the obstacles discussed earlier and thwarts movement toward real security.

The heart of this legacy is a narrowing fixation on military approaches to security. This fixation is crystallized in the triumphalist view that we won the Cold War--the forces of democracy made the necessary sacrifices during the supreme struggle and developed the military strength needed to defeat the evil forces of communism. In the minds of many leaders, the end of the Cold War provided strong reinforcement for the peace-through strength approach to security, decreasing willingness to scale back U.S. military forces. It also confirmed the superpower mentality that in an uncertain, dangerous world, it is best to be second to none in military power and to settle conflict with a mighty sword when it seems in one's interests to do so.

Although this fixation on military approaches to security is deeply rooted in fear and macho impulses, it also stems from the fact that during the Cold War, sprawling social institutions and millions of lives became centered around military production and readiness. Entire communities sprang up around weapons laboratories and nuclear production facilities constructed to halt the spread of communism, and vast numbers of workers derived their livelihood and their psychological security from these communities. Millions of soldiers invested their lives in the military, while thousands of defense corporations became dependent on the huge profits derived from military production. The result is a deep dependency at levels ranging from the personal to the institutional on military production and the military way of life. This dependency will be very difficult to break so long as a psychological issue as profound as self-preservation is at stake. Building durable peace will surely require sustained national conversion efforts that shift people, production, and spending from the military-industrial complex back into the civilian sector. Although this conversion is often discussed in terms of economics, it is equally psychological.

The fixation on military approaches to security is intimately connected to the preoccupation with enemies. For nearly half a century, fear of the communist enemy dominated thinking about security. This fear provided the psychological infrastructure which enabled the building of a vast national security industry having strong xenophobic tendencies, the spending of nearly $300 billion per year on defense, the fighting of wars in remote parts of the world, and support of regimes which, although objectionable, offered resistance to communism. Now that the communist enemy has melted away, there is a noticeable psychological gap and a tendency of policy leaders to cast about warily in search of new enemies. Instead of making deep cuts in the military budget, the national security establishment moves into the limelight an array of new potential enemies--Noriega, Saddam, Somali warlords, and Islamic fundamentalism--that can be used to justify huge military expenditures. If no dominant enemy looms on the horizon, the military establishment proclaims (as the Joint Chiefs of Staff did in 1992) that the new threat is instability, an idea that draws its strength from our subterranean fear of the other. This fear of the other which became deeply ingrained during the Cold War stimulates worst case thinking, encourages continued weapons development, and thwarts proactive security efforts such as providing significant economic aid to the struggling remnants of the Soviet Union.

But the full scope of the psychological impact of the Cold War is most apparent in the unidimensionality of current concepts of security. Throughout the Cold War, security was defined in terms of containing the enemy. Peace was thought of only in negative terms, and positive peace was dismissed as wishful thinking. Furthermore, issues such as environmental degradation, homelessness, and economic decline were explicitly not defined as primary security problems. In fact, the latter were often viewed as the tolerable costs of protecting freedom through military readiness and action. In essence, the Cold War left a legacy of psychological fragmentation, a splintering of consciousness that obscures the rich interconnections between these issues and blocks movement toward a broader view of security. This broader view must create a bridge between positive and negative peace, and it must encompass a broad array of security problems such as proliferation, ecodestruction, community degradation and violence, social inequities, poverty, hunger, inadequate health care and education, among many others. It must point the way beyond militaristic approaches toward cooperative strategies that create a psychological infrastructure for nonviolence.

Creating psychological conditions which are conducive to nonviolence is no small task. But our hopes should be lifted by the fact that ten years ago, virtually no one foresaw a rapid end to the Cold War. Deep social transformation is possible, despite its apparent impossibility at any particular moment in time. By gaining an understanding of the psychological obstacles to peace, we put ourselves in a better position to overcome these obstacles and to develop effective strategies for moving toward a nonviolent world. It is a privilege to participate in this quest for nonviolence.

REFERENCES

Anderson, J.R. (1985). Cognitive psychology and its implications (2nd ed.). New York: Freeman.

Barnet, R.J. (1972). Roots of war: The men and institutions behind U.S. Foreign Policy. New York: Penguin.

Bernstein, J. (1981). Prophet of energy: Hans Bethe. New York: Dutton.

Bronfenbrenner, U. (1961). The mirror-image in Soviet-American relations. Journal of Social Issues, 17, 45-56.

Christie, D.J., & Murphy, T. (in press). Developmental changes in nuclear and other concerns. Journal of Adolescence & Youth.

Cohn, C. (1987). Slick 'ems, glick 'ems, Christmas trees, and cookie cutters: Nuclear language and how we learned to pat the bomb. Bulletin of the Atomic Scientists, 43, 17-24.

Deutsch, M. (1983). The prevention of World War III: A psychological perspective. Political Psychology, 4, 3-31.

Diamond, G., & Bachman, J. (1986). High-school seniors and the nuclear threat, 1975-1984: Political and mental health implications of concern and despair. International Journal of Mental Health, 15, 210-241.

Escalona, S.K. (1982). Growing up with the threat of nuclear war: Some indirect effects on personality development. American Journal of Orthopsychiatry, 52, 600-607.

Frank, J. (1987). The drive for power and the nuclear arms race. American Psychologist, 42, 337-344.

Goldberg, S., LaCombe, S., Levinson, D., Parker, K.R., Ross, C., & Sommers, F. (1985). Thinking about nuclear war: Relevance to mental health. American Journal of Orthopsychiatry, 55, 503-512.

Halbertstam, D. (1972). The best and the brightest. New York: Random House.

Hesse, P., & Mack, J.E. (1991). The world is a dangerous place: Images of the enemy on children's television. In R.R. Rieber (Ed.), The psychology of war and peace: The image of the enemy (pp. 131-153). New York: Plenum Press.

Jervis, R. (1976). Perception and misperception in international politics. Princeton: Princeton University Press.

Kaku, M., & Axelrod, D. (1987). To win a nuclear war: The Pentagon's secret war plans. Boston: South End.

Khong, Y.F. (1991). The lessons of Korea and the Vietnam decisions of 1965. In G. Breslauer & P. E. Tetlock (Eds.), Learning in U.S. and Soviet Foreign Policy (pp. 302-349). Boulder: Westview.

Larson, D.W. (1991). Learning in U.S.- Soviet Relations: The Nixon-Kissinger structure of peace. In G. Breslauer & P.E. Tetlock (Eds.), Learning in U.S. and Soviet Foreign Policy (pp. 350-399). Boulder: Westview.

Lifton, R.J. (1979). Connection: On death and the continuity of life. New York: Touchstone.

Lifton, R.J. (1982). Beyond psychic numbing: A call to awareness. American Journal of Orthopsychiatry, 52, 619-629.

Lifton, R.J. (1986). The Nazi doctors: Medical killing and the psychology of genocide. New York: Basic Books.

Lifton, R.J., & Markusen, E. (1990). The genocidal mentality: Nazi Holocaust and nuclear threat. New York: Basic Books.

Locatelli, M.G., & Holt, R.H. (1986). Antinuclear activism, psychic numbing, and mental health. International Journal of Mental Health, 15, 143-161.

Nelson, A. (1985). Psychological equivalence: Awareness and response-ability in our nuclear age. American Psychologist, 40, 549-556.

Neustadt, R.E., & May, E.R. (1986). Thinking in time: The uses of history for decision makers. New York: Free Press.

Newcomb, M.D. (1986). Nuclear attitudes and reactions: Associations with depression, drug use, and quality of life. Journal of Personality and Social Psychology, 50, 906-920.

Oskamp, S. (1965). Attitudes toward U.S. and Soviet actions--A double standard. Psychological Reports, 16, 43-46.

Oskamp, S. (1968). Relationship of self-concept to international attitudes. Journal of Social Psychology, 76, 31-36.

Pruitt, D.G. (1965). Definition of the situation as a determinant of international action. In H. Kelman (Ed.), International behavior: A social-psychological analysis (pp. 393-432). New York: Holt, Rinehart & Winston.

Rumelhart, D.E. (1977). Introduction to human information processing. New York: Wiley.

Sande, G.N., Goethals, G.R., Ferrari, L., & Worth, L.T. (1989). Value-guided attributions: Maintaining the moral self-image and the diabolical enemy image. Journal of Social Issues, 45, 91-118.

Schank, R.C., & Abelson, R.P. (1977). Scripts, plans, goals and understanding: An inquiry into human knowledge structures. Hillsdale, NJ: Erlbaum.

Schatz, R.T., & Fiske, S.T. (1992). International reactions to the threat of nuclear war: The rise and fall of concern in the eighties. Political Psychology, 13, 1-29.

Schuman, H., Ludwig, J., & Kroskick, J.A. (1986). The perceived threat of nuclear war, salience, and open questions. Public Opinion Quarterly, 50, 519-536.

Schwebel, M. (1982). Effects of the nuclear war threat on children and teenagers: Implications for professionals. American Journal of Orthopsychiatry, 52, 608-618.

Schwebel, M. (1990). The construction of reality in the nuclear age. Political Psychology, 11, 521-522.

Silverstein, B. (1989). Enemy images: The psychology of U.S. attitudes and cognitions regarding the Soviet Union. American Psychologist, 44, 903-313.

Silverstein, B. (1992). The psychology of enemy images. In R.R. Rieber (Ed.), The psychology of war and peace: The image of the enemy (pp. 145-162). New York: Plenum Press.

Silverstein, B., & Flamenbaum, C. (1989). Biases in the perception and cognition of the actions of enemies. Journal of Social Issues, 45, 51-72.

Smith, M.B. (1986). War, peace, and psychology. Journal of Social Issues, 42, 23-38.

Solantaus, T. (1991). Young people and the threat of nuclear war: A literature review. Medicine and war, 7, supplement 1.

Wessells, M.G. (1982). Cognitive psychology. New York: Harper & Row.

White, R.K. (1984). Fearful warriors: A psychological profile of U.S.-Soviet relations. New York: Free Press.

White, R.K. (1991). Enemy images in the United Nations-Iraq and East-West Conflicts. In R.R. Rieber (Ed.), The psychology of war and peace: The image of the enemy (pp. 59-70). New York: Plenum Press.

Yankelovich, D., & Doble, J. (1986). The public mood: Nuclear weapons and the USSR. In R.K. White (Ed.), Psychology and the prevention of nuclear war (pp. 38-54). New York: New York University Press.

Yatani, C., & Bramel, D. (1989). Trends and patterns in Americans' attitudes toward the Soviet Union. Journal of Social Issues, 45, 13-32.

CHAPTER 3

Nuclear War Fears
Across the Life Cycle

Stephen McConnell, Barry Duncan, Debra Merrifield

"Nuclear weapons are psychological weapons whose purpose is not to be employed, but to maintain a permanent state of mind: terror in the adversary. Their target is someone's mind."

> - Jonathan Schell,
> *The Fate of the Earth*

Since the 1945 bombings of Hiroshima and Nagasaki, humankind has lived with the knowledge that the world is in a precarious balance, as peace is sought amidst the threat of complete destruction. The psychological impact of living under the threat of nuclear war is hypothesized to be significant. Researchers have attempted to delineate the effects with extant limited empirical studies for understanding the impact on individuals' lives. Unfortunately, the majority of work is theoretical and speculative due to the paucity of data.

The purpose of this chapter is to compile the facts, theories, and hypotheses about life in the nuclear age from several disciplines: psychology, psychiatry, family systems, sociology, and education. The impact of the nuclear threat is explored across the life cycle in terms of its effects upon the completion of normal developmental tasks. Concrete suggestions are offered for coping with the nuclear threat in childhood, adolescence, adulthood, the establishment of a family, and finally old age.

Each section will follow the same format. First, a summary of normal human development in each specific phase of the life cycle will be outlined. Second, research regarding the awareness of the nuclear war threat and subsequent action will be presented. Parts one and two will then be integrated to describe the developmental tasks within the nuclear context, and to discuss the impact of the nuclear threat on human development. Finally, practical activities for coping with life in the nuclear age will be suggested.

Normal Life Cycle

Erikson's (1968) stage model of development is a widely accepted description of the human life cycle. At age six, some children seem to have a preliminary awareness of the nuclear threat. Erikson's developmental stage between the ages of six and twelve proposes that children work on competency issues. Activities for mastery are important for development of Erikson's "industry" versus a feeling of inferiority, as one compares oneself to a peer group. School offers the scenario to play out the drama of mastery, evaluated by social comparison (Dinner, 1976; Pepitone, 1972).

The developmental changes charted by Erikson occur in conjunction with changes in the spheres of cognition and morality. According to Piaget (1952), children ages six to twelve display a decrease in the egocentrism of early childhood. A new skill appears as the child develops an ability to take the role of another. Problem solving increases in importance as children learn to act and interact in the world. Problem solving strategies then arise from a thinking process which is logical and concrete.

In terms of the moral development of young children, Kohlberg's (1963) preconventional stage suggests behavior is defined as "moral" or "good" as it avoids punishment or is rewarded. There is little internalization of moral standards. A child will defer to powerful people (e.g., parents, teachers) to avoid being punished. Physical consequences define the "morality" of an act.

The transition from childhood to adolescence involves shifts in several developmental areas. According to Erikson, adolescents struggle with identity issues, seeking to define themselves and their place in the world, in an effort to avoid role confusion. They begin to move away from dependence on parents to a position of competence and self-sufficiency. Sexual identity and occupational preparation are important components of an adolescent's sense of self.

Cognitive development during the preadolescent and early adolescent stages is characterized by a shift in the ability to handle abstract material (Piaget & Inhelder, 1969). With increased age, there is a move away from the concrete to a comfort with manipulating abstract information. As young people make the transition from the late stages of childhood into adolescence, there is also a change in moral development. As adolescence is entered, Kohlberg's stage of conventional morality (obeying rules in order to win praise and recognition or to maintain social order) becomes salient.

The Nuclear War Threat: Awareness and (In)Action

Research reveals that the possibility of nuclear war is acknowledged by many young people. Forty to eighty-five percent of adolescents report an awareness of the threat of nuclear war between ten to twelve years of age (Beardslee, 1986; Beardslee & Mack, 1983; Goldberg, 1988; Goldenring & Doctor, 1986). The self-reported response to an awareness and understanding of the nuclear threat is fear (Beardslee

& Mack, 1983; Reifel, 1984). Young children fear losing parents, teachers, and pets. They fear surviving a nuclear war and being alone without caretakers. Murphy & Monarity (1976) have likened such fear to a preschooler's response to an expected disaster, e.g., a tornado. These youngsters do not fear dying, but being left alone to fend for themselves. Only after age eight, when most children have some concept of their own mortality, do they fear their own deaths (Ross, 1984; Salguero, 1983).

Adolescents experience fear in terms of their future. The majority of teenagers consistently list "nuclear war" in their top three worries about the future (Goldenring & Doctor, 1983) and 31% report "often worrying" about nuclear annihilation (Bachman, 1983). Bachman's work cites a significant increase in reports of nuclear war fear for adolescents during the past decade, with 7% indicating nuclear worry in 1976, increasing four fold by 1982. Nuclear war fear is not only a phenomenon of the 1970s and 1980s. Escalona (1965) found that 40% of adolescents polled in the early 1960s expected a nuclear war within the next ten years. By 1970, 70% reported the same expectation (Escalona, 1975). The interviewers made no reference to war or war issues.

Schwebel (1982) sampled 3,000 children, approaching war issues more directly. Forty-four percent of young people expected nuclear war within their lifetimes and 95% reported concerns about that prospect. Schwebel (1982) and Escalona (1982) reported similar findings as children described feelings of helplessness and powerlessness when thinking about nuclear war. Children also expressed disbelief about having a future at all, as well as resentment toward adults.

Mack (1985) reports children's comments concerning their fantasies about the future. Children report feeling like they have "a lump in their chest" and hope "to commit suicide before the bomb hits them." They have fantasies that they "won't be 42," as life will be prematurely shortened in a nuclear holocaust. The hypothesized fear of futurelessness is supported in findings that as many as 80% of young people have changed their future plans based on an expectation of nuclear war (Goldenring & Doctor, 1985; Sandler et al., 1985). Without a guaranteed future, Mack (1984) proposes that young people do not adopt long term goals, living for the moment with no capacity to delay gratification.

Similar findings have been reported in Norway and Sweden (Raundalen & Finney, 1986). Children ages eleven to thirteen reported high levels of pessimism about the future (girls = 49.6%; boys = 54.1%). They also reported that it seemed meaningless to further their education since they would, most likely, never have the opportunity to use it.

Chivian et al. (1985) found Soviet adolescents aware of the nuclear threat an average of four to six years earlier than teens in the United States. Soviets were also better informed and could recite more accurate information about Hiroshima and radiation sickness than could American teens (Chivian et al., 1985). Research in Finland (Solantus, Rimpela, & Ossi, 1985), Sweden (Holmberg & Bergstrom, 1985) and the Soviet Union (Chivian et al., 1985) found adolescents citing "nuclear war" as their top concern for the future. Canadian teens listed fear of nuclear war in their top three worries (Goldberg et al., 1985). The experience of fear in response to an understanding of the threat of nuclear war seems to be universal.

Stillion (1986) suggests the expression of fear may be different according to age. Older children and younger adolescents (ages twelve to fourteen) report a more intense experience of fear. Older adolescents seem to control this fear reaction with denial (Beardslee & Mack, 1983; Schwebel, 1982; Tizard, 1984). Despite older adolescents' identification of the nuclear threat as a concern, only about 10% worry to such a degree that it interferes with daily functioning (Goldenring & Doctor, 1986). The remaining 90%, who report concern, may use rationalization or denial to keep their fear in check (Beardslee & Mack, 1983; Schwebel, 1982).

Developmental Tasks Within the Nuclear Context

The initial awareness of nuclear war occurs for most children during Erikson's stage four, when they are working toward mastery and competence. Information about the nuclear threat, in the absence of activities for mastery, may overwhelm a fragile and developing sense of competence. The experience of worrying about nuclear war without viable options for achieving mastery over their fears may result in problems for some children (Buban, 1986; Buban, McConnell, & Duncan, 1988). The problems may manifest themselves in the expression of feelings of hopelessness about the future, questioning whether one will be able to grow up at all. Greenwald and Zeitlin (1987) suggest that this age group may cope with nuclear war information with concrete problem solving--e.g., building rockets during play to abandon a war torn, radioactive planet. More typically, children may express a sense of despair. These feelings of hopelessness and helplessness are believed to result from a perception of themselves as having little power or control over nuclear war (Schwebel, 1982). There is still a reliance on adults, namely parents, for security and protection.

Nuclear war is conceptualized by children in concrete and literal terms because of their limited capacity for abstraction. Their descriptions include the destruction of schools and churches and all that is familiar to them. There is a shift during this stage regarding the child's handling of this anxiety-provoking information. Children's play, as a means of anxiety reduction, is replaced by the development of logical strategies and the initiation of action to combat feelings of fear. The child attempts to develop a "plan" in response to a nuclear war, including "where to go" and "where to hide." Yet, if nuclear war means total destruction, in concrete terms, the child is often left feeling overwhelmed, as there is "no place to hide." The child, at this stage, can no longer rely on immature strategies, such as make believe. There is, also, a new ability developing in this stage, to take the position of another (Piaget, 1952). This may complicate the nuclear fear experience as the child fears for family and friends, as well as for him/herself.

Moral development may also impact upon the response to the nuclear threat. Older children in Kohlberg's (1963) conventional stage of moral reasoning wish to please or win the approval of others (parents, teachers). Children may want to take a stand on nuclear war which is consistent with the parental view. Research reveals, however, that most families do not discuss nuclear war and children do not know how their parents feel about the issue (Block, 1984; Simon, 1984; Zeitlin, 1984). It may be difficult for children to bring their fears and feelings about the threat of nuclear war to their parents. Children may worry that an expression of nuclear war fear may be denounced or seen as inappropriate by their parents. Children at this age define what is "moral" and "good" by that which is pleasing to adult authority. Nuclear fears are felt by many children to be inappropriate for family discussion (Zeitlin, 1984). The "moral reprisal" for approaching the topic is feared parental punishment. The moral dilemma created is between the belief that nuclear war is wrong coupled with the belief that talking about it is also wrong.

Moral development includes an acceptance of and conformity to social rules which are believed valuable for maintaining social order. The difficulty for adolescents at this stage is in understanding that an acceptance of the social convention of nuclear war as an appropriate response to international conflict is coupled with an understanding that nuclear war means mass death and destruction. A moral dilemma is created. Adolescents want to believe in the sanctity of social laws and order but they may understand that to do so places them in grave danger.

Cognitive development in the high risk young adolescent group (ages twelve to fourteen) involves a shift in the ability to handle abstract material (Piaget & Inhelder, 1969). Nuclear war fear in this age group may reflect an increased ability to conceptualize political and world issues. However, there may not be an opportunity or an ability to perform social action (Buban et al., 1988). There is an increased understanding of the nuclear threat but without the means to activate the new awareness. Adolescents' comfortability with manipulating abstract material also enables them to become idealists, conceptualizing the way the world should be. The gap between the ideal and reality is difficult for this group to accept, especially as they confront their lack of political power.

As they age, adolescents experience a shift from competency issues to working on identity versus role confusion (Erikson, 1968). Future plans increase in importance as one begins to define oneself by "what I will be when I grow up." Yet nuclear war threatens the prospect of any future at all. Older adolescents may become angry and cynical, blaming adults for their lack of ability to manage world affairs. Or they may deny all concern about nuclear war, adopting the motto, "Eat, drink and be merry for tomorrow we die" (Frank, 1986). There is speculation that the increasing teenage suicide rate and recreational drug use may be related to this response to the nuclear threat (Schwebel, 1982).

Practical Activities for Living in the Nuclear Age

The common theme running through the nuclear fear literature is that a significant number (range from 35% to 70%) of children and adolescents are concerned about the threat of a nuclear holocaust (Bachman, 1983; Escalona, 1975). Coupled with this finding is the knowledge that young people feel better when they can discuss their fears with parents and adults (Greenwald & Zeitlin, 1987; Ross,

1984; Salguero, 1983; Zeitlin, 1984). Nuclear worry need not be a debilitating anxiety; rather, some concern may facilitate dialogue, leaving young people with a greater sense of optimism and a sense of personal control over the future (Greenwald & Zeitlin, 1987; Goldenring & Doctor, 1986; Ross, 1984; Salguero, 1983; Zeitlin, 1984). Gaining some sense of control over one's future through dialogue and action may serve to decrease nihilism and increase optimism (Goldenring & Doctor, 1986).

Dialogue is the first step in confronting nuclear fears. Yet, only about 10% of adolescents have ever talked with their parents about their concerns (Goldenring & Doctor, 1986). Often, parents believe nuclear fears are not a reality for young people. Escalona (1982) has observed that growing up in a culture which ignores the possibility of total annihilation may foster patterns of cynicism in its young people. Adolescents, who see adults as apathetic and uncaring about the threat of nuclear war, may hide their fear under the assumption that adults would not understand. The educational system can provide a critical component of the dialogue process (parental intervention is covered in the Family Section). Myers-Walls and Fry-Miller (1984) suggest a three part approach to addressing the nuclear concerns of young children. Their suggestions include: (1) providing opportunities for children to receive age-appropriate information and to acknowledge and accept their fears and anger; (2) fostering a sense of control in children through opportunities for public policy involvement, such as those provided through the Children's Campaign for Nuclear Disarmament; and (3) teaching positive and nonviolent conflict management skills to children. Snow and Goodman (1984) argue for nuclear education programs as part of high school curricula. These programs (currently available) would allow students to explore the controversial nature of the nuclear arms issue and articulate their own position.

Blackwell and Gessner (1983) also argue for concerted educational efforts directed at increasing youth awareness of the social, ethical, and technical dimensions of the nuclear threat. They call for a massive education of the citizenry through the schools, media, churches, and other organizations. The junior and senior high school student can be introduced to the issues of nuclear war through a number of simulation games, the regular curriculum, and community projects. Discussion of nonviolent conflict resolution, negotiation, prejudice, and global economics can offer students opportunities to develop an empowered view of the future.

There are a number of nuclear war resources for both parents and professionals to use with children (available from authors). Two important preliminary steps are necessary before introducing these experiences to children. First, parents and professionals are strongly urged to clarify their attitudes, values, beliefs, and feelings before attempting to work with children. The second step toward exploring children's fears of nuclear war is the development of a clear idea about where the children need to be at the end of the exercise. What are the specific goals? How are the children empowered through this exercise, so that their feelings of fear and powerlessness are addressed? The importance of these two steps is highlighted by the findings of teachers that many children have no concrete concept of peace, hold ill-founded prejudices about the "enemy," lack peacemaking role models, and express both powerlessness regarding nuclear issues and cynicism about the future (Educators For Social Responsibility, 1983).

The resources for preschool, kindergarten, and elementary children can focus on the developmental issues of prosocial behavior, verbalizing feelings, and resolving conflicts nonviolently. A group activity looking at differences among people, for example, is addressed in the Human Rainbow exercise. Children make and color masks and then form a circle, building a human rainbow around the room. Discussions focus on similarities and differences among people, as well as each child's creative ideas. Utilizing another group exercise, an altercation between preschoolers can become an opportunity for the class to explore conflict resolution. A peace zone can be designated, reserved for activities and experiences that make peace alive and exciting. Constructive methods of expressing anger, frustration, and disappointment can be modeled. Humanizing the "enemy," negotiation and cooperation can be stressed.

A Computer-based Intervention

The application of computer-based interventions in education is now a fact of life. Tom Snyder Productions, Inc., of Boston, MA, has developed The Other Side, a computer game that challenges players to prevent a simulated nuclear war through cooperative means. The use of such a computer game directly addresses the concrete to formal operational shift of the older child and younger adolescent by providing an activity, in the form of the game, that encourages their mastery of nuclear fears.

Children are usually unsuccessful in their initial attempts to cooperate (resulting in "a world so polluted no one could live in it...Game Over") (Vincent, 1986). The game is an effective tool for teaching children about nuclear issues, international affairs, the subtle complexities of negotiation, win-lose and win-win strategies, and outcomes. The Other Side can be played by a child and parent at home or by teams of students in the classroom.

Adults and the Nuclear War Threat

Normal Life Cycle

Freud, Spock and Piaget have comprehensively charted childhood and puberty. Erik Erikson put the final touches on an epigenetic chart to include adolescence, young adulthood, adulthood and maturity. Erikson and three important life-cycle scholars--psychiatrist Roger Gould (1978), psychologist Daniel Levinson (1978) and psychiatrist George Vaillant (1977)--have reached remarkably similar conclusions about post adolescent life. The main features:

16-22: *Leaving the Family.* Identity vs. role confusion is the main developmental task. Who am I and where do I begin and end are the dominant issues.

The peer group becomes paramount in an effort to assert one's individuality and break the hold of the family.

23-28: *Reaching Out.* Though the search for personal identity continues to be a dominant feature of the 20's, this period is also an age of reaching toward others. The capability to develop intimacy and make commitments is tested and stretched The growing adult is powerful, expansive and keyed on mastering the world.

29-34: *Questions, Questions.* Assurance wavers, as life begins to look more difficult and painful around age 30. Self-reflection churns up new questions: "What is life all about?" "Is this it?" "I thought I would have arrived by now!" There is a wrenching struggle among incompatible drives: for stability, attachments and roots, for freedom from all restraints, for upward mobility at work.

35-43: *Mid-life Explosion.* Death will come; time is running out. This is the first emotional awareness of "I will die." Like a second adolescence, all values are open to question, and the mid-lifer wonders, is there time to change? There is "one last chance to make it big" in one's career. The mid-life crisis does not have to be catastrophic. It does herald a new stage of growth.

44-50: *Settling Down.* A stable time: the die is cast, decisions must be lived with, and life settles down. A few old values and a few friends become more important. The successful mid-lifer does not stagnate but emerges to help, nurture, teach and serve the next generation.

After 50: *Emotional Integration.* Mellowing brings an acceptance of one's one and only life cycle with no substitutions. There is a sense of some world order and meaning, often accompanied by an increasing spiritual awareness. Having taken care of things and people and adapted to triumphs and disappointments, a core of solidness--integrity--is felt. In such final consolidation, death loses its sting. A lack of accrued integration is signified by despair and fear of death.

The Nuclear War Threat: Awareness and (In)Action

The great majority of adult Americans report little everyday worry about the nuclear threat with no impact on future plans because nuclear war simply will not happen. Yet, many individuals and groups within our society have become concerned and actively involved in opposing nuclear proliferation. Indeed, a Gallup poll in 1981 showed 72% of the American public wanted the U.S. and U.S.S.R. to stop building nuclear weapons (Rogers, 1982). Later Gallup polls (1983 and 1986) also found the majority of adults supporting a mutual arms freeze. However, most people do nothing to prevent nuclear war despite their concern because they don't believe they can do anything about it (Fiske, 1987).

With a paucity of empirical research on adults and nuclear war, theory and speculation have filled the vacuum. McGraw and Tyler (1986) and Frank (1986) have characterized five different reactions to the threat of nuclear war by adult sub-groups. The survivalists' basic premise is nuclear war cannot be prevented, but it can be survived. The activists' basic premise is: nuclear war can be prevented, but it cannot be survived. The romanticists believe the basic goodness of humanity will save us all. The disarmers, modern day abolitionists, seek to totally empty the nuclear war arsenals. The eliminationists look to the Star Wars defense plan to enable a surprise attack on the enemy, intercept its missiles, and secure an ultimate "win" for our side.

Lifton (1982) has described the "illusions of nuclear war." The illusion of control is evidenced by the belief that limited nuclear war is possible. The illusion of foreknowledge predicates it is possible to prepare people psychologically, as with a flood or tornado. The illusion of preparation is played out with civil defense programs with plans for evacuation and temporary shelters. Following the U.S. ethos of strength and power, the illusion of a "tough" America remains calm amidst--if not impervious to--worldwide panic. With "peace through strength," there is the desire to protect one's own, yet the capacity to destroy all others. Finally, there is the illusion of recovery which posits a return to a pre-war level of cultural functioning.

Excessive use of the denial defense mechanism and an apathetic, business-as-usual attitude toward the threat of nuclear destruction can lead to a phenomenon called psychic numbing. A person can become emotionally insensitive about the prospect of war and life in general. There is a dulled sense of aliveness, morality, sensation and stimulation. There is a loss of a sense of awe and appreciation for life's beauty and vibrancy. Feeling overburdened and threatened by the prospect of nuclear war, the focus narrows to aspects of life which are controllable: work, raising children, household chores, and other matters of consequence to the complete exclusion of consideration of larger societal issues.

What are the specific reasons why people care (about the nuclear threat) but do not act? Obviously, there is a clear inconsistency between attitudes and behavior. Gilbert (1988) trenchantly outlined the dynamics of inaction and noninvolvement. He posited seven psychological factors that interrupt the connection between concern about nuclear arms policies and subsequent action:

(1) Antinuclear is anti-American. Individuals who actively oppose nuclear arms policies may have to defend their commitment to the national interest and perhaps face questions regarding their sense of patriotism.

(2) The demands of daily living. After coping with work, school, family, friends, chores and responsibilities, many individuals would rather relax than pursue activism.

(3) Lack of perceived economic consequences. Spending for nuclear arms and other military projects has yet to noticeably affect the economic interests of the influential middle and upper classes.

(4) Lack of salient risk. Nuclear war is an abstract possibility until the moment is too late. Being only a possibility, it is relatively easy to minimize and deny the risk involved.

(5) Expertism. Individuals have a tendency to defer to experts to determine nuclear policy because of the technical complexity of the issues.
(6) Maze of objectives. Though the peace movement is united in its basic commitment to reduce the threat of nuclear weapons, the various groups are not coordinated and promote divergent goals. With a plurality of objectives, an individual's certainty in working for a particular goal is reduced.
(7) Helplessness. The individual feels powerless and believes one's actions cannot significantly influence government policy related to nuclear arms.

Developmental Tasks Within the Nuclear Context

The avoidance of nuclear war is a powerful issue in today's world, yet most people do nothing to prevent it. The basic task of adulthood, to be powerful and productive members of the society, may be thwarted by feelings of powerlessness in response to the nuclear threat. Powerlessness includes pessimism and cynicism about efforts to avert nuclear war. This is accompanied by a gradual shift from an internal to an external locus of control (Rotter, 1982). This sense of powerlessness has been likened to the fatalistic experience of the Medieval human, finding him/herself at the mercy of famine and plague, going on with life but awaiting certain death. A generalized, free-floating anxiety and vague feelings of futurelessness and hopelessness may be present (Wear, 1987). Dreams, with nuclear annihilation as a predominant theme, may occur. Dealing with the nuclear problem certainly means acknowledging one's own vulnerability and confronting one's own mortality.

The nuclear threat has and is taking its human toll. For example, surveys of ten thousand American and foreign college students discovered one out of six have already changed their future plans because of the threat of nuclear war (Johnson & Bacik, 1987; Johnson, Taylor & Witford, 1987). Among American students, the most common change in plans is a decision not to get married or have children. On the other hand, some senior citizens may reaffirm life and look after the next generation by trying to reduce the likelihood of nuclear war.

In summary, the nuclear threat ripples throughout the life cycle and subtly touches us all, yet few of us notice, and fewer still respond. Most people go through life as if the nuclear threat were nonexistent. They compartmentalize a wall between their everyday world and the world of a nuclear holocaust.

Psychologists' Attitudes and Activities Regarding Nuclear War

Psychology, a specific subset of the general population, has not been exempt from the concern and controversy surrounding nuclear armament issues. On August 25, 1982, the American Psychological Association's (APA) Council of Representatives passed a resolution for a nuclear freeze and a return to a productive civilian economy.

The attitudes and activities of APA members regarding nuclear arms were later investigated (McConnell et al., 1986). The findings indicated that current peace-related activities of the majority of respondents included reading relevant literature (79.1 %), signing petitions (53.5%), and participating in informal discussion (67.3%). However, the majority of respondents did not participate in the other activities include in the survey: distributing relevant literature, making financial contributions, volunteering time in an organization to promote awareness of nuclear arms, participating in marches or demonstrations, and taking a leadership role to organize groups and activities. The majority of respondents (83.2% to 99.7%) had not given time, energy, or money to the various peace-related professional organizations. Almost 17% were connected with the Union of Concerned Scientists, followed by Physicians for Social Responsibility (10.8%), followed by Psychologists for Social Responsibility (8.4%), and the National Peace Academy (4.7%).

Seventy-six and one-half percent of the respondents believed nuclear war is not inevitable. Fifty-six percent of the respondents indicated they would not want to survive an all-out nuclear war. Respondents were asked to comment on reasons why they would or would not want to survive. Of those who provided a reason for wanting to survive an all-out nuclear war, the most frequently occurring theme addressed the intrinsic value of life itself at any cost. Of those who provided a reason for not wanting to survive, the highest percentage was concerned that life would be lacking in quality following a nuclear war.

Those respondents with no antinuclear activities were asked to comment on factors contributing to their noninvolvement. The greatest number fell into "other priorities" (lack of time, money, or energy). Other factors were "apathy" (feelings of indifference, learned helplessness, denial, and powerlessness) and a belief in the deterrent effect of nuclear arms.

Practical Activities for Living in the Nuclear Age

Most adults read (relevant literature), watch (TV), and talk (in informal discussions) about nuclear arms and the possibility of war. Many adults would like to do more, but may be inhibited by lack of knowledge of the range of alternatives available that enable a small but significant contribution to be made. A broad array of options follows (McConnell & Duncan, 1987).

Adults can practice nonviolence and ensure their families respond to conflict creatively without violence. They can be open to information about the nuclear issue, reflecting on it for oneself and discussing it with others, from church to civic groups. They can be aware of the issues and use the power of the democratic system by voting one's beliefs. Getting involved with local grassroot community groups can also give one support for examining the nuclear threat. Activities might include letter writing to Congressional representatives and newspaper editors, raising nuclear concerns. Encouragement may be offered to schools to incorporate nuclear war and peace topics as well as conflict resolution into the curriculum. Teaching guides come from the National Education Association and Educators for Social Responsibility. Communities can establish themselves as a Nuclear Free Zone, which prohibits the development, funding and usage of nuclear weapons within designated borders.

Currently, world-wide, there are over a thousand Nuclear Free Zones. At the state level, there are various groups which recognize that we live in a world which needs to learn how to respond to conflict creatively without violence. Education along this line is encouraged at the university, corporate and judicial levels with alternate dispute resolution programs. Nationally, it is possible to write letters to the President. He might be requested to accept the 1983 recommendation of 11,500 physicists--including 22 American Nobel Laureates--to halt all further testing, production and deployment of nuclear weapons. Congressional representatives could be asked to support the No First Use Resolution, which holds that the United States will never institute a nuclear confrontation.

The National Peace Institute Foundation welcomes membership and support from individual citizens. The United States Institute of Peace recognizes that we live in a global society that needs to learn how to satisfy honor and principles without resorting to violence. The Institute embodies the heritage and ideals of the American people for peace. It has started to develop a range of effective options, in addition to armed capacity, that can leash international violence and manage international conflict.

International involvement could include letter writing to Mr. Mikhail Gorbechev, 4 Storaya Ploshchad, Moscow, U.S.S.R., and supporting the cultural exchange of artists, scientists, students, government officials, children, and special citizens' study groups. It is also possible to join a tour to Russia and China and become a citizen ambassador. In addition, international law can be strengthened and cooperative enterprises encouraged through the United Nations. The U.N.'s superordinate mission is the welfare of the world (good planets are hard to find) as it tries to soften the concept of "sovereign" countries. A statement, in favor of a more personalized and maybe safer world, could also be made by participation in the Soviet-American Photo Exchange. A picture of you and your family in the living room of your home is sent to a Soviet family who in turn sends a similar photo to you. Both families keep each other's picture displayed at all times in their living rooms.

Families and the Nuclear War Threat

Normal Life Cycle

The most widely accepted delineation of the family life cycle is that of Duvall (1977), which has been elaborated upon by Carter & McGoldrick (1988). Duvall separates the family life cycle into stages addressing the events related to the comings and goings of family members: marriage, the birth and raising of children, the departure of children, retirement, and death. Childrearing is emphasized as the organizing element of family life.

Carter & McGoldrick (1988) suggest that each stage requires an emotional process of transition and change in family status to enable the family to proceed developmentally. In families with young children, the key principle of the emotional process of transition is the acceptance of new members into the family. Acceptance requires several family status changes, including adjusting the marital relationship to make space for children, joining with spouse in childrearing, financial, and household tasks, and realigning relationships with extended family to include parenting and grandparenting roles.

The shift to this stage of the family life cycle requires that adults now move up a generation and become caretakers of the younger generation. Given that fewer than 10% of families fit into the traditional norm of working father, stay-at-home mother, and children (Friedan, 1985), the central struggle of this phase in the modern dual career marriage is the disposition of child care and domestic responsibilities. The issues of gender and the impact of sex role expectations weigh heavily and it may not be surprising that this is the family stage with the highest divorce rate.

In families with adolescents, the key principle of the emotional process of transition is increasing flexibility of family boundaries to include children's independence and grandparents' frailties. Changes required include the shifting of parent/child relationships to permit adolescents to move in and out of the family, refocusing of the adults on midlife and career issues, and the beginning shift toward the care of the older generation (Carter & McGoldrick 1988).

The shift to this stage of the family life cycle represents a new era because it marks a redefinition of the children within the family and of the parents' role in relation to the children. Parents must essentially transform their view of themselves to allow for the increasing independence of the new generation while maintaining appropriate boundaries and structure to foster continued family development. The central event in the marital relationship is often the midlife exploration of one or both spouses of personal, career, and marital satisfactions and dissatisfactions.

The next stage of the family life cycle involves the launching of children and a redefinition of the marital relationship. The key principle of this emotional process of transition is the acceptance of a multitude of exits from and entries into the family system. This stage requires that the rules of the marital dyad be renegotiated and the development of adult relationships between grown children and their parents be recalibrated. The realignment of relationships to include in-laws and grandchildren must also be addressed and the possible disability and inevitable death of parents endured (Carter & McGoldrick, 1988).

Because of the low birth rate and long life span of most adults, parents launch children almost twenty years before retirement and therefore must find other life activities. Parents not only must deal with the change in their own status as they make room for the next generation and prepare to assume grandparent positions, but also with a different type of relationship with their own parents, who may become dependent and require caretaking.

The Nuclear War Threat: Awareness and (In)Action

Literature addressing the familial response is almost entirely conceptual and speculative; only limited quasi-research data exist. Most research with families has been restricted to interview formats.

Parental influence on children's abilities to cope with threatening experiences is a significant variable regarding children's responses to the nuclear threat (Rutter, 1981; Tizard, 1984). The presence of a supportive family network can insulate children from psychological distress due to threatening social forces. Based on a review of stress, coping, and development, Rutter (1981) has identified parental attitudes and children's cognitive appraisals of stressful experiences to be very important to the children's successful adaptation. Parental behaviors have a direct impact on their children's ability to develop a sense of mastery over their nuclear war fears.

Children report learning about the nuclear threat through the media rather than through avenues that foster opportunities for dialogue, questioning, airing of fears, and provision for emotional support. Children come to be aware of a danger that adults in their lives are not openly discussing. Regardless of the manner in which the threat is presented--through brief news shows, documentaries, or entertainment features (e.g., The Day After)--the adult world does implicitly acknowledge that the threat is indeed present. At the adult/child level of communication, the nuclear threat is not denied in the sense that it is repressed or unacknowledged, nor is it dismissed as lacking a credible reality base. Rather, the communication seems to be established with little opportunity for a sender-to-receiver feedback loop.

Parents may diminish the opportunity for dialogue with children regarding nuclear concerns through responses which essentially close down communication. Parental responses of this nature may be viewed as "denying strategies" and include discounting (e.g., there is nothing to worry about, there won't be a war); invalidating (e.g., you're too young to worry; when you're grown up, you'll understand); and implying that nuclear concerns are not normal (e.g., you should be worrying about your homework/messy room and not filling your head with such hysteria) (Duncan, Kraus & Parks, 1986). Denying strategies also include silence and other nonverbal cues that communicate that the topic is too threatening to risk an open discussion (Buban et al, 1988; Duncan et al, 1986).

These denying strategies are not only reflective of adult denial, but more importantly emerge as a protective device (Block, 1984; Simon, 1984; Zeitlin, 1984). Zeitlin, in interviews with parents and children, found that children may utilize a denial strategy to protect parents from their own vulnerability and anguish. Simon also notes the mutuality of the protective strategy. The parents do not want to upset their children and the children do not want to challenge the helplessness of their parents. The nuclear issue thus becomes a collective family secret--everyone knows about it, but no one will talk about it. Wetzel & Winawer (1986) also describe the nuclear threat as a family secret; not a secret about the past, but rather about the future. Greenwald & Zeitlin (1987) assert that such a family secret or "nuclear taboo" is self-perpetuating and holds the family system in balance by enabling the parents to avoid their own feelings and fears.

Studies of human systems, including governmental systems, may lend some understanding to parental feelings of powerlessness regarding the nuclear threat.

Today's parents are individuals who have coexisted with the nuclear threat for all, or almost all, of their lives. Many parents were introduced to the threat at a time when surviving a nuclear war was considered possible and something for which to be prepared. In addition, the threat was introduced as being best left to experts; not only was this apparent message to surrender nuclear concerns to experts explicitly communicated, but also implicitly via the secrecy associated with weapon development and deployment (Morawski & Goldstein, 1985). Such a system involving high levels of secrecy and control at the top tends to produce powerlessness and childlike feelings for those lower in the hierarchy (Zeitlin, 1984). Parents who learned to relegate responsibility to the experts also may have learned powerlessness regarding coping with the nuclear threat. Parental responses that characterize denying strategies seem to continue deferring to experts and therefore may continue to foster powerlessness.

The methods parents developed to resolve their nuclear war fears are learned by their children. The result of this pattern is cyclical perpetuation of the problem. As Fisch, Weakland, and Segal (1982) state, the continued use of unproductive behavior (parents denying the significance of children's fears of nuclear war, as well as their own fears) is based on "culturally standard solutions for culturally defined problems" that are the product of implicit learning and thus quite resistant to change.

Ross (1984) describes the familial response as a "collective mourning" process. Initially, family members are overcome by fear and are essentially in a state of denial. If information is allowed in, it is met with apprehension, anger, and sadness (similar to denying strategies). The difference--between collective mourning and the grief process following a death--is the loss has not yet occurred with the nuclear threat.

Developmental Tasks Within the Nuclear Context

The developmental emotional transitions and family status changes of the normal family life cycle can be boiled down to a basic task: to produce and train new sets of human beings to be independent, form new families, and repeat the process, as the old set loses power, declines, and dies (Hoffman, 1988). This basic family developmental task considered in the context of the nuclear threat, confronts the family with a paradoxical situation. on one hand the family must protect its own to fulfill the basic task yet this protective function must unfold despite the ever -present capacity for the family's total destruction (Greenwald & Zeitlin, 1987). Parents are essentially faced with not only confronting their own mortality, but also their inability to protect their children from death in a nuclear war (Salguero, 1983; Wetzel & Winawer, 1983).

The nuclear threat challenges the basic task of the family and represents an assault on generativity, or the adult need to establish and guide the next generation (Greenwald & Zeitlin, 1987). Parenthood is a powerful impetus for adult development; it provides an opportunity to refine, re-define, and express who we are, to learn what we can be, and to become someone different (McGoldrick, 1988).

Almost no discussion in the developmental literature addresses the importance of children in the redefinition of one's adult identity (Daniels & Weingarten, 1983). From a family life cycle perspective, children are not only the core organizing element of family functioning, but are also a major factor in parental growth and development.

Given the importance of parenting to an adult's perception of his/her identity and definition of successful family functioning, the impending threat of nuclear war offers a significant impediment to family development. The parental role is itself threatened by parent's inability to provide a safe environment for children. Adults have responded by attempting to protect their children through the denying strategies discussed above. Wetzel & Winawer (1986) suggest that the resulting family secret deters family development by diffusing the interaction between the generations, thus, creating difficulty for the necessary transition to the next phase of the life cycle.

Practical Activities for Living in the Nuclear Age

Salguero (1983) proposes that a goal for families seeking to confront the nuclear issue includes undoing denial by simply talking about fears or feelings about the threat of nuclear war. The family can discuss what, if anything, the members wish to do in response to this threat. Through this process, families can begin to take control of the issue and not passively accept an uncomfortable situation. Wetzel and Winawer (1988) hypothesize that parental discussion serves to give parents a feeling of being in charge and re-establishes trust in the family.

Reifel (1984) and Myers-Walls and Fry-Miller (1984) suggest that a key for a parent/child nuclear war discussion is good parental listening skills. There must be listening about the child's fears without discounting them. There should, however, be reassurance of a child's irrational fears, for example, fear of a bomb under the bed. Parents should share their own fears in turn, which includes ways in which they cope (Myers-Walls & Fry-Miller, 1984). To facilitate such a discussion, parents will have needed to do much work of their own in dealing with their own nuclear fears.

Greenwald and Zeitlin (1987) propose that parents should confront three issues of their own before dealing with their children's fears. First, parents could relive their own childhood nuclear memories and their early feelings. Then, the need to acknowledge the sense of helplessness and the inability to protect their children in the face of an all-out nuclear war could be explored. Finally, parents can acknowledge their own level of responsibility and their role in changing or supporting the situation.

The common themes running through the literature regarding alternative familial response are (Simon, 1984): (1) the nuclear issue should be a permissible topic for family discussion; (2) members should be up to date on relevant facts; (3) the family should accept that activism, regardless of political position, may be the only viable remedy for nuclear anxiety. In support of these general themes, children report that they feel better when allowed to freely discuss their nuclear fears with their parents (Greenwald & Zeitlin, 1987; Ross, 1984; Salguero, 1983; Zeitlin, 1984).

Children who become involved and active do not report a reduction of nuclear fear per se, but rather do report optimistic preventive attitudes and look for a brighter future (Jacobson, 1984; Myers-Walls & Fry-Miller, 1984).

A specific method of facilitating parent and child discussion is the *Ten Myths About Children's Nuclear Fears: A Guide for Parents* (available from the authors). This guide contains tips for parents for constructive conversations with children about nuclear issues. The guide also offers parents the opportunity to consider nuclear issues and explore their own feelings and thoughts. The Ten Myths and the accompanying accurate information address children's perceptions about war, peace, "the enemy, and what is normal and abnormal for children. For example, myth number eight is: Children who worry about nuclear war must be worriers and worry about everything. The tandem accurate information is: Children who worry about nuclear war do not worry about everything. In fact, they worry the same amount as their peers do about other issues.

The literature about children's nuclear fears is almost unanimous in the suggestion for parents to encourage children to express their concerns and ventilate their fears. It is interesting to note that it is the *process*, characterized by parents encouraging expression and validating the fears in the supportive umbrella of the parent-child relationship, that is of importance to the reduction of children's fears and not the content of what the parents say or their political position. Children's nuclear fears may represent a unique meeting ground for militarism and pacifism; children's fears offer a situation in which the solution does not depend on one's position about the nuclear issue, but rather on one's parental love and involvement. In essence, then, reducing children's nuclear fears is not a political issue, but rather a parental one which does not entail the necessity for a belief in nuclear disarmament or proliferation.

Conclusion

Current research findings suggest that significant numbers of children and adolescents are concerned about the threat of nuclear war (Beardslee & Mack, 1983; Goldenring & Doctor, 1986). Their sense of powerlessness and cynicism is reduced when they can engage in dialogue and action with adults and parents (Greenwald & Zeitlin, 1987; Ross, 1984; Salguero, 1983; Zeitlin, 1984). However, most adults and parents are not open to "nuclear talk," denying its importance and assigning responsibility for issues of war and peace to "the experts" (Duncan et al., 1986). Hence, developmental task completion for both groups is impeded. Children are not given the opportunity for action to develop a sense of mastery. Adults, unwilling to support young people in examining their nuclear concerns, fail to complete their own work in generativity. Adults also fail to attain empowerment in this area, instead submitting to the mundane regimen of daily chores and the powerlessness of the denial of their nuclear concerns. There is still hope, however, as the nuclear threat continues to be in the forefront of current political debate. The recent rapprochement between Russia and the United States and the nuclear arms reduction treaty signed by the superpowers signal that good planets are indeed hard to find and we better preserve this one.

Nuclear war fears have been studied for 25 years or so. Yet, our understanding of their impact on daily living is in its infancy. Data is limited by generally poor research design and quasi-experimental techniques used to evaluate nuclear fears. These include: (1) systematic surveys, (2) questionnaires, and (3) interviews. Such studies are confounded by self-report and weak of experimenter control of external variables. Beardslee (1986) suggests that research needs to increase concern with representative samples evaluated with in-depth interviews. Prospective longitudinal studies are needed to evaluate the impact of the nuclear threat over time. Research should also scrutinize more closely the effects of educational material and media information on nuclear fears. Increased attention to the adult/child interaction is also needed, to better understand its effect on nuclear fears.

Many people believe war is intrinsic to human nature; this belief discourages action for peace. The International Colloquium on Aggression in Seville, Spain made a statement on human violence, offering hope for the preservation of this earth from a nuclear holocaust. The Seville Statement on Violence (1987) singles out five widely held beliefs as having Q scientific basis: the belief that we have an inherited tendency to make war; that we are genetically programmed to make war; that there has been an evolutionary selection for aggressive behavior more than for other kinds of behavior; that humans have a "violent" brain; and that war is caused by instinct. These positions were documented with findings from the biological and social sciences. This international committee of twenty biological and social scientists of five continents and twelve nations concluded that "biology does not condemn humanity to war," nor does any other intrinsic quality. "Humanity can be freed from the bondage of biological pessimism...." Making war is a learned cultural behavior. "The same species who invented war is capable of inventing peace. The responsibility lies with each of us."

REFERENCES

Bachman, J.G. (1983). How American high school seniors view the military. Armed Forces, 10 (1), 86-104.

Beardslee, W.R. (1986). Perceptions of the threat of nuclear war: Research and professional implications. International Journal of Mental Health, 15 (1-3), 242-252.

Beardslee, W.R. & Mack, J.E. (1983). Adolescents and the threat of nuclear war: The evolution of a perspective. The Yale Journal of Biology and Medicine, 56, 79-91.

Blackwell, P.H. & Gessner, R. (1983). An inquiry into adolescent perceptions of living in the nuclear age. Youth and Society, 15, (2), 237-255.

Block, D.A. (1984). What do we tell the kids? Family Therapy Networker, 8, 30.

Buban, M.E. (1986). Children's fears of nuclear war: A proposed intervention strategy. Unpublished manuscript. Wright State University.

Buban, M.E., McConnell, S.C., & Duncan, B.L. (1988). Children's fears of nuclear war: Group intervention strategies. The Journal of Specialists in Group Work, 13 (3), 124-129.

Carter, B. & McGoldrick, M. (1988). The changing family life cycle (2nd ed.) New York: Gardner.

Chivian, E., Mack, J.E., Waletsky, J.P., Lazaroff, C., Doctor, R., Goldenring, J.M. (1985). Soviet children and the threat of nuclear war: A preliminary study. American Journal of Orthopsychiatry, 55 (4), 484-502.

Daniels, P. & Weingarten, K. (1983). Sooner or later: The timing of parenthood in adult lives. New York: Norton.

Dinner, S. (1976). Social comparison and self evaluation in children. Unpublished doctoral dissertation. Princeton University.

Duncan, B.L., Kraus, M.A., & Parks, M.B. (1986). Children's fears and nuclear war: A systems strategy for change. Youth and Society, 18 (1), 28 44.

Duvall, E.M. (1977). Marriage and family development (5th ed.). Philadelphia: Lippincott.

Educators for Social Responsibility (1983). Perspectives: A teaching guide to concepts of peace. Cambridge, MA: Author.

Erikson, E.H. (1968). Identity, youth and crisis. Toronto: Norton.

Escalona, S.K. (1965). Children and the threat of nuclear war. In M. Schwebel (Ed.), Behavioral Science and Human Survival (pp. 201-209). Palo Alto, CA: Science and Behavior Tools, Inc.

Escalona, S.K. (1975). Children in a worrying world. American Journal of Orthopsychiatry, 45, 765.

Escalona, S.K. (1982). Growing up with the threat of nuclear war: Some indirect effects on personality development. American Journal of Orthopsychiatry, 52, 600-607.

Fisch, R., Weakland, J.H., & Segal, L. (1982). The tactics of change. San Francisco: Jossey-Bass Inc.

Fiske, S.T. (1987). People's reactions to nuclear war: Implications for psychologists. American Psychologist, 42 (3), 207-217.

Frank, J.D. (1986). Psychological responses to the threat of nuclear annihilation. The International Journal of Mental Health, 15 (1-3), 65-71.

Friedan, B. (1985). How to get the women's movement moving again. New York Times Magazine, November 3.

Gallup poll (1983). Public opinion 1983. Wilmington, DE: Scholarly Resources.

Gallup poll (1986). Public opinion 1986. Wilmington, DE: Scholarly Resources.

Gilbert, R.K. (1988). The dynamics of inaction. American Psychologist, 43, 755-764.

Goldberg, S. (1988). Children's nuclear fears: Myth and reality. Center Review, 2 (1), 4.

Goldberg, S., LaCombe, S., Levinson, D., Parker, K.R., Ross, C., Sommers, F. (1985). Thinking about the threat of nuclear war: Relevance to mental health. American Journal of Orthopsychiatry, 55 (4)1 503-512.

Goldenring, J. & Doctor, R. (1983). Adolescent concerns about the threat of nuclear war. In J. Goldenring & R. Doctor (1986), Teenage worry about nuclear war. International Journal of Mental Health, 15 (1-3), 72-92.

Goldenring, J. & Doctor, R. (1985). California adolescents' concerns about the threat of nuclear war. In L. Solantaus, E. Chivian, M. Vartanyan & S. Chivian (Eds.), Impact of the threat of nuclear war on children and adolescents: Proceedings of an international research symposium. Boston, MA: International Physicians for the Prevention of Nuclear War, pp. 112-133.

Goldenring, J. & Doctor, R. (1986). Teen-age worry about nuclear war: North American and European questionnaire stu&es. International Journal of Mental Health, 15 (1-3), 72-92.

Gould, R. (1978). Transformations: Growth and change in adult life. New York: Simon & Schuster.

Greenwald, D.S., & Zeitlin, S.J. (1987). No reason to talk about it. New York: W.W. Norton & Company.

Holmberg, P.O. & Bergstrom, A. (1985). How Swedish teenagers think and feel concerning the nuclear threat. In L. Solantaus, M. Rimpela & R. Ossi (1985). Social Epidemiology of the experience of the threat of war among Finnish youth. Social Sciences and Medicine, 21, 145.

Hoffman, L. (1988). The family life cycle and discontinuous change. In Carter and McGoldrick's (Eds.), The changing family life cycle (2nd ed.) New York: Gardner.

Jacobson, (1984). Beginnings. Harvard Educational Review, 54 (3), 337-341.

Johnson, R.N. & Bacik, L. (1987, April 20-24). Student attitudes about disarmament and the nuclear threat. Paper presented at the IV European Conference of the International Society for Research on Aggression, Seville, Spain.

Johnson, R., Taylor, B. & Witford, J. (1987, July). The politics of peace: Student perceptions in Mexico and Nicaragua. Paper presented at the International Society for Political Psychology, San Francisco.

Kohlberg, L. (1963). Moral development and identification. In H.W. Stevenson (Ed.), Child psychology: 62nd yearbook of the national society for the study of education. Chicago: University of Chicago Press.

Levinson, D.J. (1978). The seasons of a man's life. New York: Ballatine Books.

Lifton, R.J. (1982). Beyond psychic numbing: A call to awareness. American Journal of Orthopsychiatry, 52, 619.

Mack, J.E. (1984). Resistances to knowing in the nuclear age. Harvard Educational Review, 54, 260.

Mack, J.E. (1985). The psychological impact of the nuclear arms race on children and adolescents. In T. Solantaus, E. Chivian, M. Vartanyan, and S. Chivian (Eds.), Impact of the threat of nuclear war on children and adolescents. Proceedings of an international research symposium. Boston, MA: International Physicians for the Prevention of Nuclear War, pp. 9-16.

McConnell, S.C., Brown, S.D., Ruffing, J.N., Strupp, J.K., Duncan, B.L., & Kurdek, LA. (1986). Psychologists' attitudes and activities regarding nuclear arms. American Psychologist, 1, 725-727.

McConnell, S.C. & Duncan, B.L. (1987). A Blueprint For Peace Efforts. The American Psychological Association Monitor, 18, (10), 4.

McGoldrick, M. (1988). Women and the family life cycle. In Carter and McGoldrick's (Eds.) The changing family life cycle (2nded.). New York: Gardner.

McGraw, K.M. & Tyler, T.R. (1986). The threat of nuclear war and psychological well being. International Journal of Mental Health, 15 (1-3), 172-188.

Morawski, J.G., & Goldstein, S.E. (1985). Psychology and nuclear war: A chapter in our legacy of social responsibility. American Psychologist, 40 (3), 276-284.

Murphy, L.B. & Moriarity, A.E. (1976). Vulnerability, coping and growth: From infancy to adolescence. New Haven, CT: Yale University Press.

Myers-Wells, J., & Fry-Miller, K. (1984). Nuclear war, helping children overcome fears. Young Children, 39 (4), 27-32.

Pepitone, E.A. (1972). Comparison behavior in elementary school children. American Educational Research Journal, 9, 45-63.

Piaget, J. (1952). The origins of intelligence in children. New York: International Universities Press.

Piaget, J. & Inhelder, B. (1969). The psychology of the child. New York: Basic Books.

Raundalen, M. & Finney, O.J. (1986). Children's and teenager's views of the future. International Journal of Mental Health, 15 (1-3), 114-125.

Reifel, S. (1984). Children living with the nuclear threat. Young Children, 39 (5), 74-80.

Rogers, C.R. (1982, August). Nuclear war: A personal response. APA Monitor, pp. 6-7.

Ross, C. (1984). Growing sane under the nuclear shadow: What parent and child have to say to each other. Therapy Now, 18-21.

Rotter, J.B. (1982). The development and application of social learning theory. New York: Praeger.

Rutter, M. (1981). Stress, coping and development: Some issues and some questions. Journal of Child Psychology and Psychiatry, 22 (4), 323-356.

Salguero, C. (1983). Children and the nuclear threat: A child psychiatrist's personal reflections. The Yale Journal of Biology and Medicine, 56, 93-96.

Sandler, R. Roth, K., McGlone, J., Wertz, T., Balasubramanyan, R., & Uiera, J. (1985). The impact of the threat of nuclear war on adolescents in the midwestern United States. In T. Solantaus, E. Chivian, M. Vartanyan & S. Chivian (Eds.), Impact of the threat of nuclear war on children and adolescents: Proceedings of an international research symposium. Boston, MA: International Physicians for the Prevention of Nuclear War, pp. 112-133.

Seville Statement on Violence (1987). Medicine and War, 3, 191-193.

Schell, J. (1982). The fate of the earth. New York: Avon Books.

Schwebel, M. (1982). Effects of the nuclear war threat on children and teenagers: Implications for professionals. American Journal of Orthopsychiatry, 52, 608-517.

Simon, R. (1984). The nuclear family. Family Therapy Networker, 8, 22-27.

Snyder, T. (1985). Personal Communication.

Solantaus, T., Rimpela, M. & Ossi, R. (1985). Social epidemiology of the experience of the threat of nuclear war among Finnish youth. Social Sciences and Medicine, 21, 145.

Stillion, J.M. (1986). Examining the shadow: Gifted children respond to the nuclear threat. Death Studies, 10, 27-41.

Tizard, B. (1984). Problematic aspects of nuclear education. Harvard Educational Review, 54 (3), 271-281.

Vaillant, G. (1977). Adaption to life. New York: Ballatine Books.

Vincent, B.T. (1986). A study involving the use of a simulation game, The Other Side, in a sixth grade classroom, unpublished manuscript.

Wear, T.C. (1987). Nuclear denial disorder. The Humanistic Psychologist, 15, 218.

Wetzel, N.A. & Winawer, H. (1986). The psychological consequences of the nuclear threat from a family systems perspective. International Journal of Mental Health, 15 (1-3), 298-313.

Zeitlin, S. (1984). What do we tell mom and dad? Family Therapy Networker, 8 (2), 31-38.

CHAPTER 4

What Moves the Peace Movement:
Psychosocial Factors in Historical Perspective

Milton Schwebel

The peace movement (PM) has helped shape the thinking of the public on issues of war and peace in a number of countries, both in the 1980s and 1990s and in earlier periods since the founding of the first peace organization in 1815. Yet, the focus of political psychology and peace research has been primarily on policy and decision makers rather than the PM, peace activists and others. This article seeks to rectify some of the imbalance, first by examining the role of social movements (SMs), of which the PM is one, and then by analyzing three aspects of the PM. The end purpose is to propose ways to enhance the PM's effectiveness.

The Role of Social Movements

SMs have been defined as concerted-action groups that aim to bring about social change. They may be comprised of organized groups without necessarily having any formal superordinate organization. Essential to their effectiveness is that members have a sense of belonging and of solidarity (Heberle, 1968).

Without the fanfare of the 1960s or the early 1980s, SMs have risen to prominence in recent times. This has probably occurred because social needs have not been adequately addressed or have been ignored and neglected over long periods by unresponsive governments. The SMs assume the very roles that governments are perceived to be performing inadequately (e.g., protecting the environment), or they take on new roles called forth by newly evolving problems that are unaddressed by governments (e.g., protecting gay and lesbian rights).

Several reasons explain the vaunted position of SMs. First is the belief that any change in the status quo will occur only when the public demands it. For the most part, political leaders do not take the initiative; they act affirmatively only as they respond to the public's demand. Interests that profit from unfettered sale of guns, from exploitation of the environment, or abuse of civil rights as in real estate sales, are likely to maintain their hold on elected officials until the swell of public opinion makes resistance to change politically untenable. For example, massive demonstrations and other shows of public opinion (such as nuclear freeze resolutions passed by ten states and many communities) led Ronald Reagan to change his rhetoric about limited nuclear war and perhaps his stance about negotiated arms reductions.   Personal interviews with many officials in the Johnson and Nixon administrations led Small (1988) to conclude that the antiwar movement was a major player in leading the government to withdraw from Indo-China.

The public demands change when people understand that change is feasible and possible.   Toward that end the public must be well informed, a function performed by SMs, and the second reason for the prominence.   As early in the nuclear age as 1946, in a study of a representative sample of American adults, Woodward (1948) found one out of eight "greatly worried" about the atomic bomb, and three of eight less worried.   Almost every subject referred to "the terrifyingly destructive power of the bomb." Yet subjects were not motivated to take action.   To Woodward, the apathy seemed to "stem primarily from a feeling of helplessness, a belief that there is little or nothing the individual can do about the problem" (1948, p. 6).   If people are not to take "a completely apathetic attitude toward the whole problem and resign themselves to Fate...[they] must not only see the possibility of constructive action, but must also see what they as individuals can do to help solve the problems" (1948, p. 14). That is the role of SMs.

The third reason is that SMs, as a rule, provide constructive approaches to problem solving.   In one sense, the operation of active SMs is a safeguard against the violent eruptions of displaced anger that are costly in lives and property. "Watts" and "Newark" are symbols of such outbursts a generation ago, and "Los Angeles" is the contemporary code word. SMs usually provide useful alternatives to helplessness and rage.   They help people recognize the causes of their problems and the rational and politically effective modes of responding to them.

The rapid increase in SMs is no temporary upsurge of populism, but, rather, a permanent feature of political life. According to Gleditsch (1990) this development is due to the following: The party systems in industrialized nations were established to address other issues than those which confront them today and are unable to respond to the new ones; the reduction in the work week for some sectors of the population allows people more time to devote to other activities.

Another reason for increased activism is that people in industrialized democracies, and even, to the surprise of the world, in the former Soviet Union and Eastern Europe, are not static in terms of their educational and political development. Dynamic changes occur as a result of increased education, international exchange of information, and the public information media, including the alternative media. As long ago as 1974, in a study by Jeffries, each new age cohort showed a heightened awareness of the nuclear threat.   In examining those born in three successive generational periods, each new generation showed more negative attitudes toward nuclear war.   One interpretation borrows from Sigel's (1989) study of political socialization suggesting that individual political development is a product of continuous interaction with social structures: and it borrows also from Erikson's (1975) idea that not only does an historical period impact on individuals; the latter also impact on the period, helping to shape it by their activity. Presumably, as people become more knowledgeable and politically sophisticated, they are more likely to be active in shaping their political destiny. Hence, the higher educational level in the United States, and elsewhere, may well be a significant factor in the increase in the number of SMs and their membership. And it may explain a recent new trend wherein SMs strive for recognition of a people's existence and search for a collective identity (Escobar & Alvarez, 1992). In the most developed societies, in Sztompka's (1991) view, "they become the crucial agents of change" (p. 152).

Recognition of an upsurge in the activity of SMs has been accompanied by some appraisals of the PM which claim that it has reached a pivotal moment in its history. A number of researchers, according to Young (1990), view the decade of the 1980's as the period when, at least in many western and northern countries, the "peace movement ... established its permanent presence in society as a long term and global human project" (pp. 6-7).

Defining "Peace Movement"

According to Dieter Lutz of Hamburg University's Institute of Peace Research, PM refers to "a number of persons, groups, and organizations standing up for peace. Their status is autonomous and independent, their collective attitude is moulded by critics and protest, their engagement ... aims at forming public consciousness with regard to the problems of peace or activities in dealing with the problems of peace" (quoted by Rupprecht, 1990). The PM is associated with efforts to achieve peace through nonviolent means, and through cooperation, rather than competition, among nations.

As defined, PM is an umbrella term subsuming both individuals and peace organizations (POs). When thousands marched in New York or demonstrated in Washington in the eighties, many among them were unaffiliated individuals who shared a "collective attitude," were "standing up for peace" and seeking to shape public opinion. They, and the POs represented there, were "independent and autonomous." The same may be said about the PM in the nineties, both during the publicly active period of the Persian Gulf War and the more quiescently active period thereafter.

Three Aspects of the Peace Movement

As an approach to investigating what moves the PM--for the purpose of enhancing it and increasing activism--I will examine three interrelated aspects of the PM: individuals, POs, and historical perspective/social context.

Individuals

In attitude and participation, individuals relate to the PM in diverse ways, in accordance with their respective constructions of political reality. These involve their

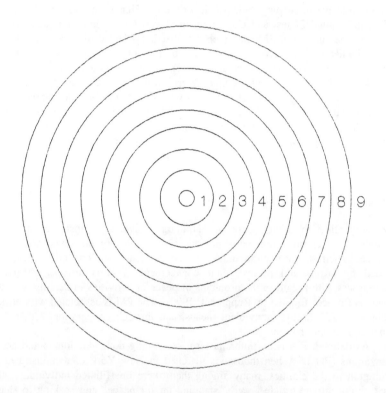

1. Unconventional   peace activists
2. Conventional   peace activists
3. Passive peace sympathizers
4. Alienated   peace sympathizers
5. Politically   alienated citizens
6. Alienated   anti-PM   sympathizers
7. Passive anti-PM   sympathizers
8. Conventional   anti-PM   activists
9. Unconventional   anti-PM   activists

Figure 1. A Peace Movement Typology

cognitions about conflict and its resolution, the trustworthiness of their leaders, their social values, and their sense of political efficacy. Some individuals are positively related to and deeply involved in the PM, some, indifferent, and others, sharply antagonistic. Figure 1, a PM typology, is a pictorial representation of nine categories of attitudes toward and involvement in the PM. The aim of the PM can be defined as that of stimulating movement of those in the inactive and antagonistic categories toward categories involving activism. The nine categories are given below.

1. *Unconventional peace activists.* These individuals are at the core of the PM. They help create POs, develop policies aimed at changing public opinion, and strategies to achieve their purposes. Because they are vital to the peace movement, it is worth examining the various motives that may move them to activity in the peace movement.

When people believe that their *cherished values* are in jeopardy, such as believing that basic rights are being denied, or the legal system is working unfairly, or the government is unresponsive to the public's call for a more energetic peace policy, they may seek redress through the power of a group. Disaffection with established order or with the policies of a government in power provokes unconventional political activity, as studies in the United States and West Germany revealed (Kinder and Sears, 1985). The sense of *duty and responsibility*, let us say to one's children or grandchildren, or to people in war-torn and oppressed countries, may also be a motivating force. The consequences of a *costs/benefits* appraisal may lead people to the conclusion that the costs in time and energy and the sacrifices frequently entailed in the life of the unconventional activist may be more than offset by gains. Participation in peace activism may be so *central to their lives* that they cannot forego their involvement (Kinder and Sears). Participation adds meaning to their existence. Some veterans associate war, along with its horrors, as a time of excitement. One veteran of the French Resistance, living comfortably 15 years later, characterized her life as "unutterably boring" and added that although she did not love or want war, "at least it made me feel alive as I have not felt alive before or since" (LeShan, 1992, p. 78). Activism for people like her may be the psychological and moral equivalent of war, to borrow from William James. *Political efficacy*, that is, the conviction that their actions mean something and have a palpable effect on policy, is believed to be an important component of the activist's motivation (Watanabe & Milburn, 1988).

A composite portrait of the unconventional peace activist reveals a person whose whole way of life is influenced by the cause of peace. Peace consciousness, being so central to the individual's cognitions, is never very distant whether the person is at the work place or at home, at a PO meeting or the theater. Seeing cherished values eroded or outrightly rejected, the individual feels responsible and duty-bound to oppose the government and believes that one way or the other the benefits will make the efforts and sacrifices worthwhile, for even the act of struggling for what is right--the sacredness of human life--is repayment enough. As one activist expressed feelings about activism,"...in that sense it's given me an inner peace I've never had before" (Locatelli & Holt, 1986, p. 151). Not only is the unconventional activist buoyed by his or her beliefs and values, he or she feels powerful and confident that actions even of one individual, in collaboration with others, really make a difference.

2. *Conventional peace activists.* Conventional peace activists share views and values similar to those of the unconventional activists but implement them in conventional ways. Rather than organizing demonstrations or picketing missile bases, they seek to influence the policies of the established political parties, perhaps by striving to have a voice in choosing candidates. Little is known about them in respect to the PM. However, in a survey on activism in general in the United States, Verba and Nie (1972) found that 11% belonged to the category of conventional activist. That may appear to be a small percentage. Yet, conventional activists, even if they are little more than one in ten, can play a highly important role because, on the one hand, they share the values of their unconventional counterparts, and on the other, they have entree to the corridors of power.

Their role, and their relationship to the unconventionals, may be conceptualized as being reciprocal. The unconventionals, on the outside, attract the attention of the media, and, through them, the public at large. Constituents in the general public begin to react to the claims of the unconventionals and, becoming restive about a particular issue, voice their opinions to their representatives. Meanwhile, the conventionals, on the inside, have been at work within their respective parties, seeking change in policy and encouraging positive responsiveness to constituents. The insiders, being a small minority, are often in the position of proposing an unpopular policy and face the danger of being isolated and alienated. As an example of a conventional activist at the upper levels of power, Senator Wayne Morse, for a time the only one in that chamber of Congress to speak out against the U.S. intervention in Vietnam, was in the position of the lonely conventional activist.

Because the role of conventional activist, like the unconventional, involves risk--one of the costs of being an activist, even of the conventional type--individuals are unlikely to assume it unless they are strongly motivated. In all probability, all of the motives that drive the unconventionals, with the exception of disaffection, may well be operative with conventionals.

3. *Passive peace sympathizers.* The vast array of people who are not activists but who vote for peace candidates or who, by their vote, support such policies as a nuclear freeze, belong in this category. They perform the functions of a citizen in a responsible manner in that they are thoughtful to the degree of holding a theoretical bias--in their case, favoring an anti-war, pro-peace national policy--and they act on their bias in the most basic democratic expression, namely, by going to the polls. The significance of their behavior is shown by the fact that in the 1980 presidential election in the United states, Ronald Reagan was elected with 44 million votes while 74 million eligible voters did not go to the polls.

Why are these people passive sympathizers rather than activists of one kind or another? Several different factors deserve consideration. As mentioned earlier, the substantial growth in social movements has been attributed in part to the shorter work week achieved since World War II in the advanced industrial nations. While millions have benefitted from those changes, many others, in the United States, at least, have not, because declining real incomes have compelled them to work overtime or at two jobs, depriving them of time and energy for political involvement. Besides that, the shortened work week has been accompanied by increased chronic unemployment and underemployment. While these conditions may provoke a few to take political action, for most people the result probably is to undermine morale. If those conditions lead to any action, it is likely to be a type that is injurious to the individuals themselves or to others, rather than constructive social activism. At the other social-class end of the occupational continuum, some potential recruits to activism are so overburdened with work that virtually no time or energy remains, even when principles and preferences dictate that they be politically active.

Still other explanations for passivity are related to educational level of the population. In their study of nuclear-related political activism among adults, Watanabe and Milburn (1988) reported that higher education "results in greater feelings of political efficacy (both general and nuclear), greater political interest, and greater general political activity" (p. 468). As noted above, greater general political activity was found to be the strongest predictor of nuclear (peace) activism. Consequently, level of education must be recognized as a predictor of activism. Using attainment of the bachelor's degree in the United States as the criterion of "higher education," 21.4% of the adult population in 1991 (compared with 10.7% in 1970) met that standard. If college attendance is the criterion, the percentage reaches 38.8 (compared with 21.3 in 1970). Either way, the proportion is probably in line with that of the two activist groups combined.

Under different historical circumstances in the United States, those with less than a "higher education" might well have had a higher degree of political activism. Perspectives about peace and other social issues, we may assume, are shaped through the interaction of already internalized values and the information and attitudes of the news media to which individuals are subjected. The stored memory and elicited attitudes as well as the accustomed modes of reasoning that people bring to any new situation, such as the rapidly growing crisis and outbreak of war in the Persian Gulf in 1991-92, mediate their assimilation of the "news." Generally speaking, those whose education has not gone beyond high school are less likely than others to have had the experience of challenging the assertions of authoritative figures. Furthermore, the alternative media are not likely to be available to them.

In other countries such as the Scandinavian and Germany, where trade union membership is high, for example, over 90% in Sweden and about 45% in Germany, the union news media may provide alternative views to those of the government or mainstream television and print media. In the United States, however, where the labor union movement suffered serious setbacks during the Reagan administration, including Reagan's presidential actions to disrupt the air controller's strike days after his election, membership is less than 17% and preoccupied with issues of survival. Of course, as the AFL/CIO leadership's stance during the Indo-China War testifies, a vocal labor union press does not automatically translate into an active antiwar editorial policy. Nonetheless, a stronger union movement could provide workers with a different perspective from that in the mainstream news and attitude-shaping media and could also generate a greater sense of political efficacy. The established media's acceptance during the Persian Gulf War of government control over the news shows the need for alternative media to help counteract passivity.

4. *Alienated peace sympathizers.* These individuals, committed in principle to a peaceful nation and world, have given up on the political system. Having lost whatever sense of political efficacy they might have possessed, they have retreated from virtually all forms of action related to the struggle for peace. They belong to no organizations, sign no petitions, attend no demonstrations, contribute no funds and vote in no elections. Like millions of others who stay away from the polls on election day, they are politically disaffected: "What's the point in voting? It doesn't change anything." Like millions of others who are bitter because poverty, unemployment, racism etc. go on unabated no matter who is elected, they are bitter as well because they feel powerless to alter policies which they regard as antagonistic to peacemaking, such as selling arms to the opposing parties in the Middle East.

Their reasons (or rationalizations, depending on the observer's values) are easily substantiated. While many in the peace movement, and some out of it and even antagonistic to it, argue that the avoidance of nuclear war and a third world war was due in no small part to the effectiveness of the peace movement, the alienated peace sympathizers are on strong ground in pointing to the record of wars, casualties and destruction that figure in recent history. They are surely unaware of the statistical evidence that their chance of being hit by a truck on the way to the election polls is greater than the chance that their one vote will affect the outcome of the election (Verba & Nie, 1972). Yet, their intuition that their individual vote will not make a difference is valid. The challenge for the peace movement is how to motivate and persuade them that their votes by the hundreds of thousands do make a difference.

5. *Politically alienated citizens.* The politically alienated are disaffected and feel powerless and hopeless about any possibility of influencing government policy. Their interpretations of government behavior--that it is unresponsive to citizens' wishes--provide them with a rationale for their own behavior. While they share alienation with the prior group--the alienated peace sympathizers--they do not share that group's attitudes about peace.

Among the politically alienated are some individuals who probably suffer from an even greater separation from the political process than those just described: They are so preoccupied with survival that they are hardly aware of political issues and unmotivated to vote in an election. Theirs is not a reasoned (or rationalized) or principled withdrawal from political activity. It is an uninvolvement of necessity.

6. *Alienated anti-PM sympathizers.*

7. *Passive anti-PM sympathizers.*

8. *Conventional anti-PM activists.*

9. *Unconventional anti-PM activists.* These four anti-PM categories, which reflect a mirror image of the first four, are composed of people who believe that the PM does a disservice. They may have learned to ascribe unpatriotic motives to those who identify with it, and especially to unconventional activists.

For some, the characterization of "anti-PM activist" is not entirely correct. Some in these four categories may not be objecting to the values of peace activists but rather to their methods, i.e., the fact that the unconventionals challenge the authority of government leaders who are presumably better informed and thus can make better judgements. Furthermore, the unconventionals sometimes engage in behavior that is anathema to some in the anti-PM groups. Whatever the individual case may be--value difference, authoritarian personality, xenophobia--the consequence is to place them in opposition to the efforts of those in the peace categories (groups 1-4 above).

Summary: The Peace-Movement Typology

Taken together, the nine categories seem to be comprehensive enough to cover the diverse attitudes and actions (or lack thereof) associated with peace-seeking through citizen action. The relationships between and among these categories can be variously conceptualized. In my depiction, both in Figure 1 and the narrative descriptions, the concentric circles represent distance or deviance from the center point, the unconventional activists. That schema is appropriate in a paper aimed at a deeper understanding of the dynamics of the PM. However, for other purposes a different perspective can be taken: The nine groups can be seen forming something equivalent to an asymmetrical distribution, with the curve skewed in the pro-peace direction, at least in the mid-1980's in the United States and perhaps much of the world. In that form the two types of activists are at polar ends of the continuum of peace attitude/action.

No matter how one organizes the relationships among these categories, the significance for the peace movement may be expressed in the following questions: How can the peace movement be enlarged? What moves each concentric circle in Figure 1 closer to the center? Or, what skews the distribution ever greater in the peace direction? To seek answers to these questions we turn to the next two sections.

Peace Organizations

Individuals represent the first aspect of the PM. Peace organizations (POs) are the second. They form the basic structure of the PM and enable it to satisfy some of the psychosocial needs of individuals. Whether or not they are membership POs, their leaders, boards and staff provide direction and maintain communication with individuals. They perform this function through publications, public meetings, demonstrations, and other activities deemed appropriate to the objectives of the PM.

Role of POs. A major role of POs is to keep peace issues alive in any and all political circumstances. Their stability and continuity are a form of national insurance, serving to protect the interests of the public in regard to keeping the peace through conflict resolution, even when public interest in the PO wanes. When wars, hot or cold, come to an end, the understandable tendency to drop one's guard leads to a falling off of interest in and support for POs. Yet, it is at that very time, as the periods of turbulence following the termination both of the Cold War and the Persian Gulf War painfully demonstrated, that the kind of vigilance that POs provide is important in maintaining public awareness.

Keeping peace issues alive must translate into keeping them in the public eye. Those political leaders who favor intimidation and the threat and use of force know that the general population is generally averse to military conflict. To avoid the necessity of gaining popular approval and the risk entailed in falsifying the circumstances in order to justify their actions, leaders prefer covert operations. POs are among a nation's best safeguards against such deception, providing they are active and sufficiently influential to bring information about illegal or covert government behavior to public view.

Goals of POs. To perform its role effectively, the PO must be guided both by short-term goals (such as disarmament and conversion to civilian production) and long-term goals (eradicating the causes of war). During the long years of the Cold War one could hardly expect members, and the public at large, to be disinterested in the threat of nuclear missiles. They were frightened by the real dangers, and the short-term goals were to reduce that threat by use of treaties, freezes, nuclear test bans and the like. They wanted change now, not next year or in a decade.

The Cold War has ended but there are other short-term goals such as safety on our streets and peace-making in violence-ridden areas in the world. Still, short-term goals are not enough. Rigby (1991) has stressed the importance to the peace-seeking community of a vision of the future to which it might aspire. A tension exists, he said, both among peace researchers and within the PM between responding to immediate threats and concerns on the one hand and devoting energies to the larger challenge of preventing conflicts. Gandhi, too, was unsure about a proper balance between working for the short-term goal of village reconstruction and the long-term one of national independence. There is no simple resolution to the tension "between those who advocate the need actively to campaign against war-making and war-preparation, and those who place greater emphasis upon the longer-term task of working to eradicate the ultimate causes of war, wherever these might be located" (p. 324). In Rigby's view these causes have their roots in basic values and human relationships. These are characterized by domination and exploitation "of women by men, of wage labour by capital, of one country by another...We need to see the whole of our daily life as an arena of struggle" (pp. 341-342).

Role of Peace Research. Even at the height of the Cold War, Rigby's colleague, the chairman of the Peace Studies Department at the University of Bradford, James O'Connell, looked beyond issues of nuclear disarmament, recognizing as he did "the centrality of peacemaking: the requirement for co-operation and community in pursuit of the universal aims of security, justice and freedom" (Woodhouse, 1991, p. 345). When some peace researchers, like Rigby and O'Connell, tend to give equal weight to long-term as well as immediate problems, at least some POs are likely to do the same because of the relationships between the researchers and the PM. For example, O'Connell explains that the British PM's greater effectiveness now than a generation ago (as demonstrated by its wider influence) has been due to its being better informed and, as a consequence, better able to "carry on discussion and argument with governments and other ruling groups" (1991, p. 121). To some degree at least, O'Connell adds, that greater effectiveness must be attributed to the scholarship and influence of peace researchers. Well-informed POs--to a considerable degree informed by peace researchers--can define goals for themselves that can be perceived as realistic and achievable. These goals can be spelled out in ways that represent something that serves as an inducement to involvement: Visions of what the world and their society can be like. Such goals and visions can have appeal because they may represent the values many people hold dear--the values that motivate people to be conventional and unconventional activists.

Attracting and retaining members. POs use other ways to attract and hold members. They engage in carrying forward implementation of the values that members hold dear. They avoid extravagant claims which have the effect of undermining the credibility of the organization in the public eye and the membership's confidence in its leadership. However they do not hesitate to claim political victories when these are justified. In that connection, after citing Small's (1987) evidence on the effectiveness of the anti-Vietnam war movement, Gleditsch (1990) recommends that the PM consider "the deliberate adoption of a strategy where it claims its victories publicly" (p. 87).

In considering what moves the PM, one is bound to inquire about the factors that lead some people to remain active and those that lead others to drop out. In his comparative analysis of the British and Danish peace movements, in which he employed both telephone and personal interviews to obtain data, Krasner (1990) addressed that question. He found that members of organizations remained active for several reasons: They derived satisfaction from expressing strongly held beliefs. They had a highly developed "sense of commitment which may be associated with religious or ideological factors, or with what I have called, 'personal political development'" (p. 189). They valued the social support they felt as part of a cohesive group.

The implications are clear. People may join POs (and other SMs) for one or more reasons that may be intellectual, moral, religious or ideological in character. The structure and processes of POs may enable members to satisfy important social and relational needs. POs that arrange to accommodate all of those needs, including the expressive and the relational, are likely to be more successful than otherwise in gaining and retaining members.

Another conclusion of Krasner's seems to have had confirmation in the aftermath of the cold war. Single-issue organizations can be viable only as long as the issue remains a burning one. Once that "freeze" or "test-ban" loses its potency, POs invested in one or the other alone are likely to suffer heavy attrition unless they choose another agenda. Multi-issue organizations are less threatened when one of their issues has lost public attention.

People drop out of the PM for a variety of reasons, according to Krasner's findings. These are: disappointment with the results of their efforts; boredom and fatigue; dissatisfaction with the ways the POs function; and conflicts within the POs. The obvious implications are that peace organizations should address such potential causes of attrition, seeking first to prevent them. If that is not possible, they should, try to alleviate them.

In fact, the first locus of peacemaking should be within the PO itself. Internecine conflict can be disastrous. Leaders must find ways to accommodate differences within the boundaries of the POs' goals. The Nuclear Freeze movement in the United States brought together people with highly diverse political views who shared this one objective, if no other. POs that aspire to a permanent existence need to adopt for their internal use the measures for communication, negotiation and mediation that they recommend to their governments for dealing with external affairs.

Starting in the 1960s there has been a new type of organization devoted to peace and other social concerns--those identified with particular professions or occupations. These have especially valuable features that may contribute to their long-term survival. For one, members start with a bond. For another, they are more likely to see a close link between their daily work and the purposes and objectives of the organization. Still another is that they may find opportunity to implement in their work their values and strongly held beliefs related to peace and other social issues.

No list of qualities of a peace organization can be complete without presenting one of the earliest to be identified, at least in the modern era. Woodward (1948), as quoted earlier, said that people must understand that constructive actions can be taken to cope with the dangers of the atomic age. They must also be told what they can do to solve the problem. No challenge is greater for peace organizations than that of helping people comprehend the immediate and long-term problems--have a vision of a better future--and what they can do to help achieve that future.

But how does an organization tell its members what they can do without at the same time establishing a top-down relationship? Alan Touraine, a French sociologist, has answered that question in one way. He has introduced a method that helps members of social movements answer that question for themselves. As Spencer (1991) describes his method, a pair of researchers "engage in dialogue with a group in a deliberate effort to shape its aspirations and self-interpretation in a direction that will forward their social movement" (p. 218). Touraine's method is suggestive, at least, of roles of members of peace and other social organizations involving them in shaping the organization and identifying what they can do to work toward their short and long-term goals.

Historical Perspective and Social Context

Cognitions about peace do not come with the genes: They are constructed and thereafter subject to modification as a result of internal and external changes. The social context for peacemaking continues to change, as it has since biblical days, Aristotle's Greece, 1815 (a pivotal year), 1945 and even 1990. One of the important functions of both peace researchers and POs is that of responding to the new circumstances. For example, the PMs in the world had to reorganize their thinking after Hiroshima. Their overarching goal could remain unchanged but not their understanding of the nature of potential conflict and its consequences. Likewise, the end of the cold war and the collapse of the Soviet Union necessitated restructuring to accommodate these changes and develop appropriate modes of peacemaking.

Having an historical perspective and recognizing the significance of the social context in which one operates are vitally important to peace movements. An historical perspective gives individuals and POs a sense of continuity that might be verbalized as follows: We have roots and are part of a long history. Our predecessors were respected men and women, many of whom made great sacrifices to establish an anti-war tradition. The obstacles, resistance, apathy and ridicule that we sometimes confront are not new. Our predecessors faced and often transcended them. They, too, experienced the waxing and waning of active membership and public support.

An historical perspective provides a lesson in the patience and perseverance that successful participation demands. Those new peace activists who believe that hard work will yield quick developments--like a peaceful eastern Europe or mid-east, or peaceful urban centers in America--are likely to become "summer patriots," quick to abandon the movement when their unrealistic expectations are unfulfilled. POs that fail to clarify the geopolitical realities do a disservice to themselves, their members and the public. History suggests that there is no foreseeable end to the challenge of peacemaking, especially if one's vision of it is shaped by the ultimate form of it in Galtung's (1968) definition: first, negative peace (the absence of organized violence), next positive peace (some cooperation, combined with occasional outbreaks of violence) and, finally, unqualified peace (a pattern of cooperation and the absence of violence).

An historical perspective is like a moving picture showing change over time. Social context is like a still picture, with the projector frozen at a given time. Both peace researchers and PMs are interested in having analyses of that still picture of the here-and-now circumstances with which they are confronted. They want to understand all of the many factors that at any given time affect human consciousness and peacemaking and are likely to be influential in mobilizing people inside and out of POs and the PMs. In the United States, the recession and accompanying hardships of the early 1990s, including extensive unemployment, are circumstances that understandably arouse resistance to reduction in arms production. Political rhetoric about "new jobs" and allotments for "retraining" will not overcome the threat of economic and psychological insecurity; hence, the following statement by the president of the American Economic Association: "We are thus unlikely to get adequately deep cuts in defense budgets unless we can deal with unemployment in a way that will promise those displaced by the cuts that they will find it easy to slip into new jobs" (Vickrey, 1992, p. 6). Analyses of 1983's social context, e.g., hostile relations between the two nuclear superpowers, and booming economies in Asia, Europe and the U.S., are useful for historical perspective but inadequate for 1993's peace-movement planning and operations.

History of the PM. Aspirations for peace have probably been held since the human species first had the intellectual powers to conceptualize a future different from its present: in Biblical times the hope of beating swords into ploughshares, in ancient Greece the demand for peace on the part of the women in Aristophanes' play "Lysistrata," who refused to sleep with their warrior husbands until they had laid down their arms.

In the intervening millennia people prayed for peace, and scholars reflected on its possibilities. Still, even early in the 1700s war was thought to be a necessary evil, "necessary to keep in check yet greater evils" (Howard, 1978, p. 21). Not until 1815 were the first organizations devoted primarily to the prevention of war established (Curti, 1929). Almost simultaneously, although without knowledge of the others, peace societies were established in New York City, Warren County, Ohio, Massachusetts and London, England. Within a few years POs sprang up in Philadelphia, Raleigh, North Carolina, Rhode Island, Vermont, Maine, Connecticut, Georgia, Indiana, Nova Scotia and eleven other locations in Canada, as well as in Glasgow and Ireland. By the mid-1820s there were 50-odd societies in the United States, and the Massachusetts society, which was probably the most influential, was sending its publications to Calcutta, Ceylon, France, Great Britain, Holland, Russia, the Sandwich Islands and South America.

In asking what moves the PM, several lessons from its history are instructive. The first is about its origins. Curti (1929) wrote that in 1815 the world was weary of war; that hardly anyone alive could recall any substantial period of peace. People were ripe for peace. Still, that is not a sufficiently powerful explanation considering that at prior times such a movement did not arise, although earlier generations had more than their fill of warfare. Nor can the argument be made that only then, early in the 19th century, did ideas come forth for a world order that could manage the relations among nations. Long before, others had paved the way, including Dante who in the 14th century proposed a world empire as a means of ending war. The difference in 1815 probably was the Enlightenment and its consequences. And one of its great consequences, as significant to SMs now as in the past--and the first lesson--was that people felt freer to think for themselves, organize and shape their own futures, even when their governments considered those initiatives to be offensive.

A second lesson is about the waxing and waning of the PMs (see Chatfield, 1992; Howard, 1978). By 1828 the American Peace Society was founded; as past wars receded into memory and suffering was remote, interest and participation in the PM waned. Agents attributed the "lamentable apathy" to "want of proper information respecting its claims and its wants" (from Advocate of Peace, 1841, quoted by Curti, 1929, p. 44). But the explanation, while understandable on the part of dedicated and sacrificing leaders, is incomplete, at best. In hindsight, with the experience of the post World War II peace movement, we know that in the absence of a powerful threat, the general public's attention is elsewhere. The second lesson is: Only when such threat actually inheres in current circumstances, when that fact can be made clear, and when, furthermore, people know what they can do, and that what they do can make a difference--only then are we likely to avoid "lamentable apathy."

A third lesson is about the role of women. Men established the first organizations. Yet within a few years women were actively involved and on a basis of equal terms with men, unlike their usual position in philanthropic organizations at the time. They participated in local branches and attended international congresses in Europe. Their active participation in the peace movement was encouraged, sometimes with a mythical degree of optimism. For instance, the editor of the Massachusetts Society's Friend of Peace antedated by about a century and a half the current widely held view about women's nurturing and connecting qualities (Gilligan, 1982). However, he apparently allowed wishful thinking to color his expectations, predicting that with thirty years of their "faithful and united exertion war might lose all its fascinating charms, and be regarded by the next generation with more abhorrence than the people of today look back on the gladiatorial combats of Rome, the papal crusade, or the flames of martyrdom" (1818, quoted by Curti, 1929, p. 23). Were he alive today at least he could take comfort in the third lesson: Women have been playing prominent leadership roles over the last few decades, and that, consistent with his view, a higher percentage of them than men, favor anti-war actions.

A fourth lesson is on the relationship between the PM and other SMs. The effects of the enlightenment and democratic processes led to the formation of other SMs at about the same time as the PM was established. For example, Thomas Gallaudet initiated a movement to establish a school for deaf mutes; the American Colonization Society was founded to protect the interests of Afro-Americans; the McLean Asylum for the Insane was formed; and the Prison Discipline Society to better conditions in prisons was organized. The conditions were present then, as in the 1960s and the 1980s, to ignite public interest and initiatives. Curti explains that the early PM was an expression of more than an antiwar reaction. It flowed from a general humanitarian development that had its origin before the wars and that now gave expression to the public's disgust with the nation's social woes and determination to alter the situation. SMs were the consequence. One movement was that of the abolitionists whose responsiveness to the peace movement--more than that of any other group--revealed something evident today--the fourth lesson: Efforts at social change, whether in the domains of the environment, social equality and justice, or domestic and international peace, go forward together. Today, that underlying principle has brought together about 75 organizations into an Alliance for Our Common Future (among them, Psychologists for Social Responsibility), which focuses on reversing the nuclear buildup, challenging and changing U.S. budget priorities, supporting and strengthening the United Nations, and promoting sustainable development and environmental protection worldwide.

A fifth lesson is about the problem of communicating with the public. Peace activists then, like today, had no great success in getting the positive attention of the communication media and had to rely on their own resources. A dramatic example of the difficulties encountered in the past and of the earnestness and sacrifice of the early Peace activists may be found in the experience of Noah Worcester. Founder of the Massachusetts Peace Society and author of *Solemn Review of the Custom of War*, he could get no publisher and, although desperately poor, assumed half the risk for its publication. First appearing on Christmas Day, 1814, the book went through five editions and by 1846, more than a dozen reprintings in the U.S. alone.

Peace publications then, as now, attempted to bring to the public information that got short shrift, if any attention at all, in the established communications media, such as the cruelty of our conduct in the war against the Florida Native Americans and the crass extravagance of American army officers (the equivalent of $700 toilet seats!). Nor was the economic motivation for war ignored. Evidence was presented in peace society publications showing that the war was protracted because of the speculation of contractors. And the peace movement's sensitivity to the oppression of less powerful groups was revealed not only in its abolitionist leanings but also in its attitude toward the treatment of Native Americans. The editor of the Calumet in 1831 called it shameful that the government was creating "'an American Poland' by dispossessing the Cherokees and extermin[ating] a people at home while lamenting the downtrodden Greeks or Poles in Europe" (Curti, pp. 63-64). The fifth lesson is that today, too, in an age of instant transmission of news and a plethora of media outlets, the peace movement must still struggle relentlessly to reach the public.

Concluding Remarks

Through the news media and film, people get an endless flow of reminders of war and other forms of violence, which is not surprising considering that there have been 12 to 25 wars per year since World War II (Brogan, 1990). At the same time, a literature to train students in peacemaking (Johnson & Johnson (1991) and to strengthen citizen power in American foreign policy (Hilliker, 1990) is being built. What is lacking is an updated vision of the future. What moves people to the PM and makes activism and the POs central to their lives, we have seen, are their cherished values; what politically disaffects them is their government's failure to implement those values. Where are the visions that millions can value today? The early peace activists were inspired by their mental picture of a world government, a legacy of earlier centuries. Many generations worked to help realize that goal and succeeded to the extent of the founding of the United Nations. What is the vision of the United Nations of the future? The World Court? Other organizations? The relationships among nations, ethnic groups, races, sexes, age cohorts, and between humans and the environment?

Projecting into the future is no simple task. In 1990, in a pilot study on how peace researchers think about the future in contrast with the past and the present, I interviewed three widely published scholars. Although they reported virtually no experience in future studies, still, when pressed, they showed that information, available in the past enabled them to predict some future changes, like the ethnic conflicts in the old Soviet Union.

A vision of the future need not be based on prediction. It represents an aspiration. POs and the PM, joining with other SMs, could go beyond the aspirations of our early 19th century ancestors and shape a vision suitable to the 21st century--a vision that would give new meaning and purpose to the movements. This represents a challenge, for as the respected World War II General Omar Bradley said, "We know more about war than we do about peace--more about killing than we do about living" (LeShan, 1992, p. 99). The arts and humanities have taught us about hating, killing, loving and surviving: Tolstoy's *War and Peace* and Remarque's *All Quiet on the Western Front*, Picasso's *Guernica*, Hemingway's *For Whom the Bell Tolls*, and Shute's *On the Beach;* but they have not given much of a vision of a future without killing. Elsewhere I have defined moral creativity as the conscious transformation of moral values and their associated affect into artistic products (Schwebel, in press). That transformation has been made to a considerable degree to condemn the ills of the world, but not much in depicting more of the positive aspects of human life, giving a sense of what a better world could be like. True, the Breugels' paintings show the joy of Flemish communal life, Beethoven's Eroica Symphony gives expression to his sympathies for republicanism in grand and noble terms, Ibsen's *Doll House* anticipates the women's movement of almost a century later. But one is hard put to find outstanding modern examples of future visions of humankind.

Besides visions of the future there is the continuing need for inquiry to help move the PM. Several avenues follow logically from the three major aspects of the PM described above. Presented as questions, they are the following:

1. Bearing in mind the concentric circles in Figure 1, what are the psychosocial factors that move people (of both sexes, varying social classes and racial and ethnic groups, at different developmental stages) from the periphery of interest and involvement toward the center of peace activism?

2. What are the dynamics of POs that attract unconventional and conventional activists and inactive sympathizers and maintain their interest and support even during non-crisis periods? What modifications in POs would vitalize the inactive and convert the opposed?

3. By what means can a peaceful way of life, visions of a peaceful future, and the history and literature of peace occupy a greater part of human consciousness?

REFERENCES

Brogan, P. (1990). World conflicts: Why and where they are happening. London: Bloomsbury.

Chambers. J.W. II (1991). The eagle and the dove: The American peace movement and United States foreign policy, 1900-1922, 2nd edition. Syracuse: Syracuse University Press.

Chatfield, C.C. (1992). The American peace movement: Ideals and activism. New York: Twayne Publishers.

Curti, M.E. (1929/1973). The American peace crusade. New York: Farrar, Straus & Giroux.

Erikson, E. (1975). Life history and the historical moment. New York: Norton.

Escobar, A. & Alvarez, S.E. (1992). Introduction: Theory and protest in Latin America today. In A. Escobar & S.E. Alvarez (Eds.), The making of social movements in Latin America (pp. 1-15). Boulder: Westview Press.

Galtung, J. (1968). Peace. In D.L. Sills (Ed.), International encyclopedia of the social sciences. Vol.ll (pp. 487-496). New York: Macmillan.

Gilligan, C. (1982). In a different voice. Cambridge: Harvard University Press.

Gleditsch, N.P. (1990). The rise and decline of the new peace movement. In K. Kodama & U. Vesa (Eds.), Towards a comparative analysis of peace movements (pp. 73-88). Brookfield, Vermont: Gower.

Heberle, R. (1968). Types and functions of social movements. In D.L. Sills (Ed.), International Encyclopedia of the social sciences, Vol. 14 (pp. 438-444). New York: Macmillan.

Hilliker, G. (1990). Citizen power in U.S. foreign policy: A strategy to communicate consensus. In F. Korzenny & S. Ting-Toomev (Eds.) Communicating for peace: Diplomacy and negotiation (pp. 217-233). Newbury Park, CA: Sage.

Howard, M. (1978). War and the liberal conscience. New Brunswick: Rutgers University Press.

Jeffries, V. (1974). Political generations and the acceptance rejection of nuclear war. Journal of Social Issues, 30, 119-136.

Johnson, D.W., & Johnson, R.T. (1991). Teaching students to be peacemakers. Edina, MN: Interaction Book Company.

Kinder, D.R. & Sears, D.O. (1985). Public opinion and political action. In G. Lindzey, & E. Aronson (Eds.), Handbook of social psychology, 3rd edition., Vol. 2. New York: Random House.

Krasner, M.A. (1990). Decline and persistence in the contemporary Danish and British peace movements.: A comparative political analysis. In K. Kodama & U. Vesa (Eds.), Towards a comparative analysis of peace movements (pp. 169-192). Brookfield, Vermont: Gower.

LeShan, L. (1992) The psychology of war: Comprehending its mystique and its madness. Chicago: Noble Press.

Locatelli, M.G. & Holt, R.H. (1986). Antinuclear activism, psychic numbing, and mental health. International Journal of Mental Health, 15, 143-161.

Rigby, A. (1991). Peace as a way of life: The life and ideas of Wilfred Wellock (1879-1972). In T. Woodhouse (Ed.), Peacemaking in a troubled world (pp. 323-343). New York/Oxford: Berg.

Rupprecht, F. (1990). Peace movement in history and at present. In K. Kodama & U. Vesa (Eds.), Towards a comparative analysis of peace movements (pp. 45-52). Brookfield, Vermont: Gower.

Schwebel, M. (in press). Moral creativity as artistic transformation. Creativity Research Journal.

Sigel, R.S. (1989). Conclusion: Adult political learning - A lifelong process. In R.S. Sigel (Ed.), Political learning in adulthood. Chicago: Chicago University Press.

Small, M. (1988). Johnson, Nixon, and the doves. New Brunswick, N.J.: Rutgers University Press.

Spencer M. (1991). Advocating peace. In P. Harries-Jones (Ed.), Making knowledge count: Advocacy and social science (pp. 209-222). Montreal & Kingston: McGill-Queen's University Press.

Sztompka, P. (1991). Society in action: The theory of social becoming. Chicago: Chicago University Press.

Verba, S. & Nie, N.H. (1972). Participation in America: Political democracy and social equality. New York: Harper.

Vickrey, W. (1992). Disarmament, unemployment, budgets, and inflation. ECAAR News Network, 4, 17.

Watanabe, P.Y. & Milburn, M.A. (1988). Activism against Armageddon: Some predictors of nuclear-related political behavior. Political Psychology, 9, 459-470.

Woodhouse, T. (1991). Conclusion. In T. Woodhouse (Ed.), Peacemaking in a troubled world (pp. 344-349). New York/Oxford: Berg.

Woodward, P. (1948). How do the American people feel about the atomic bomb. Journal of Social Issues, 4, 7-14.

Young, N. (1990). On the study of peace movements, Introductory presentation. In K. Kodama & U. Vesa (Eds.), Towards a comparative analysis of peace movements (pp. 3-14). Brookfield, Vermont: Gower.

CHAPTER 5

The Differential Psychological Effects of Positive and Negative Approaches to Peace

Richard V. Wagner

World peace is an elusive phenomenon. Part of the reason for its elusiveness lies in our penchant for defining peace in the context of war. But peace is not merely the absence of war (Galtung, 1985). If it were, we could say that the U.S. and the U.S.S.R. were at peace throughout the 1950s and '60s and '70s and '80s. Many of us lived through those forty years and it certainly didn't feel like peace. Instead, we were living through the avoidance of war.

Of course, it is critically important to understand the psychological processes that underlie the attempt to avoid war, but that is not my focus in this paper. Rather, I want to comment on the distinction between *positive* and *negative* approaches to peace. I will do so by extrapolating from psychological analyses of critical differences between positive and negative goals and positive and negative means of reaching those goals.

When I first began working on these important distinctions, it was in the context of the U.S.-U.S.S.R. nuclear confrontation. The implications of positive as opposed to negative goals and means of attaining those goals were relatively clearcut. The nuclear arms race was recognized, by proponents and opponents alike, as a negative means of maintaining a negative state of peace known as Mutually Assured Destruction. However, the "invisible hand" has changed the context, and what was relatively clearcut no longer is.

When we talk about approaches to peace, we are referring to behavior and to goals. The important role that goals play in determining behavior is well-established in psychology. Goals focus our attention, affect our level of motivation, and influence the choices we make to attain them (Lewin, 1935). How goals affect behavior depends partly upon whether they are goals of avoiding a negative state (hereafter referred to as "negative goals") or of attaining a positive state ("positive goals"). This is the distinction Maslow (1968) makes in designating deficiency (D) and being (B) need states, and that Atkinson and Raynor (1974) make in referring to the fear of failure and the hope of success. It's the distinction between peace as the absence of war and peace as social justice, between curative treatment and the promotion of health (Dyson, 1984). It's the distinction Cohen and Arnone (1988) make between conflict management, which attempts to contain conflict, and conflict resolution, which focuses on building peace, and that Kimmel (1985b) makes between peacekeeping and peacemaking or peacebuilding. Perhaps the most critical difference between positive and negative goals is that negative goals are essentially *reactive*. They are a reaction to aversive conditions, and their aim is to reduce or eliminate those conditions.

Negative, reactive political goals have certain features that can affect our progress toward peace. First, negative goals are likely to be narrowly defined and limited by the assumptions and definitions which underlie the aversive situation (Kimmel, 1985a, August). My brother-in-law reminded me recently that "there's a bully born every day," and we all know how you handle bullies! As a result, his and my subsequent discussions of peace *were* narrowly defined and limited. Positive, nonreactive goals, on the other hand, can be more innovative; they concern the construction of something new and, as a result, are not bound by the constraints of the aversive situation. My brother-in-law and I were not about to think innovatively.

Second, negative, reactive goals, deriving from existing assumptions, are likely to be more concrete than positive goals (Plous, 1988). We have found it relatively easy to propose concrete measures to negate a threat. When Saddam Hussein invaded Kuwait and threatened Western oil sources, we knew just how to deal with him: military threat and retaliation. Such measures are conceivable; policymakers know what setting deadlines and deploying and using troops mean. Positive goals, on the other hand, tend to be much more ambiguous and intangible. Let us look at several examples of proposed positive goals. Equitable distribution of world resources. How equitable? Distributed to whom by whom? Social justice for Palestinians. Meaning what? Justice, a socially-determined concept, differs from culture to culture. "A world where there may be more freedom, more food, and more opportunity for every human being" ("The Challenge," 1983). More food is relatively concrete, but freedom and opportunity are subject to wide variations in definition "Building community" (Herman, 1992). Wonderful, but "community" seems an elusive notion. Laudable as these positive goals may be, they are conceivable only in a vague, almost utopian sense and are, therefore, difficult to develop into policy.

Third, negative, reactive goals, based on existing assumptions and being more concrete, are likely to lead to readily available short-term objectives. Again, look at the example of the Iraqi threat to our interests in the Middle East. Our short-term solution is known to us all and its long-term repercussions are disquieting. Positive objectives, like building cooperative relations among adversaries, are long-term goals which have lower priority in their demand on the time and energy available for solving international problems.

To summarize, I have argued that negative reactive goals develop within an existing framework and are more concrete and aimed toward short-term objectives. They are, therefore, more easy to conceive and implement than positive goals. As a result, negative goals actually have certain advantages. Concrete, specific goals lead to high performance and satisfaction, relative to more ambiguous goals. Because they are short-term, they can be attained more quickly and provide immediate reinforcement for one's efforts (Weick, 1984). Positive, long-term goals, on the other hand, are likely to produce frustration and the danger of being overwhelmed by the enormity of the task. In our current, crazily realigning world, that frustration can affect our ability to produce the innovative solutions necessary for ultimately resolving the dangers intrinsic to our nuclear age.

Despite the short-term advantages of negative goals, we must not lose sight of the ultimate advantage of positive goals. Once reached, positive goals can be much more easily maintained than can negative goals--a crucial factor in the context of a world as dangerous as ours. Although the goals are often defined as if they were end-states, they are in reality on-going processes. For example, international "peacekeeping" (Sommer, 1985) and "peacebuilding" (Galtung, 1985), negative and positive goals respectively, are processes that must be constantly in operation. Peace kept up or built today must be further kept up or built tomorrow. However, keeping peace and building peace differ greatly in how they are maintained. Those who are being "kept at peace" must be constantly monitored; otherwise they might revert to war. Those who are building peace, on the other hand, are engaging in cooperative relations--"*mutually reinforcing* elements blended into an integrated system" (emphasis added) (Sommer, 1985, p. 91). Monitoring cooperative relations is not necessary; the rewards are intrinsic to the process.

Additionally, *failure* to keep peace has drastically different consequences from failure to build an effective peace. An unkept peace can lead to mass destruction of populations and, still, to nuclear annihilation, whereas an unsuccessful attempt to build peace merely means we have slipped backward--at worst, to where we began--and allows the opportunity to begin again. The difficulties in maintaining negative goals make it essential that our ultimate aim be the promotion of peace and not merely the long-term maintenance of mechanisms for avoiding war.

Further, negative goals constantly focus our attention on the possibility of war, thereby producing fear and, possibly, debilitating anxiety (Lifton & Falk, 1982). Such anxiety can have two deleterious effects. First, it can reduce the quality of the psychological processes critical to progressing toward peace: problem-solving flexibility, focussed attention, abstract ability, and complexity in cognition (Holsti, 1972). Second, extrapolating from the research on the fear of failure (Birney, Burdick, & Teevan, 1969), high anxiety based on fear can produce either extremely cautious or extremely risky decisions about resolving the threat of war. Taking extreme risks in a world with the capability of mass destruction is obviously undesirable; so, too, is exercising the overly extreme caution that can, ultimately, lead to inaction. Assuming that we cannot continue on our present political course without an ever-increasing danger of war, some risks must be taken in developing, proposing, and enacting solutions. People positively oriented toward the goal of peace may be more capable of developing appropriate proposals than people preoccupied with their fear of destruction.

Positive and Negative Means Toward Goals

The *means* used to attain goals can also be classified as either positive or negative. Positive means promise rewards while negative means threaten punishment. Positive means are, as Ralph White (1988) has stated, "inherently attractive and morally unobjectionable" (p. 193). There is an extensive literature (e.g., Deutsch, 1983) on the differential effectiveness of positive (i.e., promises) and negative stances (i.e., threats) in intergroup relations. Pruitt and Rubin (1986) note that promises and threats each have advantages and disadvantages in producing the outcome the promising or threatening party wants. The distinction between positive and negative means is, in many respects, parallel to the distinction between positive and negative goals.

Threats, like negative goals, tend to be more concrete and specific than promises. As a result, they are seen as conveying more information, producing greater compliance, and therefore are often the preferred means of conducting intergroup relations (Pruitt & Rubin, 1986; Rubin & Lewicki, 1973). On the other hand, negative means have at least three disadvantages. First, they produce emotions (anxiety, despair, insecurity) that diminish the constructive, rational thinking of the threatened party and increase the chances of an irrational, preemptive, or retaliatory response (Allison, Carnesale, & Nye, 1985; Holsti, 1972; Janis, 1985). Threats may in fact produce the exact opposite of the response intended--reactance in action, as we have witnessed recently in the Middle East. Promises, on the other hand, can promote hope and "a whole range of positive human responses to intractable problems" (Dyson, 1984, p. 3). Second, threats tend to promote distrust. As a result, the threatener must be ever on guard that the party threatened is complying. Promises, if fulfilled, promote trust and a relaxation of wariness among the parties. Third, threats promote counterthreats (Pruitt & Rubin, 1986), thereby feeding into what Morton Deutsch (1983) calls the spiralling, malignant process of escalation.

The correspondence between positive and negative means and goals is an important, albeit complex one. A negative means, with its destructive emotional effects and its increase in counterthreats and distrust, is unlikely to lead to a positive goal. A positive means, on the other hand, can be effectively used both to approach a negative goal and to reduce some of the drawbacks of negative goals. Osgood's (1962) GRIT proposal is an excellent example. It is primarily a positive method, demonstrating faith and respect for the adversary. But it is directed toward a negative goal because it involves alternating, unilateral, small-scale retreat from specific threatening positions (e.g., removing Serbian troops from the Croatian capital of Zagreb, thereby reducing the chances of confrontation). The result of a series of such alternating, unilateral retreats might be an increase in trust, setting the stage for achieving more positive goals and reducing the need for monitoring compliance by one's adversary. Nonviolence is, of course, another positive means of approaching peace--though one must be careful about how contentious the nonviolent approach is.

Now a few words about positive and negative goals and means to those goals in the context of a world *without* the U.S.-U.S.S.R. confrontation. The removal of the confrontation has led to the perception that the threat of nuclear holocaust has vanished. There are several consequences of the apparent removal of that threat.

First, the meaning of world peace has changed because the psychological nature of conflict has changed. No longer is conflict evaluated in the context of U.S.-U.S.S.R. rivalry. No longer is nuclear stalemate/MAD the principal goal of U.S. policy. Second, the site and nature of conflict has changed. The nuclear confrontation led to our concern and involvement in countries in danger of Communist "take-over." The fear of new Communist governments is gone and many of those conflicts have been resolved, at least temporarily. In addition, the major power rivalry masked a number of other enmities--primarily ethnic in nature. With the dissolution of the Soviet state and the resulting removal of the threat of nuclear war, these antagonisms have burst forth. Most conflicts today, as Kenneth Boulding (1992) has noted, are intranational, not international. We need to study ethnic conflict more than ever. Unfortunately, there is not the pressure *in the United States* to understand ethnic rivalry--in the absence of superpower, ideological contention, it is all too easy to ignore intranational, ethnic conflict.

Fear of war that will touch the U.S. homeland has diminished, which should mean, could mean that we can now reorient and focus on peacebuilding rather than constantly worrying about peacekeeping. The urgency to find solutions to international conflict and promote peace has subsided. How quickly we forget. The recent U.S., Russian, and Byelorussian negotiations which have culminated in nuclear treaties were merely a footnote in the news. We must not let ourselves forget. We must take advantage of the diminished nuclear threat and expand our efforts to build a world of peace.

REFERENCES

Allison, G.T., Carnesale, A., & Nye, J.S. (Eds.). (1985). Hawks, doves, and owls: An agenda for avoiding nuclear war. New York: Norton.

Atkinson, J.W., & Raynor, J.O. (1974). Personality, motivation, and achievement. New York: Halsted Press.

Birney, R.C., Burdick, H., & Teevan, R.C. (1969). Fear of failure. New York: Van Nostrand-Reinhold.

Boulding, K. (1992, May). Nonviolence in the 21st century. Paper presented at the Symposium on Nonviolence: Social and Psychological Issues, Utica, NY.

The challenge of peace: God's promise and our response. (1983, June 17). National Catholic Reporter, pp. 5-28.

Cohen, S.P., & Arnone, H.C. (1988). Conflict resolution as the alternative to terrorism. Journal of Social Issues, 44(2), 175-189.

Deutsch, M. (1983). The prevention of World War III: A psychological perspective. Political Psychology, 4, 3-31.

Dyson, F. (1984). Weapons and hope. New York: Harper and Row.

Galtung, J. (1985). Twenty-five years of peace research: Ten challenges and some responses. Journal of Peace Research, 22, 141-158.

Herman, T. (1992, May). Comments at the Symposium on Nonviolence: Social and Psychological Issues, Utica, NY.

Holsti, O.R. (1972). Crisis escalation war. Montreal: McGill-Queens University Press.

Janis, I.L. (1985). International crisis management in the nuclear age. In S. Oskamp (Ed.). Applied Social Psychology Annual, Vol. 6 (pp. 63-86). Beverly Hills, CA: Sage.

Kimmel, P.R. (1985a, August). From antiwar movements to antiwar organizations. Paper presented at the meeting of the American Psychological Association, Los Angeles.

Kimmel, P.R. (1985b). Learning about peace: Choices and the U.S. Academy of Peace as seen from two different perspectives. American Psychologist, 40, 536-541.

Lewin, K. (1935). A dynamic theory of personality. New York: McGraw-Hill.

Lifton, R.J., & Falk, R. (1982). Indefensible weapons: The psychological and political case against nuclearism. New York: Basic Books.

Maslow, A.H. (1968). Toward a psychology of being. New York: Van Nostrand.

Osgood, C.E. (1962). An alternative to war and surrender. Champaign, IL: University of Illinois Press.

Plous, S. (1988). Disarmament, arms control, and peace in the nuclear age: Political objectives and relevant research. Journal of Social Issues, 44(2), 133-154.

Pruitt, D., & Rubin, J.Z. (1986). Social conflict: Escalation, stalemate, and settlement. New York: Random House.

Rubin, J.Z., & Lewicki, R.J. (1973). A three-factor experimental analysis of promises and threats. Journal of Applied Social Psychology, 3, 240-257.

Sommer, M. (1985). Beyond the bomb: Living without nuclear weapons. New York: The Talman Company.

Weick, K.E. (1984). Small wins: Redefining the scale of social problems. American Psychologist, 39, 40-49.

White, R.K. (1988). Specifics in a positive approach to peace. Journal of Social Issues, 44(2), 191-202.

CHAPTER 6

Moral Exclusion and Nonviolence:
The Japanese American Internment

Donna K. Nagata

The events of wartime trigger images of extreme violence and aggression. Once a country has been attacked, retaliation is a frequent response. The principles of nonviolence are rarely considered. When the Japanese bombed Pearl Harbor on December 7, 1941, it did not take long for the United States to declare war on Japan. The aftermath of Pearl Harbor from a military perspective is widely known. Less widely known are the consequences of that attack for thousands of Japanese Americans at that time. Considered a military risk because of their Japanese ancestry and proximity to the West Coast, more than 110,000 Japanese Americans were removed from their homes and interned in isolated concentration camps for periods of up to four years. Denied the right to trial or due process, nearly two-thirds of the internees were U.S. citizens, born in this country. The internment affected more than 90% of the mainland Japanese American population.

Ironically, although the government cited proximity to Japan as a reason to evacuate the West Coast Japanese, those in Hawaii were not subjected to mass internment. Less than 1% of Japanese Hawaiians were interned even though they comprised nearly one-third of the territory's population at that time (Ogawa & Fox, 1986). The fact that Japanese Hawaiians were so numerous made mass internment impractical. In addition, the U.S. military there depended upon their services to operate (Commission on Wartime Relocation and Internment of Civilians, 1982).

In 1980, the Commission on Wartime Relocation and Internment of Civilians (CWRIC) investigated the facts and circumstances surrounding the Japanese American internment, and made recommendations based upon their conclusions. The Commission's final report stated that, in fact, there was no evidence to support the military necessity of incarcerating the Japanese Americans and that a "grave injustice" had been committed (CWRIC, 1983). Their recommendation that the government pay $20,000 redress to each surviving internee was eventually passed by Congress and authorized by President Reagan in 1988.

The treatment of the Japanese Americans does not seem violent when compared to acts of combat or genocide. Nonetheless, the extreme abrogation of their rights raises important issues regarding the conditions which determine our moral standards of inclusion and exclusion from justice, as well as our definitions of violence and nonviolence. This paper describes how the internment represented the moral exclusion of an ethnic minority group within their own country. Factors contributing to this exclusion are discussed as well as the long-term consequences of this exclusion for Japanese Americans. Finally, contrasts will be drawn between the processes leading to the internment and the philosophy of nonviolence proposed by Gandhi in India, where Indians were also subjected to severe exclusion under British rule.

Factors Contributing to the Moral Exclusion of Japanese Americans

Opotow (1990), citing Deutsch (1974, 1985), notes that the scope of justice is bounded by one's sense of moral community. Those who are included within one's moral community are seen as being more moral and virtuous than those who are outsiders. Those who are excluded from this community ..."are perceived as outside the boundary in which moral values, rules, and considerations of fairness apply (Opotow, 1990, p. 1)." Opotow points out that moral exclusion is most likely to occur during times of conflict and when there is a sense of unconnectedness between groups. The consequences of exclusion are severe:

> Those who are morally excluded are perceived as undeserving, expendable, and therefore eligible for harm. Although both those inside and outside the moral community can experience wrongful harm, harm inflicted on insiders is more readily perceived as an injustice and activates guilt, remorse, outrage, demands for reparative response, self-blame, or contrition. When harm is inflicted on outsiders, it may not be perceived as a violation of their rights, and it can fail to engage bystanders' moral concern (Opotow, 1990, p. 13)

Moral exclusion in itself does not necessarily lead to overt violence. Indeed, exclusion occurs along a continuum of severity (Opotow, 1990). Subtle exclusionary acts would not be seen as violent. On the other hand, history provides, unfortunately, many examples where initially subtle forms of exclusion are the precursors to torture, genocide, and mass killings (Staub, 1990). Subtle forms of nonviolent exclusion can, under the proper conditions, lead to violent actions. The exclusion and incarceration of Japanese Americans may not seem violent in itself. America's concentration camps were not death camps. Still, the policies and attitudes underlying the treatment of Japanese Americans reflected both aggression and hostility.

Multiple factors contributed to the exclusion of Japanese Americans from the moral community of most Caucasian Americans, setting the stage for the internment (Nagata, 1990b). Anti-Asian and anti-Japanese sentiment existed long before the attack on Pearl Harbor. Negative racial stereotypes portrayed the Japanese as subhuman, unassimilable, untrustworthy, and inferior to Caucasian Americans. Formal legislation restricted the immigration of Japanese to the United States, prohibited the immigrant Japanese (referred to as "Issei") from becoming American citizens, and prevented them from owning land. Informally, there were segregated swimming pools and social clubs. Opportunities for upward mobility were rare even for second generation (Nisei) Japanese Americans who were citizens born in this country (Kitano & Daniels, 1988). In many ways, Japanese Americans were already excluded from the white mainstream society prior to the war.

The panic and hysteria following Pearl Harbor fueled pre-existing antagonism and stereotypes. The vast majority of Caucasian Americans supported the idea of internment (Coombs, 1986; Johnson, 1988), excluding the Japanese Americans from the scope of their moral community. The internment was upheld by the Supreme Court, supported by Congress, and even favored by the majority of members of the American Civil Liberties Union of Northern California and the American Communist Party (Daniels, 1988). And, although liberal church leaders called for tolerance and reminded others of the loyalty of Japanese Americans, "even the sympathetic did little to try and shape government policy or to forestall mass evacuation" (Taylor, 1986b, p. 123). For Caucasian Americans in agriculture along the West Coast, economic factors also contributed to the press for removing the Japanese. Japanese American farmers had become increasingly successful raising labor-intensive truck crops and the desire of Caucasian farmers to take over the land and crops of Japanese Americans played a central role in the move towards internment. "The mass removal of the Japanese provided a fortuitous opening for achieving the principal aim of exclusionism and colonialism-economic gain (Okihiro and Drummond, 1986, p. 174)."

Neither citizenship nor past evidence of loyalty or law-abiding behavior mattered. Exclusion was based upon ethnic heritage alone. A famous quote from Lieutenant General John L. DeWitt in 1943, leading proponent of the internment, captures the prevailing sentiment at that time: "The Japanese race is an enemy race and while many second and third generation Japanese born on United States soil, possessed of United States citizenship, have become 'Americanized', the racial strains are undiluted... A Jap's a Jap... You can't change him by giving him a piece of paper (Commission on Wartime Relocation and Internment of Civilians, 1982, p. 66).

The particularly racist nature of the Japanese American exclusion is clear when one considers the fact that neither German Americans nor Italian Americans were subjected to mass incarceration even though the United States was at war with Germany and Italy. German and Italian Americans remained inside the boundaries of the moral community. Why? Certainly the racial similarity between these ethnic groups and other Caucasian Americans played a central role; there existed a sense of connectedness that never existed between Caucasian Americans and Japanese Americans. Additionally, the large size and political clout of the German American population made it unlikely that they would be excluded. In 1940, the number of families with at least one German-born parent was approximately six million (Commission on Wartime Relocation and Internment of Civilians, 1982). During the same year, Japanese Americans numbered only about 127,000 in the continental United States (Thomas, 1952). Isolated socially and geographically, they had no political power. The Issei were ineligible to vote since they were prohibited from becoming citizens, and most Nisei at the time were too young to do so (Kitano, 1969).

The vast majority of Caucasian Americans, then, clearly saw Japanese Americans as "the enemy," deserving of exclusion. There were, however, individuals who differed in their perceptions of the internment (Nagata, 1990b). Some who supported the internment emphasized the need for humane treatment, including Japanese Americans within the sphere of a moral respect for human life while simultaneously excluding them from the moral sphere of democracy. Others argued that the internment was "for their own good," necessary to protect Japanese Americans from racial violence. In this case, Japanese Americans were included under a morally justified paternalism which continued to deny them the right to determine their own destiny.

The Long-term Effects of Exclusion

The consequences of internment affected all who were incarcerated. The extent of economic losses alone, have been estimated to be in the billions of dollars (Commission on Wartime Relocation and Internment of Civilians, 1982; Taylor, 1986a). Particularly relevant here are the long-term social psychological effects suffered by internees and their offspring. Although there are no empirical studies evaluating the impact of internment on the Issei and Nisei, autobiographies and descriptive studies reveal numerous effects (e.g., Mass, 1986; Morishima, 1973; Tateishi, 1984). Testimonies by former internees at the hearings before the CWRIC, nearly 40 years after the camps, revealed the continued pain and sense of loss reported by Japanese Americans. Feelings of shame and embarrassment were frequently reported. Although they had done nothing wrong, these internees, like the victims of rape, felt that somehow they were responsible for their fate (Hansen & Mitson, 1974). Most tried to assimilate as much as possible after the war, minimizing their Japanese heritage. They worked hard to "prove" that they were good Americans and tried to put the past behind them. Others felt betrayed by their country and expressed disillusionment with America as well as a general skepticism of democracy.

Internment also physically changed the nature of Japanese American communities. Beginning in 1943, Nisei who answered affirmatively to a mandated loyalty oath began to receive clearance to leave the camps and resettle in areas outside the restricted zones of the West Coast. As a result, populations of Japanese Americans emerged in cities such as Chicago, New York, and Denver where few Japanese Americans lived previously.

The effects of the internment, however, extend beyond those who were incarcerated. The author's own research (1990a; 1991; in press) found that the severe exclusion of Japanese Americans during World War II has had continuing consequences for the postwar generations of Japanese Americans today. Survey data taken from a national sample of over 500 third generation (Sansei) sons and daughters of former internees indicated that when compared to peers who had neither parent interned, Sansei who had parents in camp were significantly less confident about their rights in this country, expressed a greater preference for Japanese Americans over Caucasian Americans, and were more likely to agree that a future internment of Japanese Americans was possible. In addition, twice as many of the Sansei whose fathers had been interned reported that their father died before the age of 60 than Sansei whose fathers were not in a camp.

The Sansei also felt the emotional aftermath of the camps. When asked to indicate how much their parents suffered from the internment, the average response was 4.63 on a scale ranging from (1) "Very Little Suffering," to (5) "A Great Deal of Suffering." Sixty-eight percent gave a rating of 5, the highest possible score. Similarly, the Sansei reported continued feelings of anger about their parents' internment. Respondents were provided with the statement "When I think of my parents having been in camp I feel angry" and asked to rate their reactions on a scale where (1) = "Strongly Disagree" and (7) = "Strongly Agree." Here, the average rating was 5.96, reflecting a high level of anger.

The Internment and Gandhi's Principles of Nonviolence

At first glance, the treatment Japanese Americans in this country and the treatment of Indians under British colonialism seem entirely unrelated. Clearly important historical differences exist between the two. Indians, for example, were the majority population while Japanese Americans were a minority group in the United States, and the nature of oppression in India was much more extensive. There are, however, similarities as well. Both Indians and Japanese Americans were colonized within their countries, systematically excluded from the moral community of a group in power. The following conditions which characterize a colonial model of governance can be seen as relevant to the Japanese Americans and Indians alike:

1) There is forced, involuntary entry.
2) There are attempts towards acculturation, in contrast to the more natural processes of intergroup interaction. The colonizing power carries out a policy that constrains and transforms the indigenous values, orientation, and ways of life of the indigenous population.
3) Members of the colonized group are administered and controlled by representatives of the dominant group.
4) There is racism (Blauner, 1972; as cited in Kitano, 1986; p. 154).

Kitano (1986) labels the internment years as a period of "domestic colonization" for Japanese Americans. Not only was relocation forced, but policies within the camps deliberately sought to diminish the Japanese culture and to acculturate internees to mainstream American values (James, 1987). Just as the social and economic livelihood of Japanese Americans was dominated by the Caucasian American majority, the lives of Indians suffered under British rule. British policies deliberately subverted Indian customs (D'Cruz, 1967) and destroyed Indian industries and trade, as well as the traditional Indian educational system (Sanderlal, 1972). Interestingly, the British framed these acts as necessary in order to include the Indians within the community of their Empire. However, Erikson (1969) points out: "While the British Empire may have promised to Indians and others a wider identity supervised by an elite of British choosing and training, it neglected to cultivate (as America neglected to do for the American Negro) those components of identity which neither a defined group nor an individual can do without (p. 267)." Exclusion, rather than inclusion, characterized the plight of Indians.

In response to the oppression of Indians, Gandhi proposed nonviolence. His philosophical and religious beliefs provide an interesting contrast to the exclusive policies of the British colonialists in India and the pro-internment majority of Caucasian Americans in the United States.

The basis for much of Gandhi's beliefs stemmed from "Satyagraha," a term which referred to a soul-force, truth-force, or love-force. Satyagraha was a spiritual and moral approach based upon nonviolent, non-cooperation (D'Cruz, 1967). While moral exclusion is based upon the definition of boundaries between groups, conflict, and unconnectedness (Opotow, 1990), Gandhi's teachings stressed the need for "perfect trust" in others and the unity of humanity (Erickson, 1969). In Gandhi's (1984) words, "For a nonviolent person, the whole world is one family (p. 48)." He also believed that focus should be placed not upon the differences between groups in conflict, but rather upon the ability of opponents to "acquire a more inclusive identity" with each other. Hence, Gandhi repeatedly stated that he did not hate the British because he believed in freedom as they did (Dean, 1959). In contrast, the internment of Japanese Americans, like the colonization of Indians, was based upon an emphasis on group differences, exclusive identity boundaries, and devaluation of the excluded group.

Given Gandhi's emphasis on the unity of humanity, one might question why the Christian churches, who presumably shared a similar philosophy, did not more actively protest the internment of Japanese Americans. Taylor (1986b) states that many churches were misled into thinking the internment was justified. While the more liberal churches, such as the Quakers, Congregationalists, and Methodists took greater action than other Protestant groups, most of their efforts occurred after the internment had already been decided (e.g., helping Japanese Americans to store their belongings when leaving for camp or, later on, assisting in the resettlement process after camp). A representative from the pacifist-oriented American Friends Service Committee (AFSC) who did testify in Seattle before a government panel advocated voluntary relocation to an inland area already populated by Japanese rather than mass internment. However, despite the AFSC's pacifist aims "...its concerns were primarily specific--humanitarian and individualistic, rather than general--with the policy as a whole" (Taylor, 1986b; p. 128).

Ironically, one Quaker who did actively demonstrate his philosophy of pacifism and nonviolence at the time was a Japanese American, Gordon Hirabayshi (Irons, 1983). Hirabayshi, then a senior at the University of Washington, Seattle, refused to register for the evacuation and eventually spent five months in jail for doing so. In a statement listing his objections, he noted that the order to evacuate denied all persons of Japanese ancestry of the right to live and he considered it his duty to refuse the order in accordance with his democratic and religious principles.

Summary

The Japanese American internment illustrates a form of moral exclusion based upon long-standing racism and colonial attitudes. These factors, combined with conflict between Japan and the United States following Pearl Harbor and subsequent military and government pressures, created an atmosphere where the principles of nonviolence such as those proposed by Gandhi, failed to emerge. Fear and the persistence of underlying prejudice towards Japanese Americans prevented even groups who traditionally advocated justice and pacifism from actively challenging the incarceration.

We have seen that moral exclusion involving historical racism can be especially severe. Its consequences affect not only those who are excluded, but also the offspring of those individuals. Third generation Sansei Japanese Americans continue to feel the effects of their parents' past exclusion, even though the Sansei now occupy a position of greater inclusion, experiencing significantly less prejudice and discrimination. Unfortunately, the current climate of tension between the United States and Japan suggests that many Caucasian Americans are again sensitized to the differences between themselves and the Japanese, rather than focusing upon, in Gandhi's terms, the unity of humanity. Japan-bashing, references to Pearl Harbor and "sneaky Japs," and increased anti-Japanese hate crimes are emerging. In some cases, hostilities have been directed towards Japanese Americans. These dynamics, reminiscent of World War II, are cause for alarm.

At the same time, however, the passage of the Redress Bill in 1988, which formally acknowledged and apologized for the injustice of the internment decades earlier, signaled to many Japanese Americans a critical step in their inclusion into the American justice system. This, combined with the postwar reduction of overt legal, economic, and social barriers against Japanese Americans, has increased their sense of empowerment. Hopefully, the success of their nonviolent response to moral exclusion will encourage all Americans to closely examine the current stereotypes and prejudices which exist and prevent these attitudes from developing into more pervasive and violent forms of exclusion.

REFERENCES

Blauner, R. (1972). Racial oppression in America. New York: Harper & Row.
Commission on Wartime Relocation and Internment of Civilians (1982). Personal justice denied. Washington D.C.: U.S. Government Printing Office.
Commission on Wartime Relocation and Internment of Civilians (1983). Personal justice denied: Part 2-recommendations. Washington, D.C.: U.S. Government Printing Office.

Coombs, F.A. (1986). Congressional opinion and war relocation, 1943. In R. Daniels, S.C. Taylor, & H.H.L. Kitano, (Eds.) Japanese Americans: From relocation to redress (pp. 88-91). Salt Lake City, UT: University of Utah Press.

Daniels, R. (1988). Asian America: Chinese and Japanese in the United States since 1850. Seattle: University of Washington Press.

D'Cruz, E. (1967). India: The quest for nationhood. Bombay, India: Lalvani.

Dean, V.M. (1959). New patterns of democracy in India. Cambridge, MA: Harvard University Press.

Deutsch, M. (1974). Awakening the sense of injustice. In M. Lerner & M. Ross (Eds.), The quest for justice: Myth, reality, ideal. Canada: Holt, Rinehart & Winston.

Deutsch, M. (1985). Distributive justice: A social psychological perspective. New Haven, CT: Yale University Press.

Erikson, E.H. (1969). Gandhi's truth: On the origins of militant nonviolence. New York: W.W. Norton.

Gandhi, M. (1984). The quintessence of Gandhi in his own words. New Delhi, India: Madhu Muskan.

Hansen, A.A. & Mitson, B.E. (1974). Voices long silent: An oral inquiry into the Japanese American evacuation. Fullerton, CA: California State University Oral History Program.

Irons, P. (1983). Justice at war: The story of the Japanese American internment cases. New York: Oxford University Press.

James, T. (1987). Exile within: The schooling of Japanese Americans: 1942-1945. Cambridge, MA: Harvard University Press.

Johnson, S.K. (1988). The Japanese through American eyes. Palo Alto, CA: Stanford University Press.

Kitano, H.H.L. (1969). Japanese Americans: The evolution of a subculture. Englewood Cliffs, NJ: Prentice Hall.

Kitano, H.H.L. (1986). The effects of evacuation on the Japanese American. In R. Daniels, S.C. Taylor, & H.H.L. Kitano (Eds.) Japanese Americans: From relocation to redress (pp. 151-158). Salt Lake City, UT: University of Utah Press.

Kitano, H.H.L. & Daniels, R. (1988). Asian Americans: Emerging minorities. Englewood Cliffs, NJ: Prentice Hall.

Mass, A.I. (1986). Psychological effects of the camps on the Japanese Americans. In R. Daniels, S.C. Taylor, & H.H.L. Kitano (Eds.) Japanese Americans: From relocation to redress (pp. 159-162).

Morishima, J.K. (1973). The evacuation: Impact on the family. In S. Sue & N. Wagner (Eds.) Asian Americans: Psychological perspectives (pp. 13-19). Palo Alto, CA: Science and Behavior Books.

Nagata, D.K. (1990a). The Japanese American internment: Exploring the transgenerational consequences of traumatic stress. Journal of Traumatic Stress, 3, 47-69.

Nagata, D.K. (1990b). The Japanese American internment: Perceptions of moral community, fairness, and redress. Journal of Social Issues, 46, 133-146.

Nagata, D.K. (1991). The transgenerational impact of the Japanese American internment: Clinical issues in working with the children of former internees. Psychotherapy, 28, 121-128.

Nagata, D.K. (in press). Legacy of injustice: Exploring the cross-generational effects of the Japanese American internment. New York: Plenum.

Ogawa, D.M. & Fox, E.C., Jr. (1986). Japanese American internment and relocation: the Hawaii experience. In R. Daniels, S.C. Taylor, & H.H.L. Kitano (Eds.) Japanese Americans: From relocation to redress (pp. 135-138). Salt Lake City, UT: University of Utah Press.

Okihiro, G.Y. & Drummond, D. (1986). The concentration camps and Japanese economic losses in California agriculture, 1900-1942. In R. Daniels, S.C. Taylor, & H.H.L. Kitano (Eds.) Japanese Americans: From relocation to redress (pp. 168-175). Salt Lake City, UT: University of Utah Press.

Opotow, S. (1990). Moral exclusion and injustice: an introduction. Journal of Social Issues, 46, 1-20.

Sanderlal, P. (1972). British rule in India. Bombay, India: Popular Prakashan.

Staub, E. (1990). Moral exclusion, personal goal theory, and extreme destructiveness. Journal of Social Issues, 46, 47- 64.

Tateishi, J. (1984). And justice for all: An oral history of the Japanese American detention camps. New York: Random House.

Taylor, S.C. (1986a). Evacuation and economic loss: Questions and perspectives. In R. Daniels, S.C. Taylor, & H.H.L. Kitano (Eds.) Japanese Americans: From relocation to redress (pp. 163-167). Salt Lake City, UT: University of Utah Press.

Taylor, S.C. (1986b). "Fellow-feelers with the afflicted:" The Christian churches and the relocation of the Japanese during World War II. In R. Daniels, S.C. Taylor, & H.H.L. Kitano (Eds.) Japanese Americans: From relocation to redress (pp. 123-129). Salt Lake City, UT: University of Utah Press.

Thomas, D.S. (1952). The salvage. Berkeley, CA: University of California Press.

CHAPTER 7

A Social Psychology of Rules of War:
A Research Strategy for Studying Civilian-Based Defense

Jeffrey A. Mann

Progress in understanding behavior is sometimes advanced by framing a question differently. In this vein, the notion of "civilian-based defense" frames questions about conflict differently. It raises rich, fresh, and testable questions about the psychology of nonviolent and violent conflict. The following two sections of this chapter aim to illustrate this perspective. The first section clarifies what civilian-based defense refers to. It explains how the concept of civilian-based defense brings questions about the dynamics of nonviolence into the realm of international conflict. The second section suggests a route by which research psychologists might study civilian-based defense. As an illustration, this section presents two empirical projects, and highlights the study of "rules of war" as one psychological assumption that may be tested about civilian-based defense. Overall, this chapter aims to illustrate that current psychological theory can contribute to a study of civilian-based defense, and the notion of civilian-based defense can challenge current psychological theory to address new questions.

Nonviolence and Civilian-based Defense

There are several ways of thinking about nonviolence (Sharp, 1979). Some theorists emphasize a "spiritual" nonviolence, focusing on nonviolence as a lifestyle, and a philosophy for persuading others to genuinely accept one's views. Others emphasize a "pragmatic" nonviolence, focusing on nonviolence as a technique for coercing acceptance or tolerance from others. Few theorists reject the value of both of these elements, but most emphasize one or the other in their study. Gene Sharp (1979), for example, highlights the coercive elements that are available in nonviolent action. Sharp does not dismiss the value of a spiritual nonviolence for one's own life, or for interacting with others (e.g., Sharp, 1973, p. 706). But he emphasizes the coercive power available through nonviolent action. Sharp emphasizes that if social relations require cooperation, then each party wields a nonviolent power in the form of noncooperation. To withhold cooperation is power. It can be a coercive power because it has the capacity to alter another's behavior without relying on the other party's goodwill or change of heart. By highlighting a coercive, non-spiritual version of nonviolence, Sharp emphasizes that masses of people can engage in nonviolent action without first being required to adopt a fully nonviolent lifestyle, or a comprehensive rejection of violence.

One extension of this view has lead Sharp (1980) and others (e.g., Roberts, 1968) to propose a radical application of nonviolence. These writers propose that such coercive nonviolence can be planned and organized on a nationwide scale, and in theory, could be used by a country to defend itself in a unique way in war. This notion of using nationwide, planned, organized nonviolence is called civilian-based defense.

Clearly, civilian-based defense, or CBD as it is abbreviated, is a radical proposition. However, sometimes, progress in understanding behavior is made simply by framing a question differently. And CBD frames questions about conflict differently. By imagining what would have to occur for such nonviolence to work, we will likely gain a greater understanding of the dynamics of nonviolent and violent conflict.

Among the questions that CBD raises, one fundamental issue is: What would constrain a rogue government from simply killing any opponents who resisted nonviolently? Sharp (1980) emphasizes that one powerful constraint is social complexity and dependence. Unless an invader is willing to kill or deport everyone in a country, and bring in its own citizens, an invader is dependent on the native populace to run the country. However, several writers (e.g., Atkenson, 1976) have argued that this is a partial, but far from a comprehensive, constraint. For example, what if an invader is willing to repopulate a country with its own people? Or, what if an invader is not interested in gaining productivity from a country, but is interested simply in occupying and eviscerating the country to prevent it from developing into a threat? In these cases, what would stop a rogue government from simply killing any opponents who resisted nonviolently?

The Psychology of the Observer in CBD

Sharp (1973) proposes there is a second constraint. It is the reaction of observers. It is here, in understanding the psychology of observers' reactions, that I think there are rich psychological questions. For example, would observers be outraged at violence against nonviolent opponents? Would observers sanction political leaders to stop such violence? Sharp (1973) proposes that they would and frequently have. In Sharp's (1973, pp. 657-658) words, the psychology of the observer is as follows:

> Cruelties and brutalities committed against the clearly nonviolent are likely to disturb many people and to fill some with outrage. Even milder violent repression appears less justified against nonviolent people than when

employed against violent resisters...wider public opinion may turn against the [violent] opponent, [and] members of his own group may dissent...

Sharp (1973) reports many compelling historical case studies as evidence to support this dynamic. But Sharp does not emphasize cases that do not support this dynamic. The intention of his book is to provide a theory of nonviolent power, and to demonstrate compellingly that effective nonviolent action is possible--that it has happened historically with a wide variety of nonviolent means, and in a wide variety of contexts. Sharp identifies some conditions that may influence observers' reactions (e.g., Sharp, 1973, pp. 726, 740, 754), but it is not his intention to elaborate a psychology of these conditions. Nevertheless, there are several strategies for examining the facilitative and inhibitive conditions for the proposed dynamic, and for examining the psychology of these conditions.

One strategy is to use the scientific method, and to test hypotheses about nonviolence and CBD. Social psychologists generally use experimentation and other methods that allow one to systematically test hypotheses and observe both confirming or disconfirming evidence. The following section describes two studies conducted to test versions of Sharp's hypothesis. Clearly, these studies are not definitive tests of Sharp's hypothesis--no few studies could be. Rather, these studies illustrate the psychological hypotheses that can be derived from Sharp's and others' rich theorizing about civilian-based defense, the psychological theories that can inform our thinking about observers' reactions to CBD, and social psychological research methods that may be used to complement other disciplines' methods for approaching CBD.

Study One

The first study, conducted with Sam Gaertner at the University of Delaware, is an experiment that tested Sharp's hypothesis in the context of a CBD scenario. Briefly, we transformed Sharp's proposed dynamic into a hypothesis that we could operationalize experimentally. We labelled Sharp's quote "a rule of proportionality," and stated it as follows:

> The use of force is deemed appropriate to the extent that levels of force between groups are equal or proportional; conversely, the use of force is deemed inappropriate to the extent that levels of force are disparate or excessive (Mann & Gaertner, 1991, p. 1794).

This rule of proportionality raises issues from current social psychological theory. Briefly, it addresses theory on justice judgments, and proposes that observers care about procedural justice in conflict, i.e., whether the procedures used in conflict are fair (e.g., Lind & Tyler, 1988). This rule of proportionality is plausible. But, there are several reasons why observers might not be concerned with using proportionate force. In our study, we tested one such factor. We wanted to know whether observers are biased to be more lenient to their own group's violations than other groups' violations of a rule of proportionality. If observers are to constrain a government's excessive violence, it is ingroup observers--the constituents of the excessive government--who often have the most power to sanction the government. Certainly independent observers can have an impact. But, if observers will only see force by an outgroup as excessive, and rarely see force as excessive when committed by its ingroup, then that would limit the power observers have to constrain a government's excessive violence. Several theories of intergroup relations (e.g., Realistic Conflict Theory, Sherif & Sherif, 1969, and Social Identity Theory, Tajfel & Turner, 1979), predict that observers will be biased to be more lenient toward their own country's excesses than another country's excesses (see Mann & Gaertner, 1991 for a more detailed prediction).

Overall, then, we tested two hypotheses. First, would observers follow what we have called a rule of proportionality? Second, would observers be more lenient towards their own country than other countries? This first study we conducted with an experiment.

We presented psychology undergraduates (half men, half women) with a news transcript describing a fictitious military invasion of Nigeria, a country we assumed most students knew little about. We manipulated three independent variables in the study in a 3 x 2 x 2 factorial design. The first variable was the Invading Country. In 1/3 of the transcripts, the invader was the U.S.; in 1/3, it was England; and in 1/3, it was the old Soviet Union--this study was run in 1986 when the Soviet Union still existed as a single country. We expected that our U.S. subjects would be more lenient in judging their own country than in judging England, or the Soviet Union.

The second variable was the Invader's Tactic. One-half of the transcripts described the invaders as using highly violent tactics (i.e., shooting and killing 400 defenders); the other half described the invaders as using moderately violent tactics (i.e., forcefully arresting 400 defenders). The third variable was the Defender's Tactic. One-half of the transcripts described the defenders as using moderately violent tactics (i.e., weakly and sporadically shooting at the invaders); 1/2 described the defenders as using nonviolent tactics (i.e., nonviolently demonstrating and blockading streets).

We expected that the more disproportionate the force, the more inappropriate it would be rated. Thus, invader's use of highly violent tactics against nonviolent defenders would be rated most inappropriate, e.g., more inappropriate than invader's use of these same tactics against moderately violent defenders. Similarly, the most proportionate exchange of force (i.e., invader's moderately violent force versus defender's moderately violent force) would be rated most appropriate. Again, overall, the more disproportionate the force, the more inappropriate it would be rated.

Following is an abbreviated version of one condition of the news transcript. In each transcript, the cause of the U.S. or British invasions was to defend the Nigerian government against a minority communist attempt to nationalize the economy. The cause of a Soviet invasion was to defend Nigeria against a minority capitalist attempt to privatize the economy. In the present example, England is the Invading Country, the Invader uses highly violent force, and the Defender uses nonviolent force--it is an exchange of disproportionate force that is intended to capture the sense of civilian-based defense.

...[In an effort to restore order to Nigeria, a country reportedly threatened by communist subversion,] British troops off the coast of Nigeria landed in that country today. In confrontations in the streets of [Nigeria's] capital city, British troops...clashed with thousands of civilian Nigerians. The Nigerian Embassy...reports that 400 unarmed civilian Nigerians were killed when British troops fired on the Nigerian civilian defense force, a force designed to use organized nonviolence to defend Nigeria...[T]housands of unarmed Nigerian civilians trained and organized by neighborhood districts, stationed themselves with signs, and some with loudspeaker systems, in designated streets of the capital city to demonstrate to British forces that they pose no military threat to England, [and] they support the independence of their government against British military intervention...Streets in the capital were already lined with posters stating the government's policy to defend Nigeria with organized nonviolent action. According to reports...400 unarmed civilian Nigerians have been shot and killed and hundreds others have been injured. The British Foreign Office reports that no British troops have been injured...(Mann & Gaertner, 1991, pp. 1798-1799).

Again, this is an abbreviated version of one condition in the study. After reading one condition of the scenario, main dependent variables asked subjects to rate the perceived appropriateness of the invader's force and defender's force.

What did we find? Consistent with the rule of proportionality, the more disproportionate the force, the more inappropriate the tactic was rated. As Table 1 shows, invader's highly violent force was rated most inappropriate when used against nonviolent defenders (see Table 1). Invader's force was rated more inappropriate in this exchange than if they had used the same tactics against moderately violent defenders, and than if they had used less violent tactics (i.e.,"moderately" violent) against the nonviolent defenders. Also, as expected, in the most proportionate exchange of force (i.e., moderately violent invaders versus moderately violent defenders), the invader's force was rated least inappropriate. These results were consistent with a rule of proportionality.

As expected, we found that the inappropriateness of the Invader's force did depend on whether it was the U.S., England, or the Soviet Union invading Nigeria. Subjects rated tactics by the Soviet invaders ($M = 5.77$) as significantly more inappropriate than identical tactics by either the U.S. ($M = 5.10$) or England ($M = 5.01$). There was no significant difference between ratings of the U.S. and British invaders. One way to explain this pattern is that it is consistent with a Realistic Conflict Theory of intergroup bias. This theory suggests that subjects will be biased against groups with which their group has a competitive relationship, e.g., as the U.S. did with the Soviet Union, and that subjects will be biased in favor of groups with

TABLE 1
Mean inappropriateness of invader's force (Mann & Gaertner, 1991)

				Invader's level of force			
Moderately violent (forceful arrest)		Highly violent (lethal shooting)	
Defenders moderately violent (weakly shoot)	Defenders nonviolent (blockade)	Defenders moderately violent (weakly shoot)	Defenders nonviolent (blockade)
4.11[a]	5.15[b]	5.60[c]	6.30[d]

Note. 1 = appropriate, 7 = inappropriate. Means with different superscripts differ significantly at p < .05.

TABLE 2
Percentage of each type of rationale underlying an evaluation (Mann & Powers, 1991)

	Evaluation		
Rationales	Justified (n = 2)	Unjustified (n = 36)	Ambiguous (n = 35)
Noncombatant immunity	0	64	0
Military Necessity	100	0	6
Chivalry	0	3	0
Patriotism	0	0	0
Noncombatant Immunity and Military Necessity	0	6	0
Noncombatant Immunity and Patriotism	0	6	0
Noncombatant Immunity, Military Necessity, and Patriotism	0	3	0
None	0	18	94

which their group has a cooperative relationship, e.g., as the U.S. did and does with England (see Mann & Gaertner, 1991, for a fuller comparison of Realistic Conflict Theory and Social Identity Theory predictions). Clearly, subject-observers were more lenient towards their own country and another cooperative country than towards the competitive Soviet Union. Notably, however, the bias among the countries was relative rather than absolute. U.S. and British tactics were judged as less inappropriate than Soviet tactics, not as appropriate. Intergroup bias appeared to lessen subjects' tendency to follow the proposed dynamic, but not to completely erase this tendency.

Overall, the study found some support for a rule of proportionality, and the potential that observers would be inclined to criticize their country's and other country's use of excessive force against nonviolent opponents. Clearly this is just one study, and it leaves many questions still to be answered. For example, would observers act on their evaluation that a country used an inappropriate level of force? Under what conditions, would observers be willing to do something following this evaluation? Would this finding generalize to other subjects, perhaps subjects from another culture? Many more questions are possible.

Clearly, there are advantages and disadvantages to studying nonviolence through experimentation. One of the potential disadvantages is that one can be uncertain if the results would generalize to the "real" world. There can be some doubt if an experiment captured the emotional intensity of the phenomenon, or the real-world costs and rewards that occur with the phenomenon (see Mann & Gaertner, 1991, however, for evidence suggesting that most subjects believed the validity of the news transcript). In this event, other quantitative research methods are available for examining the psychology of observers' reactions to nonviolence.

Study Two

In a second study, conducted with Melissa Powers, at Wheaton College (Mann & Powers, 1991), we examined American observers' reactions to the My Lai massacre of the Vietnam War. We used the quasi-experimental method of archival content analysis to understand observers' reactions to a real-world event where a government used excessive force against innocent civilians.

The My Lai massacre was the killing of several hundred S. Vietnamese civilians in 1968 (Hersh, 1970). A platoon of U.S. soldiers entered the village of My Lai expecting to find and kill enemy guerilla troops. Instead, they found only unarmed civilians, and under persistent orders from their commanding officer, Lt. William Calley, a small group of these soldiers systematically assembled and shot several hundred of these civilians. In this tragic event, the Vietnamese victims were not "nonviolent" activists, but they were individuals who were not violent--they were innocent civilians. Active nonviolent resistance is not synonymous with the passive, absence of violence. This was not CBD. But observers' reactions to the use of force against unarmed opponents in war should help us understand reactions to force against nonviolent opponents.

We know from studies at the time ("Gallup Finds," 1971; Kelman & Lawrence, 1972) that most Americans disapproved of the My Lai killings. They did not justify the killings, despite the fact that most opposed Lt. Calley's legal prosecution. In our study, we wanted to know why most Americans thought the killings were wrong. By condemning the killings, American observers were implying that there are rules in war--there are things you cannot do in war. We wanted to know why Americans believed this--what were the rationales underlying Americans' criticism of the killings? We proposed four rationales that we thought would be most salient in observers' criticisms. We derived these rationales from Just War theory, a classic religious doctrine on war-time morality, and American military law (O'Brien, 1981). We wanted to test if these rationales were in fact salient to the observers.

The four rationales are principles in the laws of war. They are labelled (1) military necessity, (2) noncombatant immunity, (3) chivalry, and (4) patriotism. Briefly, if military necessity was salient, subjects' rationale for condemning the killings would be that the killings were unnecessary for victory. That is, subjects' statements would emphasize that killing is justified if it is essential for victory, killing is not justified if it is not relevant to achieving victory. If noncombatant immunity was salient, subjects' rationale would be that the victims were noncombatants. That is, subjects' statements would emphasize that soldiers are legitimate targets, but civilians should be excluded from intentional attack. If a third principle of war, chivalry, was salient, subjects would emphasize that the victims should have been treated in accord with tradition. That is, unarmed civilians, or disarmed soldiers, should be taken prisoner, not summarily executed, because that is tradition, and separates soldiers from murderers. As a fourth principle, we proposed that subjects might not emphasize any of these rules of war, but rather would respond on a more emotional level of stereotypes. A subject might emphasize simply that the killings were wrong because they "violate American values," or "Americans don't do that." We called this rationale "patriotism," and thought of it as a way that observers might think about right and wrong without being intuitively aware of formal rules of war.

We wanted to assess which, if any, of these four rationales was salient in observers' criticism of the My Lai killings. We turned to an historical source that recorded people's thinking about the killings at the time the killings became public. We used the U.S. Congressional Record, a source containing all speeches presented on the floor of the U.S. House and Senate. Speeches in the Congressional Record were not responses to a fabricated news report, or recollections of old reactions; these were archival reports of people's responses at the time the killings became public. Unlike use of the experimental method, there can be no doubt that this archival method captures subjects' responses in their natural context.

Our goal was to understand subjects' rationales as objectively as possible. Therefore, we used the method of content analysis, which lead us to develop an explicit coding system for classifying subjects' rationales (see Mann, Powers, & Rubery, in press, 1991 for a detailed description of the coding system). First, we coded whether subjects explicitly evaluated the killings as justified or unjustified, or were ambiguous in their evaluation. Then, we coded subjects' rationales for their evaluation. As noted earlier, we coded whether subjects' statements emphasized the rationale underlying a principle of military necessity, noncombatant immunity, chivalry, patriotism, or some combination of these four rationales. We had two coders independently rate subjects' rationales so we could assess whether our classification system was explicit, and reliable (as subsequently, our high levels of inter-rater reliability indicated). What did we find? Why did observers criticize the My Lai killings?

Briefly, among those speeches that criticized the killings, we found that the single most frequent rationale for criticizing the killings was noncombatant immunity (i.e., 64% of these speeches, see Table 2). To our surprise, few politicians emphasized military necessity, chivalry, or patriotism, or any other combination of these rationales. For example, Rep. Koch (1969) stated,

...A tragedy took place in the village of Songmy (i.e., My Lai) where Vietnamese civilians, men, women, and babes in arms, were massacred by American Army personnel. If we did not know it before, we know it now, that the ability to commit war crimes is not restricted to the Germans...(p. 35652).

For Rep. Koch, the view that civilians were killed is the essence of his argument. He offers no other justification for why these killings in war were different than any other killings in war--why these were "war crimes."

What is the implication of this finding for nonviolence and CBD? My Lai makes it clear that many observers are willing to recognize their own country's excesses, at least when they are committed in the face-to-face manner of the My Lai killings, in the context of a war like Vietnam, among an American sample, and at a time when most were dissatisfied with the progress of the war. More importantly, though, I think the current study tells us something about how American observers define an excess in war. In their public responses, our sample did not struggle with or emphasize many of the principles raised in Just War Theory and American military law. What was singularly salient was that the My Lai victims were noncombatants. What if the victims had been actively and nonviolently resisting, rather than passively nonviolent? Would observers then have seen them as a potential enemy that justifies the use of force? The evidence is suggestive, but not conclusive. The My Lai victims were unarmed civilians, and their noncombatant status, most salient to our subjects, would be the same for actively nonviolent opponents. Subjects' lack of emphasis on military necessity, and great attention to noncombatant status, suggests that given similar circumstances with nonviolent opponents in war, most American observers like our sample would be inclined to criticize such killings.

Overall, then, using a different research method, we found some further evidence generally consistent with the proposed psychology of the observer. Under certain conditions, it seems most observers believe there are procedural rules in war, and perhaps in conflicts involving nonviolent opponents. Under certain conditions, war is not a state of nature where "anything goes." The samples we have studied have some norms about how conflict should be fought. Clearly again, there are many questions to pursue. For example, are there conditions where observers believe rules should be broken? What if many lives of one's countrymen can be saved by fighting "unfairly?" Then, would the ends justify the means? There are more questions, and I hope these can be pursued in the future.

Conclusions

In summary, there are three general ideas proposed in this paper. First, I have tried to clarify how the concept of CBD brings questions about the dynamics of nonviolence to the realm of international conflict. Second, I have tried to show that the notion of CBD raises many psychological questions about both violent and nonviolent conflict. Psychological theories about procedural justice, and intergroup relations, as well as about bystander intervention, may all contribute to, and be challenged by, this context. In addition, asking what constraints there are on conflict--whether observers have rules about conflict--seems relevant to understanding both violent and nonviolent conflict. Third, I have tried to show that different quantitative social psychological research methods can be applied to study nonviolence and CBD. Sharp's work, and others', on nonviolence are rich in hypotheses. Psychologists can study those hypotheses with their unique methods, and complement the methods used by historians, political scientists, and sociologists.

One does not have to "believe in" nonviolence and CBD to study their psychology (though, of course, one could). As non-conventional methods of social influence, these propositions frame questions about conflict differently. And sometimes progress in understanding behavior can be made by framing a question differently.

REFERENCES

Atkenson, E.B. (1976). The relevance of civilian-based defense to U.S. security interest. Military Review, vol. LVI, no. 5 and 6, pp. 24-32, 45-55.

Gallup finds 79% disapprove of verdict. (1971, April 4). New York Times, p. 56.

Hersh, S. (1970). My Lai 4. New York: Random House.

Kelman, H.C. & Lawrence, L.H. (1972). Assignment of responsibility in the case of Lt. Calley: Preliminary report on a national survey. Journal of social issues, 28, 1, 177-212.

Lind, E.A. & Tyler, T. (1988). The social psychology of procedural justice. New York: Plenum Press.

Mann, J.A. & Gaertner, S.L. (1991). Support for the use of force in war: The effect of procedural rule violations and group membership. Journal of applied social psychology, 21, 22, 1793-1809.

Mann, J.A. & Powers, M.H. (1991). My Lai and procedural rules of conflict: Why Congress criticized U.S. troops in war. Paper presented at the 62nd annual meeting of the Eastern Psychological Association, New York City, N.Y.

Mann, J.A., Powers, M.H., & Rubery, R.M. (in press). Procedural rules in international conflict: A content analysis of reactions to the My Lai killings. Social justice research.

O'Brien, W.V. (1981). The conduct of just and limited war. New York: Praeger.

Roberts, A. (1968). Civilian resistance as a national defense. Harrisburg, PA: Stackpole Books.

Sharp, G. (1973). The politics of nonviolent action. Boston, MA: Porter Sargent.

Sharp, G. (1979). The types of principled nonviolence (pp. 201-234). In G. Sharp, Gandhi as a political strategist. Boston, MA: Porter Sargent.

Sharp, G. (1980). "The political equivalent of war"--Civilian-based defense (pp. 195-262). In G. Sharp, Social power and political freedom. Boston, MA: Porter Sargent.

Sherif, M. & Sherif, C. (1969). Ingroup and intergroup relations: Experimental analysis. In M. Sherif & C. Sherif, Social psychology. New York: Harper and Row.

Tajfel, H. & Turner, J. (1979). An integrative theory of intergroup conflict. In W. Austin & S. Worchel (eds). The social psychology of intergroup relations (pp. 33-47). Monterey, CA: Brooks/Cole.

CHAPTER 8

Children as Peacemakers: Promoting the Development of
Cooperation and Conflict Resolution

Jill Alexander and Stephen C. McConnell

"The Psychologists' Manifesto: Human Nature and the Peace: A Statement by
Psychologists," issued in 1945, described ten basic principles to consider in planning
for permanent global peace (cited in Jacobs, 1989). Children as the coming
generation should be the primary focus of attention: "Children are plastic; they will
readily accept symbols of unity and an international way of thinking in which
imperialism, prejudice, insecurity and ignorance are minimized" (Jacobs, 1989, p.
127). The thesis of this chapter is to explore elements relative to children and peace,
more specifically delineating ways to promote children's development of cooperation
and conflict resolution.
  Conflict is an inevitable part of everyday life, existing on multiple realms
including internal, interpersonal, intergroup, and international. Conflict can lead to
change, adaptation, and development both individually and interpersonally (Johnson,
1990). While productive conflict can be the catalyst for feelings of expansion and
for new ideas and ways of living together, it also has a less positive side, and its
consequences can be destructive. It can damage friendships, families, social
institutions, and in contemporary times, the human species itself (Smith, 1990; Macy,
1983).
  The central concept in most major theories of human development involves
conflict, identifying conflict as dynamic, critical moments of successfully or
unsuccessfully adapting or progressing (Schantz, 1987). Conceptually, conflict has
been equated with aggression; however, Schantz (1987) suggested that while
aggressive behavior occurs most often in the context of social conflict, it is only one
of many types of responses that may occur in a conflictual situation. Contrastingly,
a state of conflict denotes when parties of an interdependent relationship have
incompatible behaviors or aspirations, and this incompatibility is outwardly expressed
with one person opposing another person's behavior or goals (Smith, 1990; Schantz,
1987).
  Commonly, peace is associated with passivity and 'being nice'; however,
peace is not the absence of conflict, but has been defined as an active and creative

process involving ways people can act on problems and challenges without being emotionally or physically damaging (Hudson, 1984) and can work to resolve conflicts whereby both sides benefit (McGinnis and McGinnis, 1985;Yelsma & Brown, 1986). Even so, when people are overcome with fear, anger, or other difficult feelings, when they lack a sense of their personal worth, and/or have no practice in addressing alternatives, most people find it difficult to react creatively to conflict (Judson, 1984).

In the realm of conflict resolution, responsible behavior generally involves one's resources and proclivities toward prosocial and moral behavior. The more experience children have in different ways of doing things and the more they are encouraged to think, the more answers they are able to draw from their own resources when in a crisis (Boulding, 1980). However, similar to adults, a child who has few ideas about what to do next tends to sulk, strike out, or avoid conflicts (Strayer & Strayer, 1976; Judson, 1984)).

Applying social and developmental psychological knowledge is relevant to the understanding and control of social conflict and to the promotion of strategies for facilitating children as peacemakers. A review of the literature regarding children and their issues, conceptions, strategies and outcomes of social conflict will be presented. Gender influences and the context of interpersonal relations will also be reviewed. Moral and prosocial development and their related determinants and influences, including parental styles of interaction will be related to children's conflict resolution. Finally, a model for clinical application based on a children's and parent's group approach will be suggested.

Children and Conflict

Schantz (1987) utilized an effective outline for delineating her review of empirical literature regarding interpersonal conflicts of children in natural settings. Schantz's framework is utilized in this paper, consolidating what the literature offers regarding the issues, conceptions, strategies, and outcomes as well as incorporating gender components and the context of unilateral and mutual interactions relative to the examination of conflict and its resolution. While much of the psychological literature has focused on the study of the individual's characteristics and behavior, the studies discussed will tend to view conflict in the social realm. Conflict, in general, will be defined as mutual resistance between two or more people (Schantz & Schantz, 1985) or as occasions where one child attempts to influence a second child who resists and the protagonist persists.

Children's Issues of Conflict

There are a variety of goals or issues that are catalysts of conflict in children's relations with each other. In her review of the research findings, Schantz (1987) found the following issues to be prevalent at various ages: (1) during the toddler and preschool years, the greatest percentage of conflicts seems to involve the possession and use of objects; (2) the second largest category appears to be distress over another child's actions or lack of action; (3) social intrusiveness, which could be an unprovoked attack or an interference of a child's activity; and finally, (4) violating conventional or moral rules provokes conflict. Schantz and Schantz (1985) found that developmentally as children get older, an increasingly smaller proportion of conflicts are about the physical environment (objects and space) and a larger percentage involve control of the social environment, including conflicts over ideas, facts, or beliefs as well as actions.

In some studies, successful problem solutions were more predictable when strategies were considered in relation to specific goals (Krasnor & Rubin, 1983; Renshaw & Asher, 1983; Schantz & Schantz, 1985). There may be simultaneous goals in any one conflict episode, such as having control over persons or objects, wanting a favorable outcome for oneself, or wanting to create or maintain positive relationships with one's adversary (Nelson & Aboud, 1985). Renshaw and Asher (1983) found that for 8 through 12 1/2 year-old children much of the work of social interaction consists of participants constructing goals as they proceed, sometimes with an initial dispute not remaining as a primary issue.

Children's goals or issues relative to social conflicts appear to vary with age. However, since children tend to construct goals as they proceed, if their goal is not conducive to do so, children may not succeed in being cooperative, even if they know how to cooperate (Renshaw and Asher, 1983).

Children's Conceptions of Conflict

Children's conceptions or notions about social conflict influence children's conflictual interactions. Shantz and Shantz (1985) examined the relations between a set of social-cognitive conceptions and various aspects of interpersonal conflict between 6-and 7-year old children. Three types of social conception were assessed: (1) children's understanding of persons and how they understand their adversary; (2) social rules, representing the larger, regulatory social context within which conflict occurs, and rule infractions which often lead to conflict; and (3) conflict-resolution strategies involving children's specific knowledge of alternative ways to solve peer conflicts.

The results indicated that social-conceptual level of functioning is related to some aspects of conflict (Schantz & Schantz, 1985). Children with higher person conceptions tend to engage in a lower percentage of person fights than do those with lower person conceptions. It was suggested this could mean that the more the child conceptualizes peers in psychological, individualized terms, the less the child tries to control his/her peers' behavior. Additionally, children who had more advanced rule conceptions and whose rule conceptions were more consistent experienced more success than less advanced children.

Selman (cited in Schantz, 1987) provided a developmental analysis of conflict concepts and conflict resolution strategies, utilizing a social understanding model based on perspective coordination for types of conflict concepts children and adults hold. Developmental levels were described as: (1) behaving from a physical and momentary "here-and-now" orientation, resolving conflicts by stopping interactions or using physical force; (2) having an appreciation of the subjective and psychological consequences of conflict, although applying to only one person in the conflict; (3) gaining bilateral understandings of conflict, still conflict is not yet seen as a mutual disagreement nor as needing a mutually satisfying agreement; (4) apprehending that specific conflicts reside within the relationship itself and that solutions need to be mutually satisfying; and (5) integrating a balance of independence and dependence in friendships and recognizing symbolic and unstated ways of handling conflicts.

Selman and Demorest (1984) tested their model by examining the trends of interpersonal negotiation strategies of two nine year-old emotionally disturbed boys who participated in pair therapy. Concerned with how people coordinate other's thoughts, feelings and motives in conjunction with their own in attempting to balance inner and interpersonal disequilibrium, they addressed components which operate in interpersonal behavior. One component, the action orientation, referred to an individual's strategies being oriented toward transforming the self and/or other person in returning an interaction to equilibrium. Individuals try to transform the thoughts, feelings, or actions of another in the other-transforming orientation, while transforming ones own in the self-mode. In the lower strategy levels, the child's approach is more rigid, whereas in the higher levels, there is a more integrated interplay between the two orientations.

Observations suggested it is therapeutically sound to match children with predominantly opposite orientations and that children can learn, at least in the safety of the therapeutic context, that strategies of opposite orientation may not harm the self or other (Selman & Demorest, 1984). Neither orientation is adaptive in itself, as both strategy types can maintain an imbalance. Too much conflict was generated when matching two-other transformers, making it difficult for therapeutic work to occur, and matching two selftransformers generated a lack of interaction.

Children's conceptions about conflict not only influence how often and to what degree children experience success in their engaged conflicts, but also appear to be associated with the strategy orientations children employ. Thus, focusing on children's understanding of persons and social rules and promoting more balanced action-orientation strategies appear to be beneficial goals to effective conflict resolution.

Children's Conflict Strategies and Outcomes

One social conception of conflict presumes that the child's goals are to overcome another's opposition or resistance. A limitless variety of prosocial or antisocial behaviors may be viewed as tactics or strategies for how a child overcomes another's resistance and a variety of outcomes may occur.

Children have been found to display and understand varied nonverbal gestures and affective repertoires in their conflict resolution processes, and these types of emotional reactions tend to motivate partner's subsequent actions (Camras, 1977;

Camras, 1980; Sackin & Thelen, 1984; Matsumoto, Haan, Yabrove, Theodorou & Carney, 1986). Aggressive facial expressions have been observed in disputing kindergarten children (Camras, 1977), and were associated with persistence by the expressor to retain possession of a desired object followed by hesitancy on the part of a challenging child to continue attempts to gain the object. Challenging children were also observed to hesitate when nonaggressive facial expressions, usually signalling sadness, were emitted by their partners.

Preschoolers have been observed to settle the majority of their social conflicts without adult intervention (Hay & Ross, 1982), with submissive or appeasement behaviors, such as crying, flinching, withdrawing, and request cessation, tending to be the most common method of conflict termination. Although submissive behaviors are believed to help maintain a social hierarchy, Strayer & Strayer (1976) suggested that early dominance relations are modified through social learning. Additionally, a small percentage of conflicts ended with children playing together in a cooperative way following the occurrence of placating or conciliatory behaviors.

Sackin and Thelen (1984) identified live types of conciliatory behaviors: (1) a cooperative proposition or verbal indication of friendly intentions and suggestions for cooperative interaction; (2) an apology expressing regret; (3) a symbolic offer where one child offers something to the other that was not immediately available; (4) object offering; and (5) grooming, or touching in a friendly or helpful manner. They examined whether such conciliatory behaviors function to initiate peaceful associative relations in kindergarten-age children rather than the separations that commonly follow fighting. Results showed most of the agonistic encounters ended with a subordinate behavior and separation. In striking contrast, eighty percent of the conciliatory gestures led to peaceful together outcomes.

The least successful tactics appear to be a child's insistence on his/her way and the use of either physical or verbal aggression (Eisenberg & Garvey, 1981; Schantz & Schantz, 1985; Hay & Ross, 1982). Hay & Ross (1982) found in observing conflicts over a period of three days that it was the loser of the last conflict that was more likely to initiate the next conflict. They suggested that winning a conflict is not necessarily rewarding and is not a promoter of higher rates of initiating conflict. However, an increase in the loser initiating conflict may be due to prior outcome dissatisfaction and a desire to regain a sense of affirmation.

Successful tactics tend to reflect sensitivity to another's intentions and needs and adjust to them. However, young children accused of violating rules of all types seldom ignore a challenge nor respond ambiguously or with defiance (Walton & Sedlak, 1982). Most often they respond with a reason or justification. Giving a reason tends to end an interchange or to be followed by the other child suggesting a compromise. Schantz and Schantz (1985) found approximately half of the strategies they observed involved assertions, negations, expressive nonverbal behavior, and ignoring of the other child, and a child's success was associated with a relatively high use of commands and low use of requests.

Researchers have also reported the relation between conflict strategies and outcomes and friendship (Renshaw & Asher, 1983; Nelson & Aboud, 1985; Hartup,

Laursen, Stewart & Eastenson, 1988; Matsumoto et al., 1986; Schantz & Schantz, 1985). More likable children seem to have more sophisticated strategies available for achieving positive-outgoing goals, and less popular children more often suggest avoidance and hostile goals (Renshaw and Asher, 1983). Schantz and Schantz (1985) found that although more antagonistic behaviors are strongly related to high social impact, higher likability was associated with engaging in fewer conflicts and less use of physical aggression. Interestingly, success in winning conflicts was not associated with social preference nor social impact.

Nelson and Aboud's (1985) results supported that third and fourth grade children responded differently to conflict with a friend than with a nonfriend. Measuring content discussion and changes in answers from before and after a problem-solving interaction, children received more explanations and critical evaluations from their friends.   Whether a friend or nonfriend duo, initial disagreements in the discussion produced greater response alterations than agreements; however, more positive changes occurred when the disagreement was between friends than nonfriends. This finding is interesting in that it indicates that, whether with a friend or nonfriend, disagreement is a catalyst for change beyond what is stimulated by a discussion, suggesting that children at least in this age range are more likely to come to a new solution after disagreement.

Children's strategies are related to the outcomes they experience and reveal information about how children attempt to achieve their goals in a conflictual interaction (Schantz, 1987). Although the ability to communicate friendly gestures is associated with the ability to cooperate, positive outcomes were also related to more active, assertive and affirming behaviors rather than to passive or conforming ones. The above findings offer evidence to suggest that from an early age successful resolution of a conflictual episode is a mutual endeavor.

Gender Differences and Children's Conflicts

The significance of the role that gender plays relative to children's conflict and its resolution has been studied in various contexts. Many researchers have shown males and females differ in their orientations to settling differences (Gilligan, 1982; Pearson, 1985; Brock-Utne, 1985; Kilmann & Thomas, 1975), and qualitative differences have also been noted in prosocial and cooperative behavior (Radke-Yarrow, Zahn-Walker & Chapman, 1983). Boys tend to play outdoors in team sports and fantasy games, and girls tend to play indoors with dolls and board games (Pearson, 1985). As a result of these differences in play, boys tend to be more assertive, competitive, verbally and physically aggressive, achievement oriented in their activities, and more concerned with control and uniqueness (Yelsma & Brown, 1985). Females tend to learn to avoid conflicts, take on a peacekeeper role, use more accommodating and facilitative strategies and expressions of support and solidarity.

Although there were no gender differences in social-cognitive functioning of the children they studied, Schantz and Schantz (1985) did find that gender played a significant role in children's conflicts. Girls' proclivity to engage in person control conflicts and boys' in object control ones are consistent with traditional notions of socialization. Girls are reared to be relatively more socially oriented and boys more object or task oriented. The major predictors of rate of conflict were gender as well as age with boys and older children tending to get into more conflicts than girls and younger children. The results add to the general findings from studies on aggression that boys are more likely to engage in higher rates of fighting and use more physical aggression in conflict resolution attempts (Parke & Slaby, 1983; Brock-Utne, 1985).

Although socializing can be homogenizing and conforming, Pierce and Edwards (1988) chose a written fantasy activity to analyze gender differences of 9 to 14 year-old students, under the premise that creativity is an area where it can be safe to deviate from the norm. Students were asked to invent a story about anything they would like with no restrictions, and their story content was coded for the kinds and resolutions of conflicts, gender characteristics, use and degree of violence, and degree of reasoning to solve problems. Results indicated significant differences between girls and boys in ways conflicts were resolved. Violent resolutions to problems, such as murdering the opponent and physical restraint, were more likely to be chosen by boys than by girls. Girls resolution strategies were more varied, employing reasoning, analysis, trickery and avoidance. Girls more often allowed conflicts in their stories to resolve themselves.

Some researchers argue that females express aggression indirectly (ignoring, excluding, refusing, avoiding) whereas males use direct aggression (Parke & Slaby, 1983). Others state that females are not less indirectly aggressive than males, but that as a result of socialization experiences, females are more susceptible to guilt and anxiety over expressing aggression; thus, inhibition of their aggression may result in some situations (Frodi, Macaulay & Thome, 1977; Parke & Slaby, 1983).

Kilmann and Thomas (1975) described two basic communication orientations as being influential in conflict management: individual assertiveness, which leads a person to be concerned about satisfying one's own needs while recognizing the rights and needs of others during interactions; and cooperativeness, which reflects the degree to which a person attempts to adjust or satisfy the needs and concerns of the other person. They found effective conflict management fit a model based on an individual's ability to balance communication abilities, accessing qualities of both assertiveness and cooperation associated with masculine and feminine roles respectively. Yelsma and Brown (1985) also found that gender-role classification was more of a discriminator of communication behavior and predisposition to conflict management than was biological sex classification.

Gender differences and children's social conflicts are determined to a significant extent by socialization factors; however, it appears that both orientations and actions of males and females offer contributions to conflict and its resolution. The above information has implications regarding how children are influenced by role models as well as regarding potential ways to enhance children's self-assertiveness within cooperative relations.

Unilateral Versus Mutual Interactions

A variety of researchers have examined the context of interpersonal relations and how it affects conflict resolution procedures (Levya & Furth, 1986; Hunter, 1984; Youniss, 1981). An interpersonal context effect theoretically proposes two extreme types: unilateral (authority) relations, in which there is minimum of rational exchanges of ideas and conformity is expected on the part of the subordinate party; and mutual (peer) relations, in which reciprocal or collaborative idea exchanges promote understanding.

Levya and Furth (1986) examined adolescents', ages 11, 13, 15 and 17, understanding of societal conflict and of compromise resolution in the context of peer and authority relations. Adolescents were asked to develop dialogues by continuing conversations from eight conflict stories that were counterbalanced for presentation in peer or authority contexts. Various degrees of non-compromise, routine, and constructive or consensus-seeking solutions were observed.

The results were that the interpersonal context in each of the conflict issues displayed a consistent trend with the peer context showing a higher number of constructive compromise responses and a lower number of non-compromise responses in comparison to the authority context (Levya & Furth, 1986). Many adolescents in describing conflicts in authority situations explicitly stated that the adults would win the conflict based on the fact that they were in a position of power. Since no one was in a position of power in the peer context, compromise strategies were more likely to be created. Supposing that the world of peers merges into the world of adults and that authority relations gradually move to mutuality in the course of development, it was expected that the differences between peer and authority conflict resolution scores would be greater for younger than older adolescents. However, this interactive effect did not occur; rather there was an insignificant increase in constructive compromise responses between 13 and 17 year-olds.

Hunter (1984) investigated unilateral and mutual interaction patterns in the contexts of parents and friends exerting direct influence on adolescents and in terms of whether adolescents seek social verification from parents or friends. Friends were viewed to interact more mutually than parents who were seen to interact more unilaterally than peers. Greater knowledge, expertise and nurturant concerns, especially when adolescents wanted to verify their views against their parents' more experienced views, appeared to be the important bases for social influence from parents. On the other hand, the socializing interactions with friends were most often in the form of mutual social verification based on similarity of experience, mutual understanding, and co-constructing shared knowledge without the constraints of having to defer to superior judgements.

While peers do tend to share similar life experiences, perhaps too much is being made of this interpretation. Youniss (1981) stated that parent-child relations of childhood and adolescence exemplify a unilateral authority relationship in which parents strive to impart an already-constructed knowledge to their children. Children are expected to accept a reality that is imposed on them, whereas in the mutual reciprocity relationship, they have the opportunity to actively construct and verify their own reality with someone whose ideas can be challenged and tested along with their own. If promoting resolution skills is desirable, parents becoming more mutual and not predominantly unilateral in their interactions would be beneficial.

Summary of Children and Conflict

It is clear that as participants in conflict, children construct a variety of goals and display an impressive amount of knowledge about social rules, person conceptions, and social strategies. The underlying dimensions that appear to change with development include: temporal orientation (from here-and-now to future interactions); the conflict focus (from physical behaviors to people in a relationship); and understanding of relationships (from unilateral to mutual). Further, children are aware and responsive to their adversaries during conflict and clearly demonstrate that many social processes are in play as children negotiate their differences.

Implications for intervention include focusing on more than overt behaviors alone. Evidence indicates that there are underlying cognitive, affective, motivational and relational processes which intervention needs to address in order to facilitate children's effective and flexible use of negotiation strategies. A focus on children's sense of power or affirmation, goals, and communication and relationship styles may help, especially for those children who lack friends. Reframing the 'win-lose' concept to both partners having fun, sharing information, affirming each other, or coming up with new alternatives rather than on winning or avoiding the conflict, may facilitate cooperation. Addressing how families can increase more mutual parent-child relationships appears relevant to promoting the development of conflict resolution skills.

Moral and Prosocial Development

Fully addressing theoretical frameworks is beyond the scope of this paper. However, a brief description of moral and prosocial development is beneficial to the incorporation of a later proposed model of intervention.

The psychoanalytic concept of identification, which is the means by which societal values are thought to be internalized, has been widely employed in research on prosocial behavior. Freud stated that identification generally underlies empathic relations with other persons and results among other things in a person limiting his aggressiveness toward those with whom he has identified himself (cited in Radke-Yarrow et al., 1983).

Learning theories deal with overt behavior acquired through direct reinforcements and modeling. Skinner felt behavior was controlled by environmental contingencies, and Bandura further specified this position by showing that prosocial behavior is acquired through observation and imitation (cited in Radke-Yarrow et al., 1983).

Cognitive-developmental theory emphasizes children's understanding of themselves and others as mediating the development of moral and prosocial behavior. Piaget (1965) delineated hierarchical developmental stages of moral reasoning, and stated that an awareness of self arises in relation to others. He viewed young children as egocentric, lacking an understanding of particular differences between the self and others, especially perspective differences. According to Piaget, experiencing reciprocal interaction between equals leads the child out of egocentrism.

Kohlberg (1969), influenced by Piaget, elaborated a developmental stage model describing the progression of children's moral reasoning. He was not particularly concerned with behavior, but was more concerned with the ideas that may guide behavior, such as moral reasoning pertaining to laws, rules, authority, responsibility, equality and justice. Kohlberg suggested that persons construct representations, transform and organize information into mental conceptions, and go beyond convention to establish moral codes of their own. His theory was predicated on the belief that cognitive development was inherently a process of discovering forms of logical reasoning based on an individual's ability to self-reflect.

Contemporary Moral Developmental Perspectives

In general, cognitive theorists have not dealt in detail with the links between children's understanding of themselves and others and their moral or prosocial acts. One of the questions posited by contemporary theorists is whether moral reasoning is the primary condition necessary for moral acts (Radke-Yarrow et al., 1983; Youniss, 1981; Blasi, 1980; Hogan, 1984; Gilligan, 1982).

Contrasting to theories that view moral development as primarily due to cognitive development, investigators who have addressed young children's moral actions rather than their judgments about dilemmas have shown that young children appear capable of a range of morally sensitive behaviors (Radke-Yarrow et al., 1983; Matsumoto et al., 1986). Others have suggested that much of the basic conceptual moral structure of children is present by age 5 (Ferguson & Rule, 1988; Schultz, Wright & Schleifer, 1986). If children fail to justify their moral judgements in a mature fashion, it is not necessarily because they lack the concepts, but they may not be able to display that understanding in every circumstance.

Blasi (1980) agrees that cognition plays a central role in moral functioning, but that morality ultimately lies in action. His review pointed out that there are a number of conceptual and methodological problems in implementing the cognitive-developmental approach where moral thinking is the guideline for predicting moral behavior, such as the tendency to treat qualitatively different stages as if they were on a quantitative dimension and the remoteness of moral reasoning stages from the content of specific actions and from the motivational or affective context of the individual. Blasi found that some of the most important functions of cognition, that is the creation of meaning and the determination of the truth, are not recognized in moral functioning research and argued for addressing a process approach to moral or personal consistency, which refers to the agreement between what an individual states about his actions and the actions themselves.

Gilligan and her colleagues (1982; 1988), whose work came out of Kohlberg's moral developmental position, proposed that interpersonal concerns and justice constitute two specific types of moral orientation which are associated with gender. Kohlberg's focus on fairness and rights, which Gilligan refers to as justice reasoning, is predominately an orientation held by males. However, Gilligan found that women do not consider fairness as primary, but that they are motivated by relations or a care mode of reasoning.

Some researchers have found no significant gender differences regarding moral orientations (Walker, 1989; Smetana, Killen & Turiel, 1991), but cite evidence that children appear to have context specific criteria regarding moral judgements (Walton, 1985; Smetana, Killen & Turiel, 1991). Smetana et al. (1991) found that for 8 to 14 year-old children, concerns with justice and interpersonal relations co-exist in judgements of boys and girls and the application of judgements is dependent on situational variables.

Youniss (1981) offered a discussion of contemporary moral development theories and suggested an alternative based upon a social constructionism. Proposing that a split of cognition and affectivity was detrimental to addressing morality, the elements of a constructionist model view the individual as conceived through membership in communicative relations. In this context, affect is defined as the commitment persons make to work for the common good, managing themselves to maintain community without sacrificing their own autonomy.

An individual confronts reality discovering that there are multiple interpretations including his own (Youniss, 1981). This choice point can be met with alternative responses: to adopt the interpretations which other persons hold, especially of those who are considered authorities and all-knowing; to utilize one's own reasoning in an interpretative manner, inferring the views of others and constructing moral codes by means of reflective reasoning; or to recognize that a multiplicity of views is an opportunity for problem solving. In a communicative relations model, the construction of moral codes is neither through imitation nor self-reflection, but through cooperation. Since people face multiple views including their own, an alternative to settling differences or creating order is to approach conflictual views as a communication problem. The discovery and use of ways to facilitate communication, such as negotiation, debate and discussion, help individuals to see that consensus offers validation.

Youniss (1981) further points out how Piaget acknowledged the inadequacy of cognition based on self-reflective reasoning and discussed placing children in communicative relations in order to have children construct moral codes through discourse. Piaget agreed that in unilateral communication and transmission of knowledge from adults to children, children's contribution to dialogue is minimal, and their views are abandoned to adopt those of their parents. Unilateral communication does not help children to recognize subjective biases nor to view themselves as agents, since they have such a small role in co-constructing moral codes.

However, children's friendships are examples of communicative relations in which mutual understanding, or consensus, and mutual respect, or community, are clear developmental achievements (Radke-Yarrow et al., 1983).

Traditional cognitive positions view autonomy as an individual's self-reliance on conclusions reached through laws of reason (Youniss, 1981). In the constructionist view, communicative relations are not a lower position from which one grows out of towards independence, but remain viable throughout life as means to revise and verify one's moral position. Thus, autonomy is redefined as within the bounds of mutual dependence and learning one's individual freedom is conditional to other's behavior and freedom.

Moral and Prosocial Development Summary

Many theories propose that social-moral reasoning progresses from constraint (fear of punishment) to cooperation (consensus seeking), attributing this development to cognitive growth without addressing an interpersonal emphasis. There appears to be an interactive relation between children's social, cognitive and moral development or between intrapersonal and interpersonal processes (Youniss, 1981; Schantz, 1987; Piaget, 1969; Selman & Demorst, 1984; Gilligan, 1982). Youniss (1981) expanded the traditional interpretation of cognitive theory by strengthening it with social affectivity and constructionism, proposing that the roles of social conflict in children's development are based in communicative relations where a child learns his/her sense of self and autonomy in relation to his/ her interdependence with others. The significant correlations between compromise resolution and moral reasoning in peer but not in authority contexts provides support for the viewpoint that the avenue to mature morality is found primarily in peer relations (Levya & Furth, 1986). However, opportunities for children to experience constructive and enhancing negotiations in authority contexts do exist, and their effects on moral and prosocial development deserve consideration.

Parenting Influences

Parenting practices occur within and are effected by larger contexts, including the structures of educational, economic, political and media systems along with the norms of the culture and society. Even so, parents as socializing agents in children's lives have a special impact due not only to being involved in children's early experiences, but also to the continuity of their interactions across time (Hetherington & Parke, 1986). Parents inevitably have more power than children, having control of more resources as well as more knowledge, skills and physical power. Despite the fact that parenting practices need to adapt to the individual child and to different circumstances, there are certain key concepts relevant to all parenting in terms of promoting children's conflict resolution abilities (Jorgenson, 1985; Radke-Yarrow et al., 1983).

Parents socialize children by serving as models for imitation (Hetherington &

Parke, 1986; Maccoby & Martin, 1983). The process of identification, or feeling similar to another person, is based on the premise that individuals find gratification in responding in ways they believe others would want. There is an important distinction between observational learning and identification versus reward and punishment processes of socialization. When enforcement comes through reward and punishment usually they are intended to shape behavior. On the other hand, imitation and identification often occur without the parent intending to influence the child. Many parents verbalize a set of values and exhibit another, which is not an effective approach to positive socialization.

Becker (cited in Maccoby & Martin, 1983) examined and classified the consequences of different kinds of parental discipline using a fourfold typology of parenting based on the dimensions of parental control and emotional relationship with the child. The ultimate goal of discipline is considered to be self-regulation rather than regulation by external agents (Hetherington & Parke, 1986). Baumrind studied Becker's typology (cited in Hetherington & Parke, 1986) and found the following patterns.

Indulgent-permissive parenting refers to lax and inconsistent discipline and encouragement of children's free expression of impulses (Hetherington & Parke, 1986). This style has been associated with uncontrolled, impulsive behavior in children.   A neglecting parental style frequently involves ignoring and being indifferent and uninvolved with children. Parental rejection and permissiveness are often associated with aggressive behavior due to children's associated frustration in lack of response to their needs. Parents become a poor source of reinforcement and consequently are less effective in teaching self-restraint.

Authoritarian parents were found to be rigid, power-assertive, harsh and unresponsive to children's needs.   Power-assertive disciplinary tactics are often associated with aggression and hostility in children (Maccoby & Martin, 1983; Hetherington & Parke, 1986). While they may avoid parental contact and exhibit minimal overt aggression in the home toward a threatening parent, children tend to displace their aggression to others outside the home where they are less fearful of retaliation (Parke & Slaby, 1983).

Advocated as the most beneficial, an authoritative-reciprocal parenting style is referred to as a pattern of family functioning where children are required to be responsive to parental demands and parents accept a reciprocal responsibility to be as responsive as possible to children's reasonable views and demands.   This discipline style includes: clear standards and firm enforcement of rules; lack of yielding to child coercion; an expectation of mature behavior from the child; encouragement of the child's independence and individuality; and bidirectional communication between parents and children (Hetherington & Parke, 1986; Maccoby & Martin, 1983). This style of discipline has been associated with the development of self-esteem, competence, internalized control, and cooperative relationships.

A critique by Lewis (cited in Maccoby & Martin, 1983) questioned Baumrind's emphasis on parental control and argued that perhaps parent control or child compliance were being measured rather than child competence. Lewis found that if firm parent control is subtracted from the pattern of behaviors characterizing authoritative parenting, children do not become less competent.

Numerous authors promoting the facilitation of cooperation and conflict resolution in children point to the need for an alternative way to view parental discipline as mutual (Judson, 1984; Dorn, 1983; McGinnis & McGinnis, 1985; Miller, 1986). Conceptually, parents and children work together where no one wins and no one loses by sharing decision-making, problem solving and practicing healthy communication skills. Ideally, the outcome is mutually enhancing interactions that enlarge both parent's and children's lives.

Parents learn to exert influence through use of explanations and reasons instead of authority or power, as power hierarchies and their accompanying manipulation are antithetical to personal affirmation (McGinnis & McGinnis, 1985). Affirmation is viewed as an essential component to developing a sense of personal competence and to promoting a sense of community. The use of explanations or reasons by parents appeals to the child's desire to be more mature and to his/her concern for others, enabling the child to internalize social rules and to discriminate appropriate behavior in specific contexts (Hetherington & Parke, 1986).

Parenting Influence Summary

The structure of social contexts of development seem to reveal positive approaches to conflict resolution based on the notion that most non-conflictual states between children depend on the individuals having, to an important degree, shared knowledge, goals, expectations, rules and values (Schantz, 1987). Children whose conflict strategy orientations are more balanced, meaning they take into account both their own and others' needs and perspectives, experience more success. Gender orientations, or motivations, concerning individuality (masculine) and affiliation (feminine) were also found to each contribute to the process of effective conflict resolution. Conflict resolution from an early age is clearly a mutual endeavor among children; even so, mutual child and parent interactions can also offer benefits. In this regard, authoritarian and mutual parental discipline styles have been associated with children's sense of competence and behavior.

Most formal conflict resolution training for children comes from education professionals. However, teaching peaceful associations in a setting where children are taught to compete against each other for such things as attention and grades has been considered difficult (Brock-Utne, 1985). There is an impetus for the family to be the primary teacher. Maccoby and Martin (1983) proposed families be examined in terms of conflict and whether parent's or children's goals prevailed or a balancing of shared goals was established through negotiation. Interventions which promote the understanding and learning of parenting strategies and of child and parental roles which provide more of a communicative process view of mutual development and adaptation may encourage more balanced negotiations. In addition, interventions which facilitate children's development of cooperation and effective conflict resolution may also be beneficial.

A Model for Application

Based on the premise that groups have the advantage of being a small, insulated piece of the world in which present behavior can be experienced and new behaviors can be explored, a group model is proposed as an ideal way to promote the elements of constructive conflict resolution, generalizable to daily interactions (Yalom, 1985; Oaklander, 1988). The following group formats for children and parents are designed to be implemented in clinical settings, such as mental health agencies and private clinicians' offices, where service providers have expertise in child and family development and dynamics. Clinicians also need to be able to incorporate components of group therapy including: stated therapeutic goals; an explicit time limited framework; structuring around common needs and problems of group members; and a process-orientation in order to take advantage of the group's potential for enhancing an individual's sense of competence (Yalom, 1985). Structured activities and theme work are also well suited for group settings, and opportunities can be created for family-centered discussions and problem solving.

Group Themes

Various writers have proposed elements that contribute to the atmosphere for resolving conflict and to enhancing a family's ability to prevent destructive conflict and manage conflict in constructive ways (Judson, 1984; Hopkins & Winter, 1990; Prutzman, Stern, Burger & Bodenhamer, 1988; Macy, 1983; Johnson, 1990; Ing & Gabor, 1988; Gordon, 1970). A constructive process is created through an atmosphere of affirmation, communication, cooperation, problem solving, and community. These elements will be discussed below as key themes to include in both children and parent group formats. Specific elements and considerations will then be identified for each group and described in separate sections.

Affirmation and Self-awareness. Feeling affirmed is part of promoting conflict resolution in a group and family environment, as people need a sense of their own goodness, power and confidence. Children and adults are able to express feelings and thoughts better if they feel positive about themselves. Having a sense of positive self-esteem makes it easier to acknowledge the positives in others, including people with whom one is in conflict, and helps exploration of alternatives to problems. Teaching children to be aware and sensitive to the views and feelings of others can be an effective way of preventing aggression and promoting peaceful behaviors (Hetherington & Parke, 1986). Activities in the group can be designed to identify positive things about oneself and others.

Communication. Learning to communicate feelings and thoughts, including needs and problems, as well as sharing information with others in productive and creative ways is important to conflict resolution. Structured activities can support effective communication strategies including: active listening; observational skills including nonverbal messages; speaking skills, including assertiveness and offering feedback.

Sharing information and ideas increases a person's power. Therefore, sharing or exchanging information helps to distribute power instead of keeping it with only some of the people (usually adults in a unilateral approach) and increases one's ability to understand interactions. In a group, it can build a group's problem solving power, as one person's sharing can be a catalyst to another's thinking and result in a variety of alternatives.

Cooperation. Structuring cooperative and prosocial activities in a group setting provides opportunities for individuals to work together toward the same goal and to have discussions about competition and cooperation. Cooperative activities where each person is needed to fulfill the activity tend to build trust and a sense of community in a group. During the course of cooperative games, children who do not get along seem to forget the aspects of the image they hold of each other and react according to the needs of the activity (Luvmour & Luvmour, 1990). Cooperative games also provide opportunities to learn about sharing, turn taking, supporting one another, and following rules and limits.

Problem-solving. One of the most effective approaches to negotiating a solution is through promoting a win-win approach to resolving conflicts as it maximizes the degree to which each individual's needs are met and helps diminish potential negative affective and-interpersonal outcomes (Johnson, 1986; Gordon, 1970). A problem solving sequence which promotes the above generally involves identifying and mutually defining the problem, generating alternative problem solutions (brainstorming methods), evaluating the options, deciding upon a solution to implement, and later evaluating or modifying the chosen option. Role playing in groups is a well-known method of learning these types of skills.

In an article on gender issues and conflict resolution, Berman (1990) discusses how most conflict resolution training focus on the above rational type of problem solving approach which is not negative, but is incomplete. Thinking more contextually, she highlighted the need to incorporate that there are different ways of constructing a problem and the need to listen to how children and adults frame problems. Group members can benefit from attending more to the relationship and process and less to the solution.

Distinguishing between process and content conflict interventions, process interventions involve helping those who are conflicting to resolve their disputes without actually suggesting any particular resolution (Pruitt, 1981). Contrastingly, content interventions involve actual suggestions of possible solutions. Most alternatives in social conflict are not fixed and sometimes are not even known to the participants, but instead are invented during an encounter (Smith, 1987). This has implications not only for children's problem-solving, but also for adults who intervene in child-child conflicts, suggesting that parents learn ways to encourage children discovering solutions to conflicts since the best outcomes are supported by their prior process.

An area of frequent conflict especially with children is rules. "Rules" sometime connote rigid restrictions and resistance, and some conflict resolution trainers suggest language alternatives, such as 'policy' or 'responsibility' as useful words (Judson, 1984). Groups can address what policies are needed in the group to help everyone involved interact in caring and safe ways with each other and the environment. As one area where individuals can mutually agree and adapt when needed, this practice in the group can be applied to the home setting.

Supportive community. A group atmosphere allows people to work together on problems and assumes that everyone has something to contribute and is part of the solution. Providing opportunities to understand and accept that different people have different responses to particular situations and to develop skills for interacting with a variety of people directs children toward gaining social responsibility. Opportunities for prosocial endeavors support children's realization of the value of each individual's contribution to society. Further, a parent group frequently can be a catalyst to further social action, inspiring adults in efforts to organize changes for their children and themselves (Judson, 1984; Macy, 1983).

The Children's Group

The children's group will utilize semi-structured fantasy and creative mediums to support the expression and resolution of conflict. This type of framework allows opportunities for children to enact and resolve conflicts via fantasy and feelings elicited by group activity in a safe setting and provides enough structure to expand the range of children for whom therapy is available (Smith et al., 1985). The children's group can adjust activities according to the age range selected and should include both males and females who vary in action-orientations in order for group members to interact and learn from a mixture of interpersonal styles. Diagnostic criteria can be broad, excluding only children with severe developmental impairments that would be overwhelmed by the use of fantasy and unable to interact with peers (Smith et al., 1985). Individual goals for children can also be included such as: relaxing the need to control others; increasing tolerance for conflict; improving self-image and expression of feelings; increasing peer involvement; and applying goals to specific home and school situations.

Creative activity allows children the opportunity to experiment with roles, try new things, practice skills, and exercise their imaginations in a situation in which there is minimal risk (Oaklander,1988; Smith et al., 1985). Children internalize conflict resolution lessons more successfully when they are engaged on an emotional as well as cognitive and social levels, and creative mediums and symbolic images provide effective ways to achieve this (Yaffe, 1990). Engaging in social pretend play has also been associated with young children's social competencies, peer acceptance and negotiation skills (Doyle & Connolly, 1989). Through group activities and fantasy, therapists can learn about children's interpersonal relations in general and what is going on in the child's life from his or her perspective (Oaklander, 1988). Mediums to draw opportunities from can include: painting; drawing; music making; group collages; fairytales (including rewriting resolutions); imagery and relaxation activities; skits and melodramas; and puppetry.

Guidelines to consider incorporating into a children's conflict resolution group include: no cliques; including everyone; no putdowns nor attacking behavior; and the permission to pass when a child does not want to share. Providing time to process activities and to evaluate the group, encouraging children's feedback, is important. This shows children that the group is for them, and by incorporating feedback into future activities, that their input is valued. Member's awareness of the number of group sessions (10-12) and termination can be used to discuss endings and issues related to keeping friends.

The Parent's Group

A parent group can provide help in the understanding of certain child developmental patterns and can offer a place to explore new ideas and thinking about parenting with others who have similar feelings and concerns. Dorn (1983) feels parent groups should encourage parents to draw on their own experiences as children and to set goals for themselves in the group, such as learning what they do right, as well as what they need to learn, what they can learn from their children, and how they can grow along with them.

Wichert (1989) states it is essential for parents (and group facilitators) why want to promote peaceful associations to clarify their values regarding personal feelings they have about issues and behaviors of people, such as competition, which tend to influence children receiving mixed-messages. Parents' values about gender roles and expectations of their daughters versus their sons is one area that can be addressed. Discussing with parents their feelings about instilling values of affiliation in boys and values of assertiveness in girls supports children potentially addressing conflicts and their resolution with a more balanced orientation.

The following parent group topics are also suggested:

Discipline. Discipline is a form of helping children to eventually become more self-managing and monitoring. Children benefit from participating in deciding consequences for unacceptable behavior (McGinnis & McGinnis, 1985). Parents can help children concertize ways in which the family can help children to remember behaviors that are desired. The effects of punishment can also be addressed.

Violence in the media and community. Parental attitude is essential in helping children deal with violence in the media and community. Children become accustomed to viewing acts of aggression on television without learning consequences, and violence is seen as excitement rather than as suffering or loss (Parke & Slaby, 1983). It can also effect children's attitudes and lead them to see violence as an acceptable and effective way to solve social conflicts. Parents can help to lessen the impact of television and community violence by talking about what their children view and ask about, helping children understand possible reasons for people's actions and addressing alternatives.

Mutual problem solving with children. When children come to adults with a problem, it does not mean they necessarily expect them to solve the problem. A mutual parenting style helps children experience the process of problem solving as an inventive process, requiring negotiation and common agreement, and does not keep the power, decision-making and enforcement in the hands of the adults (McGinnis & McGinnis, 1985). To avoid power struggles, parents need to go into situations with their children without having an already planned outcome. Regularly shared decision-making and problem solving time which supports children's equal participation is helpful. Structuring evaluation time in the group can act as a model for parents to practice mutual problem solving with their children.

Conclusion

Children learn early that social conflict is inevitable and can be frightening and injurious. As participants in conflict, children display an impressive amount of knowledge about conflict conceptions, strategies and their potential outcomes. Evidence indicates that there are underlying cognitive, affective, motivational, moral and relational processes which intervention needs to address in order to facilitate children s cooperation and effective use of conflict resolution behaviors. A model was presented for intervention based on the premise that when children are taught to respond to conflict, fighting, and differences of opinion through active listening, dialogue, problem solving, and cooperation, it empowers them by broadening their repertoire of available responses.

Children's socialization is influenced by a myriad of factors, and the models available to children influence to a significant degree their goals and obstacles and the success or failure they experience. Although much is known about parenting styles, future investigation of how families deal with social conflict and the effects of mutual parenting styles, specifically regarding shared goals, is necessary. Similarly, research based on contemporary theories of moral development which focus on moral actions and communicative relations needs to further address parental contexts in order to better understand the effects on children.

Application of the extensive knowledge about conflict and its resolution needs to be utilized outside of educational environments to promote the development of children's cooperation and conflict resolution from birth. An intervention model was also proposed to promote parent's facilitation of these processes. By addressing personal values about issues related to the nature of parent-child interactions and conflict resolution and practicing a mutual parenting style, parents can offer their children an alternative to experiencing conflictual interactions as invigorating and powerful. Through mutually enhancing relationships, peaceful associations can become vital, too. Children, in turn, become better able to respond to everyday conflicts with an enhanced sense of choice and individuality. By gaining a concrete understanding of values of cooperation and interdependence, children can be educated for survival and strategies for living in our changing society and world.

REFERENCES

Baxter, L., & Sheperd, T. (1978). Sex-role identity, sex of other, and affective relationships as determinants of interpersonal conflict management styles. Sex Roles, 4(6), 813-825.

Berman, S. (1990, December). Pay attention to the "care voice." The Fourth R: The Newsletter of the National Association for Mediation in Education. Promoting the Teaching of Conflict Resolution Skills in Schools, 30, 1-6.

Blasi, A. (1980). Bridging moral cognition and moral action: A critical review of the literature. Psychological Bulletin, 88 (1), 1-45.

Boulding, E. (1986). Assumptions, images and skills. In R.K. White (Ed.), Psychology and the prevention of nuclear war. New York: New York University Press.

Brock-Utne, B. (1985). Educating for peace: A feminist perspective. New York: Pergamon Press.

Camras, L.A. (1977). Facial expressions used by children in a conflict situation. Child Development, 48, 1431-1435.

Camras, L.A. (1980). Children's understanding of facial expressions used during conflict encounters. Child Development, 51, 879-885.

Dorn, L. (1983). Peace in the family: A workbook of ideas and actions. New York: Pantheon Books.

Doyle, A.B., & Connolly, J. (1989). Negotiation and enactment in social pretend play: Relations to social acceptance and social cognition. Early Childhood Research Quarterly, 4, 289-302.

Eisenberg, A.R. & Garvey, C. (1981). Children's use of verbal strategies in resolving conflicts. Discourse Processes, 4, 149-170.

Ferguson, T.J., & Rule, B.G. (1988). Children's evaluations of retaliatory aggression. Child Development, 59, 961-968.

Frodi, A., Macaulay, J., & Thome, P.R. (1977). Are women always less aggressive than men? A review of the experimental literature. Psychological Bulletin, 84 (4), 634-660.

Gilligan, C. (1982). In a different voice: Psychological theory and women's development. Cambridge: Harvard University Press.

Gilligan, C., & Attanucci, J. (1988). Two moral orientations: Gender differences and similarities. Merrill-Palmer Quarterly, 34, 223-237.

Gordon, T. (1970). P.E.T. Parent effectiveness training: The tested new way to raise responsible children. New York: P.H. Wyden.

Hartup, W.W., Laursen, B., Stewart, M.I., & Eastenson, A. (1988). Conflict and the friendship relations of young children. Child Development, 59, 1590-1600.

Hay, D.F., & Ross, H.S. (1982). The social nature of early conflict. Child Development, 53, 105-113.

Hetherington, E.M., & Parke, R.D. (1986). Child psychology: A contemporary viewpoint (3rd ed.). New York: McGraw-Hill.

Hogan, R. (1974). Dialectical aspects of moral development. Human Development, 17, 107-117.

Hopkins, S., & Winters, J. (Eds.). (1990). Discover the world: Empowering children to value themselves, others and the earth. Philadelphia: New Society Publishers.

Hunter, F.T. (1984). Socializing procedures in parent-child and friendship relations during adolescence. Developmental Psychology, 20(6), 1092-1099.

Ing, C., & Gabor, P. (1988). Teaching conflict resolution skills to families. Journal of Child Care, 3, 69-80.

Jacobs, M.S. (1989). American psychology in the quest for nuclear peace. New York: Praeger Publishers.

Johnson, D.W. (1990). Reaching out: Interpersonal effectiveness and self-actualization (4th ed.). New Jersey: Prentice-Hall.

Jorgenson, D.E. (1985). Transmitting methods of conflict resolution from parents to children: A replication and comparison of blacks and whites, males and females. Social Behavior and Personality. 13(2), 109-117.

Judson, S. (Ed.) (1984). A manual on nonviolence and children. Philadelphia: New Society Publishers.

Kohlberg, L. (1969). Stage and sequence: The cognitive-developmental approach to socialization. In D.A. Goslin (Ed.), Handbook of socialization theory and research. (pp. 347-480). Chicago: Rand McNally.

Krasnor, L.R. & Rubin, K.H. (1983). Preschool social problem solving: Attempts and outcomes in naturalistic interaction. Child Development, 54, 1545-1558.

Levya, F.A., & Furth, H.G. (1986). Compromise formation in social conflicts: The influence of age, issue, and interpersonal context. Journal of Youth and Adolescence, 15(6), 441-452.

Luvmour, S., & Luvmour, J. (1990). Everyone wins: Cooperative games and activities. Philadelphia: New Society Publishers.

Maccoby, E.E., & Martin, J.A. (1983). Socialization in the context of the family: Parent-child interaction. In E.M. Hetherington (Ed.), P.H. Mussen (Series Ed.), Handbook of child psychology: Vol 4. Socialization, personality, and social development, 4th ed. (pp. 1-101). New York: Wiley.

Macy. J. (1983). Despair and personal power in the nuclear age. Philadelphia: New Society Publishers.

Matsumoto, D., Haan, N., Yabrove, G., Theodorou, P., & Carney, C.C. (1986). Preschoolers' moral actions and emotions in prisoner's dilemma. Developmental Psychology, 22(5), 663-670.

McGinnis, K., & McGinnis, J. (1985). Parenting for peace and justice. New York: Orbis Books.

Miller, J.B. (1986). Toward a new psychology of women. Boston: Beacon Press.

Nelson, J., & Aboud, F.E. (1985). The resolution of social conflict between friends. Child Development, 56, 1009-1017.

Oaklander, V. (1988). Windows to our children: A gestalt therapy approach to children and adolescents. New York: Center for Gestalt Development.

Parke, R.D., & Slaby, R.G. (1983). The development of aggression. In E.M. Hetherington (Ed.), P.H. Musser. (Series Ed.), Handbook of child psychology: Vol 4. Socialization, personality, and social development, 4th. ed. (pp. 547-642). New York: Wiley.

Pearson, J.C. (1985). Gender and communication. Iowa: W.C. Brown Publishers.

Piaget, J. (1965). The moral judgement of the child. New York: Free Press.

Pierce, K., & Edwards, E.D. (1988). Children's construction of fantasy stories: Gender differences in conflict resolution strategies. Sex Roles, 18(7/8), 393-404.

Pruitt, D.G. (1981). Negotiation behavior. New York: Academic Press.

Prutzman, P., Stern, L., Burger, M.L., & Bodenhamer, G. (1988). The friendly classroom for a small planet. Philadelphia: New Society Publishers.

Radke-Yarrow, M., Zahn-Waxler, C., & Chapman, M. (1983). Children's prosocial dispositions and behavior. In E.M. Hetherington (Ed.), P.H. Mussen (Series Ed.), Handbook of child psychology: Vol 4. Socialization, personality, and social development, 4th ed. (pp. 469-546). New York: Wiley.

Renshaw, P.D., & Asher, S.R. (1983). Children's goals and strategies for social interaction. Merrill-Palmer Quarterly, 29, 353-374.

Sackin, S., & Thelen, E. (1984). An ethological study of peaceful associative outcomes to conflict in preschool children. Child Development, 55, 1098-1102.

Schantz, C.U. (1987). Conflicts between children. Child Development, 58, 283-305.

Schantz, C.U., & Schantz, D.W. (1985). Conflict between children: Social-cognitive and socio-metric correlates. In M.W. Berkowitz (Ed.), Peer conflict and psychological growth: New directions for child development (3-21). San Francisco: Jossey-Bass.

Schultz, T.R., Wright, K., & Schleifer, M. (1986). Assignment of moral responsibility and punishment. Child Development, 57, 177-184.

Selman, R., & Demorest, A.P. (1984). Observing troubled children's interpersonal negotiation strategies: Implications of and for a developmental model. Child Development, 55, 288-304.

Smetana, J., Killen, M., & Turiel, E. (1991). Children's reasoning about interpersonal and moral conflicts. Child Development, 62, 629-644.

Smith, J.D., Walsh, R.T., & Richardson, M.A. (1985). The clown club: A structured fantasy approach to group therapy with the latency-age child. International Journal of Group Psychotherapy, 35(1), 49-64.

Smith, W.D. (1987). Conflict and negotiation: Trends and emerging issues. Journal of Applied Social Psychology, 17(7), 641-677.

Strayer, F.F., & Strayer, J. (1976). An ethological analysis of social agonism and dominance relations among preschool children. Child Development, 47, 980-989.

Walker, L.J. (1989). A longitudinal study of moral reasoning. Child Development, 60, 157-166.

Walton, M.D., & Sedlack, A.J. (1982). Making amends: A grammar-based analysis of children's social interaction. Merrill-Palmer Quarterly, 28, 389-412.

Wichert, S. (1989). Keeping the peace: Practicing cooperation and conflict resolution with preschoolers. Philadelphia: New Society Publishers .

Yaffe, K.R. (1990, June/July). Building bridges through drama and theater. The Fourth R: The Newsletter of the National Association for Mediation in Education, Promoting the Teaching of Conflict Resolution Skills in Schools, 27, pp. 1-6.

Yalom, I.D. (1985). The theory and practice of group psychotherapy. New York: Basic Books.

Youniss, J. (1981). Moral development through a theory of social construction: An analysis. Merrill-Palmer Quarterly, 27, 385-403.

CHAPTER 9

Resiliency and its Relationship
to Productivity and Nonviolence

Joanne M. Joseph

What do Ralph Bunche, Gandhi and Eleanor Roosevelt have in common? They are examples of productive and resilient leaders dedicated to the tenets of human equality, world peace and action through nonviolence. As individuals, they were self-disciplined, compassionate, flexible and tolerant of individual differences. What explains the personality types of these fine leaders? Researchers have searched for a personality structure that explains the basic nature of nonviolent productivity. However, the exact nature of a nonviolent personality is not well understood (Kool and Keyes, 1990).

Recently psychologists have examined the characteristics of individuals who deal constructively with stressful situations. These people are able to extract the prosocial opportunities from change, and personal direction and wisdom from adversity. The personality type is referred to as "resilient." The traits, beliefs and behavior patterns of resilient children has been summarized by Emmy Werner (1984). Suzanne Kobasa's work (1982) on the stress-resistant adult provides one structure for understanding the traits that make-up the resilient personality type. This resilient core appears related to both productivity and nonviolent action strategies. Therefore, a study of resilience may provide insight into the makings and development of a productive and peaceful personality.

In this chapter, I will summarize the attitudes and traits that contribute to psychological resilience. I will then address the relationship that exists between resilience, productivity and nonviolent action strategies. I will conclude with ideas about how resilient, productive and nonviolent traits can be promoted in youth and reinforced in the adult population.

Psychological Resilience

The research on resilient children comes from a variety of sources. Some of the major findings are from studies that have followed the same children from infancy through adolescence (Block and Block, 1980; Block, 1981; Murphy and Moriarty, 1976;, Werner and Smith, 1982). Clark (1983), Garmezy (1983), and

Table I: Characteristics of Resilient Children

(1) Proactive Problem Solving Style.

(2) Positive orientation to change and adversity.

(3) Positive dispositions.

(4) Coherence.

Robert Cole (1986) have studied the lives of minority children who succeed in school, despite discrimination and inherent disadvantages. Others, Anthony (1974) have looked at the traits and factors surrounding resilient children from highly dysfunctional and violent families and still others have examined the resilient survivors of wars and concentration camps (Moskovitz, 1983). Emmy E. Werner (1984) has summarized all of these studies to find that resilient children share four central characteristics. Table I summarizes these characteristics.

Resilient children take a proactive rather than a reactive or passive approach to problem solving. They assume responsibility for their life situations. This is in direct contrast to children who wait for others to do for them or react in a hostile and impulsive manner to stressful situations. This proactive approach to problem-solving requires children to be self-reliant and independent while at the same time socially adept enough to get appropriate help from adults and peers. Eleanor Roosevelt learned early in life to be independent. She dealt with the emotional rejection of her mother and grandmother by getting involved with projects and prosocial activities and by finding alternative sources of unconditional love (father in early life and teachers during childhood and adolescents). In so doing, she was able to find a refuge from the social rejection of her mother and grandmother and alternative sources of positive feedback to fuel her own sense of self-esteem and self-efficacy.

Resilient children construe personal adversity in positive and constructive ways. They are not immobilized by their negative condition. They allow the anger they feel for the injustice to spur them on towards a broader social or personal goal. In other words, the anger does not result in hostility. Hostility constricts the person emotionally and cognitively (Mandler, 1982). Resilient children find the "windows" of opportunity in bad situations. As a child, Ralph Bunche was angered by the contrast he saw between the affluent white aristocrats and the poverty of the hard-working blacks. He was incensed by the discrimination he felt on the train where Afro-Americans were restricted to poor accommodations and derogatory comments. He did not allow this sense of injustice to either emasculate him as a person or drive him to act-out in hostile and destructive ways. Instead, he developed a high degree of self-control and committed himself to the fight for human equality and international understanding and peace. As a result, Ralph Bunche became one of the world's leading scholars on race relations and was one of the major forces behind the establishment of the United Nations. His ability to direct his anger and frustration constructively allowed him to successfully negotiate a peace settlement between the Arab states and the then new state of Israel. This peace lasted twenty years. For these efforts Ralph Bunche was awarded the Nobel Peace Prize in 1950.

Resilient children tend to have positive dispositions. They are adaptable and socially adept. They usually establish a close bond with at least one care-giver during infancy and early childhood. Ralph Bunche had a particularly close bond with his maternal grandmother and Gandhi with his mother. These adults are powerful models of resilience and provide reinforcement for resilient behavior.

Resilient children develop a sense of what Antonovsky (1979) calls coherence. Coherence is the basic belief that life has meaning and I as a person have at least

Hardiness

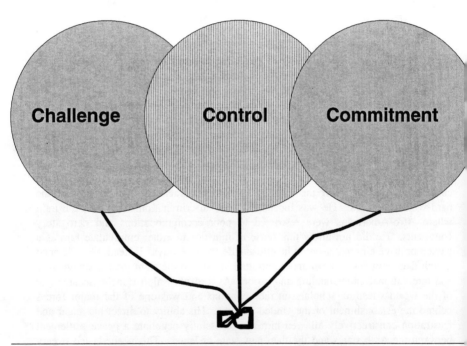

Figure 1: Components of Hardiness

some control over what happens to me. In the research conducted by Ayala-Canales (1984) and Moskovitz (1983), children subjected to the trauma of war and concentration camps were able to love and behave compassionately toward others despite the hate and horror that surrounded them. They are able to do this because they construe a higher purpose for their lives. Gandhi could tolerate the punishments that were either self-imposed or imposed by others because he believed in "spirit over matter and principles over possessions." (Fischer, 1950).

The research on stress-resistant adults has uncovered similar resilient characteristics. Suzanne Kobasa (1982) refers to resilient adults as "hardy." She defines hardiness as: "*a constellation of personality characteristics that function as a resistance resource in the encounter with stressful life events.*" (Kobasa, 1979, p. 168.)

This personality construct has three main components: control, challenge and commitment. A hardy individual is hypothesized to be both stress resistant and goal-directed. Hence, a hardy personality is more likely to be physically and mentally healthy as well as generally successful and competent.

The concept of hardiness is derived from the existential school of thought. According to the existential perspective, the major goal of human existence is personal meaning that comes from the ability to choose. Stress and life changing events are viewed as decision-making challenges. These decision-making challenges allow the individual to develop authenticity. Authenticity is the appropriate and productive channeling of one's awareness and energies. Authenticity enables an individual to thrive in stressful environments, because authenticity allows for productive self-direction. It is this basic existential conception of choice, challenge and commitment that led Kobasa to propose the construct of hardiness.

Components of Hardiness

Kobasa defines challenge as: "the belief that change rather than stability is normal in life and that the anticipation of change are incentives to growth rather than threats to growth." (Kobasa et al., 1982, p. 170). Perceived in this way, change is interpreted as an opportunity for growth and development. Events that appear to have a negative consequence or a potential for negative outcome are construed as opportunities for self-development. Louis Fischer (ibid) describes two incidences early in Gandhi's life that changed the course that his life would take. These episodes are good examples of Gandhi's challenge orientation. The first incident occurred when Gandhi intervened with a British official on behalf of his brother Laxmidas. Gandhi was physically expelled by the agent's messenger from the room. This level of disrespect and discrimination represented a change for Gandhi. He allowed this situation to direct him toward a prosocial goal: "For the first time his life had at least negative direction: he knew what he did not want to do. The episode intensified his abhorrence of the petty intique, palace pomp, subservience, and snobbery which pervaded the governments of the tiny principalities of Kathiawas." (Fischer, 1950, pp. 20-21). The other episode occurred in Maritzburz, South Africa.

Here Gandhi was again forcefully removed from first class accommodations because his skin color was brown and not white. Gandhi refused to acquiesce and take the third class accommodations. Likewise, he refrained from engaging in overt physical aggression. Gandhi was not threatened by these incidents. He was angered by them but--he channeled that anger toward a "resolution to combat the dread disease of color prejudice....In the end he won a great victory for freedom." (Fischer, 1954, p. 22). This challenge orientation is what Emmy Werner refers to as a positive orientation. Resilient children use this positive orientation to manage traumatic and personally negative situations.

A challenge orientation requires cognitive flexibility and openness. Cognitive flexibility is one of the essential features of productive problem-solving. As a result, a flexible thinker has the ability to generate more and better alternatives. This ability contributes to productive nonviolence because it allows the individual to integrate incongruous experiences and fully use available resources.

Commitment is defined as "the ability to believe in truth, importance and interest values of what one is doing and the willingness to exercise influence or control in the personal and social situations in which one is involved." (Kobasa, et al., 1982, p. 171) Kobasa argues that committed persons have a developed sense of purpose which lead them to identify with relevant events and persons. In times of adversity, commitments motivate the person to persevere. Commitments give meaning to human suffering and struggle. Resilient children develop commitments early in life and use them to develop their sense of coherence. Eleanor Roosevelt was able to deal with her personal disappointments because she had a political agenda--the fight for women's rights, world peace and racial equality.

Control, the third component of the "hardy personality," is defined as the belief that personal destiny is the result of one's own efforts and attributes. Psychologists refer to this attitude as an internal locus of control. This internal locus of control is related to the proactive strategies employed by resilient children and individuals who have an internal locus of control possess what Albert Bandura (1982) calls a sense of self-efficacy. They assume responsibility and take action because they have confidence that their own actions will result in movement toward their goal. Internal locus of control reinforces a sense of challenge and strengthens commitment. Ralph Bunche assumed responsibility early in life for contributing to the family's income. This sense of responsibility was nurtured by the hard life and obstacles that he faced early in his life. As a result, Ralph Bunche developed a generalized sense of self-efficacy. This strong sense of responsibility and confidence in his ability to persevere was crucial for the challenges and hardships that faced him as an adult.

Kobasa, Maddi and Couringtron (1982) argue that these three characteristics--challenge, commitment and control--are not mutually exclusive. They together convey the dimensions of a hardy personality who when faced with a stressful life event will take charge of the situation, construe the stressor as a challenge and work to bring resolution to the stressor that is consistent with the individual's commitment to goals.

Appraisal of the Hardy Construct

Kobasa (1979), Kobasa, Maddi and Kahn (1982), and Kobasa Puccetti (1983) have all shown that "hardiness" distinguishes between stress-resistant and non-stress resistant business executives. Other researchers have identified problems with the "hardiness" theory and research (Funk and Houston, 1987; Hull, Van Treuven and Virnelli, 1987) . The concerns raised by these researchers include measurements of hardiness, the unitary vs multidimensional quality of the concept, and the exact causal connection between hardiness and health. They conclude that hardiness is poorly measured and that the evidence regarding its casual connection to stress resilience is equivocal at best. Despite these objections, the research does clearly indicate a difference between hardy and nonhardy individuals when hardiness is defined in terms of cognitive appraisal (Rhodewalt, Zone, 1989) and/or involves individuals who are committed to goals. (Howard, Cunningham and Rechnitzer, 1986). Hence, while "hardiness" as a construct needs further methodological elaboration, the concept itself appears to be useful for understanding of at least some of the aspects involved in stress-resilient and goal directed behavior. Hardiness seems to have best predictive ability when it is conceptualized as a cognitive orientation to view change or adversity as a challenge and when it includes commitment and goals. Belief that one has the ability and resources necessary to meet the challenge of the stressful situation and to meet the goals enhances both the probability that an individual will engage in positive appraisal of a stressful situation and maintain a commitment to the goals. It is this adaptive mechanism behind "hardiness" that may be related to productive nonviolence.

Resilience and Productive Nonviolence

Productive nonviolence refers to those goals and behaviors that are prosocial in nature and which promote personal growth, interpersonal understanding and social change through peaceful means. Prosocial actions are designed to promote justice, equality and general humanitarian concerns for the community at large. Personal growth refers to the intellectual, moral, skillful and spiritual development of the person over a lifetime. This personal growth results in a higher level of self-control, in more effective problem-solving capacities, in an increased level of cognitive flexibility and in an ever increasing ability to experience personal satisfaction and peace. Interpersonal understanding includes the ability to understand and respect individual differences among peoples, resulting in a greater level of tolerance and compassion for others. Social change is the willingness to assume responsibility to effect the changes necessary in self and society in order to insure a physically safe and socially peaceful world. Peaceful means are techniques that are designed to influence people through negotiations, empathetic appeal, education, moral example, public peaceful protest, political lobbying, and in extreme cases, noncooperation with morally unacceptable public law.

How does resilience relate to productive nonviolence? Resilience seems to be a precondition for productive nonviolence. A person who engages in productive nonviolence needs to have an internal locus of control, a non-hostile sense of challenge and strong sense of commitment to personal and social goals. Associated with these resilient traits are beliefs of self-efficacy for effecting change in self and society and an "other-orientedness" marked by a need to compassionately understand one's fellow man. These traits are certainly evident in the characters of Eleanor Roosevelt, Ralph Bunche and Gandhi. They are also evident in the expressed beliefs and behaviors of peace activists. I have already discussed the resilient aspects of Roosevelt, Bunche and Gandhi. Fiske (1987) distinguished peace activists from the ordinary population of citizens. Peace activists engage in proactive measures to promote antinuclear activity. The ordinary citizen expresses a concern about nuclear activity but does not act on these beliefs. A strong difference between the peace activist and the ordinary citizen is a sense of political efficacy. The activists' "sense of political efficacy is linked to a broad sense of personal, rather than external control over life events in general." (Fiske, 1987, p. 213) Antinuclear activists have clear and strong commitments to antinuclear activity and world peace. When these goals are threatened through nuclear build-ups, the activists are motivated to action. They see the challenge behind the threat. They assume the responsibility directly and believe that their political activity will result in favorable outcomes for their cause. These behaviors and beliefs are characteristic of the resilient personality and are indicative of those individuals who stand as moral and humanitarian models.

What difference is there in the resilient characteristics of productive nonviolent types and other strong personalities like type A's and the pro-defense activists'? There are two categories of type A personalities. Some type A's are self-initiators, hard working, energetic, driven by goals and non-hostile. There are others who are also driven, hard working but hostile and easily threatened by situations and others who either challenge, or, are thought to challenge their goals. The hostile type A's are less stress resilient physically and mentally when compared to non-hostile type A's (Taylor, 1991). Personalities like Hitler have features that on the surface seem resilient but, closer examination indicate hostile type A characteristics. Hitler was externally oriented--hence his need to control others. He was committed to the notion of an "Aryan pure race" but this commitment was based on his sense of ethnic insecurity. His insecurities and fear about loosing control led him toward a coercive use of power and ultimately toward his own self-destruction and the destruction and suffering of millions of other individuals.

Fiske (1987) points out that individuals who are pronuclear defense have little belief in their efficacy to avert nuclear war and generally hold the belief that historical forces and not themselves determine the fate of their world. What might we conclude from this brief analysis? The lack of resilient characteristics, especially those connected with internal locus of control and challenge, may contribute to an individual's need to use coercion. This observation is consistent with Leon Rappoport's (1989) personality analysis of Heydrich and Gordon Liddy. Insecurities about one's own efficacy to control one's own fate coupled with the inability to channel anger productively results in a cognitive rigidity which allows for dehumanization and social egocentricism. The cognitive rigidity also constricts the individual's ability to think creatively about solutions to the real problems. This in turn further erodes feelings of self-efficacy. Violence is a natural outlet for anger. When dehumanization and social egocentricism are also present, other people and property become the target of the anger.

In summary, a productive nonviolent personality is a resilient personality. They are committed to humanitarian goals (as opposed to just self-serving goals) and are cognitively flexible thinkers with the skill to direct their anger and concern toward productive peaceful solutions. It is the direction that the resilient characteristics take that differentiate nonviolent productive individuals from other leaders and personalities.

Socializing Resiliency and Productive Nonviolence

The question of how to promote and reinforce resilience and productive nonviolence in children and adults is the subject of current interest and research (Arnold, 1989). The research on resilient children and nonviolence has given us valuable insight into the environmental factors that contribute to those personality traits. A full discussion of these factors is beyond the scope of this paper. I have chosen therefore to outline some of the directions that research and programs designed to promote resilience and nonaggression should take.

The research on antinuclear activists (Fiske, 1987) and nonviolent personality types (Kool and Keyes, 1990) indicate that making the attitudes and beliefs salient promotes the corresponding behaviors. For example, peace activists think more, discuss more and read more about issues related to nuclear war and war in general. Buddhist and Quakers are predisposed by their philosophy to be nonviolent because nonviolence is at the core of their teachings and stories. This makes nonviolence a salient issue. To make resilient attitudes and productive nonviolent behaviors more salient, socializers of children and the major socializer of adults (media) need to first pay more attention to those attitudes and behaviors that promote resilient productive nonviolence. One way of making these attitudes more salient is to provide more media coverage of persons and events that behave in these productive ways. Another solution is to find and construct stories that have these values as their themes. Unfortunately, the stories that children and adults hear (via newspapers, T.V., movies, books etc.) are very weak from the perspective of these resilient productive nonviolent values. This is problematic because as Joseph Campbell (1988) argues in *Power of Myths*, stories give people the prototypes for good and evil, for heroes and for how to conduct oneself and experience reality. Similarly, Vitz (1990) argues that stories are important vehicles for the socialization of moral values and concerns.

The research on resilience and nonviolence suggests that an internal locus of control and feelings of personal and social self-efficacy are important contributors to productive nonviolence. To have a feeling of personal self-efficacy, an individual needs to be able to think flexibly, to take a challenge perspective and to be able

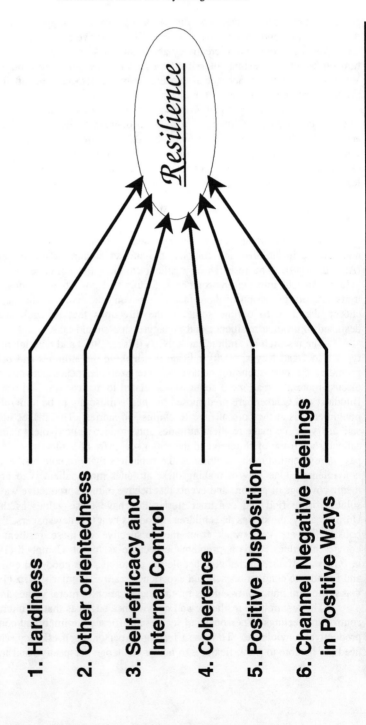

What Goes Into Resilience

Resilience

1. Hardiness

2. Other orientedness

3. Self-efficacy and Internal Control

4. Coherence

5. Positive Disposition

6. Channel Negative Feelings in Positive Ways

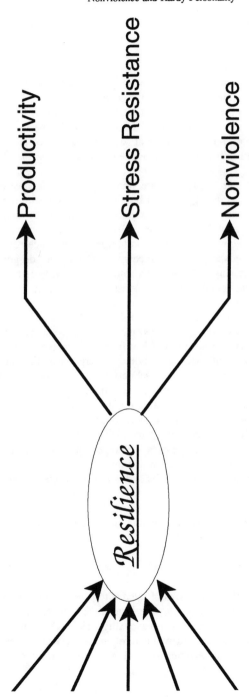

Figure 3: Outputs From Resilience

effectively problem-solve. Good models and good stories can provide individuals with the examples they need to be flexible and to generate and choose appropriate solutions. Social support for resilient productive nonviolent choices reinforces the sense of personal and social efficacy.

Resilient children exhibit a level of social sensitivity to the needs of others that is characteristic of nonviolent personality types. Emmy Werner (1984) describes a "required helpfulness" in the backgrounds of resilient children which contribute to their social sensitivity. Required helpfulness has an additional benefit--it empowers an individual and reinforces a person's sense of social efficacy. Social self-efficacy is a factor that consistently distinguishes nonviolent responders on the NVT (Kool and Sen, 1984).

Social sensitivity and helpfulness are reinforced by society when society rewards individuals for engaging in prosocial behaviors. Social institutions enhance social sensitivity when they encourage programs and activities that promote multicultural and multiracial understanding and tolerance. Society encourages social efficacy when it gives persons forums and opportunities to introduce social change. In other words, society needs to give more media coverage to the "do-gooders" and to those individuals who manage adversity in a resilient way. We need more stories and we need hero types that exhibit the characteristics of a resilient, productive and nonviolent personality. Society needs to decrease the number of media models that enact characteristics antithetical to the tenets of resiliency. To use Joseph Campbell's terminology "we need new myths". We need more productive stories and models. The stories and the models who are most salient in our newspapers and in our T.V. programs often lack the kind of social sensitivity or interpersonal tolerance that are required for productive nonviolence. Our schools need to encourage cooperative learning and discourage destructive competitive attitudes. Cooperative learning environments promote interpersonal understanding, tolerance and helpfulness--ingredients we find in resilient, nonviolent personality types. Parents need to be good models for their children. Parents who extend themselves to others and who show tolerance for other peoples different from themselves give their children resilient expectations and guides to live by.

In conclusion, resiliency, productivity and nonviolence are attributes that can be learned and nurtured by the society. Just how should this be done? This is an open question that begs for innovative ideas, research and dedicated resilient types willing to assume the responsibility for finding the methods to communicate the resilient and nonviolent values and behaviors.

Conclusions and Summary

Resiliency is a relatively new area of interest to psychologist and sociologist. Resilient individuals are individuals who are productive and peaceful despite the difficulties and stressors they face. As a personality trait, resilient individuals are hardy. They have a strong sense of internal control and self-efficacy. They are able to channel their negative emotions in positive and productive ways and they are able to commit to meaningful goals. As a group, resilient individuals have a strong sense of coherence, a positive disposition and are "other oriented". These characteristics relate to the kinds of traits that are observed in individuals who are productive and nonviolent. Resilience promotes productivity and nonviolence. Resilience is also a stress inoculator.

Resiliency can be socialized and nurtured by social institutions--family, church, school and society in general. The media, broadly defined as newspapers, T.V., movies and stories is a major socializer of values. These values are either reinforced or discouraged by the significant persons in our environment.

The challenge of the 90s must be to find ways of nurturing resiliency and nonviolence. The recent riots in L.A. are living proof that this country is in need of a value "overhaul". The principle component behind resiliency along with the humanitarian and equalitarian values of nonviolence are guide posts that might be used to move our society in a more positive and productive direction.

REFERENCES

Antonovsky, A. (1979). Health, Stress and Coping: New Perspectives on Mental and Physical Well-being. San Francisco: Jossey-Bass.

Anthony, E.J. (1974). The Syndrome of the Psychologically Invulnerable Child. In The Child in His Family: Children at Psychiatric Risk, Eds. E.J. Anthony and C. Koupernik, New York: Wiley.

Arnold, L. (1990). Childhood Stress. New York: John Wiley.

Ayala-Canales, C.E. (1984). The Impact of El Salvador's Civil War on Orphan and Refuge Children. M.S. Thesis in Child Development. University of California at Davis.

Bandura, A. (1982). Self-efficacy mechanism in human agency. American Psychologist, 37, 122-147.

Block, J. (1981). Growing Up Vulnerable and Growing Up Resistant: Preschool Personality, Preadolescent Personality, and Intervening Family Stresses. In C.D. Moore (ed), Washington, D.C.:U.S. Government Printing Office.

Block, J.H. and Block, J. (1980). The Role of Ego-Control and Ego-Resiliency in the Organization of Behavior. In W.A. Collins (ed), The Minnesota Symposium on Child Psychology 13: Development of Cognition, Affect, and Social Relations. New Jersey: Erlbaum.

Campbell, J. and Moyers, B. (1988). The Power of Myth. New York: Doubleday.

Clark, R.M. (1983). Life and School Achievement: Why Poor Black Children Succeed or Fail. Chicago: University of Chicago Press.

Coles, R. (1986). The Moral Life of Children. New York: Atlantic Monthly Press.

Fischer, L. (1950). The Life of Mahatma Gandhi. New York: Harper

Fiske, S.T. (1987). People's Reaction to Nuclear War. American Psychologist, 42, 207-217.

Funk, S.C. and Houston, B.K. (1987). A Critical Analysis of the Hardiness Scale's Validity and Utility. Journal of Personality and Social Psychology, 53, 572-578.

Garmezy, N. (1983). Stressors of Childhood. In N. Garmezy and Rutter (eds), Stress Development and Coping. New York: McGraw-Hill.

Howard, J.H., Cunningham, D.A. and Rechnitzer, P.A. (1986). Personality (Hardiness) as Moderator of Job Stress and Cornonary Risk in Type A Individuals: A Longitudinal Study. Journal of Behavioral Medicine, 9, 229-243.

Hull, J.G., Van Trreureb, R.R. and Virnelli, S. (1987). Hardiness and Health: A Critique and Alternative Approach. Journal of Personality and Social Psychology, 53, 518-530.

Kobasa, S.C. (1982). The Hardy Personality: Toward a Social Psychology of Stress and Health. In G.S. Sanders and J. Suls (eds.), Social Psychology of Health and Illness. New Jersey: Erlbaum.

Kobasa, S.C. (1979). Stressful Life Events, Personality and Health: An Inquiry into Hardiness. Journal of Personality and Social Psychology, 37, 1-11.

Kobasa, S.C., Maddi, S.R. and Courington, S. (1981). Personaliity and Constitution as Mediators in the Stress-illness Relationship. Journal of Health and Social Behavior, 22, 368-378.

Kobasa, S.C., Maddi, S.R. and Kahn, S. (1982). Hardiness and Health: A Prospective Inquiry. Journal of Personality and Social Psychology, 42, 168-177.

Kobasa, S.C. and Pucetti, M.C. (1983). Personality and Social Resources in Stress Resistance. Journal of Personality and Social Psychology, 45, 839-850.

Kool, V.K. and Keyes, C.L. (1990). Explorations in the Nonviolent Personality. In V.K. Kool (ed.). Perspectives on Nonviolence, New York: Springer-Verlag.

Kool, V.K. and Sen, M. (1984). The Nonviolence Test. In D.M. Pestonjee, (ed), Second Handbook of Psychological and Social Instruments. Aherndabad: Indian Institute of Management.

Mandler, G. (1982). Emotion and Stress: A View from Cognitive Psychology. In L. Ternoshok, C. Van Dyke, and L.S. Zegans, (Eds.), Emotions in Health and Illness. New York: Grune And Stratton.

Moskovitz, S. (1983). Love Despite Hate: Child Survivors of the Holocaust and their Adult Lives. New York: Schocken Books.

Murphy, L. and Moriarty, A. (1976). Vulnerability, Coping and Growth from Infancy to Adolescence. New Haven: Yale University.

Rappoport, L. (1989). Power, Personality, and the Dialectics of Nonviolence. In V.K. Kool (ed.) Perspectives on Nonviolence. New York: Springer-Verlag.

Rhodewalt, F. and Sone, J.B. (1989). Appraisal of Life Change, Depression, and Illness in Hardy and Nonhardy Women. Journal of Personality and Social Psychology, 56, 81-88.

Taylor, S.E. (1991). Health Psychology. New York: McGraw-Hill.

Vitz, P.C. (1990). The Use of Stories in Moral Development. American Psychologist, 45, 709-720.

Werner, E.E. (1984). Resilient Children. Young Children. November, 68-72.

Werner, E.E. and Smith, R.S. (1982). Vulnerable, but Invincible: A Longitudinal Study of Resilient Children and Youth. New York: McGraw-Hill, 1982.

CHAPTER 10

Transforming Myths of War to Create a Legacy of Peace

Michael Britton

Leaving a legacy of peace to the next generation is no small task. In the larger world, no serious unresolved claims must be left, no long standing hatreds still brewing, no institutions still operating on principles guaranteed to generate future conflicts. In addition, the cognitive base handed on, the ideas on which the next generation will draw, must involve ideas that generate collaboration, humility as to the limits of any group's wisdom, and modesty on the part of nations in regard to the claims they make on each other as well as the actions they take towards each other. While the cognitive part of the mind exerts a powerful, and perhaps decisive influence on the actions that people will take in the future, there is another part of the mind that influences behavior and that we can influence in the next generation, a part which I will address here: the realm of imagination.

The imagination responds to military affairs, both in the form of past events and anticipated future ones. Military realities in the external world become part of our imagination, not only in each of us as individuals but in whole societies. How those military matters are imagined by a people becomes something that can predispose them to respond enthusiastically to future calls to war, or can predispose them to look for other, more constructive, life-affirming tasks to engage in as a people. By influencing how military matters live in the imaginations of the next generation, we can lay a groundwork in their psyches for embracing the next opportunity for war or a groundwork for aggressively pursuing collaboration and cooperation in their relationships with other nations. It is very important that we do not neglect this choice.

While leaving a legacy of peace for the next generation is no small task it is nonetheless a task, something we are responsible for working at, whether we like it or not. My concern has to do with identifying the full spectrum of ways we can shape both the thinking and the external world faced by the next generation, so as to empower them to invest their energies in building a network of inter-national relationships that are constructive and life-affirming. In this chapter, I will be focusing on one slice out of that total spectrum, namely how we influence the next generation's imagination regarding military matters. We cannot escape the reality that we will influence their imagination somehow in this regard. The issue is to be conscious and responsible in undertaking to influence how their imaginations take hold of the military environment as part of a larger project on our part of giving them a genuine legacy of peace.

Part One: Imagination And Past Events

Images from wars, the military events of the past, enter the imagination of people, including the imagination of the next generation, and become a stream of images and attendant emotions, available as warrior imagery to be coopted for deadly use in the future. Imagery can decouple from actual wars and become free floating warrior imagery, creating Predators, Terminators, Aliens, Robocops, cartoon warriors, etc. The battling continues in the imagination, with military-like figures, though the wars from which it is derived are no longer mentioned. This stream of imagery keeps feelings and mind sets alive that can later be tapped as a familiar way to feel about situations, when someone wishes to stir a people to engage in a war in the future. Their imaginations have been rehearsing just such a situation, and find in the call for war something that has an emotional familiarity to it. Such a legacy given to the next generation acts as a curse upon them, an "empowering" of them to involve themselves in new killing fields.

If we do not wish to stand on the sidelines while the next generation's imagination is coopted by processes that foster future wars, that create in the next generation a shadowy readiness for, or resonance to, new calls to arms, new invitations to bloodbaths, what can be done? What can we do so that the realities that stirred up these images in the first place generate images and myths available for constructive ends instead?

Telling the Story

It is the telling of the story of past military events that is the link between the actual events and the imagination. After a war, it is a normal part of recovering from the warring and being warred on to retell the story. There is a strange mixture of silences and retellings--as in the retellings after World War II and the silences after Korea, Viet Nam, and now after the Gulf War. In reality, all wars are traumatic, and the generation involved is driven by the normal post-traumatic need both to retell the story and to be silent, to remember and also to forget the story, bury the grief, bury the outrage, and bury any shame. The question is what these silences and stories mean to the children who grow up immersed in them. In regard to the stories about the war, there is also the question of who tells and who is silent, and therefore of which stories are told. Often the women's stories remain silent: the mothers and daughters and sisters; the military wives; the nurses; the women soldiers; and the sex workers (prostitutes). In regard to the silences about the actual war, those silences may actually be filled with stories about environments that feel like war, and conflicts that involve combat, so that the felt reality is expressed even though it has been separated from the events in which the experience originated, events not mentioned. Even in the silences about the actual war, there may be much retelling of the experience of warring: the silence is not as silent as it seems.

When children are immersed in warrior imagery, their imaginations take that imagery as the material at hand to work with in building a feeling-charged framework for encountering life and making future decisions. It is inevitable that after a military action that effects a society, the story will be retold. The question is: how do you tell the story of the past in such a way that it is transformed from a military myth that potentiates future conflict into a healing myth that empowers action on behalf of life and constructive ends?

Transforming the Story for Healing the Future

I do not pretend to have a full answer to that question. Rather, I intend this paper to serve as a stepping off point for discussion and developing answers. As a springboard for future thinking and discussion, I will suggest a three-step model for shaping how we retell what we have experienced in war so that our children's generation is empowered to build a constructive life rather than burdened with a readiness for bloodshed. From this point of view, retelling can be approached as a three-part task.

Step One: Telling What Actually Happened. The first step is telling the military reality, what actually happened, and how it was personally experienced, as honestly as one can tell it. In this step the next generation is getting to know the story teller, personally, and getting to know the shaping of the storyteller's life through his or her story, the meaning events had to him or to her, how he or she handled things, the lessons taken to heart, the pride and shame and grief and fears and hopes harbored. To tell the story of D-Day, the landing on the beaches of Normandy by Allied Forces, beginning to retake Europe from Nazi domination in World War II, would be an example of a real event to be retold. I will follow that example through the next two steps to illustrate the process I am suggesting.

Step Two: From Military Story to Moral Story. In this step, the reality is retold as a collective *moral* experience or endeavor, with the military features subordinated to that dimension of the story. In that light, D-Day can be retold as the story of young people coming on the shore, pinned down by great adversity, struggling across the beaches without knowing in advance if they would succeed or fail, without knowing if they would live to see the outcome, persevering until they made it across the beach and up the cliffs, where they achieved their objectives. The story might then be recast in terms such as these:

And so it may be for you, in your generation... that often young people come onto the beaches of adult life and face great tasks. And, should that happen to your generation, you may face uncertainty and great difficulty in pursuing those tasks, but you are the heirs of the generation that persevered across the beaches of Normandy; you have the same capacity for persevering and ultimately succeeding at whatever tasks your generation may face.

The military event is translated into a story about the moral dimension of life, and transposed to the reality that the next generation may well encounter a parallel moral dimension in their lives.   And in that context, this moral story takes on an empowering (in this case, encouraging) relevance for them.

   Step Three: Identifying a Similar But Positive Collective Moral Task for the Next Generation. Next the question becomes: what moral task, devoid of military content, focused on the service of life, is the next generation facing such that the moral experience just related will be useful for their future? In the United States, for the children of those who fought at Normandy in World War II one great collective task had to do with something far afield from the military: an ideal that swept the land in regard to marriage, namely to construct a love life that integrated marriage, being in love, and sexual desire.   That became an ideal for everyone.   Yet the know-how needed to achieve that ideal was missing.   Hence great confusion and set-backs would occur.   That difficulty (lack of knowing how) and its attendant pain would be the adversity this generation would face in regard to pursuing this ideal for marital relationships built on love and desire.   The message might have been stated in terms such as these:

> This is a task your generation will face, to figure out how to build marriages that involve being in love and desire, and staying in love and desire through a lifetime. We can encourage you in that ideal, but we don't know how to tell you to achieve it. We do not know all the skills it takes to succeed. So you will have difficulty, and often feel discouraged. But persevere, as we did at our task, and you can succeed at yours. You and your generation, despite the adversity and difficulty of working out your marriages and loves, will be able to figure out those skills and attain the wisdom needed. And you will then have that legacy to hand on to your children: both the ideal we encouraged in you, and the know-how to achieve it. We had to summon up perseverance on those beaches, but that was our task. Your task is different, but remember you have the same capacity for succeeding through perseverance that we had. Go forth and succeed at this task, using the same determination we used to get across that beach in Normandy. Learn the secrets of putting marriage, being in love, and deep desire together for a lifetime.

Such a process involves a special grieving for those who knew the war first hand, for it involves letting go of the past, seeing the next generation in its own context, conceiving the good the next generation can and should strive to accomplish. And that may involve getting to live out something the generation doing the telling was deprived of by the war. This involves grieving, so as to be able to tell the story in a way that shows an acceptance of one's own life for what it has been (and might yet be), shows love for the next generation, and becomes a blessing to them.

The stream of imagery handed on in that way would have some images of D-Day and that war, that beach, that day, and the experience of the parents. But it would not be dominated by those images, or by images of warriors, Predators, and the like. Rather the bulk of the imagery would be about marriage, love and desire; focusing on putting them together successfully; anticipating difficulties; but staying focused on making love, desire and marriage flourish. The fabric of life the next generation goes forth to create then is entirely different, more life-oriented. Their imaginations rehearse loving well, rather than being fierce in bloodbaths. Faced with decisions about how to invest societal resources, or decisions about which societal projects to undertake, their imaginations look for those societal projects and policies that have a ring of emotional familiarity: the ones that bless love, rather than the ones that have to do with battles.

When veterans and parents and military wives and military nurses and sex workers labor to tell the story in this way, the contents of the images of the war itself will also be subtly altered as a result of the caring that is present in the effort to retell things for the good of the young. And so a healing can go on for those who lived through the reality as well.

The objective is for the events of the past to enter the imagination of future generations, not as a legacy of emotional readiness for future wars, but as a legacy of healing from the impact of the past war, a legacy of embracing life in all its goodness. The imagination carries seeds of good deeds and loves yet to be lived, and will therefore recognize opportunities for what they are when they appear, for the soul has been preparing for just such living. The gods bless those who give such legacies to their children.

I have illustrated this concept with World War II, a war experienced as traumatic but successful. The task will be different for wars experienced differently--for example, those experienced as traumatic and as failures, like Viet Nam; as successes that involved little trauma to Americans, like the Gulf War; and those actions that involved shame. The same empowering objective must be pursued in each kind of case, but the content of the three steps would be quite different in each instance. So this task invites more complex thinking about how to retell things. What moral lesson is empowering to the next generation in how one's own generation failed at something? Or in experiences that one's own generation feels shame for? How are such military actions retold to become a blessing that empowers the young to grow up and make life-affirming, collaborative lives together? And what happens when the young listen not only to the stories of the generals, but also the stories of the war from the sex workers, the nurses in the field, and the doctors in the field?

I am suggesting this as a stepping off point for examining the process of retelling, and for working to shape it for more positive ends. It would be a valuable next step to meet with veterans of various wars--and the other parties I have mentioned--from many countries, to work on this project and develop more detailed steps, examples, and a body of stories of old wars recast in more healing terms. For it is not possible to make a legacy of peace only by influencing the next generation in one's own country. War is a relationship event, a product of a system of interrelating by the nations of the globe. Any action designed to prevent war in the future must have a systemic breadth to it, permeating all the nations of the world with encouraging their children's imaginations in a healing direction.

Part Two: Anticipating the Future

When we speak of myth, we speak of images and therefore of the realm of the imagination. This is a large realm. We might say, imaginatively, that part of the realm of imagination is so "heady" that it extends upward and outward from the head. This is expressed when we say: "Isn't she imaginative" about a child's story. Or "Be imaginative" in regard to solving a problem. It connotes breaking with reality, making up something that is different from reality.

But there is also another part of the realm of imagination, one that extends, as it were, down and in: into the heart, the belly, the soul, the psyche, as in Jungian work. Here images arise from the depths, perhaps unasked for, sometimes with powerful feelings, sometimes in shocking or incomprehensible forms. Jungians tell us those creations of the imagination are better understood, not as departures from reality, but as a knowing of reality, as telling us truths about what is. We might say that religion and myth speak to us through that place, touch us in that place, as also does poetry. And our culture dishonors all four: religion, myth, poetry, and deep imagination. But what if we look ahead to a serious military reality, and allow ourselves to respond from this place? I would like to suggest that, again, imagination can do service to the creation of an effective legacy for peace, an effective motivational orientation to peace, if we are conscious and responsible about the imaginative anticipation we ourselves engage in, which becomes the field in which our children's imaginations are immersed, the soil in which their strivings for the future are shaped.

Imaging the Hydrogen Bomb and Its Import for the Future

The reality I have chosen to illustrate this concept is that of thermonuclear fusion bombs, also called hydrogen bombs. Most of us do not know about them through our senses. We do not see or hear them, we do not smell them like coffee in the morning. We know about them through our fact-gathering intellect. But this intellectual knowledge nonetheless is enough to generate images from the depths. I do not mean simply the literal images we can see on television of hydrogen bombs exploding, with their now familiar mushroom fireballs. Those are images originating directly from the external world, taken in through our senses. Instead I am referring to the images that well up from the inside, from the imagination, that may not look at all like the physical "real thing," but whose significance is that they size up and speak about the larger import of that external physical reality.

Most of us have no such images from within about hydrogen bombs. We may misappropriate such images from within as being about our own intrapsychic lives, in psychotherapy.   More likely, we psychically numb the spot in our imagination from which they would spring.   But that means that, since they are the same thing, we thereby also numb a spot in our hearts, our bellies, and our souls, becoming less fully responsive to life in general.   And it means we are also blocking a means for understanding the full nature of the situation this reality has created.

In either event, without images another problem develops.   That which is unimaged is also unbounded, unlimited. (Hillman, 1992).   Our response therefore tends to become one of dread without bounds.   This is a terrible stress, even when it is mostly operating just below the level of our direct awareness.   What wells up is desire for a space away from this unbounded tension, a space in which to feel relief.   Today we purchase that space by saying the Cold War is over, disarmament has begun, we can forget about the problem.   But deeper images would suggest that this is not true or helpful.

I will illustrate the alternative by turning to the imagery that arose from within one man, Robert Oppenheimer, as he reflected on the experience he had of witnessing the detonation of the first atomic bomb, of which he was said to be the father.   When he allowed something to well up, it was a quote from the sacred text of the Bhagavad Gita: "If the radiance of a thousand suns were to burst at once into the sky, that would be like the splendor of the mighty one... I am Death, the Shatterer of Worlds."   Such was the image.   If we question it, what hints does it offer us about the nature of the reality confronting us?

Oppenheimer imaged the reality of the bombs as a deity, a deity with a purpose- this deity enters our world, our civilization to transform it, and to do so in a specific way, by putting an end to it.   He is the "Shatterer of Worlds."   So this is the first thing suggested about the significance of the hydrogen bombs: they are here to shatter and put an end to our civilization.

The image of a deity also reminds me of the movie *Ghostbusters*.   A woman opens the door of her ordinary refrigerator and finds that she has unintentionally opened a door into "the other world"--not so that she can cross over, but so that it can come inrushing into the ordinary world, with a magnitude of power far beyond the mundane.   Just so, to image hydrogen bombs as a deity is to suggest the inrushing into global civilization of a power bent on transformation, with a magnitude of force far beyond that of our normal ways of civilization.   Indeed a deity is a force that cannot be stopped by human beings.   It will complete its dance, its intended transformation, no matter what people do.   Such an image hints that hydrogen bombs, which are here to put an end to civilization as it exists, will succeed at putting an end to our civilization, and that there is nothing that we human beings can do to avoid that outcome.   It is little wonder we wish to dismiss this business of imagery as fantasy, as telling us nothing about the real world.   How terrorizing to believe this is an exact description of our situation.

Yet, to image something puts limits on it.   Even to image something as a deity puts limits on the unbounded, and also somewhat humanizes it, which can allow the soul to settle a bit.   A god or goddess who comes with a purpose is something the calculating part of our minds can understand. We can think: if we dishonor the purpose of this deity, he or she will become enraged and put an end to our current civilization with as much violence as his/her rage can muster. If, on the other hand, we honor this purpose, we may please him/her, and perhaps the deity will put an end to the current civilization in a generous way, for example by bringing new meaning and civilization out of the old one, new life from the old casing, in kindly fashion. We might say that Shiva can dance the end of a civilization either way, reflecting the reality that hydrogen bombs can end current civilization and its principles either way, through massive violence such as has never been seen before, or through prompting us to develop new principles for relating globally. But the old civilization will be ended one way or the other. There is no escape from that. The only choice is which way that purpose will be accomplished. The image hints at this necessity for honoring the threatening import of hydrogen bombs in our midst.

If we chose to honor this mission of putting an end to what exists, what exactly is it that must come to an end? A civilization is multi-layered, involving many institutions--ways of doing geopolitics, economics globally and at home, ways of working, making community, loving, approaching sex, parenting, etc. *I would suggest the purpose of this "deity" is to so transform our ways in all these spheres that the will to make or use such weapons vanishes from the earth, not to return. (My reasons for this interpretation are presented elsewhere, Britton, 1992).* I do not mean simply that the bombs themselves are to be done away with, but that, in addition, we are to so transform how we go about geopolitics, economics, love, and all the rest, that the interest, the motivation, the desire to make such weapons not only vanishes now, but also does not spring up again in human minds and hearts in the future.

Surely this is a monumental task. Yet, to speak in the language of this metaphor that sprang from the depths in Robert Oppenheimer, a man quite close to the actual reality of these weapons, hydrogen bombs will cause this transformation to take place and will cause it to happen one way or the other. There is no more a way to escape this outcome than to escape a deity. The only choice is whether to perish in seeking to ignore this task, or to collectively undertake its honoring, and so to give birth to the life of a new civilization.

And, we might say, on our choice waits Kali, the earth goddess, who will eat our ashes and the ashes of our children after nuclear wars, if we dishonor this task, drinking them down into the soil with the black rains to follow a nuclear attack, using those ashes, our ashes, to feed the roots of new and strange life forms springing up from the irradiated earth. Or, if we honor the re-organizing of the principles of operating our many institutions such that they are designed to support life, then Kali will likely bless our communities with the beauty and scent of her flowers, the taste of her fruits.

A Three-Step Process

Poetic and metaphoric as this way of the imagination is, there is a process of anticipating the future that I have just illustrated and whose structure I will now spell out. This is a way of thinking, a question, and a task, which I have broken into three steps.

Step One: The Shift from Numbing to Attending. This is the turning inward, waiting for images to rise up in response to the military reality being anticipated; allowing the imagery, however at first irrelevant it may seem, to be taken seriously.

I do not mean the externally created images, the sense-impressions of hydrogen bombs, for example from watching their explosions on television. I mean whatever imagery comes from within, which may not look at all like exploding fireballs.

Step Two: Reflecting on The Imagery to Find What it May be Saying About Reality. This is the process I have just illustrated with Robert Oppenheimer's imagery. It is a kind of dialogue between our fact-intellect's knowledge about reality and our deeper soul/heart imagery. Here I illustrated that by asking: what truth do these images tell us about these bombs?

Step Three: Sharing This Process Together. By sharing the images that come up with others who are engaged in the same task, reflecting on the meaning together, working together back and forth between fact-knowledge and soul images, allowing this to cycle back inward to generating more images, and so on, the process moves from the individual level to the collective level. In addition to such work within groups, different groups working on the same task are likely to generate different images, with different concerns, feelings, and aspects of the larger truth. Bringing these into dialogue with each other empowers further inward cycling, further enriching of the imagery and the understanding, and further evolution of a collective momentum of imagery and knowing--and willing. This process that moves beyond the insight of individuals to gain a collective momentum is what we call myth, which is the process that *empowers us to act on behalf of those positive historic tasks that confront us.*

Disciplined Myth Making

The hydrogen bomb will transform the world, either putting an end to civilization over the next century or two through "small" nuclear wars or requiring civilization to put an end to warfare. We are still in denial about this inescapable choice. Past warrior myths cannot encompass it. There is a need for women as well as men to formulate this moment in mythic terms that will enable us to use this moment wisely. And in this myth-making we must look for two things: (1) *the positive historic task we are called to,* in our generation and in the next, and (2) *the flow of forces towards the hopeful outcome that we and our children can embrace.* For children who hear adults engaged in myth-making must hear (A) that the world can work out, (B) that the hopeful side can succeed, and (C) that there is an indication of the task they can embrace, the work they can do, to move things in the right direction. *Myth making must bless the next generation with hope, focus and effectiveness.*

This also makes clear that myth making must not be elevated to a superior position in how we approach life, but rather brought into dialogue with our other ways of knowing and acting in the world. People have joined together many, many times in the past--and still do so today--in the forming of evil, destructive myth that leads to killing fields. The soul level, the imagination of groups, can join in conjuring up murders, and so this work of the soul must be done with dedication to serving life and love, health and joy, in all those that will be touched by the group's actions. Myth making must be disciplined, just as our other faculties must. Myth making must be measured first and last by the criterion that it be working in the service of life, the life of all parties, not only one's own.

In any generation's myth-making, the adults must be working, in the presence of the next generation, to bring into clarity the shape of the worthy, loveable world we are collectively laboring for, along with clear direction, effective means, and merited hope. Then the legacy for the next generation can be part of a quest whose nature is clear and realistic, and whose basis rests in serving the forces of Life.

Choice

I have illustrated identifying such a task, in regard to hydrogen bombs, in the form of a call (1) to think through each *institutional* aspect of international and national life (political, economic, community, labor, love and desire, family, religion, etc), to identify the ways each fosters thinking and feeling that lay foundations for interest in weapons of mass destruction; (2) to seek institutional ways that do not produce interest in making weapons of mass destruction, by anyone, anywhere on the globe; and (3) when such ways are brought to light, to work to implement them, to re-make how we go about our lives together within our societies and among our societies such that our efforts so serve life that interest in making weapons to massively injure life disappears and never arises again. That indeed is a great historic task, a collective global mission, in which all countries, cultures, and social classes can come together in spirit and sense of identification, to serve that which is worthy, noble, and to be loved and enjoyed. *This* is a worthy vision to give the next generation globally!

Otherwise, if we insist on business as usual in our institutions, if we do not let go of the old ways and seek in the flux to serve the newly arising potential for life-serving civilization around the globe, we curse the next generation by trying to evade destiny. The gods do not smile on those who curse the children of the world.

Summary

Imagination plays an important role among the many sociological and psychological factors that shape our behavior. Its images, and the feelings they structure, create a readiness to understand the outside world in ways that fit with the world as it feels familiar within--along with a readiness to take the kind of action well rehearsed in the mind. The imaginations of a generation are influenced by military realities, whether we like it or not. Our choice is whether to let that process go its own way, for good or ill, or to understand the process and try to shape it in constructive ways.

Military events of the past take their particular shape in the imagination through the way they are retold in society. This presents us with the task of disciplining and shaping our retelling, so that we create a legacy in the imaginations of the next generation of images and feelings that are predisposed to engage the world in constructive ways rather than warring ways.

The imagination also responds to the world around us in the present by anticipating the future. By attending to the images and feelings that well up from the depths, we can know the import of future reality in ways we otherwise would overlook, and thus chart a more constructive course. Here too, a discipline is called for, so that in this process of imaging the future and forming a mythic sense of task together we serve the next generation well as a source of realism, empowerment, direction and hope. So that our collective "mything" serves life rather than evil or destruction.

Many people dismiss the task of providing the next generation with an external world and an internal psychology of ideas and imaginings that will send them forth on positive life tasks rather than set them up for warfare and tragedy as a task too ethereal, too undefinable, something that cannot be operationalized and therefore cannot be achieved. I have tried to illustrate here that this task can be operationalized. Even so nebulous a task as influencing the imagination for good has been shown here to be something that can be worked out in concrete, operational terms. To create a genuine legacy of peace is not a matter of wishing, but of a task in reality that we can and must set about. This chapter has suggested ways of beginning to identify that task in regard to one dimension of the social psychological realm, namely the imagination as a potent source of future action, for good or harm. Given that imagination will respond to military realities whether we like it or not, I have suggested ways to take responsibility and shape that influence in ways that might be a gift to the next generation rather than a curse. This choice is not a matter of ability or inability, but of the place the next generation truly holds in the hearts of this generation. It is the measure of the depth of our own hearts that we are taking.

Note on the Religious Imagery

When I first wrote this chapter, I thought of the imagery of a deity as metaphoric. But I am struck by a way in which this particular metaphor slips past being merely metaphoric. Those who invented the nuclear bombs could be said to have been doing ordinary physics (no matter how extraordinary it seemed to them), in the service of ordinary geopolitical strivings. In the course of doing this ordinary physics, these people, like the woman who opened the ordinary refrigerator door in the movie *Ghostbusters*, inadvertently opened the door on that same current of power that generated the origins of the Universe in the Big Bang. Whether one thinks of that Originating Energy as God, or the creation of God, one might well think of it as Sacred, the inrushing into existence of a force so massive and ultimately resplendent that it could scatter stars and galaxies enough to create the far reaches of this cosmos, that could breathe life into existence in some of those places--could breath pine forests out of the crests of mountains, flowering cactus out of desert sands, darting fish out of salt and fresh waters, animals and birds out of the soil of prairies and forests, and the beauty and aliveness of our bodies, our hearts, and our embodied souls that shiver with delight and awe in the presence of that Creation of which we are a part. We are the myriad tiny blossoms springing into and out of existence in the rushing into existence of this Originating Force, so massive and so resplendent that it merits the name Sacred.

While doing things with merely physical objects, these scientists suddenly created rents in the fabric of our ordinary, civilized world, rents through which comparatively tiny flashes of that Sacred Energy leap forth into our world. Witnessing those tiny flashes, we behold massive thermonuclear fireballs.

We thought we could do this, and subordinate that Sacred and Terrible Energy into our ordinary, mundane ways of going about global political jockeying. But, as with all tales of genies released from bottles or lamps, to unleash the presence of the terrible Sacred into civilization is to invite in another dimension that brings its own definition of the situation, its own parameters, which, metaphorically I have described as its own "purposes." And, given the magnitude of power unleashed, those parameters then take over the defining of the world. We are forced into a position whereby our sense of things must be reshaped and subordinated to fit within those parameters, not the other way around. We asked for a genie that would do war most mighty and terrible for us, and the genie came and said: "I have a wisdom and purpose of my own. You will learn the ways of peace, or I will lay your civilization in its coffin." This was not anticipated.

We might then speak of an unexpected encounter with the dangerous Sacred while conducting mundane business, an encounter that must be served with reverence and strength if we are not to be killed by it.

If I understand correctly, Shiva is the god whose dance affects civilizations, bringing them to birth or to death. Kali is the earth goddess who both gives birth out of her soil to the life of this earth, and welcomes that life back into the soil through the cycle of death. Taking in the dead, she will use those nutrients to give birth once again to a new cycle of earthy life. So there are two levels: earth life and civilization. These two have been at war in the civilization spawned from Europe for some time.

If we ignore the requirement to support the positive Shiva side by working to bring forth a new civilization around the globe, new ways of approaching all institutions, new principles that lead to the vanishing of any interest in terrible weapons, then civilization will likely be convulsed with small nuclear wars that will feed our ashes to the soil. But, if we honor this new birthing on the Shiva level, we might think of a wedding of Shiva and Kali, a making of civilization, globally, that loves life in all its forms, and which loves the blossoming of the Kali side, the blossoming of earth flowers and the beauty and life of earth.   When the labor of civilization serves the blossoming of life, then Shiva and Kali are wed.   In that sense, our nuclear self-endangerment perhaps expresses the anger of Shiva and Kali at being separated any longer.

One might say, therefore, that the task at hand is to wed the purposes of civilization to the loves of this earth that flower in their cycles.

REFERENCES

Hillman, J. (1992). And Big Is Ugly: The titanic dimension in art. A talk delivered in New York City.
Britton, M. (1992). Redefining Security. Unpublished Manuscript.

CHAPTER 11

Nonviolence: An Empirical Study in India

Manisha Sen

Most violent acts are deliberate and premeditated. Often they are disguised in the form of love for one's family, religion, nation or race. A common response to violence is "violence" itself.

While psychological research has grown significantly over the past several decades to describe the behavioral patterns of violent individuals and the changes they show from culture to culture and situation to situation, the personality and behavior of nonviolent individuals have not been studied extensively (Kool, 1990). There are several reasons for this lack of interest in the study of nonviolent behavior. Disagreement on the definition (Lynd, 1966) and inadequate methods to study nonviolent behavior (Kool, 1990) are the most significant reasons for our poor understanding of the concept.

In sharp contrast to violent individuals, the nonviolent individuals show aggressive behavior of their own type. They tend to keep their aggressive behavior passively verbal. Sometimes they inflict injury on themselves in protest or by fasting. Sharp (1973) has described various methods that are used in nonviolent protests, e.g., resistence, obstruction, civil disobedience, sit-ins, etc. Use of such methods show how individuals shape their behavior by consciously searching alternatives to violence to cope up with conflicts.

During mid-seventies, I collaborated with Professor Kool to study the personality and behavioral patterns of nonviolent individuals. An outcome of our endeavor was the development of a Test of Nonviolence which will be described in the first section of this chapter. In the second phase of our research we conducted laboratory studies in which violent and nonviolent subjects responded to instigations in a typical Milgram type of setting. The implications of this and similar studies will be reported in the second part of this chapter. The third section will describe how family and other social environments influence nonviolent behavior.

Section I

The inspiration to develop a Test of Nonviolence (NVT) was rooted in the behavioral characteristics of Gandhi and his followers who preached and practised nonviolence and kept their aggression passively verbal and self-oriented (e.g., fasting or other self punishment methods). In such cases a commonly accepted definition of aggression that it involves delivery of noxious stimuli to another person does not hold good. The methods used by nonviolent individuals are to weaken the moral defenses of his opponent by drawing their attention and involving their memory to let them know that he or she (the victim) was least interested in using violence against their opponent, and that the situation demands peaceful resolution rather than a violent encounter.

A profile showing contrast between violent and nonviolent individuals was presented in our study (Kool and Sen, 1984). While violent individuals' aggression flares up with instigation, the nonviolent individuals have a tendency to keep their behavior organized and controlled in the wake of aggression or provocation. A violent individual aggresses to show his power and to achieve the reinforcer, while a nonviolent individual tends to share power and part it away in goodwill. Violent people are more arbitrary and indiscriminate in their behavior patterns and readily injure others compared to their nonviolent counterparts who adopt a rational approach in conflict situations.

Our approach to view nonviolence was not guided by the traditional view that nonviolence means no aggression at all. We believed that aggression has a survival value (Kool, 1992). If individuals show preference for reducing conflict by using means other than violence, they will be satisfying the initial test of nonviolence. However, nonviolence does not mean total absence of aggression. When Gandhi recruited soldiers for the British Army to fight Hitler's genocide, his acceptance was less arbitrary, did not necessarily require all possible implements normally used to glorify war, and was free from proclivity. In short, nonviolent individuals use violence only when all other means fail to stop brutality and genocide.

The original NVT consisted of 37 forced choice items and several filler items. Each item gives the option to the subject to indicate his/her preference for a violent or nonviolent orientation to deal with a problem. A subject receives a score of 1 for endorsing an item in the direction of nonviolence and 0 in the direction of violence. Therefore, a subject's highest and lowest score on the NVT will be 37 and 0, respectively. The validity of the scale was established by correlating the NVT with Buss-Durkee scale of aggression. A strong negative correlation (-.51) was obtained with the overall scores of Buss-Durkee and the NVT scores of the subjects. On a North American sample, Kool and Keyes (1990) reported not only strong correlation between the total Buss-Durkee scale scores and the NVT, but also found statistically significant correlations between the NVT and all the subscales of Buss-Durkee with the exception of guilt subscale. They also found that the Quakers and Juvenile delinquents scored highest and lowest, respectively, on the NVT.

Several other studies have employed the NVT to demonstrate the relationship between nonviolence and dogmatism, power, attribution and morality. For details, see chapters in this book and Kool (1990).

Section II

Personality measures like the NVT face several problems if a test fails to measure behavioral characteristics predicted by the test in an experimental or a field setting. Although the use of the NVT by many scholars across several countries had given us strong support for its adequate psychometric properties, we wondered whether the NVT would help us predict the behavior of nonviolent individuals.

We began with a controversy in the literature on the issue of catharsis. Social psychologists have long been divided on whether catharsis increases or decreases aggression. The traditional empirical view of catharsis is derived from the frustration -aggression hypothesis (Dollard, et. al., 1939) that aggression of any type produces a reduction of drive which inhibits probability of further aggression. In other words, if a violent individual is allowed to express his hostility on another subject, his level of aggression is likely to reduce such that further aggression on his/her part is less likely to take place in the absence of provocation. We then wondered whether nonviolent individuals will also show a similar reduction in their level of aggression if they are allowed to aggress against a victim. In addition, we examined the role of instigation in aggression in a typical dyadic group, e.g., male-male or female-female, in which a subject aggresses against a victim in a Milgram type of experimental setting. In an earlier study, Kool (1977) observed that the level of aggression of subjects increased with increase in the level of instigation. It was argued that a similar type of instigation would lead to arousal which would be dealt with differently by the violent and nonviolent subjects, suggesting a personality-based explanation for catharsis.

High and low scoring subjects on the NVT were either annoyed or not annoyed and then requested to deliver shocks to a victim in a Milgram type of situation. In one condition the subjects had to wait for a long time before they actually participated in the experiment (annoyed, wait condition). In the other situation, a subject delivered shocks to a victim during the same period (nonannoyed, shock condition). The results of this study were consistent with our hypotheses. First, the high scoring nonviolent subjects delivered significantly lower amount of shock than their violent counterparts. Second, the subjects in both groups gave higher shocks in the wait-annoyed condition as compared to those in the shock-annoyed condition. The most interesting feature of this study was the significant interaction effect for the violent and nonviolent individuals under wait and shock conditions while they were annoyed or nonannoyed. The results showed that violent subjects grew more violent when they were annoyed than when they got a chance to express it (catharsis). A similar effect was noticed in the nonviolent subjects but the magnitude of this effect was lower than that of the violent subjects. After all, the nonviolent subjects in this study were college students who experienced guilt and tended to control their aggression but did not show all the qualities of an ideal nonviolent individual.

TABLE 1

Mean scores of aggression of authoritarian and nonauthoritarian subjects in an annoyed/non-annoyed and shock/wait condition (n = 8 in each group).

Personality	Annoyed		Nonannoyed	
	Shock	Wait	Shock	Wait
Authoritarian	73.88	152.63	50.25	67.38
Nonauthoritarian	25.13	34.00	26.88	28.25

TABLE 2

Means and SDs of Normal, destitute and delinquent groups on the NVT.

	Means (N=50)	SDs
Normal	31.84	2.84
Destitutes	28.60	4.23
Delinquents	21.90	5.71

The implications of the above study are that the traditional view of catharsis seems to hold good with respect to violent individuals but those who tend to control anger and actively seek alternate solutions, e.g. nonviolent individuals, may not show a similar cathartic effect. In other words, when the mediating variable of arousal linking frustration and aggression is offset by guilt, the role of catharsis does not seem to be prominent (Geen, 1990). It should be noted that the controversy over increase or decrease in aggression after giving a subject a chance to aggress is subject to several conditions. Our contention, as evidenced in the results, is that catharsis is largely a matter of learning how to cope up with arousal and threats, and the inputs causing excitation of inhibition or aggression are punctuated in the personality patterns of the individuals, as has been the case with our nonviolent subjects.

The second study was based on the previous study but it involved another group of subjects, i.e., authoritarians and nonauthoritarians. Because authoritarians tend to react strongly to their ego needs when threatened in an experimental setting and think of individuals in stereotyped categories (Kool, 1977), both authoritarian and nonauthoritarian subjects were tested under annoyed and nonannoyed shock and wait conditions. Consistent with the results of the previous study on violent and nonviolent subjects, the results of this study also showed the significance of personality (authoritarian or nonauthoritarians) as an important mediating variable (see Table 1). Whereas the authoritarian annoyed subjects were highly aggressive in the annoyed wait condition, their nonauthoritarian counterparts were extremely tolerant and showed relatively smaller increase in their aggression levels in identical conditions. The implications for explaining catharsis seem to be similar to those in the previous study because annoyed conditions showed the maximum differences between the two groups of both the studies.

Section III

Psychologists in general and social psychologists in particular are often criticized for their molecular approach to social problems. Violent behavior has its roots in society. Its causes are numerous. Violent behavior may arise from life experiences as individuals and as members of a family or society. The propensities towards violence or peacefulness are a result of a persons beliefs, attitudes or experiences, and these originate in the community. In this section, I will focus on social factors related to issues on nonviolence in India.

In a study by Heckel and Mendell (1981) a number of important factors were found significantly related to nondelinquent behavior: childhood happiness, freedom from conflict with parents, home stability, and freedom from abuse. Taking a cue from this study, I proceeded to measure nonviolence in the institutional delinquents, destitutes and normal subjects at home in India. Obviously, the delinquents showed the lowest scores on the NVT and the normal subjects the highest scores (see Table 2). These results confirmed the results of Kool and Keyes (1990) obtained on the institutional delinquents in the USA.

Having this finding in the background, I explored the relationship between the NVT and family environment and cop mechanism.

TABLE 3

Significant correlations between the three measures: Family environment, Coping and NVT (females)

Variable		r	p
Cohesion	Expressiveness	.54	.001
	Independence	.41	.001
	Achievement Orientation	.31	.01
	Intellectual-Cultural Orientation	.41	.001
	Active Recreational Orientation	.34	.005
	Moral Religious Emphasis	.32	.005
	Organization	.44	.001
	Turning against self	.20	.05
	Conflict	-.40	.001
	Regression	-.25	.01
Expressiveness	Turning against self	.24	.05
	Regression	-.22	.05
Conflict	Moral Religious Emphasis	-.26	.05
	Organization	-.50	.01
Control	Denial	-.20	.05
	Turning against self	-.24	.05
Independence	Regression	-.21	.05
Achievement Or.	NV	.29	.05
Intell. Cult. Or.	Regression	-.26	.01
Organization	Regression	-.22	.05

TABLE 4

Significant correlations between the three measures: Family Environment, Coping and NVT (males).

Variables		r	p
Cohesion	Conflict	-0.34	.01
	Independence	0.34	.01
	Intellectual-		
	Cultural Orientn.	0.32	.01
	Moral-Religious		
	Emphasis	0.39	.01
Conflict	Organization	-0.37	.01
Achievement			
Orientn.	Organization	0.43	.001
Intellectual-	Active-Recreation		
Cultural Orientn.	Orientn.	0.47	.001
Regression	Nonviolence	0.45	.001

The family environment was assessed by using the Family Environment Scale (FES) developed by Moos & Moos (1986). It comprises of 10 subscales that measure three broad areas: the relationship dimensions, the personal growth dimensions, and the systems maintenance dimensions. The relationship dimensions were measured by cohesion, expressiveness and conflict subscales. The personal growth dimensions were measured by the independence achievement orientation, intellectual cultural orientation, active recreation orientation, and moral religious emphasis subscales. The organization and control subscales were used to measure the systems maintenance dimension. The FES scale consists of 90 true/false items. It has an average construct validity of .49 for the 10 variables and a test-retest reliability ranging from .68 for independence to .86 for cohesion.

The Coping Operations Preferential Enquiry developed by Schultz and Waxler (1978) was used to measure coping mechanisms. It consists of 6 situations. To each situation are given 5 alternatives to be marked on a 5 point scale. The respondent has to assign a value of 1 to the most likely alternative and a value of 5 to the least likely alternative. All other alternatives are to be assigned a value from 2 to 4. The coping mechanisms assessed were: denial, isolation, projection, regression and turning against self.

The results showed that several subscales of the Family Environment Scale had significant high correlations with the NVT and coping mechanisms (see Tables 3 and 4). Among females, cohesion and expressiveness had a significant positive correlation with turning against self, but control had a significant negative relationship with turning against self. Cohesion, expressiveness, independence, intellectual cultural orientation and organization, had a significant negative relationship with regression. Achievement orientation had a significant positive correlation with the NVT. These findings suggest that where a cohesive family encourages expression of feelings and thoughts by its members, provides sufficient independence, inculcates moral and religious values, and shows considerable interest in intellectual cultural and recreational activities, there is a tendency for women to take on self-blame or attribute shortcoming to oneself. An additional important result was the positive correlation between achievement orientation and the NVT. Indian females are less likely to use regression as a cope operation when the family is cohesive, encourages expression and independence.

In the male group, on the other hand, regression and the NVT had a significant positive correlation.

The above findings suggest that factors in the family environment that seemed to be most important in determining nonviolent behavior were cohesion, expressiveness, intellectual-cultural orientation, active recreational orientation and moral-religious emphasis. Control was observed to have a negative correlation with nonviolence. The coping strategies that appeared to be coexisting with nonviolence were regression and turning against self. With education as the basis, a person could develop a personal moral-religious system based on the principles of human dignity, human worth and brotherhood.

The results of this study also raise some pertinent issues. Does family environment vary for the males and females across different cultural groups? Are coping operations related to family dimensions? Would these factors vary across different cultures? For future research, it is important to investigate the relationship between family environment factors, coping operation and aggression across cultures.

REFERENCES

Dollard, J., Doob, L., Miller, N., Mowrer, O.H., and Sears, R.R. (1939). Frustration and aggression. New Haven, Conn.: Yale University Press.

Geen, R.G. (1990). Human aggression. Pacific Grove: Brooks/Cole.

Heckel, K.V. and Mendell, E.A. (1981). A factor analytic study of the demographic characteristics of adult and Juvenile incarcerates. Journal of Clinical Psychology, 37, 430-433.

Kool, V.K. (1977). Experimentally induced aggression levels of high low authoritarians. Psychological Studies, 22, 63-68.

Kool, V.K. (1990). Perspectives on nonviolence. New York: Springer-Verlag.

Kool, V.K. (1992). Nonviolence and mainstream psychology symposium, APA, Washington.

Kool, V.K., and Keyes, C.L.M. (1990). Explorations in the nonviolent personality. In V.K. Kool (Ed.) Perspectives on nonviolence. New York: Springer-Verlag (pp. 17-38)

Kool, V.K. & Sen, M. (1984). The nonviolence test. In D.M. Pestonjee (Ed.) Handbook of psychological and social instruments. Ahemdabad, India: IIM.

Lynd, S. (1966). Nonviolence in America: A documentary history. New York: The Bobbs-Merrill Company.

Moos, R.H. & Moos, B. (1986). Family environment scale. Palo Alto, CA: Consulting Psychologists Press.

Schultz, W.C. & Waxler, B. (1978). Coping operations preferential inquiry. Firo awareness scales manual. Palo Alto, CA: Consulting Psychologists Press.

Sen, M. (1988). Nonviolence in a group with or without a criminal record. Paper presented at the International Council of Psychologists convention, Singapore.

Sharp, G. (1973). The methods of nonviolent action. Boston: Porter Sargent.

CHAPTER 12

Peace Psychology: Overview and Taxonomy

Herbert H. Blumberg

Peace psychology as such is a comparatively recent field, with no firm boundary, but including (among other things) various perspectives relating to the nonviolent avoidance of major war and the facilitating of a just and enduring peace. For some, the field also extends to various other matters--such as interpersonal harmony and the dangers of nuclear power, to take two examples.

Of the 1500 publications which we have identified (Blumberg & French, 1992)--and which exclude general works in related areas such as aggression and conflict resolution--the large majority were published after 1982. True, for many decades there have been psychologists dedicated to peace and justice (e.g., Deutsch, 1961; and Frank, 1960) and bodies supportive of relevant work--for instance, the Society for the Psychological Study of Social Issues, a division of the American Psychological Association (APA). However, the current "flow" of psychological interest in the area began rather suddenly in the early 1980s. It was then that the APA adopted various relevant resolutions, about then that Psychologists for Social Responsibility was founded, and about a decade thereafter that an APA division devoted to peace psychology was established.

Given what is now a plethora of research, one clearly important goal is to try to understand, or at least to keep track of, what has been found out and what gaps there might be. In short (and with apologies for a mixed metaphor) there is a need to get a handle on a flood of research. As part of this task, it is helpful to try to group the work into categories and to evaluate the "replicability" of the categories.

Categories within Peace Psychology

The advent of free-text bibliographic searching--particularly in a CD-ROM format, with which one could inexpensively explore much of the PsycINFO database--facilitated the "sharpening" of a peace-psychology search strategy. The bulk of retrievals can be made by selecting from works whose titles or abstracts include one or more of the following: peace+ (peace, peaceful, etc.), nuclear, disarm+, or international. (For more details, see the search strategy described in the appendix of Blumberg & French, 1992).

French located a substantial number of additional works essentially by using a "snowballing" technique--reading a variety of books, chapters, and articles, and following leads from them to other references.

The title index of our 1992 bibliography provides an initial taxonomy or classification scheme. For a list of the various categories, together with the number of publications in each, see Table 1. These categories are largely independent, but where a work was clearly relevant to two different topics, it was included in both. Note that this list is derived from the existing distribution of research; some of the "categories" may seem incommensurate and some important areas may be "missing"--a point which I shall develop briefly here and to which I shall return later.

TABLE 1

Frequency Distribution for Peace Psychology Categories

Category	Frequencies
Aggression	20
Attitudes (incl. effects of TV docs.)	204
Bibliographies	14
Children & adolescents	169
Conflict resolution	105
Education & peace studies	64
Effects of conflicts, incl. nuclear war	41
Emergency decision-making & crisis management	33
Feminist aspects	16
General (but specif. psychol.) contributions	73
Govt. policy-making; international relations; arms-race analysis	182
Images (e.g., of future, of cooperation, & of nuclear war effects)	60
Miscellaneous	68
Peace movements; war prevention	74
Peacemaking efforts; wars and crises; historical perspectives	91
Philosophical & religious aspects; morality	44
Psychodynamic aspects, mental health, anxiety, & related concepts	171
Risk assessment & reduction	19

Note. Data refer to number of abstracts in a particular category, as manifest in the title index to Blumberg & French (1992). Some items are classed in more than one category. Genocide (6 items) is here included within *Miscellaneous* rather than as a small separate category.

It would probably be a mistake to be particularly concerned about the precise number of categories. Somewhat arbitrarily, the most closely related categories could be combined and, in the opposite direction, a large category or cluster could be sub-divided into two or more smaller ones.

Not only can one sort publications into categories, but also the categories can be sorted into larger classifications. (See Table 2, other aspects of which are described below). Three of our nineteen categories represent major psychological fields; arguably, about five are psychological "sub-fields;" four are on the "interface" between psychology and other disciplines; about three more are on the interface between psychology and what might be called "solid peace-studies topics." In addition, three categories--bibliographic, feminist, and miscellaneous--cut across the larger classifications.

Notice that this classification has been compiled empirically on the basis of existing publications. Most traditional major psychological fields are omitted. Such fields--learning, motivation, and so on--are however represented within the "general psychology" works or in the groupings of "psychology subfields." Nevertheless, in some cases one can (by inspecting the literature) conclude that particular topics may be "under-researched" in peace psychology. One major question about the categories has to do with their replicability--a matter which ordinarily could be difficult to address.

However, at the time when the Blumberg-French bibliography was in page proofs, a related bibliography became available (Kramer & Moyer, 1991). Its purpose and organization were rather different, and the two works showed surprisingly little overlap in their actual contents. About one-third of the 1000 or so items in the Kramer-Moyer work are also in the Blumberg-French bibliography. Nevertheless, the classification scheme used by Kramer and Moyer is remarkably similar to that used independently in Blumberg and French's title index.

According to Cronbach (1982), there are (broadly speaking) three levels of replicability, each with its own advantages. At the narrowest level, can a research team reproduce its own findings on a subsequent occasion? For the middle level: can another team, which has read the initial report, produce similar findings in a different setting? At the broadest level, will two teams reach similar conclusions from working with similar conceptual frameworks? The present "test" of replicability is roughly aligned with this broadest level.

Table 2 shows the two sets of categories in parallel columns. The Kramer-Moyer scheme uses about twice as many categories as Blumberg and French, but the two schemes map quite closely onto each other. For example, for "children and adolescents" which is a single Blumberg-French category--Kramer and Moyer have two categories, one for children and one for adolescents.

Kramer and Moyer do have one large category, Cognitive, which fits only roughly with three Blumberg-French categories: emergency decision-making, images, and risk assessment. There are three small Kramer-Moyer categories (not shown in Table 2)--authoritarianism, detente, and illusory correlation--which account for less than 1% of their items and which Blumberg and French would have included within

Table 2
Comparison of Two Sets of Categories Related to Peace Psychology

Blumberg-French Category	Kramer-Moyer Category
PSYCHOLOGY AREAS	
Chldren & Adolescents.	Adolescents. Children.
General Psych.	----
Psychodynamics.	Defense Mechanisms. Den
	Helplessness. Numbing. Personality.
----	Cognition.
PSYCHOLOGY SUB-AREAS	
Aggression.	Aggression.
Attitudes.	Attitudes. Propaganda. (Self-fulfi)
	prophesies).
Emergency decision making [Cognitive, etc.].	Crisis management. (Decision maki Groupthink.
Images—e.g., of future, of cooperation, & of nuclear war effects [Cognitive?].	Enemy images. Stereotypes.
Risk Assessment [Cognitive].	----
ACADEMIC DISCIPLINES	
Education.	Education.
Government, international relations, arms-race analysis.	Arms control. Arms race. Civil defe Deterrence. Soviets. Strategy.
Peacemaking, wars, history.	History. War.
Philosophy, religion, ethics.	Ethics.
PEACE STUDIES	
Conflict Resolution.	GRIT. Superordinate goals.
Effects of conflict/war.	Effects—medical. Effects—physi Effects-psychological. Nuclear win
Peace movements & war prevention.	Peace.
ADDITIONAL	
Bibliography.	----
Feminist approaches.	----
Miscellaneous. (Genocide).	----

Note. Categories in parentheses appear to be partially relevant. Words in square brackets represent comments which we have added.

Miscellaneous (a category not found in Kramer and Moyer's work). Also, three of the Kramer-Moyer categories--negotiation, strategic defense initiative, and Three Mile Island--are somewhat beyond the remit of the Blumberg-French work, dealing as they do with a general topic, with weaponry as such, and with nuclear power. Finally, Blumberg and French's numerically small feminist and bibliographic categories have no explicit counterpart in Kramer and Moyer's work.

In order to give an idea of the content of the peace psychology categories, two abstracts from each area are displayed in the Appendix. They were selected as follows. For text analysis and other purposes, the first twenty abstracts in each Blumberg-French category were extracted and divided into two groups--"odd-numbered" (i.e., the first, third, ..., nineteenth work) and "even-numbered" (second, fourth, ..., twentieth). The odd-numbered works were used for exploratory analyses of various kinds, and the even-numbered ones used to confirm the findings from the exploratory analyses. (For a few small categories, a little less than twenty works were available for use.) In most cases, the Appendix shows two of the ten odd-numbered items for each category. The two were selected to give an idea of "good or representative research." Exceptionally, the items displayed in the general cross-psychology category were deliberately chosen as two landmark compilations in the field, one edited by White and the other by Wollman. Readers are encouraged to browse through the Appendix in order to gain their own impressions of the field.

Because each category is about equally represented in the Appendix, large categories are very much under-represented. (This is also the case for the sets of ten abstracts from which they were derived and which are used for some of the analyses described below). This represents a "deliberate over-sampling of areas of high variance." That is, the Appendix is intended to provide an impression of the contents of all of the categories, large and small. In general, two examples (rather than one) are provided for each category in order to provide a crude "error term"-that is, an indication of the variability within categories.

Classifying the peace-psychology publications into categories, and trying to combine the categories into larger groupings, represents an effort at macro-level qualitative content analysis. Such efforts are not exempt from being assessed for reliability and validity--and, as we have seen, from being compared with parallel efforts by other researchers. Let us turn now to a more micro-level quantitative textual content analysis.

Quantitative Content Analysis

Can the trial categories of peace psychology be distinguished empirically? Do they show different "themes"? Some preliminary results are based on two kinds of "word counts"--using two different computer programs. (Answering a more difficult question--how can all of the publications be assigned to [any] categories such as to maximize their discriminability--is not attempted in this paper.)

Word counts. TEXTPACK provides, among other things, simple word counts (see Weber, 1990). The most frequent words in each category were compared. However, the words within a given paper are particularly nonindependent. For instance, a single abstract of a paper dealing with "nondefensive attitudes" might use the word nondefensive several times, thus giving an inflated estimate as to how often the word occurred generally in papers on attitudes toward peace. Therefore, the abstract for each paper, rather than each word or each sentence, has been used as the unit of analysis, and I have compared the number of abstracts in each category which display particular words at least once.

Table 3 shows the frequently-occurring words from the odd-numbered sample of about ten abstracts from each category. The six columns of figures show the frequencies of some words that were common in a number of the categories. The final column shows the specific words which were frequent in particular categories.

Journal titles, such as *Journal of Social Issues*, were excluded from the text prior to tabulation. Also excluded were words of little semantic content: most prepositions, pronouns, conjunctions, etc. Different forms of the "same" word were generally counted together (e.g., human, humanity, and humankind).

Several of the cross-category words (international, peace, nuclear, and war) figured in words and phrases which were part of the search strategy used, in the first place, to retrieve and compile many of the entries in our bibliography. So it is not surprising that they are heavily represented. It is of possible interest, however, that their representation is uneven across the categories. For instance, many of the works concerned with children are devoted to dealing with their fears about nuclear risks, whereas feminist and peace-education works are more often concerned with developing a just, meaningful, and enduring peace.

Psychology, of course, is a high-frequency word in psychological publications in general. The remaining word which figures in several categories is "social." It is used as an adjective for an almost bewildering range of concepts, some of which are: attitudes, behavior, biology, change, class, commentaries, conditions, conflict, context, control, Darwinism, dilemmas, energy, environment, feminism, identity, impact, importance, interaction, issues, life, movement, order, power, process, psychology, relationships, responsibility, science, skills, support, training, upheaval, welfare, and worker.

The last column of Table 3 shows words which are frequent in only one or two specific categories. For the most part, these entries are not unexpected, but they do help to identify themes common within particular categories and they confirm the view that the categories do have lexicons which are, to a measurable extent, distinct. (Incidentally, for papers in international relations, "race" usually refers to "arms race.")

The conclusions (and the actual words which are represented) are reasonably robust and did not differ substantially when an equivalent analysis was performed on ten even-numbered abstracts. Single occurrences of a word were, however, unreliable--which is why ones are rounded to 0 in Table 3.

Table 3
Frequent words in peace-psychology abstracts

CATEGORY	Psychol.	Inter-nat'l	Peace	Nu-clear	War	Social	Other Frequent words (>3 per 10 abstr)
CHLDRN	5	5	0	9	6	0	adolescent/-s, children/-s, difference/-s, threat
GEN.PSYCH	9	4	2	7	7	0	international, research
PSYCHDYN/MentHlth	5	0	3	8	6	3	discussed/-es, health, human, threat
AGGR	6	4	5	5	4	5	aggression/-sive, group, human-kind, society/-ies, violent/-ce
ATTIT	0	4	2	4	3	3	attitude/-s, intl., study/-ies
CRIS.DEC.MKNG	5	3	0	5	3	3	accident, crisis/-es, decision/-s, examined, management, situation/-s
IMAGE (FUT, COOP, WAR)	4	0	2	7	7	3	discussed/-es, image/-s
RISK RDCTN	3	0	0	9	4	0	human, risk/-s, weapons
EDUC&PCE.STUD	3	4	7	0	4	7	education/-ing/-al, issues, school/-s, student
INTL.REL	7	5	0	4	2	2	arms, change/-s, discusses/-ed, international, politics/-ical, race, relations, soviet
HISTORCL	6	2	4	0	2	0	discusses
PHILOS/RELIG	7	2	4	6	2	0	human
CONFL.RES	6	5	0	0	0	6	conflict/-ing
CONFL.EFFCTS	6	0	0	8	6	0	effect/-s
PCE.MVMNTS	3	0	4	4	2	0	movement
BIBLIOG	5	2	4	5	3	3	annotated/-tations, present/-s
FEMINIST	0	5	6	2	4	2	attitude/-s, feminine/-ity/-ism/-ist, orientation, research, sex/-role, weapon, women
MISC	5	0	3	4	3	0	discussed/-es, new

Note. Numbers indicate how many out of ten abstracts contain a particular word. "0 means < 2.

For comparison purposes, I also compiled word counts for two "control" samples, representing near neighbors of peace psychology. The first of these is a general sample of 40 psychological abstracts. (The data are equivalent to taking a sample of 80 peace-psychology abstracts and looking up the 1000th abstract after each one in the PsycLIT database; out of the 80, the 40 odd-numbered psychological abstracts constitute a control sample for exploratory analyses). The second control sample is from a set of summaries of "general" 1990 books (with British imprints) on peace and the prevention of nuclear war (N = 78 odd-numbered and 77 even-numbered books).

Generally, the high-frequency words differed between the peace-studies and ordinary-psychology "control" samples. To a fair extent, the peace psychology abstracts shared the lexicons of both of these "neighboring" control samples.

For the psychology control sample of 40 abstracts, the following words appeared at least 10 times (after each word, no. of abstracts and no. of occurrences are shown in parentheses): behavior (5, 12), children (10, 22), development (6, 10), disorder (4, 11), each (7, 11), family (6, 17), group (7, 19), learning (4, 11), more (10, 19), not (9, 11), patients (8, 16), practice (4, 10), psychologists (2, 10), results (11, 13), stimulation (1, 10), symptoms (4, 11), therapy (2, 12), treatment (4, 10), use (8, 12), using (10, 10), yrs (10, 17).

A similarly compiled list for peace studies (war prevention) turned out as follows: analysis (11, 13), arms (15, 31), book (34, 45), British (7, 17), conflict (10, 19), control (10, 16), countries (7, 10) defence/defense (29, 55), deterrence (6, 13), development (8, 12), disarmament (8, 11), economic (13, 22), Europe (14, 26), European (14, 27) examines (9, 11), forces (7, 12), future (11, 14), history (10, 11), how (15, 17), human (9, 12), international (24, 41), issues (10, 13), looks (6, 13), major (9, 10), measures (4, 10), military (14, 30), nations (9, 13), NATO (9, 15), new (17, 22), nuclear (28, 86), peace (19, 41), policy (10, 25), political (9, 27), politics (10, 10), problems (11, 16), security (15, 26), social (8, 10), soviet (10, 16), states (11, 13), strategic (9, 22), strategy (8, 11), study (10, 10), theory (9, 11), united (13, 19), war (18, 38), weapons (17, 38), work (10, 12), world (23, 39).

Disambiguation. Although the patterns of high-frequency words do suggest the flavor of the various categories, one problem with simple word counts is that often the same word can be used in more than one sense. The General Inquirer computer programs *disambiguate* text--that is, tag many of the words according to their meanings in context--prior to performing other operations (see Weber, 1990). A short sample of disambiguated text is as follows:

DISCUSSES THE RELEVANCE OF THE SEVILLE STATEMENT ON VIOLENCE (1986), WHICH REJECTS 5 MYTHS RELATED1 TO2 THE NOTION THAT1 WAR1 IS1 A - PART1 OF HUMAN NATURE1 (HN). STUDY2IES WITH COLLEGE STUDENTS HAVE3 REVEALIED THAT1 THOSE2 WHO BELIEVE1 WAR1 IS1 INTRINSIC TO1 HN ARE1 LESS1 LIKELY2 TO1 BELIEVE1 THEY (CAN DO)1 ANYTHING PERSONAL2LY ABOUT1 NUCLEAR WAR1

Once the text is disambiguated, a typical subsequent operation is to look up the words in one of the large standard "dictionaries."

For the present work, I have used the Lasswell Value Dictionary, because it has a particularly large lexicon, makes few double classifications, and was developed for use with texts related to politics, although it is also suitable for general purposes (Zull, Weber, & Mohler, 1989).

In order to calculate the percentage of a text which falls under particular value categories, one recommended procedure has been to take the total number of words, and then subtract the number with "no semantic meaning" (prepositions, pronouns, etc.), thus arriving at "MNGSUM" (the number of words having meaning). In all of the present samples, MNGSUM includes about 70% of the total number of words. The frequencies in the various meaning-content (value) categories can then be displayed as a percentage of MNGSUM.

Table 4

Percentage of Meaningful Words in some Summary Content Categories from the Lasswell Value Dictionary

Value	Peace Psych.	Psychol.	Peace
AFFTOT (affection total)	1	2	1
ENLTOT (enlightenment total)	14	12	11
IF	1	1	1
NATIONS	0	0	1
POWTOT power total	13	6	18
RCTTOT rectitude total	1	1	1
SKLTOT (skill total)	2	2	2
TIMESP (time space)	4	4	6
WLBTOT (wellbeing total)	3	4	1
WLTTOT (wealth total)	1	1	2
TRANS (transactions)	2	2	3
TRNGAIN (transaction gain)	1	1	1
N-WORDS (actual no. of words.)	14,343	6,054	8,946
NTYPE (no semantic content)	4,666	1,875	3,180
MNGSUM (actual no. with "meaning")	9,677	4,179	5,766

Note. The first column of percentages shows averages across 18 peace-psychology categories. Content categories for which the (rounded) average is zero are not shown, nor are those for which NONE of the peace-psychology categories include more than 1%. These summary content categories not shown in the table include Anomie, AUD (audience), NEGG AFF (negative affect), NOT, OTHERS (e.g., "THEY"),   POSSAFF (positive affect), RSPTOT (respect total), Self, Selves, and TRNLOSS (transaction loss).

A list of some of the main summary value categories from the Lasswell dictionary is given in Table 4. Also displayed is the percentage of meaningful words in peace-psychology abstracts classified into each value category. (These percentages are based on the "odd-numbered" sample, but results from the "even-numbered" sample were virtually identical).

For comparison purposes, the table also shows the two "control" samples, general psychological abstracts and primarily British 1990 books on peace and the prevention of nuclear war.

Two of the value categories account for particularly large shares of the "meaningful" words, though other values are measurably represented. One of the most frequent summary values is enlightenment (manifest in words such as argued [didactically], learned, discuss, and lessons). It includes subcategories consisting of gains in enlightenment, losses, and its intrinsic pursuit-- e.g., "Lessons learned from the workshop are discussed." This value is even more highly represented in peace psychology than in the psychology and peace-studies control samples.

POWTOT (power total), the other highly-represented value, has an uneven profile across categories. Indeed, the summary value category which best discriminates among the various peace-psychology categories is POWTOT. (The overall discrimination is reliable; the correlation between odd-numbered and even-numbered samples--on POWTOT across peace-psychology categories--is .74, df = 16, p < .001). POWTOT comprises various sub-values that show "a concern for the use of power and group action for the coordination of individual pursuits" (Zull, Weber, and Mohler, 1989, p. 104). Words such as govern, mediation, peace, and under (in the sense of subordinate) are included. This value is most common in works on conflict resolution, as well as those on general peace psychology, and on international relations, and also on peace movements and war prevention. POWTOT is comparatively infrequent in works concerned with children and with psycho-dynamics and mental health, and also in bibliographic publications and those concerned with the effects of conflicts. As one might expect on the basis of the foregoing information, the psychological-abstracts control sample is much lower (on POWTOT) than peace psychology, and the peace-studies books on war prevention are higher than peace psychology.

For the remaining Lasswell value categories, rates were fairly small and did not discriminate reliably among peace-psychology categories (which is why Table 4 is not broken down into separate columns for different categories of peace psychology). Exceptionally, philosophical/religious works were high on rectitude (7% of the meaningful words were, e.g., fair [in the sense of impartial] and crime)! And works on children and on the effects of conflicts were comparatively concerned with well-being (about 6+ % manifest in words such as [relevant meanings of] live [verb] and youth).

With some data, one can successfully factor-analyze the value frequency tables. This would, in effect, inform us as to whether particular clusters of values tended to occur together, and whether the different peace-psychology categories would display characteristic frequency profiles of such clusters or factors. Such an analysis was not however reliable for the present data. Factor analyses based on the odd-numbered and even-numbered abstracts yielded different factor structures, perhaps because the number of peace-psychology categories is small compared to the number of value categories and also because only a few of the value categories showed much presence or much variance. For the present purposes, therefore, the list of values is not readily reducible to a smaller number of factors.

Missing Peace-Psychology Categories

Obviously the analyses in the present paper, dealing as they do with the "state of the art," do not dwell on peace-psychology categories which are not well-represented in the literature. One can, however, consider additional areas which are prominent in general psychology as a whole and ask whether they might fruitfully be the subject of more work in peace psychology.

Some possible examples: applications of learning theories (e.g., in explicitness of reinforcement when inviting reciprocation for tension-reducing initiatives), more systematic evaluation of motivation (e.g., of policy-makers), social processes (such as diffusion of innovation), sensation/perception (adaptation levels & limited ranges of perception), and still more crosscultural research. Also needed are more works which help consolidate the existing mass of literature.

Conclusion and Summary

Studies in peace psychology can be reasonably sorted into a set of categories that have substantial external validity as manifest in the similarity between the work of two independent research teams. Moreover, the categories can be distinguished empirically in terms of the lexicons that they use--and indeed the whole of peace psychology can be distinguished from both peace studies and psychology in genral, in terms of their overall lexicons and of the values expressed in these lexicons.

Two recent bibliographies (edited by Kramer & Moyer, 1991, and by Blumberg & French, 1992) together cover over 2000 peace-psychology pubications, mainly since 1982. Attitudes, children and adolescents, psychodynamics, and cognition are heavily represented. Also, many papers cover decision-making, images, and "general" (multiple psychological fields). Well represented is work in interfaces with international relations, also with history and the study of war and its effects, education, and also philosophy/religion/morality. Two "peace studies" topics receive much attention: conflict and its resolution, and peace movements and war prevention. The replicability of the list of categories used, and of the allocation of entries to these categories, are considered. In general, the various categories cover related, but discriminably different, material.

Acknowledgements

The Tregaskis Bequest provided a grant toward travel expenses, enabling me to present an earlier version of this paper at a symposium on "Nonviolence: Social and Psychological Issues," SUNY Institute of Technology at Utica/Rome, May 1992. I am also grateful for the facilities provided by Goldsmiths' College, University of London (my usual affiliation) and Haverford College (where I have been a visiting professor for most of the 1992-93 academic year).

TEXTPACK V and THE GENERAL INQUIRER III are both available from ZUMA, B2, 1, P.O. 12 21 55, D-6800 Mannheim 1, Germany.

The abstracts included in the appendix are extracted, as cited, from the work of Blumberg and French (1992); they are reprinted here by permission of the American Psychological Association.

Notes

Readers may also wish to consult the following book: Marianne Müller-Brettel, Bibliography on peace research and peaceful international relations: the contributions of psychology 1900-1991. Munich, London, New York, and Paris: K.G. Saur, 1993. A carefully indexed and classified (but not annotated) list of over 2500 works in English and German.

REFERENCES

Blumberg, H.H., & French, C.C. (Eds.). (1992). Peace: Abstracts of the psychological and behavioral literature, 1967-1990. Washington, DC: American Psychological Association, 1992.

Cronbach, L.J. (1982). Designing evaluations of educational and social programs. San Francisco, CA: Jossey-Bass.

Deutsch, M. (1961). Some considerations relevant to national policy. Journal of Social Issues, 17(3), 57-68.

Frank, J.D. (1960). Breaking the thought barrier: Psychological challenges of the nuclear age. Psychiatry, 23, 245-268.

Kramer, B.M., & Moyer, R.S. (Eds.). (1991). Nuclear psychology bibliography. Ann Arbor, MI: Society for the Psychological Study of Social Issues.

Weber, R.P. (1990). Basic content analysis (2nd ed.). Newbury Park, CA: Sage.

Zull, C., Weber, R.P., & Mohler, P.P. (1989). The General Inquirer III. Mannheim, Germany: ZUMA (Center for Surveys, Research, and Methodology).

Figure 1. Examples of Works from each Peace-Psychology Category

I. PSYCH. AREA

Children and Adolescents

Alvik, Trond. [Royal Danish School of Educational Studies, Copenhagen]. (1968b). The problem of anxiety in connection with investigations concerning children's conception of war and peace. *Scandinavian Journal of Educational Research*, No. 3-4, 215-233.
Discusses views on whether or not questioning children about war and peace provokes anxiety. The literature is surveyed and an exploratory study employing a 4-group pretest/posttest design to register variations in level of anxiety is presented. Results from 24 2nd-, 4th-, and 6th-grade children show that no anxiety is provoked.

Ardila, Ruben. [U Nacional de Colombia, Bogota]. (1986). The psychological impact of the nuclear threat on the third world: The case of Colombia. *International Journal of Mental Health*, 15(1-3), 162-171.
Studied the impact of the prospect of nuclear war on children [C (aged 7-8 yrs)] and adolescents [ADs (aged 17-18 yrs)] in Colombia, with 200 C and 200 ADs from the lower socioeconomic class and 200 C and 200 ADs from the higher socioeconomic class. Responses to a questionnaire and interviews were analyzed. Results are presented for each of the 4 groups. Data indicated that Ss are greatly concerned about the possibility of nuclear war and that this worry influences their way of looking toward the future. Social class differences are noted.

General (but Specifically Psychological) Contributions

[White, Ralph K. (Ed.). (1986c). *Psychology and the prevention of nuclear war.* New York: NYU press.
This book is a varied and stimulating collection of readings divided into 13 sections.: (a) psychological effects of the nuclear threat; (b) the psychology of the American people and the Soviet decision makers; (c) the deterrence model and the spiral model; (d) nonviolent paths to security; (e) 2 war-related motives: pride and fear; (f) perception and misperception

in international conflict; (g) personalities of the decision makers; (h) deterrence; (i) government decision making and crisis management; (j) escalation; (k) negotiation, bargaining, and mediation; (l) changing war-related attitudes; and (m) peace education. [See, e.g., Feshbach, 1986; Frank, 1986f; Holsti, 1986; Janis, 1986; Jervis, 1986a; Lebow, 1986; Mack & Snow, 1986; Smoke, 1986; Tetlock & McGuire, 1986; White, 1986a, 1986b, 1986d; and Yankelovich & Doble, 1986.] [CCF]]

[Wollman, Neil (Ed.). (1985). *Working for Peace: A Handbook of Practical Psychology and Other Tools.* San Luis Obispo, CA: Impact.
Emphasizes the development of personal skills in working for peace. Sections of the book are concerned with peace workers, getting organized, reducing conflict, publicity, changing attitudes, and other tools and creative projects.

Psychodynamic Aspects; Mental Health; Anxiety; Related Concepts

Antoch, Robert F. (1985). Uber einige bemerkenswerte Parallelen zwischen innerem und ausserem Frieden [On some remarkable parallels between inner and outer peace]. *Zeitschrift fur Individualpsychologie,* 10(1), 2-10.
Discusses the relationship between inner peace and peaceful social interactions from an individual psychology perspective. An open, flexible, nondefensive attitude toward one's self and toward one's social environment is a prerequisite for mental health and for a peaceful society. An exaggerated tendency toward security and protection of the status quo leads to a paralysis of interactions, to illness, and to strife, both within the individual and within society. (English abstract)

Becker, Ellen. (1987). Addressing the nuclear issue in the psychotherapy hour: A clinical and personal perspective. In K. Porter, D. Rinzler, & P. Olsen (Eds.), *Heal or die: Psychotherapists confront nuclear annihilation* (pp. 20-33). New York: Psychohistory Press.
Case vignettes and case histories. [Citation as extracted in *PsycBOOKS*, 1987, 6900-211]

II. SUB-AREA PSYCH.

Aggression, Its Nature and Effects

Davies, James C. (1989). "Nuclear weapons and the dark side of humankind": Comment. *Political Psychology,* 10(1), 177-181.
Comments on the article by J. E. Mack (see PA, Vol 75:13639) entitled "Nuclear Weapons and the Dark Side of Humankind." The present author argues that the question is more complex than simply whether or not violence is innate and suggests that environmental circumstances that help produce violence and internal, organic forces that interact with each other and with external circumstances must also be considered. Two extant theories are used to explain the widespread use of political violence: genetic psychology and the Yale frustration-aggression hypothesis. It is argued that violence is a product of prolonged and severe frustration of any and all innate drives.

Staub, Ervin. [U Massachusetts, Amherst, US]. (1988). The evolution of caring and nonaggressive persons and societies. *Journal of Social Issues,* 44(2), 81-100.
Explores ways to shape individual personalities, societies, and the relations among them, with the ultimate aim of diminishing intergroup hostility and war. This evolution requires committed individuals and groups to work for change. Certain human proclivities, such as the us-them differentiation, devaluation of outgroups, and stereotyping, are sources of intergroup hostility. Socialization practices by parents and schools that promote positive connection to and caring about people are described. Parent training and family system diagnoses can impart awareness and skills and influence parental attitudes. Institutions and culture can be shaped by creating systems of positive reciprocity among groups.

Attitudes; also, e.g., Effects of Televised Documentaries

Adams, William C.; Smith, Dennis J.; Salzman, Allison; Crossen, Ralph; Hieber,

Figure 1 (continued). Examples of Works from each Peace-Psychology Category

Scott; Naccarato, Tom; Vantine, William; & Weisbroth, Nine. (1986). **Before and after** *The Day After*: **The unexpected results of a televized drama.** *Political Communication and Persuasion*, 3(3), 191-213.
Survey of attitudes before and after the showing of the film *The Day After* surprisingly revealed no shift of attitudes toward disarmament. The only shift was a totally unexpected "rally-round-the-flag" effect, which is said to have helped President Reagan. Furthermore, behavioral measures such as communications to the White House, the Congress, the ABC network, counselling services, and antinuclear groups suggested that the film had had very little impact. [CCF]

Braithwaite, V. A. & Law, H. G. [U Queensland, Brisbane, Australia]. (1977). **The structure of attitudes to doomsday issues.** *Australian Psychologist*, 12(2), 167-174.
Employed principal components analysis followed by a varimax rotation to investigate the structure of 24 belief statements representing responses to the threats posed by overpopulation, pollution, and nuclear weapons. These items were administered to 170 undergraduates together with the Wilson-Patterson C Scale, which was included in the analysis as a marker variable. Little support was found for a general dimension of doomsday consciousness. Of particular interest was the way in which factors of concern and responsibility were orthogonal to factors of support for social action.

Emergency Decision Making and Crisis Management

Herman, Charles F. [Ohio State U, Mershon Center, US]. (1972). *International crises: Insights from behavioral research*. New York, NY: Free Press.
Presents historical, sociological, psychological, and political approaches to the analyses of international crises from World War I to the Bay of Pigs invasion. Comparative case studies of crisis, perceptions of crisis by policy makers, crisis games and simulations, and methods of coping with crisis are discussed.

Holsti, Ole R. (1986). **Crises, and ways to keep them from escalating.** In R. K. White (Ed.), *Psychology and the prevention of nuclear war* (pp. 419-431). New York: NYU Press. [Excerpts from

Holsti, O. R. (1972). *Crisis escalation war*. Montreal and London: McGill-Queen's University Press.]
Considers the effects of crisis and stress on decision making and of Nuclear War Effects and offers advice on policy implications. [CCF]

Janis, Irving L. [U California, Berkeley, US]. (1986). **Problems of international crisis management in the nuclear age.** *Journal of Social Issues*, 42(2), 201-220.
Studied the conditions under which misjudgments are made by national leaders in crisis situations (i.e., nuclear war) to provide guidelines for policymakers on crisis management during international conflicts. Symptoms of defective decision making are discussed, and evidence concerning the relationship between decision-making processes and outcome is presented. Cognitive, emotive, and affective decision rules of policymakers are reviewed.

Images—of The Future, of Cooperation, and of Nuclear War Effects

Ankarstrand-Lindstrom, Gunnel. (1984). **Framtidsperspektiv i gymnasieundervisningen: Nagra skolforsok pa temat "Fred i framtiden?"** [Future-oriented teaching in the upper secondary school: Exploring "Peace in the future?"]. *Pedagogiska Hjalpmedel*, No. 36, 62 pp.
Studied approximately 20 high school classes in Sweden in an attempt to introduce and evaluate future-oriented teaching. These future-oriented studies, which focused on the theme "peace in the future," are described using interview data from teachers and students. (English abstract)

Churcher, John & Lieven, Elena V. [Victoria U of Manchester, England]. (1983). **Images of nuclear war and the public in British civil defense planning documents.** *Journal of Social Issues*, 39(1), 117-132.
Discusses British civil defense plans for nuclear war, which embody selective and misleading images of nuclear war and of the public. Official documents intended for public mass consumption depict nuclear war as survivable, without discussing the meaning of *survival*. Planners' internal documents show more detailed and realistic appreciation of probable effects, but survival is still imagined in predominantly physical terms, and social or psychological

impact is not seriously analyzed. Attem at planning for administration of postatt society present contradicting conception the public: as a prosocial "us" antisocial "them." Together with a series elisions among such concepts as law, ord life, property, control, and persuasion, enables planners with limited imagination assume the role of guardian of the pub interest. There are potential antidemocr consequences for the present-day Bri society as plans are enacted in civil defe exercises and preparations. It is conclu that civil defense planning is not just ab saving lives in the future, but is also clos linked to national defense policy in present.

Risk Assessment and Reductio

Blight, James G. [Harvard U, Ctr Science & International Affairs, Cambrid MA, US]. (1986a). **How might psychol contribute to reducing the risk of nucl war?** *Political Psychology*, 7(4), 617-6
Considers recent attempts at nuclear reduction by psychologists. These inclu analyses of the risk of war in terms psychopathology in the way war is thou of or in the relations between superpowers; those that view risk in ter of constraints on the rationality of fore policy decision making; and those that wi it in terms of crisis and stress. The effe of this theorizing on policy making been minimal, and justifiably so because underlying assumptions and modus opera are utopian and fruitless. If psycholog wish to provide insights for policy, th will have to avoid calling conversion-like cognitive revolutions suggesting off-the-shelf solutions from th laboratories and clinics. Rather, what needed is a greater emphasis on describ the phenomenal world of the participants decisions of nuclear war and peace.

Frei, Daniel. (1983). *Risks unintentional nuclear war*. Totowa, N Jersey: Allanheld, Osmun and Co.
Excellent analysis of the factors t increase and decrease the risk unintentional nuclear war. Includes secti on nuclear accidents, decision making un stress, game theory, etc. [CCF]

Figure 1 (continued). Examples of Works from each Peace-Psychology Category

III. DISCIPLINES

Education and Peace Studies

Almgren, Eva & Gustafsson, Evy. (1974). World citizen responsibility: Assessment techniques, developmental studies, material construction, and experimental teaching. *Educational and Psychological Interactions*, No. 48, 34. Summarizes the "world citizen responsibility" project carried out at the Malmo School of Education. Extensive test batteries were constructed to study attitudes toward foreign groups and international relations. Among the older students more negative stereotypes were found, particularly towards minority groups and immigrants. Special teaching packages intended to increase the students' world citizen responsibility were developed and tested. Results give reason for optimism.

Bjerstedt, Ake. (1984). Fredsfostran, fredsundervisning, pedagogik for fred: Finns det nagot sadant, och hur skulle det ga till [Peace education: Some reflections on facts, possibilities and the need for expanded knowledge]. *Pedagogisk Psykologiska Problem*, No. 437, 152 pp. Reviews the literature on how issues of war and peace can be addressed in the schools, the methods and objectives of peace education, and the concept of global education. The anxiety and despair expressed by young children in response to internal tensions and the arms race are noted, and the importance of international understanding is stressed. (English abstract) (30 pages of references)

Government Policy-Making; International Relations; Arms-Race Analysis

Bernstein, Jerome S. (1989). *Power and politics: The psychology of Soviet-American partnership*. Boston, MA: Shambhala Publications. Provides in very practical terms a new way of understanding what is happening in Soviet-American relations and where we need to go from here. The author believes that we are entering a new political era as the result of profound psychological changes taking place behind the international scenes, and he identifies the archetypal forces that underlie these changes. Unlike most psychological writings on the subject, this book examines

the collective influences that have impelled the superpowers toward conflict and are simultaneously impelling them toward cooperation. It argues that psychology must play a dramatic role in international relations if humanity is to avoid self-annihilation. It is the act of war itself--and not specific conflicts between groups and nations--that is the greatest threat to human survival, and our realization of this fact marks a critical turning point in the evolution of civilization. In documenting this historical evolutionary shift, Jerome Bernstein discusses the role of U.S.-Soviet relations, a redefinition of war and peace in radically new terms, and the dynamic of paranoia as a nonpathological as well as pathological factor in foreign affairs. [From the jacket, as extracted in *PsycBOOKS*, 1989, 6500-94]

Bronfenbrenner, Urie. (1961). The mirror-image in Soviet-American relations: A social psychologist's report. *Journal of Social Issues*, 17(3), 45-56. The author's experience as a tourist in the U.S.S.R. gives rise to the theory of "mirror-image," i.e., that both the U.S.S.R. and the U.S. have similar distorted pictures of each other. The author suggests that these distortions may become self-fulfilling prophesies. [Abstract adapted from California State Psychological Association's Bibliography on Psychological Effects of Nuclear Developments] [CCF]

Peacemaking Efforts; Wars and Crises; Historical Perspectives

Barabantschikov, Alexandr V. (1985). [Soviet psychology in the Great Patriotic War]. *Voprosy Psikhologii*, No. 2, 12-22. Discusses the participation of Soviet psychologists in the war against Hitler. The lines of development of Soviet psychology during World War II are described. The efforts made by Soviet psychologists to achieve peace are emphasized. (English abstract)

Boyer, Paul. (1986). A historical view of scare tactics. *Bulletin of the Atomic Scientists*, 42(1), 17-19. Suggests that early antinuclear activists, in using fear to try to inspire political action, may have unwittingly contributed to anticommunist hysteria and nuclear proliferation. [CCF]

Cooper, H. A. [Neuvevidas International Inc, Dallas, TX]. (1983). Hostageology. *International Journal of Offender Therapy and Comparative Criminology*, 27(1),

94-96. Suggests that the seizure of hostages at the US embassy in Teheran, Iran from November 1979 to November 1980 not only affected the national psyche but also had a dramatic effect on the presidential election. *Hostageology* is concerned with the rescue of hostages, and hostageologists fall into 2 classes: those who favor rescue through negotiation and those who favor the use of force. Although both approaches were attempted in Iran, negotiation succeeded. It is concluded that hostage taking has far from exhausted its potential in the world, and hostageologists must attempt to rise to the challenge.

Philosophical and Religious Aspects; Morality

Brockett, Charles D. [U of the South, Sewanee, TN, US]. (1986). A Kohlbergian approach to international distributive justice: A comparison of the shared humanity and interdependence perspectives. *Political Psychology*, 7(2), 349-367. Uses L. Kohlberg's (1971, 1976) theory of moral or justice reasoning to clarify the logical and ethical differences between 2 perspectives on international obligations, the interdependence perspective and the shared-humanity perspective, and to demonstrate the greater adequacy of the latter. The implications of a shared-humanity perspective on international distributive justice are discussed, and Kohlberg's postulation of a Stage 6 level of moral reasoning is defended.

Burhoe, Ralph W. [Zygon, Winter Park, FL, US]. (1986). War, peace, and religion's biocultural evolution. *Zygon Journal of Religion and Science*, 21(4), 439-472. Presents a model of human nature as a symbiosis of genetic and cultural information, and considers how religion can generate not only altruistic social behavior among both kin and nonkin, but also, paradoxically, propel humans toward war. Uniting leaders of traditional and emerging religions is needed to bring about religious reformations and revitalization needed to create peace and order.

Figure 1 (continued). Examples of Works from each Peace-Psychology Category

IV. PEACE STUDIES

Conflict Resolution

Bazerman, Max H. [Northwestern U, J. L. Kellogg Graduate School of Management, Evanston, IL, US]. (1986). Why negotiations go wrong. *Psychology Today*, 20(6), 54-58. Describes 5 common cognitive mistakes negotiators make: (a) the "fixed-pie" assumption that there is only a fixed amount of profit or gain in what is being negotiated and that in order to win something, the other must lose something; (b) the failure to develop expertise to gain as much information about a deal as the other side has; (c) the failure to realize that continuing or escalating a conflict is a mistake; (d) overconfidence; and (e) the failure to reframe the situation positively. Negotiators who do not start out with a fixed-pie bias find it easier to avoid escalating demands and to reframe their thinking and proposals in a positive way. Negotiators who try to understand an opponent's thinking are less likely to feel overconfident in their judgment or to escalate demands needlessly. Negotiators who are aware of the tendency to be overconfident in their judgment are more likely to consider what opponents are thinking and to reframe their perceptions in positive terms.

Cohen, Stephen P.; Kelman, Herbert C.; Miller, Frederick D.; & Smith, Bruce L. [Van Leer Jerusalem Foundation, Israel]. (1977). Evolving intergroup techniques for conflict resolution: An Israeli-Palestinian pilot workshop. *Journal of Social Issues*, 33(1), 165-189. Describes a pilot workshop in which Palestinians and Israelis met with a team of social scientists to discuss the conflict in the Middle East. The goal was the evolution and evaluation of intergroup techniques for conflict resolution. Some of the features of the workshop are discussed: (a) use of separate preworkshop sessions with each party to focus on internal group processes, (b) induction of communication marked by an analytic approach to the conflict rather than the legalistic approach that generally characterizes communication among conflicting parties, (c) process observations from an intergroup (rather than an interpersonal) perspective, and (d) emphasis on symbolic issues and questions of national identity. Lessons learned from the workshop are discussed. It was found that there is a need to give greater attention to spelling out the ground rules of the

workshop beforehand; there must be advance agreement that the participants accept the organizers' forms of intervention, especially unusual forms of process intervention. On the other hand, some of the more structured techniques were found to be unacceptable. For example, explicit role reversal was perceived as too gimmicky and therefore inappropriate to the seriousness of the issues. The value of the 3rd party was confirmed, most especially in its capacity to help the adversaries respect each other's self-image (national identity).

Effects of Conflicts, including Nuclear War

Allen, Bem P. [Western Illinois U, Macomb, US]. (1985). After the missiles: Sociopsychological effects of nuclear war. *American Psychologist*, 40(8), 927-937. Discusses the physical and medical effects of nuclear war, including the effects of radiation and the possibility of a "nuclear winter," and speculates on the sociopsychological effects on persons in urban and rural areas. Issues considered include the occurrence of survival guilt and deindividuation, the foreseeable breakdown in the social and economic order, and resulting violence. The uncertainties of nuclear war and the disastrous effects of even a limited nuclear exchange are emphasized.

Chazov, E. I. & Vartanian, M. E. (1982). Effects on human behavior. *Ambio*, 11(2-3), 158-160. Interesting discussion of the likely psychological sequelae of nuclear war based on accounts of Hiroshima and Nagasaki and nonnuclear disasters. The authors conclude that adequate treatment for the wide range of psychological disorders to be expected would simply not be possible. [CCF]

Peace Movements; War Prevention

Boyer, Paul. (1984). From activism to apathy: The American people and nuclear weapons, 1963-1980. *Journal of American History*, 70(4), 821-844. Explores the factors underlying several distinct cycles of activism and apparent apathy with respect to the nuclear threat. [CCF]

Department of Psychology and Education. [U Centroamericana "Jose Simeon Canas," San Salvador, El Salvador]. (1986). Psicologia, dialogo y

paz en El Salvador [Psychology, dialog and peace in El Salvador]. *Boletin Psicologia El Salvador*, 5(22), 191-203. Discusses the possible roles of psychology and psychology in promoting peace in Salvador. The need for psychologic peace-making (in contrast to psychologic warfare) in El Salvador is emphasized.

V. ADDITIONAL

Bibliographies

Feminist Aspects of Peace

Brock-Utne, Birgit. (1985). *Educati for Peace: A Feminist Perspective*. Ne York: Pergamon. Covers definitions of peace, activiti started and led by women, peace educatio science and peace research, and feminis as a starting point for effecti disarmament. [HHB]

Jensen, Mark P. [Arizona State Tempe, US]. (1987). Gender, sex rol and attitudes toward war and nucle weapons. *Sex Roles*, 17(5-6), 253-267. Examined the relationship between sex-ro orientation and attitudes toward war an nuclear weapons of 156 male and 17 female undergraduates, using gender an measures of sex-role orientation (includi the Bem Sex-Role Inventory) to predi attitudes about nuclear weapons and use military force. Two specific and 2 class of hypotheses were tested: masculinit femininity, masculinity * feminini interaction, and gender * sex-ro orientation hypotheses. Results provi limited support only for the feminini hypothesis that attitudes toward war a associated with feminine traits. Neith masculinity nor femininity was found to the only mediator of the gender/war attitu relationship, indicating that sex-ro orientation (and especially masculinit should be given less emphasis regarding th relationship between gender and attitud toward war.

Miscellaneous

CHAPTER 13

Gandhi's Concept of Love

Ian M. Harris

Ahimsa, truly understood, is in my humble opinion a panacea for all evils, mundane and extra mundane. We can never over-do it. Just at present, we are not doing it at all. Ahimsa does not displace the practice of other virtues, but renders their practice imperatively necessary before it can be practiced even in its rudiments. (Gandhi's Essential Writings, 1970).

Gandhi's approach to love revolved around the Buddhist and Hindu concept, ahimsa, or nonviolence, which means not harming or desiring to harm others. Gandhi was influenced by Jain theology which emphasizes the sanctity of all life. To live according to the law of love was not to harm other living creatures. Love provided a very high moral ideal by which Gandhi attempted to live. In his political activities love implied doing good even to the evil doer. Ahimsa in action is love:

It is no nonviolence if we merely love those that love us. It is nonviolence only when we love those that hate us. I know how difficult it is to follow the grand law of love. But are not all great and good things difficult to do? Love of the hater is the most difficult of all. But by the grace of God even this most difficult thing becomes easy to accomplish if we want to do it. (Bose, 1948, p. 24).

Ahimsa has a negative aspect, not harming others but also a positive aspect, where it resembles the Christian concept of charity, "love for thy neighbors."
Gandhi had an unconditional love for humanity. To him love was a powerful force within the heart and soul of each living being:

Nonviolence is the greatest force at the disposal of mankind. It is mightier than the mightiest weapon of destruction devised by the ingenuity of man. Destruction is not the law of humans. Man lives freely by his readiness to die, if need be, at the hands of his brother, never by killing him. Every murder or other injury, no matter for what cause, committed or inflicted on another is a crime against humanity. (Harijan, July 20, 1931).

The love we should have for each other because of the Atma--or universal soul, that belongs to each of us--allows for social cohesion. Gandhi said in his autobiography, "To slight a single human being is to slight those divine powers, and thus to harm not only that being but with him the whole world" (Bose, pp. 27-28). Without love and the respect that comes from loving our essential humanity there would be no social order. Greed and violence would characterize human existence. In a world of no love unrestricted selfishness would create havoc. Love encourages people to care for other persons and makes possible human societies.

For Gandhi love has both a spiritual and a social power. As a spiritual force love presents the means to experience God, or truth. Loving others, or practicing ahimsa, is the highest virtue, treating all beings as oneself. Truth for Gandhi was God that pervaded all beings and unified them through love. To love God is to love the beings through which God is incarnate. "When you want to find truth as God the only inevitable means is Love, i.e., nonviolence" (Gandhi, 1937). On a social scale love provides moral principles about how to live:

> Unfortunately for us, we are strangers to the nonviolence of the brave on a mass scale....I hold that nonviolence is not merely a personal virtue. It is also a social virtue to be cultivated like the other virtues. Surely society is largely regulated by the expression of nonviolence in its mutual dealings. What I ask for is an extension of it on a larger, national and international scale. (Gandhi, 1972, back cover).

Love encourages honest relations between people and urges care for the needy and sick. Gandhi successfully used nonviolence in his campaign to free the Indian people from British Colonial domination. In the United States during the 1950s and '60s organizers in the south used nonviolent principles to help gain civil rights for black people. Love, as preached by Martin Luther King, Jr., provided a framework to transform race relations in the United States. The Quaker pamphlet, "Speak Truth to Power," based upon nonviolence provided a theoretical framework for both the Vietnam anti-war movement and the anti-nuclear movement in the United States. More recently nonviolence has been used in Eastern European countries to dismantle the Cold War and throw off the crushing hegemony of the Soviet Union. On a national and international scale nonviolence leads to notions of national defense based on transarmament, a concept advanced by the American political scientist, Gene Sharp. A defense policy based upon the principles of transarmament would train all citizens in nonviolent civil disobedience. If a country was attacked, the citizens would refuse to obey the conquerors who in turn would be rendered ineffective.

Good and Bad Loves

Gandhi, however, did not approve of all forms of love. His love of love was conditional. Love for Gandhi was like rain from the heavens. Like love, rain is a uniform gift, available to the untouchables as well as the Brahmins. All forms of life need rain in order to survive. And like rain, love helps sustain life. Most rains are nourishing. However, some rains are destructive. They come as hurricanes or typhoons and cause floods. The strong winds accompanying the rain can be devastating. Likewise, love can contain powerful passions. Passionate lovers experience torments, cares, jealousies, suspicions, fears, griefs, and anxieties. Erotic love can be addictive, so that the lover focuses only on personal needs and stays in relationships that are abusive.

Gandhi was opposed to passionate love and neglected to emphasize the important role that love based upon friendship plays in human existence. He did not seem to appreciate that all forms of love can be enhancing. After the storms of passion have subsided, an individual can return to normal life enriched, like the banks of the Ganges enhanced by flooding that comes from spring rains. After turbulent storms rivers are full, and crops can grow.

Love enhances human beings because their hearts work like an electrical battery. The greater the charge going into it, the more love a heart has to give to the world. Love expands infinitely. If you receive love from someone you have love to give to another and so on, till many people benefit from one loving act. A human being charged by the passions of love may direct love energy in many beneficial ways.

For Gandhi good loves are compassionate and dispassionate. Bad loves are passionate. Compassionate love expresses a concern for the welfare of others. Dispassionate love is love of a higher being or abstract principles like truth, justice, or beauty.

My love for nonviolence is superior to every other thing mundane or supermundane. It is equalled only by my love for truth which is to me synonymous with nonviolence through which and which alone I can see and reach truth. (Gandhi, *Young India*, February 20, 1930).

For Gandhi, love and truth go hand in hand. Truth is only half without love because my truth is right and your truth is also right. Love allows an individual to take into account another person's truth. Satya, or truth, and ahimsa are two sides of a coin:

With all respect for the traditional translation of ahimsa, I think Gandhi implied in it, besides a refusal not to do physical harm, a determination not to violate another person's essence. For even where one may not be able to avoid harming or hurting, forcing or demeaning another whenever one must coerce him, one should try even in doing so, not to violate his essence, for such violence can only evoke counter-violence, which may end in some kind of truce, but not in truth. For ahimsa as acted upon by Gandhi not only means not to hurt another, it means respect for the truth in him. (Erikson, 1969, p. 412)

Hindu tradition holds out the possibility of the ultimate realization of God through a search for absolute truth. Within Hinduism a worshipper moves from the jiva, the narrow egocentric self of an earthly creature, to the Atma, the higher self of a divine creature. Truthfulness in speech and action flows spontaneously from the love of fellow human beings. Truth and love are therefore inseparable in Gandhi's thought although some forms of love would distract from the search for the divine. Bad loves for Gandhi are passionate, driven by lust and an intense longing for union with another human being. They ground human beings in earthly pleasures and distract then from their all important spiritual quest. They grow out of need, are egotistical, and focus on bodily pleasures. Gandhi disavowed eros, or passion, in his own life with a vow of brahmacharya, or celibacy.

What is brahmacharya? It is the way of life which leads us to Brahma-God. It includes full control over the process of reproduction. The control must be in thought, word and deed. If the thought is not under control, the other two have no value...For one whose thought is under control, the other is mere child's play. (Harijan, June 8, 1947).

As a devout Hindu, Gandhi rejected passionate love based on need, which consumes people with feeling good about themselves, distracting them from achieving unity with a higher force. Erotic love invokes passionate feelings in a lover, is unstable, and potentially explosive. Gandhi had no tolerance for a type of love which has been called "limerence." Limerence is the love of teenagers, growing out of insecurity. (In Hindu this form of love is called "calf love." There is nothing serious in it because calves are immature.)

In his approach to love Gandhi was looking for a more mature love based upon positive appreciation for the divine that exists within each of us. He promoted a spiritual form of love:

Man as animal is violent, but as spirit is nonviolent. The moment he awakens to the spirit within he cannot remain violent. Either he progresses toward ahimsa or rushes to his doom. (Murti, 1970, p. 23).

This mature love enables human beings to transcend bodily needs and develop an intimate relationship with God.

Gandhi held these views because of the self discipline it took to withdraw and find within the source of all creation. Gandhi's concept of love emphasizes suffering which allows human beings to identify with the spirit that exists within all living forms. Because life is holy, it is better to use ahimsa that recognizes the power of truth within all living creatures than it is to use brute force:

It is easy to see that soul force is infinitely superior to body force. If people in order to secure redress of wrongs resort to soul force, much of the present suffering will be avoided. (Prabhu & Rao, 1945, p. 68).

The soul force, which Gandhi promoted through satyagraha (literally "holding on to the truth"), contains a compassionate love of others that leads towards perfection, as opposed to brute force based upon greed and egotism. For Gandhi, it was better to suffer an evil deed than it was to take vengeance:

It is a law of Satyagraha that when a man has no weapon in his hands and when he cannot think of a way out, he should take the final step of giving up his body. (Desai, 1953, p. 296).

To do evil to another human being is to violate the love we should have for all human beings because of the soul force that we all possess. When we suffer we should not be aggressive, so our opponent has nothing to fear. Satyagraha never destroys anybody, but rather respects the capacity for truth that exists within every human being.

Human beings have a choice about how to act. They can become violent when provoked or they can suffer. The act of suffering is itself an act of love.

It is this act of Jesus, i.e., suffering, that influenced Gandhi most. Instead of searching for the historical veracity of the life of Jesus, Gandhi asked all to emulate the sacrifice of Jesus. (Leo, 1990, p. 76).

In Christian theology Christ died so that those who live after him may experience love and redemption. This understanding of love, as self-purification and suffering, sets Gandhi apart from people who experience love as a joy and a pleasure. Most humans experience love through friendship and passion, two forms of love rejected in Gandhian thought.

Learning to Love

Love permeates all aspects of human existence and cannot easily be separated into good and bad parts. It exerts a powerful influence upon persons at all ages. As people mature, they gain different insights into love. Their experiences with love establish patterns that influence how they behave as lovers. Growing awareness of the power of love within an individual's life corresponds to stages of psychological development, providing an orientation towards love. These stages are illustrated in Table I below and will be explained in the text that follows:

TABLE I

Stages of Love Development

	Stage	Type of Love	Characteristic Tasks
I.	Embryonic	Being taken care of	Total dependence upon another
II.	Maternal	Attachment	Bonding
III.	Youthful	Friendship Kinship Esprit de corps	Sharing secrets Developing values Identity formation
IV.	Adolescent	Eros Limerence	Desire to unite Acceptance by peers
V.	Adult	Self-love Familial love Camaraderie	Take care of needs Develop family Create respect at work
VI.	Mature	Love of God, truth, human race, Earth, creation, Nature	Achieve purpose

----

　　Our initial experience of love, embryonic love, comes in the uterus, where, protected by the warm amniotic fluid of our mother, we are fed and feel secure. We come into the world crying for love. The birth experience, when we are catapulted out of the protection of the womb, is perhaps the most traumatic experience of our lives. For the rest of our years we long for the warm embrace of embryonic love.

　　The second stage of love, maternal love, comes from parents. Even though this type of love is often associated with females (mothers), it is a type of love both parents can and ought to share with their children. The human infant is helpless. Without the protection of loving adults babies can't survive. Our experiences with parents and parent figures lay a foundation for love throughout life. Infants emerge from the womb ready for attachment. In evolutionary history physical proximity to a care giver greatly increases an infant's chance of survival. The patterns of attachment formed with parents follow a person from cradle to grave. Infants and children construct mental models of themselves interacting with social partners. These models regulate a person's behavior and feelings. Confidence in the availability of attachment figures or the lack of it built up in childhood sets expectations that last through life.

Unfortunately, not all human beings receive love and care from their parents. Eric Fromm said about those children who do not receive parental love, "If mother's love is not there, it's as if all beauty is gone and there's nothing I can do to create it" (1956, p. 32). Those people who don't receive maternal love may never learn how to trust other human beings. They go through life in a state of rage, often becoming sociopaths, committing violent acts against a world that has rejected them. They don't trust authority figures and are angry at a social order that has not taken care of their basic needs. Because they haven't been valued, they find no value in life. Gandhi had this to say about those who don't receive love:

And he who is without love, that is lacks the spirit of ahimsa, who cannot look upon all living things as his kith and kin, will never know the secret of living. (Murti, 1970, p. 104).

The third stage of love, youthful love, involves friendship and communal ties. Children develop close friendships exploring the world with other children. Childhood love involves sharing secrets with intimate buddies, but not romance. Girls and boys can be close friends at this stage. Their love for each other may contain some sexual play but won't be buffeted by the strong passion of limerence which characterizes the next stage of love. They don't desire union with each other, but rather seek playmates with whom to explore the mysteries of the universe.

Youthful love, pure with no strings attached and free from value judgements, can also be described as the tribal stage, where a child identifies with a group of people and wants to be like the adults in that community. Each child seeks approval from adults who form a kinship network with certain distinct values. These early experiences in social relations with other children and adults within that tribe help mold values. Children act in ways that will get the approval of significant others and the attention they receive both from their friends and other members of the community establishes important patterns of behavior. Belonging to a particular kinship network provides an esprit de corps, a sense of group identity that reinforces values which become central to a young person's identity.

The fourth stage of love is romantic, where an adolescent searches for a parent substitute, a member of the opposite sex who can provide nurturance and comfort to assist in the difficult task of building a new nest away from the comforts of home. At this stage erotic love with its sexual overtones becomes a key dynamic. Hormones are raging through the body. Sexual organs achieve maturity, and sexual activity becomes a primitive rite of passage into adulthood. The emotions surrounding romantic love are so strong because the stakes are high. At that point in life the young lover searches desperately for a mate who can replace the commitment, love and dedication provided by parents. Adolescents also form strong bonds with their friends who help them achieve an identify independent of their parents.

The fifth stage, or adulthood involves three aspects--(1) self love, (2) family, (3) work. Developing loving relationships within these spheres are essential tasks for adults. The degree to which adults achieve success and happiness in life will depend upon the degree of loving they achieve within these three domains.

(1) Through loving experiences adults learn to love themselves. Competent adults no longer need parents. They take care of their own needs. Meister Eckhart, the thirteenth century Christian mystic, had the following to say about self love:

> If you love yourself, you love everybody else as you do yourself. As long as you love another person less than you love yourself, you will not really succeed in loving yourself, but if you love all alike, including yourself, you will love them as one person and that person is both God and man. Thus he is a great and righteous person who, loving himself, loves all others equally. (1991, p. 204).

Love of self is perhaps a most fundamental form of love that allows a person to love others. Gandhi did not encourage this kind of love because of his adherence to Hindu beliefs which diminish the value of the self as a person seeks unity with higher metaphysical forces.

(2) Each of us is born into a family and hence we develop certain patterns of familial love within our family of origin, but as adults we also develop families. "Families" here is used in the broadest sense of a support community. Each adult seeks a support community that shares his or her values and helps that person deal with the difficulties of living. "Families" also refers to intimate coupling. In the western world modern families take many different forms, including lesbian and gay couples, adults who live together but don't get married, communal living arrangements, and conventional marriages. In the Eastern world adult children often live with relatives in extended families. All of these different arrangements represent an attempt to create a secure nest. Gandhi attempted to provide such a beloved community for himself in his Ashram, rather than through his immediate family because of his vow of brahmacharya.

Love encourages human beings to form families, procreate and reproduce the human species. In this way romantic love assists the process of natural selection. In Western societies people choose a mate through romantic love. They fall in love and often marry that person. Once the limerence has subsided, a different form of love, known to the Greeks as storge, sets in. Storge implies loving affection that settle in over time. Adults who have children develop a parental love which is essential for the well-being and care of family members. This parental love contains both maternal and paternal aspects. Paternal love implies more than physical nurturance, the hallmark of maternal love. It implies care, concern, and productive activities that provide for the economic needs of family members. A father's task is to protect the hearth.

(3) Adult love also plays an important role in the economic sphere. Human beings have to work in order to support themselves. Most adults work in alienating situations where, as Marx pointed out, they are divorced from the products they produce and are treated as commodities in a labor exchange. Adults can apply love

to their jobs by creating work environments where they are treated with dignity, respected for their contributions, and respectful of the work of others. One of Gandhi's greatest contributions was to emphasize the relationship between love and economics. His approach to economics is summarized by the following remark, "The principle of nonviolence necessitates complete abstention from exploitation in any form" (Harijan, November 11, 1939). He advocated a balance of resources that would provide for basic human needs and a trusteeship relationship with the Earth.

Being an adult is difficult, trying to balance competing demands for family, work, and self love. Love helps adults deal with the loneliness, pain, and chaos of existence. Through adult love people learn to share and to give, to make generosity a daily part of life. The Native Americans have a saying that a person who gives receives nine times the value of the gift through the course of that person's life. The more love an adult gives, the richer his or her life will be.

The final stage of love, mature love, allows an individual to transcend bodily needs and to surrender to some greater force, often represented by the concept of God, which provides meaning, a purpose for living. This love, praised by mystics, transcends the senses and promotes unity with the transcendent. A love with no attachment implies a liberation from the senses; whereas eros implies drowning in the senses. For Gandhi this stage of love involved a commitment to the truth:

> One of the axioms of religion is, there is no religion other than truth. Another is, religion is love. And there can be only one religion; it follows that truth is love and love is truth. We shall find on further reflection that conduct based on truth is impossible without love. Truth-force then is love force. (Murti, 1970, p. 22).

Mature love is beyond speech and reason. It involves a love of God and a striving for self perfection pursued by deeply spiritual people.

Not all individuals go through all these stages. Research in the United States indicates that 23% of the population is avoidant of attachment to others and another 19% is anxious and ambivalent about attachment, (Shaver, Hazan, and Bradshaw, 1990) indicating that large portions of the population may never have resolved some of the essential trust issues involved in stage two of becoming a fully loving person. When children fail to form loving attachments with adults in their lives, they may never experience the higher stages of love. They are in danger of living as separate and alienated adults. And we all suffer because we live in a society that contains such bruised individuals.

Rather than celebrating love in all its richness, Gandhi would have all human beings go from stage two to stages five and six (adult and mature), skipping over stages three and four (youthful and adolescent). He had a great love of his mother but never seemed to develop the kind of attachments characteristic of young children to their friends or romantic lovers to their beloved. Although he was married at age 13, he later disclaimed his sexual passions with his row of brahmachaya. He went from a child loving his mother to an influential actor in the world of householders to a lover of the poor, working for their betterment. Gandhi, who was married and a father, in his desire to be a devout Hindu, skipped over the satisfaction that most of us experience in loving relations with others. He ignored his wife's physical needs and developed a view of love based upon sacrifice and not harming other living beings.

The Power of Love

Being a loving person implies much more than being popular and having sex appeal, as portrayed in popular culture. Since nonviolence is based upon love, it is important not to dismiss various aspects of love if we are to understand the full richness of nonviolence. A complete theory of nonviolence would celebrate all the rich varieties of love. It would view love unconditionally, embracing all forms of love because love helps us get our needs met.

Scott Peck defined love as "The will to extend oneself for the purpose of nurturing one's own or another's spiritual growth" (1978, p. 64). Love is an emotional response to that which we highly value. Love is a commitment, a passion, and intimacy. Love has many different objects. It implies care for the beloved object, a commitment to that object, a passion to be with that object, and sharing secrets with the beloved. Regardless of the object being loved, love is a dynamic experience involving cognition, emotion, and behavior. Intimacy, which is a part of love, grows with time. Intimacy promotes a validation of the self which builds confidence about the capacity for trusting relationships with others. We need faith in our own love in order to love others.

As Eric Fromm has pointed out, love in all its forms, allows us to escape from our loneliness (1946). In spite of Gandhi's reservations about friendship and eros, these forms of love help us overcome our own narcissistic orientation and self preoccupation. When we are in love, we create power and harmony. Our sexuality allows us to participate in the ultimate act of creation. When we make love we become God-like in our capacity to produce new forms of life. Sexual love, through the act of reproduction, allows us to connect to the spirit that unites us all.

Love contributes to attachment, as opposed to separation. Being in love is an enhancing experience that kindles feeling of care for others. Because of love we respond to others, transcending the prison of our own separateness. Love in all its forms requires people to be alive both to others and to the world at large.

Gandhi was wrong in discrediting friendship and eros because love in all its forms awakens moral sentiments. People in love demonstrate care and responsibility towards the objects of their love. When we love someone, we bond to that person. Being in love allows us to experience each other's humanity. Because we care for others, we do not want them to experience violence. Love fuels our rage at injustice and requires a responsible approach to life.

As Gandhi pointed out, love disarms violence. Ahimsa is the right strategy for resolving conflicts. Love is the way to mend relationships that have been torn asunder by suspicion, hurt, mistrust, hatred, or violence. Ahimsa assumes a win-win approach to conflict where each participant tries to recognize and validate the worth of the enemy. Love helps people get through times of stress and crisis and allows us to feel passionately about causes.

People do not become great lovers accidently. Eric Fromm, the American psychologist, has pointed out that love requires practice, discipline, and knowledge. To be a lover is not just to learn one behavior, like smiling at strangers, but rather implies learning a complex set of skills. Leo Buscaglia (1972), one of the strongest proponents of love in the American culture says that love is a learned phenomenon.

Anatomy of Love

The stages of love refer to a person's psychological development, how he or she experiences love. Love as a concept exists with human cultures and has many different meanings.   C.S. Lewis (1963) described four different types of love--affection, friendship, eros, and charity. Saying that love consists of these four types is similar to saying that a body consists of four different systems--the circulatory system, the skeletal system, the respiratory system, and the digestive system. Each of these systems contains many different organs and cells. Together they and many other systems make up a complex living organism. Love, a complex human emotion that contains many different components, is a rich gift to the human race. It has more to it than can be expressed with these four types. It would be as incorrect to say that love just consists of friendship as it would be to say that the body just consists of the circulatory system. Blood may be a necessary part of a living body, but it is not sufficient for life. Friendship may belong to all forms of love, but it alone does not capture the richness of this emotion.

Affection is a strong attachment or devotion accompanied by feeling. Affection does not come from choice. When people find they are stuck together over time this emotion appears. Affection opens our eyes to the goodness in others. It comes from needing to be valued. Affection includes familial love for brothers and sisters as well as a mother's concern for a child's well being. It is an emotion given willingly and freely. Affection grows out of commitment. It implies a sense of camaraderie, belonging to a team and having a sense of fellowship for others on the team. The French would say affection grows out an "esprit de corps," that comes from working with others and appreciating their efforts. Affection breeds a sense of loyalty and cooperation, a kinship that allows for social cohesion. A human being without affection has no sense of belonging and is isolated. Like the Greek love, storge, friendship settles in over time and does not require passion.

Friendship implies mutuality with another human, the sharing of secrets, and is based upon choice. People choose their friends. To the ancient Greeks philia, or friendship, was the most fully human of all loves. The Greeks looked upon romantic love as a kind of sickness, while the Western world has elevated romance to a revered place and has ignored the importance of friendship. Philia is marked by equality, enjoyment, trust, mutual assistance, acceptance, respect, spontaneity, understanding and intimacy. Friendship provides non-physical intimacy that arises out of companionship when two people share an interest. People without this kind of love are lonely. People with friends experience a sense of security that comes from connectedness to other human beings.

Eros is lust or passion and implies the feeling of "being in love," a feeling not associated with other types of love. Eros involves sexual desire for union with another person. In the *Symposium* Plato describes this kind of union as capable of creating new life and hence it leads participants to feelings of immortality. Ultimately, Plato would argue that what draws us to another person is the essence of beauty that the other person represents, which leads to appreciation of the idea of beauty itself and hence eros is the soul's attempt to achieve oneness with the source of its being. Plato would agree with Gandhi that eros is not the highest form of love. He would say that it is a mistaken attempt to achieve love of the divine.

Charity is brotherly love. It involves giving to others. The Greeks used the word "agape" to characterize this type of love, and Martin Luther King Jr. stated that this form of love was the basis of Christianity (Ansbro, 1978). Gandhi associated charity with the positive form of ahimsa:

> In its positive form, ahimsa means the largest love, greatest charity. If I am a follower of ahimsa, I must love my enemy. I must apply the same rules to the wrong-doer who is a stranger to me, as I would to my wrong-doing father or son. This active ahimsa necessarily includes truth and fearlessness. As man cannot deceive the loved one, he does not fear or frighten him or her. Gift of life is the greatest of all gifts; a man who gives it in reality disarms all hostility. He has paved the way for an honorable understanding. And none who is himself subject to fear can bestow that gift. He must therefore be fearless. A man cannot practice ahimsa and be a coward at the same time. The practice of ahimsa calls forth the greatest courage. (Bose, 1948, p. 151).

Charity is a type of unconditional love that we have for other humans because they are human. Agape allows people to feel compassion for the suffering of others. It belongs to mature love in so far as it is abstract and dispassionate, where through our rational capacities we grow to acknowledge that others, in spite of their differences, share certain aspects with us.

Ahimsa, the love of all that is alive, is very similar to agape. It is not a feeling that children are born with but one that they acquire as they grow older. Carol Gilligan called ahimsa the desire not to harm others, the highest form of morality (1982). Agape also allows for gaiaphilia, or love of the Earth, a type of spirituality that belongs to many indigenous people and is the cornerstone of the recent environmental movement.

Without charity there is hatred, violence, prejudice, depression, and fear of the future. Charity implies an unselfish love that respects the integrity and uniqueness of each human being. Charity requires fairness and respect for the rights of others. It is the selfless giving love of angels. In its highest form it implies submission to the will of God. God loves the unlovable.

Gandhi embraced two of Lewis' four types--affection and charity. The sentiments of love contained within these types allowed Gandhi to live in the realm of householders and care for his fellow human beings. By ignoring the other two types, friendship and eros, Gandhi did a disservice to those human beings who experience those forms of love. Love in all its forms awakens human beings to care. It stimulates trust within the human heart and directs individuals away from private concerns.

Loveness

Putting all these forms of love together creates a new entity, a state of living in love and being in love, a state of loveness. Various social experiences can be graded in terms of loving or hateful. The more loving experiences an individual has, the more that individual will be capable of love. Vice versa, the more hatred an individual receives, the more hateful that individual will be, unless that hatred is mitigated by love. The goal of human existence should be to make real the promise of love. An enriched human society will draw upon all the forms of love to nourish its members. Becoming aware of the constituent elements of loveness provides a conceptual framework for building a social order that promotes all different aspects of love. Gandhi commented that human beings seem to use love but don't acknowledge its power:

> I claim that even now, though the social structure is not based on a conscious acceptance of nonviolence, all the world over mankind lives and men retain their possessions on the sufferance of one another. If they had not done so, only the fewest and the most ferocious would have survived. But such is not the case. Families are bound together by ties of love, and so are groups in the so-called civilized societies called nations. Only they do not recognize the supremacy of the law of nonviolence. It follows, therefore, that they have not investigated its vast possibilities. (Harijan, February 22, 1942).

Each person has a need for significance. People who do not have a feeling significance may obtain it in destructive ways. To love someone makes that person feel significant. Those who don't feel significant lash out at others, often in violent ways. Thus, the lack of love creates violence. Love can heal wounds that otherwise fill human beings with hatred and insecurities. Human beings who aren't loved don't trust each other and create paranoid worlds filled with enemies. Because of their fears, they need to destroy their enemies, and hence begin the endless cycles of revenge and hatred that dominate human existence. As Gandhi and Martin Luther King Jr. both pointed out, the only way out of those cycles is through love.

People concerned about creating a just society would use loveness as a guide when setting priorities. Just as the concept of infinity provides a basis for the form of mathematics known as calculus, the concept of loveness should form a basis for social arrangements. It should be a goal that directs social decisions and guides behavior. Responsible adults would make sure all children are raised in love with decent housing, clothing, food, and shelter. Citizens should be trained to protect human and civil rights. When an individual was hurting, other citizens would gather around that person offering love and support. A truly loving society would increase the amount of loveness it supplies its members. It would see that the Earth was nourished as well as all the animals, water, plants, and air that make up our world. People would base their decisions upon how their actions would increase the amount of loveness in a given community rather than upon private motives for greed or profit. Martin Luther King Jr. pointed out that the goal of life should be to create a beloved community, where all members care for each other (King, 1963). The challenge of existence requires growing out of the pure love of the womb and creating a loving environment. The experience of embryonic love haunts human consciousness and creates a desire to live in a state of loveness. With loveness as a guide and a knowledge of all the complex aspects of love, human beings may be able to create beloved communities that allow each individual to live up to his or her potential.

In Western traditions love of God is faith in God. In Eastern traditions love of God is experience with the oneness of all creation, inseparably linked with the experience of love in every act of creation. For Gandhi love involved a dispassionate love of the truth and not a passion for individual humans. Gandhi's spiritual training led him to dedicate himself to loving the truth, to living for the truth, and to promoting loveness:

> I am an irrepressible optimist. My optimism rests on the belief in the infinite possibilities of the individual to develop nonviolence. The more you develop it in your own being, the more infectious it will become till it overwhelms your surroundings and by and by might oversweep the world (Harijan, January 28, 1939).

REFERENCES

Ansbro, John. (1978). Martin Luther King Jr. Paulist Press.
Bose, Nirmal Kumar. (ed.) (1948). Selections from Gandhi. Ahmedabad: Navajivan Publishing House.
Buscaglia, Leo. (1972). Love. New York: Ballentine Books.
Desai, Mahadev. (1953). The Diary of Mahadev Desai. vol I. Ahmedadbad: Navajivan Publishing House.
Eckhardt, Meister (translated by R.B. Blakney, 1991). New York: Harper & Brothers, New York.
Erikson, Erik H. (1969). Gandhi's Truth: On the Origins of Militant Nonviolence. New York: W.W. Norton & Co.
Fromm, Eric. (1956). The Art of Loving. New York: Harper and Row.
Gandhi, Mahatma. (1930). Young India, February 20, 1930.
Gandhi, Mahatma. (1937). Young India, December 31, 1937.
Gandhi, Mahatma. (1972). Gandhi: All Men are Brothers. UNESCO: World Without War Publications.
Gilligan, Carol. (1982). In a Different Voice. Cambridge, MA: Harvard University Press.

Harijan, July 20, 1931.
Harijan, January 28, 1939.
Harijan, November 11, 1939.
Harijan, February 22, 1942.
Harijan, November 22, 1946.
Harijan, June 8, 1947.
King, Martin Luther Jr. (1963). Strength to Love. New York: Harper and Row.
Leo, Anthony. (1990). Christ's Influence in Gandhi's Life. Gandhi Marg, 12 (1) (April-June) pp. 72-76.
Murti, V.V. Ranana ed. (1970). Gandhi's Essential Writings, New Delhi: Gandhi Peace Foundation.
Prabhu, R.K. and U.K. Rao, eds. (1945). The Mind of Mahatma Gandhi. London: Oxford University Press.
Peck, Scott. (1978). The Road Less Traveled: A New Psychology of Love, Traditional Values and Spiritual Growth. New York: Simon and Schuster.
Shaver, Phillip, Cindy Hazan and Donna Bradshaw. (1990). Love as Attachment: The Integration of Three Behavior Systems. In R. Sternberg & Barnes (eds.), The Psychology of Love. New Haven: Yale University Press, pp. 68-99.
Washington, James. (1986). A Testament of Hope: The Essential Writings of Martin Luther King Jr. San Franciso: Harper & Row.

CHAPTER 14

Nonviolence in the 21st Century

Kenneth E. Boulding

The 20th century has seen almost unprecedented change in the total system of Planet Earth. The world human population has increased at least three times. There has been an enormous increase in human knowledge and human artifacts. In cosmology we have expanded into virtually the ends of the universe in space and time. In biology we have come to understand the genetic basis of life and the real meaning of heredity. We are still a long way from knowing exactly how the genotype produces the phenotype: a fertilized egg, a chicken; a fertilized human egg, Einstein. We have developed aerial warfare and the nuclear weapon, we have increasingly become a single world economically--the volume of international trade increased six times between 1950 and 1980--we have established the United Nations, however small and weak it may be. We have a world communication system; a fair proportion of the human race can now talk to anybody anywhere in the world almost immediately. We have mapped Venus and Mars and sent our artificial eyes to the edge of the solar system. We have almost gotten rid of empires. There has been a real spread of democratic institutions around the world, though the process is very incomplete.

We have seen two world wars, the rise and collapse of both fascism and communism. We had a grave world depression from 1929 to 1933, and in spite of the enormous growth in population, the per capita gross world product--whatever that is--has almost certainly increased, though with widening disparity between the rich temperate zones and the poor tropics.

A really striking phenomenon in the 20th century--not enough noticed by historians!--has been the rise of organized nonviolence as an instrument of social and political change. Something like this has happened many times in human history, but in the 20th century it became conscious, thanks due largely to Gandhi, who was certainly the philosopher, almost we might say the Newton of nonviolence, who played a dominant role in liberating India from British rule and liberating Britain from the burden of empire. We could argue indeed that the power of nonviolence in the world has increased almost throughout the 20th century: a great change in race relations in the United States inspired by Martin Luther King, who was a disciple of Gandhi; the expulsion of Ferdinand Marcos from the Philippines, the extraordinary economic expansion of Japan under the military domination of the United States.

Finally, the almost entirely nonviolent transformation of the Soviet Union and the Eastern European Communist countries, with the exception of Romania, certainly indicates a crumbling of the power of organized threat in the face of the withdrawal of legitimacy from existing rulers by very large numbers of ordinary people. We still have, of course, close to 200 independent national states, all but one (Costa Rica) committed to national defense by an organized military. Each year, however, something new is happening in the world that never happened before, particularly in regard to the general structure of power. There has been a decline in "power over" or dominance, which is largely though not entirely the power of threat, and the rise of "power to do" or "empowerment," which is the ability not only to get what we want but to change what we want when we find that what we want is not really worth wanting. The rise in feminism and the shift from male domination of women into mutual partnerships between them is another remarkable aspect of the 20th century.

In order to understand what is going on, we need to examine both the conscious and the unconscious processes of the great complex, overall system of Planet Earth. The conscious processes are those which are guided in some degree by decision. Decision involves a choice among the different conscious images of the future. The extent and the magnitude of these images reflects the power of the decision maker to change the world through some kind of action. A prisoner in a jail has little power over the prisoner's own behavior, and very little power over others. The president of the United States, by contrast, has the power to declare war, and to order the military force of which he is the commander-in-chief to risk their lives, to kill larger numbers of other people and to destroy property. He may not have the power to be re-elected except through the control which he may have over his public image. Therefore, power is clearly a very complex phenomenon.

I distinguish "three faces" of power (Boulding, 1989) though these categories are by no means unambiguous or complete: The first of these is threat power, which involves the threatener saying to the threatened, "You do something I want or I'll do something you don't want." The power of the law rests on rather specific threats, which can have a considerable effect on human behavior. Thus, the law says, "Put a coin in the parking meter or else you will be fined." Or "Calculate and pay your income tax obligation according to the rules or you will get into serious trouble." Military threats are apt to be much more vague: "You do something unspecifiedly nasty to me and I will do something unspecifiedly nasty to you!" Their weakness in influencing behavior has something to do with the indeterminacy and uncertainty of the threat, as the recent Iraq war showed very clearly. The dynamics of the threat system depends very much on the response of the threatened. One response is submission, as when I pay my income tax. Another is defiance--"I am going to drive over the speed limit" or "I won't pay my income taxes." Then, of course, what happens depends on the response of the original threatener. If the threat was in the first place a bluff, as it often is, there may be no response, or, of course, the threatener may try to carry out the threat.

Another response is flight, which depends on the principle that the power of the threatener is a diminishing function of the distance between the threatener and the threatened. This has been very important in human history and probably accounts for the spread of the human race all around the world. A fourth possibility is counterthreat: "If you do something nasty to me, I'll do something nasty to you," which may lead into deterrence, that is, abstention on the part of the original threatener from carrying out the threat. It may lead to a breakdown, for instance, in war if each tries to carry out the threat on the other. A last possibility, important in the theory of nonviolence, might be called "disarming behavior," which seeks to turn the threatener into a friend, drawn into a larger community which includes the threatened. This is very important in the theory of nonviolence.

A second form of power is economic power, most simply defined as what the rich have more of than the poor. This sometimes emerges out of the successful use of threat power, as in the conquest of land. On the whole, however, economic power comes out of the skills of production and exchange and the distribution of economic power is very largely the result of a long history of different human experiences in learning and in luck. In pure exchange, economists believe, either participant has a veto. The seller can refuse to sell and the buyer can refuse to buy. This means that exchange will not take place unless both parties feel at the time that they will both be benefitted. There can be exceptions to this, especially in the case of superior threat power on the part of one of the parties, as in the labor market.

The third, and I argue the most important, source of power is what I have called "integrative power." This is the power of legitimacy, persuasion, loyalty, community, and so on. In a very real sense power is a gift to the powerful by those over whom the power may be exercised, who recognize the power as legitimate. Threat power and economic power would be hard to exercise if they were not supported by integrative power, that is, if they were not regarded as legitimate. King George III had the illusion that he had the power to tax the American colonists, who then proceeded to withdraw legitimacy not only from the tax but from the monarch himself. The sources of integrative power are very complex and rather obscure. Why the French in Quebec submitted to an alien monarch, whereas the English speakers further south did not is an interesting question. The ability to persuade is clearly important. History has something to do with it. Old legitimacies have a certain tendency to persist. Payoffs have something to do with it. We tend to regard as legitimate those structures from which we feel we can benefit. On the other hand, there is the phenomenon that I have called the "sacrifice trap," that if we make sacrifices for anything it is hard to admit that they were in vain, and that may enhance the legitimacy of the imposer of the sacrifice. We see this in the case of the military. Sometimes, however, the sacrifice is perceived as too great and there is a revulsion or an overturn of legitimacy.

All actual exercise of power tends to involve all three "faces," but they can co-exist in very different proportions. Threat power is certainly dominant in the military, but unless it has a certain base in economic power, of course, the means of destruction and threat cannot be produced. Unless a military organization has "morale," and if it ceases to believe in the legitimacy of its officers and generals and admirals, no amount of internal threat on ordinary soldiers or sailors can be effective. The greater the internal threat, the more likely there is to be a revolt and rebellion. This happened sometimes with the French army in the First World War, when ordinary soldiers simply refused to obey orders they knew were designed for their sacrifice. The economic power of property is supported by the threat power of the law, yet where property becomes illegitimate, as it did, for instance, in Russia in 1917, no amount of threat power can preserve it. In democratic elections, while economic power may be used to some extent to buy votes, and even a certain amount of threat power in terms of possible loss of jobs and so on, the overwhelming source of power is legitimacy. Threat does not make people vote for you, and people may be suspicious of wealthy candidates.

It is often the unconscious processes of history that govern the way in which power in any of its forms comes to be exercised. We are too much accustomed to thinking of history as consisting of the decisions of the powerful and their effects. All history books tend to be written in terms of military victories, leaders like Genghis Khan or Napoleon, and so on. This leads to a neglect of the unconscious processes which come out of the underlying dynamics of human learning and interaction. It could be argued indeed that conscious decision processes in history, which make for empires, wars, revolutions, and so on, can often be seen as interruptions in the underlying unconscious processes of the accumulation of human knowledge, inventions and technology, the rise of religions and ideologies, changes in culture and ethics, which come out of the small decisions of large numbers of ordinary people, not out of the big decisions of the powerful. I believe very profoundly that there is a real world, in spite of some possible evidence to the contrary, and that if our image of the world does not correspond to the reality, we are a little more likely to change it than if it does, that is, there is an instability of error, though this may be very long-run, and a very real power of truth. The Inquisition in the Catholic Church, the KGB in the Soviet Union, the mentality of Nazi ideology have all faded.

Economic development itself is a learning process, spread over very large numbers of people, and an attempt to impose development from above often slows it down. Japan is a good example. While it is true that the leaders of the Meiji Restoration around 1870 removed previous obstacles to development imposed by authority, the actual development was the result of the learning processes in the ingenuity of very large numbers of people. The rise of the Japanese military interrupted this development to a small extent by the Korean and Chinese conquests, and to a disastrous extent in World War II. Nevertheless, the defeat of Japan in World War II removed the obstacles to development which the military were imposing. One can see even World War II as an interlude in the economic development of Japan, for where Japan is today, or where it was even by the late 1960s, is just about where it would have been if its development had proceeded at the pre-war pace and there had not been a Second World War.

The Soviet Union is an even more interesting example of an imposed development, because it was imposed by a tyranny which, under Stalin, surpassed even the Spanish Inquisition, then gradually lost legitimacy, until the whole structure collapsed almost overnight, with virtually no violence. The empires of the European powers are another case in point. The historical evidence suggests that the empires of the British, the French, and the Dutch slowed their internal economic development of the imperial powers in the 19th century. The countries that got rich in Europe after the middle of the 19th century were not those who went in for empire, but countries like Sweden and Denmark, who stayed home and minded their own business well. Germany is another striking example. It was the cultural center of Europe in the 18th century, with Bach, Beethoven, Kant, Hegel, and so on. Its economic development after the middle of the 19th century, again, like Japan, was largely a product outside of government. Then when the military took over after Bismarck, even more under Hitler, even though Hitler did achieve full employment, the economic results of all this were catastrophic. And like Japan after its military defeat, economic development proceeded at an accelerated pace until it again about caught up with where it would have been if there had not been the two world wars.

The Ottoman Empire is another good example of the economic failure of military success. Its conquest of Byzantium in 1453 was followed by a long period of economic and cultural decline, for almost 500 years, whereas disorganized and rather powerless Europe literally went off finally into outer space. Spain is another example. Its huge empire crippled it both economically and culturally, and it made practically no contribution to modern science until the 20th century. The modern world indeed came out of the politically disorganized and rather powerless triangle between northern Italy, Britain and Sweden, and while the development of the modern world helped to create European domination over the rest of the world, domination did not produce it. It grew out of a learning process which involved very large numbers of fairly ordinary people, on the whole separate from the political system. The rise of modern science represents the establishment of a subculture that denied the use of threat as a means of persuasion and power. The agricultural and industrial technical revolutions likewise came out of people who were not politically powerful. Many actually dissociated themselves from the political system.

Societal evolution, like biological evolution, can be influenced by political power but it is not guided by it. Human power, indeed, distorts the ecosystem in favor of human values, as when a farmer makes his land grow wheat instead of prairie grass. Government in many ways is rather like social agriculture, discouraging weeds like crime and encouraging the growth of organizations and behaviors which are favorable to ultimate human values. Farmers, of course, can destroy the soil on which they work; governments have often destroyed the social soil which supports them. The ecosystem is the most fundamental system. It may be distorted by human power, but still remains an ecosystem, still guided to a large extent by Adam Smith's famous "invisible hand." The wild woods have no "government," although on an increasingly crowded earth they may only exist because government prevents their destruction by private people. Government and the exercise of human power may still have to be used to distort ecosystems towards higher human valuations. The "invisible hand" can sometimes turn into an "invisible fist." The intrusion of a parasite may destroy a forest. The ecosystem of commodities (which is the economy) can go into positive feedback processes like those which produced the Great Depression of 1929-1933. Using a visible hand, or even occasionally using a visible fist, may be defensible.

Where, then, does nonviolence fit into this large picture? Almost unconscious nonviolence in the form, for instance, of disarming behavior, the sort of thing that turned Hagar the Horrible into a courtier's gentleman, has been very important in human history. Indeed, I would argue that most human development has been nonviolent. At least 90 to 95% of human activity is nonviolent--or what I have called "unviolent"--in terms of growing crops, making things, exchanging things, raising children (there is a little violence in this), and so on. Organized nonviolence, however, is very largely a 20th century development, beginning with Gandhi, who was perhaps the first nonviolent philosopher and theorist, stressing the power of truth and the capacity of undeserved suffering to produce shame in the perpetrators of it. I remember Gandhi making his famous visit to Lancashire when I was young. In spite of the fact that his boycott of imported English textiles in India was affecting the Lancashire economy adversely, he made a great impression on the people. I remember a popular song which went something like this: "We don't like the black shirts, we don't like the brown shirts, we don't like the red shirts, but here's to Gandhi with no shirt at all."

Popular songs, indeed, are a very interesting indicator of what is happening to integrative structures. The fact that World War I produced exciting war songs, while World War II produced practically none, and the Vietnam War produced mostly anti-war songs, with the possible exception of country music, certainly indicates that a profound change has been taking place in the legitimacy of war. Even the Gulf War, while it produced a lot of popular enthusiasm, did not, I think, produce much in the way of war songs.

A feature of nonviolence in the 20th century, for which we owe a great deal to Gandhi, is the movement of what might be called "informal and unorganized nonviolence" into "formal and organized nonviolence" as a political tool. Besides the three faces of power mentioned above, a case can be made for introducing a fourth face, which is organizational power. This involves the development of organizations, ranging from churches to governments and corporations, which have members and usually some sort of hierarchy. It is hard indeed to have a large organization that does not have some sort of hierarchy. Organizations, like any structure, beyond a certain point exhibit diminishing returns to scale, which is why small is often not only beautiful but has survival value. The cockroach survived the extinction of the dinosaurs and may even survive our extinction.

Certain changes in organizational structure, however, tend to increase the size at which the diseconomies begin. I have argued (Boulding, 1984) for instance, that the tremendous rise in the size of organizations of all kinds since about 1870, especially corporations and governments, has a lot to do with the invention of the telephone, which enabled upper members of a hierarchy to communicate with a great many more lower members than had previously had been the case. It is hard to imagine running either General Motors or the United States government in which the main means of communication were young boys running around with slips of paper, or letters that took weeks to arrive! The development of computers and the FAX may push this point at which diminishing returns to scale begin to an even larger size, though this is not wholly clear.

As we move into organizational structures, both the social and the biological ecosystems tend to shift in the direction of hierarchy and "bosses," and the various forms of human power may become more important. The rise of nonviolence in the 20th century, however, is an indication of the fact that even with increase in organizations the power mix is coming to include much more integrative power and much less threat power, with economic power perhaps somewhere in between. I have sometimes argued that if we are looking for any single element in the social system on which everything else depends--something which we should probably not do--the best candidate would be integrative power in the shape of legitimacy, for without legitimacy neither threat power nor economic power is very effective. People don't get rich by bullying, but by complex interactions with the market and other people. Even when threat is used in the form of bullying, it tends to weaken because of the erosion of legitimacy. Even the Gulf War may have increased the hostility towards the United States all around the world. Military defeat, as we saw earlier, often results in more cultural and economic development on the part of the defeated than on the part of the victors.

The prospects for organized nonviolence in the 21st century, therefore, look rather good. The problem here is that organizations for nonviolence tend to be temporary, put together for a particular occasion or objective, and if that objective is fulfilled, the organization tends to disintegrate. Gandhi's own organization is a good example. Gandhi's "victory" over the British and the establishment of an independent India led to the virtual dismemberment of the Gandhian movement and to an appalling civil war between Muslims and Hindus resulting in millions of casualties. It produced also an India which really rejected Gandhian principles and became what might almost be called a "Victorian European nation," with a large military force and a constant threat of war with Pakistan and China. I was in India during the war with China and witnessed a huge military procession in Delhi, with regiments of women in saris doing the goosestep and a most moving display showing the dove of peace defending her young!

The continuing power of the military may very well be the result of its embodiment in permanent organizations even in peacetime--armies, navies, and air forces--which have a very distinctive culture of their own, and which train the people in them to believe in the legitimacy of war in almost any form, a belief which can easily be expanded when there is a war. The peacetime military organizations also can have very profound effects on civilian government. There are many examples of the military taking over civilian government in a coup, though these military governments do seem to be a little unstable and there is a noticeable tendency after a while for a civilian government to return. Perhaps this is because the military is not really very good at government, as they are so specialized in threat, whereas government involves the careful exercise of integrative and economic power. The military may be skilled at having integrative power over their own soldiers, but that does not necessarily give them integrative power over the general public. It is a very fundamental principle of democracy indeed that military power must be subordinate to civilian power. Beyond a certain point, if the military dominates the civilian power, this is the end of democracy, though ironically enough it was Hitler's integrative power over the German people, that is, his rhetoric, that produced the re-militarization of Germany and the Second World War. Here again, military defeat often de-legitimates military power and permits the restoration of civilian power, which is much more successful in stimulating cultural and economic developments.

A very interesting question for the 21st century, therefore, is whether organized nonviolence can develop into a permanent organization for training and developing specialists in the art. There are small signs of this in institutions like peace brigades and the development of what is almost like a new profession-conflict management, mediation, and so on--but so far this is very small scale. Some European governments, especially, have become interested in what is sometimes called "defensive defense," that is, internal means of dealing with external threat and even occupation, without creating a threat to the threatener. This may lead to the organization of "disarming behavior" and training for nonviolent responses to violence before violence occurs. One would certainly like to see a major development of this kind in the 21st century.

It is not impossible, therefore, that the 21st century may see a real blossoming of the organization of nonviolence, though this may face some of the difficulties that the military have in maintaining their legitimacy and morale when there is no war. In the military this has developed into practice maneuvers, marching exercises, and so on, which can keep the members of the military from being bored during peacetime. Whether we can do this for organizations of nonviolence is an interesting question which only the future can answer. Nevertheless, it is not unreasonable to have real hope for more sophisticated and organized structures of nonviolence in the 21st century. We may eventually view the 20th century as the seeding ground for development of this kind.

REFERENCES

Boulding, K. E. (1984). The Organizational Revolution: A Study in the Ethics of Economic Organization. New York: Harper & Brothers; reissued: Westport, Conn.: Greenwood Press.
Boulding, K. E. (1989). Three Faces of Power. Newbury Park, Calif.: Sage Publications.

CHAPTER 15

Feminist Debates about Nonviolence

Lynne M. Woehrle

The relationship of feminists to nonviolence, its theory and its practice, provides a healthy tension of debate and discovery for both the women's movement and the peace movement. This chapter explores the difficulties women face in accepting nonviolence as a strategy. Four debates about nonviolence as theory and action are raised within the context of a feminist standpoint. The debates considered in this chapter include: (1) what feminists mean by the term "nonviolence"; (2) the ability/resources that women and men have to be nonviolent; (3) the value of military participation for women; and (4) the value of nonviolence as a means for ending sexist oppression.

I use the concept of a "debate" to suggest that women express a multiplicity of views on the subject of nonviolence both as a theory and as a practice. I find the idea of a debate a positive way to express this diversity, thereby presenting it as intentional and valuable rather than seeing it as disappointing that there is not unity. Some women differ on the meaning of nonviolence; others on its potential as a strategy; still others question its validity at all. What I want to emphasize is that as women we have particular social experiences that shape how we view nonviolence and that for the most part these experiences have not been seen as critical to the development of theories of nonviolence as a philosophy and as a strategy for social change. My goal is to begin to sort out the many levels these debates occupy.

Within feminism and within nonviolence it is possible to distinguish both short-term and long-term goals. While there are significant differences in the short-term, the long-term goals are strikingly similar. Both are praxis based on socio-political analysis which seeks the elimination of oppressive systems in our society. The model from which this chapter is built is that there are feminists and there are nonviolence activists/theoreticians, and then there are also those who integrate the two categories. Two important assumptions underlie this chapter: (1) that both feminism and nonviolence are theoretical constructs as well as practical strategies; and (2) that each can be considered as ends as well as a means.

These four debates suggest two critical points which must be considered. First, that where active nonviolence is concerned there may be a difference between how we act on an individual basis, and the actions we take as a result of membership in a group or a movement. For example, a woman who is alone and is attacked sexually will probably find that strict adherence to the philosophy of nonviolence may well entail submission to rape. Survivors often share that the terror of one moment can be a lifelong experience of violence. However, community actions such as "take back the night" marches or the establishment of safe houses suggest that nonviolence may be a powerful tool of education and empowerment against rape.

Secondly, it is important to consider the relationship of ends and means. For example, are we willing to accept as adequate the short term gains in education, and perhaps respect that women may achieve with participation in the military? Are we really satisfied with shoring up a masculinist institution? Rather, if we are actually intent on revolutionary ends, what means will radically alter how humans relate to each other and thereby provide for the end to all oppressions?

This chapter takes the stance that reform of the present system is limited in its possibility for actually ending sexist oppression. This analysis is based on the belief that wide-ranging institutional change is necessary for women's complete liberation. For instance, the perpetuation of violence against women at all levels of society is based not only on the division of labor by sex-defined categories, but it also depends upon institutions such as the military which promote the objectification and devaluation of women.

Employing the term "feminist" includes a great variety of women. In recent years, parts of the western tradition of middleclass feminism began to include issues of race and class within the feminist agenda. Specifically, we learned from our sisters of color and/or the lower classes, that oppressions are inseparable in the analysis of the patriarchal tradition. The goal of feminist unity in diversity remains as yet unachieved, however there are growing, important pockets of radical discussions which are making direct and indirect links between race, gender, and class.

It is important to point out that many of the women who make us aware of connections would prefer not to be called "feminists" because the term is seen as representative of a movement of white, middle and upper class women, and one which excludes men. Women of color, low income, and non-western cultures who experience more layers of oppression are challenging feminists to consider what we want our relationship to be with men. Feminism, they suggest, need not be adversarial, but rather should strive to be inclusive.[1]

DEBATE # 1: What do feminists mean by the term "nonviolence"?

As feminists what do we mean when we say that we believe in nonviolence? Who are the "we" that are making this commitment and how do we define nonviolence? In what context is this commitment based and who is included? Who is excluded? Are we nonviolent in all situations? Who or what do we study to learn nonviolence? Why do we choose nonviolence? Is this a strategy? Is it a way of life?

Each of these questions challenges a person who represents herself as nonviolent to clarify what that means. This chapter explores these questions in relation to perhaps the most critical question of all: If we are feminists must we also adhere to the principles of nonviolence? In my experience there is not an easy answer to this question but it is important to explore at both the individual and group level.

The theoretical constructs of nonviolence are various, but most include the idea of breaking the cycle of violence by refusing to return violence for violence. Furthermore, the goal is to see the potential for good in one's enemy or oppressor and to challenge that person and yourself to seek truth and justice, thereby setting aside violence. Overall a nonviolent person is committed to the idea that violence against others is wrong and is not the means to human liberation. Moreover, nonviolence is often regarded as the strategy of the oppressed. Those in power may hold superior weaponry, and be willing to fire, but what is the point if eventually no one is left to control. Thus the power of the state to a certain extent depends upon the consent of the governed.

The use of nonviolence can include actions such as rallies and protests of all sizes, as well as organized defense against dictatorial government such as in China in 1989, or attempts to block an invasion such as in Czechoslovakia in 1968. Nonviolent action often includes specific training for the participant on issues such as: nonviolent physical resistance, communicating with arresting officials or antagonists, or the legal basis and ramifications of nonviolence.[2]

The literature suggests that nonviolence is chosen by feminists for many reasons: it is a means of breaking the cycle of violence; it is a moral method of social change which is not passive nor violent; it requires human commitment but not military might; and it seeks to change but not to completely destroy relationships. Employing nonviolence entails breaking from our traditional patterns of resolving conflicts; patterns which distribute power to the strongest and the most violent. In many instances, nonviolence allows feminists to frame the conflict in our own terms. This allows us to point out that military might or muscle do not have to be central to the process of human relationships, nor are they necessary for the functioning of society.

Often part of a feminist agenda is the creation of new structures and systems which are non-hierarchical and nonviolent. This means making decisions by consensus, rotating roles and responsibilities, working as groups or communities for more than just the individual good. For example, the women's peace camp at Greenham Common (Britain) and the Women's Encampment for a Future of Peace and Justice (Romulus, New York), are more than ongoing protests of nuclear weapons and militarization; they are experiments in a new, feminist, non-hierarchal and nonviolent lifestyle (Cook and Kirk, 1983; Cataldo et al., 1987).

There are three terms it is important to expand on in understanding what feminists mean by nonviolence: passivity, self-defense, and suffering. In defining nonviolence which includes women's experiences each of these terms must be discussed. For nonviolence to be persuasive it must attend to the realities of those who adopt it. Moreover, nonviolence is hardly a new concept for women or for feminist action. Pam McAllister cites women as using nonviolent action as early as 1300 B.C. in Egypt when the Hebrew midwives disobeyed the Pharaoh (McAllister, 1988, p. 222).

Often nonviolence, perhaps because it connotes an absence of violence--taken as a lack of action--is believed to be synonymous with passivity. Yet as nonviolent theory and action suggest, nonviolence is both a principle and a technique based on mental and physical activity (Feminism and Nonviolence Study Group, 1983, p. 26). The distinction between passivity and nonviolence is important in showing that adhering to nonviolence does not mean submitting or being a coward.[3] Nonviolence means not accepting oppressive behavior from another, but it also means responding in a way that does not demand submission from the other in return (Deming, 1968, p. 202).

For example, at a workshop on nonviolence, I heard a story about a woman who while walking across Central Park in New York City at dusk, with an armload of books, realized that she was being followed by a man. As he drew near to her and was about to speak, she turned to him and placed the books in his arms, expressing relief that he was there to help with her heavy load. He walked with her silently and at the entrance to her apartment building she took the books and thanked him for his help. Before he walked away he admitted that he had really planned to "mug" her, but that her actions caught him by surprise.

Feminists do not stand alone in their decision to reject passive nonviolence at the level of self-defense. Even the male prophets of nonviolence, such as Gandhi and Martin Luther King Jr., believed that there was a point at which one might be forced to turn to violence in the interest of individual self-defense. Women experience these personally violent situations more often than men. Thus feminists can, and many do, advocate nonviolence within an understanding of its limitations in situations that would lead to self-sacrifice, especially in cases of sexual violence.

In Gandhian nonviolence, the concept of suffering plays an important role. The Feminism and Nonviolence Study Group of Britain points out that while many of the male philosophers advocate voluntarily seeking suffering:

> For women, however, physical and emotional suffering is rarely sought, it is already much more a part of existence. Women are battered, sexually abused, do 60 percent of the world's work and own less than 10 percent of the world's wealth (Feminism and Nonviolence Study Group, 1983, p. 36).

The important issue is not to compare who does the most suffering, but to ask whether nonviolent action based on suffering is predicated on an understanding of the particular experience of women. Furthermore, is current thinking about nonviolence responsive to the more complex subordination of women of color or poor women?

Thus a significant debate remains: should we seek suffering and can or will we suffer for causes that are not our own? And how is seeking suffering to show one's commitment to nonviolence different from the rites of passage to manliness demanded by the military? (Feminism and Nonviolence Study Group, 1983, p. 36). More importantly, what particular training do women require so that we can learn to distinguish between the suffering which comes with the choice of nonviolent action and the submissive bearing of all pain, a habit to which women are so acculturated.

Perhaps feminists choose nonviolence because it is predicated on the integration of theory and practice. Many feminists embrace nonviolence because they believe that in the long run violence will work to the advantage of the status quo and they refuse to play by the rules of the oppressors. Feminists who choose nonviolence find that it changes the rules, and perhaps this is why it is such a revolutionary tactic.

DEBATE #2: The ability/resources that women and men have to be nonviolent

This debate might also be named the question of whether there is such a force in society as the image of the "Moral Mother". There is disagreement among feminists over whether women are inherently more peaceful than men, and men inherently more violently aggressive than women. This debate might also be framed as a question of nature versus nurture.

Building on the traditional Hobbes-Locke debate over whether human nature is basically good or basically bad, the question of the Moral Mother raises whether there is a genital basis for the emergence of good or bad in human beings. The debate is over the validity of traditional dualisms which associated:

women	men
peace	war
passive	active
feminine	masculine

These dualisms entrap women in submissive, inactive, passive roles. They also entrap society into the acceptance of war, as the male half the population is believed to have it in their nature.

The explanation forwarded by some feminists for women's peacefulness is that it lies in their ability to be mothers. In other words, women are believed to have a special biological connection to the significance of life. The argument then follows that the mother is "moral by default" (di Leonardo, 1985, p. 602). Micaela di Leonardo describes this "Moral Mother" image:

...nurturant, compassionate, and politically correct the sovereign, instinctive spokeswoman for all that is living and vulnerable. The Moral Mother represents the vision of women as innately pacifist, and men as innately warmongering. It is she who will take the toys away from the boys (di Leonardo, 1985, p. 602).

This compassionate protection of life, supposedly innate to women is called "preservative love" by Sara Ruddick (1983, p. 479).[4] This love is developed from the responsibility of a mother to preserve and protect her child. Preservative love, Ruddick (1983) argues, is the basis for "women's distinctive peacefulness" (p. 479). Women learn preservative love from being daughters and from being mothers, and thus we learn the pacifism which opposes fundamental military values (Ruddick, 1983, p. 479).

The complexity of this debate is that though the Moral Mother argument is framed as values which are learned, at its base is the biologically-framed assumption that only women, by virtue of being daughters and mothers, can learn the love which preserves life. This appreciation for life is an affirmation of women's social and biological role as life-givers and as mother-nurturers. Beyond these roles women are allowed few sources of self-esteem and power. The question is whether there is a biological determinant which sets those who make the Moral Mother argument apart from those who argue that women are more peaceful because of our socialization. While most often feminists claim some sort of special link between women and peace, there are even feminists who argue that women are not really more peaceful than men.

Three major critiques of the biological determinism of the Moral Mother argument exist in feminist literature. First, it is argued that a stance of biological determinism forces women into the passive role and men into the aggressive role. Sexism is entrenched and encouragement is given to the traditional system of the dominant-submissive hierarchy (diLeonardo, 1985, p. 601). This alignment of morals with a certain gender places morality in a static relationship with humanity.

A second critique of the Moral Mother stance is that there is much contradictory data which show that women do serve in the military, do desire combat roles, and can be taught to be "good soldiers" (Kanogo, 1987; Enloe, 1983; Randall, 1981). Women are enlisting in militaries and joining guerrilla armies because they believe it will achieve the equality of women with men and change the image of woman as passive and weak (diLeonardo, 1985, pp. 602-603). In other words, at least in the short term, there are women who are willing to revoke "preservative love" in the interest of ending sex-based inequalities.

A third argument that can be made against the Moral Mother position is that it leaves out those women who choose not to or cannot be mothers. It also assumes the morality and integrity of the mother no matter what her values, ideology of parenting, or personal experiences might include. The protection of the sanctity of motherhood may very well set women up to be failures when they cannot live up to the myths. Furthermore, in a time when many men and women are transforming their lives to decrease the sexual division of labor in society, the Moral Mother argument excludes the possibility that fathers can be compassionate and can be primary caretakers.

DEBATE #3: The value of military participation for women

Perhaps one of the most intriguing debates is the question of whether women should serve in the military. All participants in the debate seem to agree that war and the military are predominantly male entities, especially combat roles (diLeonardo, 1985, p. 600; Enloe, 1983, p. 150; Randall, 1981, p. 66). In its simplest form the debate is over whether or not the feminist agenda is furthered by women's participation in the military. One of the complexities of the debate is the difference between serving in a state military organization and serving in a revolutionary guerrilla force. At another level the debate is over whether equality with men is the same goal as ending sexist oppression.

Three basic arguments are made to connect women's equality with participation in military organizations:

1.   In many countries, military service is considered a duty in exchange for the right of citizenship.
2.   Women, to be equal to men, must show that we are capable of providing our own defense.
3.   It is thought that the conscription of women would change male and female relations, allowing women more genuine respect and along with that, "eliminate the restrictions on power and mastery that now afflict us" (Ruddick, 1983, p. 482).[5]

Underlying the argument for the feminization of the military is a current of belief in the superior morality of women, and that a military with more women will be more peaceful (Ruddick, 1983, p. 482).

Interviews with women in the FSLN (the Sandinista revolutionary army), and data on the Kenyan women involved in the Mau Mau guerrilla forces reflect this vision that women's participation would garner equality for them. In each case individual women did gain much respect, but there is little evidence that gender relations were significantly transformed. (MacDonald, 1987; Kanogo, 1987; Randall, 1981). Cynthia Enloe suggests that women do experience relative equality in guerrilla forces because in wartime all help is needed. Moreover, a revolutionary military needs to be decentralized, and operate with less formal hierarchy in order to insure mobility and security (Enloe, 1983, p. 160). She notes, however, that as the war progresses, and the revolutionary army is winning, a process of institutionalization begins.

Part of this process is to establish the difference between combat and non-combat (or support) roles. This is a gendered distinction, and as the guerrillas grow into a state military due to power changing hands, women are placed once again in "the rear" which is the non-combat zone (Enloe, 1983, pp. 160-161). Thus women who serve in combat do so in very particular situations, such as in pre-state Israel (Yuval-Davis, 1985, p. 655), in the FSLN (Randall, 1981), or in the Mau Mau uprising (Kanogo, 1987). Nonviolent feminists question if this means that while a woman serves in a combat role the gender distinctions are broken down, or if she merely looked upon temporarily as an honorary male (Enloe, 1987, p. 535).

The primary motivation for state militaries to recruit women is the inadequate and declining pool of manpower. This problem is faced by the military elites in wartime, and also currently in the Western hemisphere due to demographic changes. Government studies in several North Atlantic Treaty Organization (NATO) countries suggest the increasing use of women in militaries can be attributed to three factors: (1) falling birth rate; (2) increasing militarism/the general militarization of society; and (3) the rise of demands for women's equality (Chapkis, 1981, p. 4). Militaries increasingly employ women in administrative (i.e. clerical) positions and in other noncombat jobs. For example, in the Israeli Defense Forces, often cited for having broken down the traditional combat/non-combat sexual division of labor, in the 1980s over two-thirds of the women served as clerical workers (Enloe, 1983, p. 155). Furthermore, the combat roles, which women are excluded from, are at the top of the military hierarchy for gaining job promotions. Since most of the top positions require combat experience, women are left unqualified and often unpromoted (Tiffany, 1981, p. 39).

Thus the women who advocate the "right to fight" and full equality in the military, are faced with many limitations. Wherever a military force has the human resources and weaponry to distinguish "the front" (combat zone) and "the rear" (non-combat zone), women are allocated to the rear in support roles, freeing more men for the front. Women are, whenever possible, excluded from combat, not due to inability or incompetence (Randall, 1981), but because combat is the ultimate test of masculinity and a core piece of the male identity (Enloe, 1983, p. 13). Moreover, men must often be coerced to kill and two motivations the military uses are: (1) if a man does not succeed in basic training, or kill in combat, he is insulted by being called a "woman" or a homosexual (i.e. effeminate); and (2) men are reminded that they are in the military to protect their way of life, and women and children (Michalowski, 1982). Therefore, to allow women in combat would cause this rationalization to be nonsensical.

The misogynous ideology and language of military training, the rampant homophobia of the military lifestyle, the combatant/noncombatant distinction in all but some revolutionary guerrilla forces, and the military's image as a proving ground for masculinity, place the "right to fight" advocates on shaky ground as far as having a strategy for eliminating sexist oppression. There is little to suggest that in the long term women's participation in the military gains anything for feminists as a group. Perhaps in the short-term, particularly in revolutionary forces, military participation earns respect for individual women and helps them to enter decision-making roles, and, certainly most recent revolutions have promised increasing equality for women. However, the success stories are the exception. A big deal is made of the image of a woman guerrilla with a gun on her back and a baby strapped to her front. If this is the path to equality, then as Cynthia Enloe (1983) asks: where are the men with babies strapped to their fronts?

DEBATE #4: The value of nonviolence as a means for ending sexist oppression and empowering women

Since a majority of women experience some level of sexual harassment during their lives, it is useful to analyze the healing process of survivors of sexual assault and rape to clarify why the concept and practice of nonviolence is not necessarily an obvious choice for women.[6] Sexist oppression is more often than not enforced through violent means. What affinity for the nonviolent agenda do women feel when faced with physical, mental, and emotional violation? What do women who have been treated violently need in order to accept a nonviolent strategy?

One of the responses feminists made in the 1970s to the growing incidents of sexual assault and rape was the establishment of rape crisis centers and therapy groups for survivors of sexual violence. A function of these support services is to move the survivor through a process of regaining self-esteem including: the claiming of a positive self-concept, the ability to trust again, and a positive view of her sexuality. The healing process deals with: the elimination of self-blame for the attack(s), the survivor's rejection of her own body, the difficulty many survivors have in separating sex from acts of violence of a sexual nature, and learning how to maintain self-confidence and trusting relationships.

Violent acts of a sexual nature are examples of male dominance which is often associated with male virility and sexuality. Sexual assaults and rapes are acts of domination and attempts to prove control or ownership and ability to dominate. The person assaulted is exploited as a resource for the creation of the individual power of the rapist(s).

The healing process for survivors involves four central issues: control, assertion, boundaries, and trust. The first three are functions of re-establishing one's self-respect and they rely on creating a sense of autonomy. The fourth one is an issue of building relationships and learning (again) to enter into community, a process which limits the type of autonomy one may have. Each of these has implications for the ability of a survivor to accept the philosophy of nonviolence and to participate in nonviolent actions such as civil disobedience.

Nonviolence entails responding in ways that de-escalate a violent situation by breaking the cycle of violence. According to research on rapists by Nicolas Groth (1979), passive reactions to the rapist tend to encourage the escalation of the violence. He found through interviewing rapists that they were most likely to be deterred by either violent responses or other actions which reminded them of their victim's humanity. Much like the soldier in combat, dehumanization of the victim is important in the process of committing such a violent act. The challenge a nonviolent woman faces is how to actively preserve herself in a violent situation without using unnecessary violence.

Concepts like "community" and "interdependence" may trigger fear of vulnerability and raise the issue of control, and the fear of losing it. The mechanisms survivors often use for protection are: establishing boundaries, creating emotional and physical distances from other people, and using anger to prevent the development of communality or interdependence. The idea that nonviolence will eventually elicit a positive response from the aggressor may be especially difficult for a survivor of assault, rape, or torture to rely on in a violent situation.

Furthermore, principled nonviolent activists differ over at what point self-defense becomes a rationalization for violent responses to violent aggression. The protection mechanisms of survivors against further victimization are based on separation and distrust. Nonviolence is built on community and trust. A feminist agenda which through nonviolent principles, challenges autonomy and emphasizes interdependence and trust without recognizing how difficult this may be in practice, can be very threatening to survivors. Until a survivor reaches a point of regaining self-respect and a sense of respect from others, which assure her of an autonomous self, how can she participate in a relationship of interdependence such as that required by nonviolent confrontations. As long as the inequality of women and men exists, the decisions that women make about being nonviolent are different from those that men make. This is true for any social groups that are in relations of inequality.

Differences Between Individual and Group Action

Where active nonviolence and feminist activism are concerned there may be a difference between how we act as individuals and the actions we take within our identity as a member of a specific group or movement. Feminism and nonviolence are both methods for political action, that is action which takes place in the public sphere. The feminist statement that the personal is political means that to speak of personal experiences is a means of finding patterns of oppression which have wider social significance. What we do to bring social change as a group, whether the actions are by individuals or en masse, is a political action and the framework for our vision.

While choosing to live a principled nonviolent lifestyle may seem like an individual act, it is a political action as part of a group. That group consists of those who not only speak of what an alternative system of relationships might entail, but also attempt to live that future in the present. At this juncture of my argument the issue of self-defense becomes relevant. To what extent will a principled nonviolent feminist maintain a sense of individual security?

If I am sexually assaulted, though my politics may be about an ideal future, my present situation demands a reaction of self-defense that may include my taking violent action. An individual rape victim does not have the public visibility of the protesters in the Civil Rights Movement in the United States; an act of nonviolence in the moment of attack does not make her heroic and more moral to the public eye. Moreover, in the one-to-one situation of sexual assault it may well be that the only not-violent act possible is submission and not nonviolence. I must emphasize the distinction between acting without violence and acting nonviolently. The latter includes a much narrower range of actions as specified by years of development of theory and social action techniques.

Another conclusion that can be drawn is that while it may be hard to act nonviolently alone, we can act politically with nonviolence (in affinity with a group), against sexual assault and rape. At the political level a range of nonviolent actions are available. Public outcry, marches, court cases, rape crisis centers, anti-rape education, and community safe houses are ways to use nonviolent action against sexual assault and rape. It is also possible for self-defense training to be a political act. For instance in the 1970s the wave of self-defense courses for women were in part individually practical, but they also contained the political statement that women will not take anymore violence against our bodies.

It is probably safe to say that when a woman is attacked she does not take the time to consider how her reactions fit the wider political agenda. This provides an important distinction between self-defense and an act of civil disobedience. In the latter case one may be in a psychological situation akin to those of sexual assault, but there is a sense in civil disobedience of making a political choice to act with a group toward a political purpose. On the contrary, rape and sexual assault happen during daily functioning, and thus one's immediate response is not necessarily in the wider range of political action.

Group membership and a sense of political purpose in the public sphere are important factors in distinguishing between specific instances of self-defense which may require violent reaction and the use of nonviolent action techniques to achieve social and political changes. Feminists, and women in general, live an experience which can elucidate more precisely the relationship of self-defense and nonviolence. This is an important contribution since to date most literature on nonviolence is very nebulous about self-defense and what it includes. In the future we need more analysis among advocates of nonviolence about the issue of self-defense; the experiences of women could provide an important voice in such a discussion.

Ends and Means In A Feminist Approach

In any discussion of social change, consideration of the means and ends of a movement is critical. How various feminists differ over means and ends is clearly raised in the selection of strategy. Besides differences in whether we decide to act violently or nonviolently, there are differences over the specifics of short-term and long-term goals. Thus while all feminists might agree that our ultimate goal is to end sexist oppression, what we envision that statement as meaning may differ dramatically from one feminist to the next.

When sexist oppression is defined as the prevalence of inequality between men and women in access to resources, power, and privilege, the ends may be stated as "equality." It is obvious that except for perhaps in the realms of emotions and parenting, current society affords men, especially heterosexual white men, the upper end of what is desirable as a safe and comfortable lifestyle. Thus the claim made by some feminists for "equality" means forwarding women's entry into the male system. However, "equality" in a male-dominated system is an end which can only be achieved by means which require women to act and think as males.

If sexist oppression is defined as one part of upholding the myth of male superiority, the ends brought by the elimination of the myth are very different from women becoming male. The ends envision social transformation to a society without a hierarchy of difference and without group-defined domination. Those ends do not re-invent white patriarchy, replace it with patriarchy of some other color, or create some version of matriarchy. Rather these are long-term ends of changed attitudes and social transformation. The means to these ends require work on two levels. First we must try to live the future in the present to make it functional and to gain social acceptance of the ideas. Second we must take action in the present that makes the present itself a more egalitarian society. For instance as discussed above, living nonviolently may at times raise a direct tension with providing for individual safety. In other words, we cannot allow ourselves to be sexually assaulted or raped on the premise that to react violently in self-defense threatens the achievement of our ends. At the same time we cannot mythologize violent responses as nonviolent activity. The important nonviolent means to ending rape and sexual assault are those that place the issues in the public sphere where political action can be taken to eliminate them.

The means of a nonviolent feminist are a revolutionary program for social transformation. It is critical that our movement is clear on what is meant by sexist oppression, what are the ends, and what are relevant and acceptable means. What we envision as our ends will make a crucial difference in how we choose our means and in how long we expect it will take to liberate all women.

Conclusions

This study of the literature on women and war and women and nonviolence leads to seven important conclusions in relation to the four debates outlined above. The first conclusion is that feminists should be concerned about how nonviolence is defined. In particular we should ask about who formulated the definition, and consider whether it reflects the experiences of women in all of our diversity. Moreover, our experiences should be considered important resources for the development of nonviolent theory and action.

A second conclusion is that the argument for the Moral Mother, or the natural, biologically located peacefulness of women is a deterministic approach to understanding the relationship of gender and militarism. Moreover, there is evidence, such as women's military service, and changing conceptions of fathering which contradict that women are a natural and exclusive source of preservative love. Therefore claiming a close relationship of women to peace is not irrelevant, but it should be done carefully and in the context of ideas about gender socialization.

Thirdly, the increasing militarism of women suggests that while the Moral Mother argument is not that persuasive, there is a need for nonviolent feminists to convince women of the importance of rejecting military values. In addition, it is important for the furtherance of the feminist agenda that women refuse to support the military in any way. This conclusion rests on the acknowledgement that militaries are entrenched in proving masculinity and protecting patriarchy.

The fourth conclusion is that as far gaining women's equality permanently and on a wide scale, military service has proven to be a waste of energy and a dead end for most women. The military is based on hierarchy and systems of achievement which value masculinity. As such the military is yet one more institution where women can succeed only by way of becoming honorary males. Therefore we must be careful to make clear what we mean by "equality."

A fifth conclusion is that in creating a feminist understanding of nonviolence as theory and in practice, it is important that we develop language and techniques that empower women. We must build confidence that to choose nonviolence is not to choose inaction, but to choose a practical and revolutionary tactic which with determination will lead us toward social transformation.

Sixth, the feminist standpoint that the personal is political is useful for nonviolent feminists in clarifying the difference between our actions for individual safety and our actions in affinity with nonviolent feminism. We are not the first to query over the issue of self-defense, however, we may well have the most experience and resources for analyzing the prevalent concerns. Distinguishing between the individual and group oriented action provides a greater significance for adhering to a principled nonviolent lifestyle because then the action is undoubtably public and political.

Finally, the diversity of ends and means among feminist approaches to ending sexist oppression suggest that it is critical that activists and theoreticians are clear about definitions and strategies. The discussion of ends and means and the healthy tensions that can evolve are positive for both feminist and peace movements. We must think practically about what means will achieve our desired ends. What we lack most of all at this time are the details of our preferred future and how we will actually achieve social transformation.

ENDNOTES

[1] All feminists should make a point of reading African-American and Latina feminist literature. A good place to start is with Feminist Theory: From Margin to Center by Bell Hooks (1984), MA: South End Press.

[2] In The Politics of Nonviolent Action, parts 1-3, Gene Sharp at great length details nonviolent action techniques as well as case histories of nonviolent protests. The Politics of Nonviolent Action, (1973), MA: Porter Sargent.

[3] Gandhi helped clarify this issue by referring to his action as satyagraha, literally meaning "truth force" by which he implied the idea of "clinging to the truth" which produces an active image of nonviolence.

[4] "Preservative love is a caring for or treasuring of creatures whose well-being is at risk" (Ruddick, 1983, p. 479).

[5] See the previous section for the arguments about gender-specific morality.

[6] The information in this section is drawn from informal conversations with survivors of sexual assault and members of the anti-rape movement in the United States.

REFERENCES

Cataldo, Mima, Ruth Putter, Bryna Fireside, Elaine Lytel. (1987). The Women's Encampment for a Future of Peace and Justice. PA: Temple University Press.

Chapkis, W. (ed.). (1981). Loaded Questions: Women in the Military. Amsterdam and Washington, D.C.: Transnational Institute.

Cook, Alice and Gwyn Kirk. (1983). Greenham Women Everywhere. Boston: South End Press.

Deming, Barbara. (1968). On Revolution and Equilibrium. Liberation, February.

DiLeonardo, Michela. (1985). Morals, Mothers, and Militarism: Anti-Militarism and Feminist Theory, Feminist Studies, 2, 599-617.

Dworkin, Andrea. (1976). Our Blood. New York: Harper and Row.

Enloe, Cynthia. (1983). Does Khaki Become You?: The Militarization of Women's Lives. Boston: South End Press.

Enloe, Cynthia. (1987). Feminists Thinking About War, Militarism, and Peace. In Beth B. Hess and Myra Marx Ferree (eds.), Analyzing Gender: A Handbook of Social Science Research. Newbury Park: Sage.

Feminism and Nonviolence Study Group. (1983). Piecing It Together: Feminism and Nonviolence. Devon, UK: Feminism and Nonviolence Study Group.

Groth, Nicolas. (1979). Men Who Rape: The Psychology of the Offender. New York: Plenum Press.

Hooks, Bell. (1984). Feminist Theory: From Margin to Center. Boston: South End Press.

Kanogo, Tabitha. (1987). Kikuyu Women and the Politics of Protest: Mau Mau. In Sharon Macdonald, Pat Holden, and Shirley Ardener (Eds.). Images of Women in Peace and War: Cross-cultural and Historical Perspectives. Edited by UK: Macmillian.

Macdonald, Sharon. (1987). "Drawing the Lines: Gender, Peace and War: An Introduction" In Sharon Macdonald, Pat Holden, and Shirley Ardener (Eds.). Images of Women in Peace and War: Cross-cultural and Historical Perspectives. Edited by UK: Macmillian.

McAllister, Pam. (1988). You Can't Kill The Spirit. PA: New Society.

Michalowski, Helen. (1982). The Army Will Make A Man Out of You. In Pam McAllister (ed.) Reweaving the Web of Life: Feminism and Nonviolence. PA: New Society.

Pierson, Ruth Roach. (1987). 'Did Your Mother Wear Army Boots?': Feminist Theory and Women's Relation to War, Peace, and Revolution. In Sharon Macdonald, Pat Holden, and Shirley Ardener (Eds.). Images of Women in Peace and War: Cross-cultural and Historical Perspectives. Edited by UK: Macmillian.

Randall, Margaret. (1981). Sandino's Daughter's: Testimonies of Nicaraguan Women in Struggle. Edited by Lynda Yanz. Canada: New Star Books.

Ruddick, Sara. (1983). Pacifying the Forces: Drafting Women in the Interests of Peace. Signs, 8 471-489.

Sharp, Gene. (1973). The Politics of Nonviolent Action: Parts 1-3. Boston: Sargent Press.

Sheehan, Joanne. (1986). "Nonviolence: A Feminist Vision and Strategy", War Resisteis League publication.

Stiehm, Judith (Ed.). (1983). Women and Men's Wars. Oxford and New York: Pergamon Press.

Tiffany, Jennifer. (1981). Equal Opportunity Trap. In W. Chapkis (ed.) Loaded Questions: Women in the Military. Amsterdam and Washington, D.C.: Transnational Institute.

Yuval-Davis, Nira. (1985). Front and Rear: The Sexual Division of Labor in the Israeli Army. Feminist Studies, 2 649-675.

CHAPTER 16

The Center for Nonviolence:
Working Toward Gender, Racial and Economic Justice

Richard L. Johnson

The Center for Nonviolence in Ft. Wayne, Indiana has been offering nonviolent alternatives to battery, rape, pornography and militarism since 1981. In the early years, as Men for Nonviolence, the focus was primarily on community education and weekly groups for batterers. In 1985, women began offering groups for formerly battered women, and the name was changed to the Center for Nonviolence. In 1987, the youth program began, which now offers groups for children and young people from six to 17, both males and females, both perpetrators and survivors of domestic violence.

Those of us who began Men for Nonviolence in 1981 had all been active in social justice movements, and most had been meeting in a men's consciousness raising group, patterned after women's CR groups, since the mid-seventies. We began in the late seventies to offer classes on what men could do against rape, and we participated in actions to dramatize governmental indifference to the oppression of women, but we wanted to develop new ways to counter personal and institutional sexism in our community. I went to a Men and Masculinity conference in Milwaukee in October, 1979 and met men from RAVEN in St. Louis, which offered groups for batterers based on a pro-feminist analysis of domestic violence. I brought the idea back to Ft. Wayne, we discussed it at length in 1980, and we began offering services in 1981.

From the beginning, we worked with women at the Ft. Wayne Women's Shelter and the Rape Crisis Center as well as with other feminists involved in a number of different organizations. We saw ourselves as men who wished to take personal responsibility to end, or at least reduce, male violence and other forms of patriarchal power. And we believed that rape, battery and pornography, which are primarily perpetrated by men, were connected as well to militarism, another patriarchal form of power and control that deforms the lives of men, women and children, both civilians and soldiers.[1] Most of us had been active in peace groups during the Vietnam war, when women had begun to confront us about our sexism. We believed then, and we continue to believe now, that love and community are essential to nonviolent change. As Martin Luther King, Jr. stated, "at the core of nonviolence stands the principle of love."[2] Gandhi spent many years in ashrams in both South Africa and India seeking to ground his work in a community based on **ahimsa**, and King sought as well to create the "blessed community," where Christians and non-Christians could work together toward an end of violence.

Over the years, we have found many impediments to the creation of love and community, both within ourselves and the men, women, and children we seek to serve. In this paper I discuss the three impediments that divide us the most-- gender, race, and economic class--, and I examine our successes and failures in working toward gender, racial, and economic justice. I focus primarily on the present, with some references to the past, and on the future.

As a participant/observer at the Center, I have thought about and discussed the issues raised here with others many times over the years. Recently I interviewed the five full-time staff members and eight part-time co-facilitators of groups for men, women, and young people.[3] As a teacher/researcher in Peace Studies, I believe we need many more case studies of groups engaged in nonviolent action. It seems to me that this examination of the Center for Nonviolence can be useful because the issues of gender, race, and economic class are important in most nonviolent struggle and because there are also unique features of this program. To my knowledge, the Center for Nonviolence is the only organization in the United States that combines an effort to end domestic violence and militarism. As a result of our community's response to our work, we have focused more on domestic violence in Ft. Wayne than on any other form of violence; but we are also engaged in solidarity work with peace and justice activists in other countries as well, as I discuss below.

Even though I am analyzing gender, race and economic class separately, they are, of course, interrelated. Studies have shown that all three factors play a role in violence. Elaine Ciualla Kamarck, a senior fellow at the Progressive Policy Institute, cites a study that found "the absence of the father is more strongly related to the propensity to engage in violent criminal behavior than either race or poverty."[4] That mothers are disproportionately responsible for the care of children is a clear result of family gender roles. But economic class is central as well, for William Julius Wilson connects the number of fatherless families to economic trends that have led to high joblessness among black men. And these economic trends are in part a result of racism that places a majority of African-American men and women in this country into an economic underclass.[5]

Gender Justice

Social perceptions about gender create one of the deepest human divisions. Male-dominated societies have defined women as the archetypal Other for millennia, and male violence continues to be one of the primary ways that men enforce women's lower social status.[6] Many batterers in our program tell us that the only people they have ever abused are their partners. They give us that information to convince us that they are naturally nonviolent, but their partners are so difficult to live with that their violence is justifiable (or not really violence at all, since "she made me do it"). We respond that our training as males leads us to use violence to control women and that blaming the victims of our violence is simply another strategy to deny responsibility for our own actions.

On an individual and societal level, it is women who have initiated and continue to mount the central challenge to male violence. There would be no institutional response to battery if battered women did not report the violence against themselves and their children and if women had not founded shelters and other institutions to protect women and children and to force the perpetrators to enter programs for batterers or to go to jail. Patriarchal attitudes that justify violence against women continue to be virulent in our society, and they influence the minds of men and women.[7]

Paula Wilhauck, one of the co-facilitators at the Center for Nonviolence, dramatized how powerfully patriarchal ideas affect our interpretation of events in our lives. A few years ago, her former husband and she were having an argument late one night in their car. He beat and threatened to kill her, but she was able to get away from him and hide in a deep ditch next to the road. She walked several miles to their house to protect her children, but when she arrived, he attacked her with a knife. If her daughter had not intervened, he would have killed her.

But she did not question his actions. He was the man, and she had internalized the belief that "man is my God." It was not until she joined a women's AA group and other support groups, including one at the Center for Nonviolence, that she understood that she had a right as a human being to be treated with respect.

The founders of Men for Nonviolence were white, college educated men, mostly professionals, who were profoundly concerned about gender-based violence. We believed that we could seek advice and counsel from feminists--both professionals in area agencies and the women with whom we lived--, and that any blindnesses we might have had on gender issues would be overcome through our great desire to listen to and learn from women. We were wrong. Patriarchal assumptions run so deep through our social institutions and through our own minds that it is not possible, in our collective understanding, to confront and reduce male violence effectively within a male organization with even the best intentions among its members.

One of the most serious problems we face as male co-facilitators of batterers groups is our tendency to bond with the men. We were shocked to discover that we could fall prey to male bonding in our groups. Since we had been working for years on gender justice, we believed that we would be immune to batterers' denigration of women. However, meeting as we do for 29 weeks with men, and coming only rarely in direct contact with the women they battered, it is far too easy for us to be taken in by their perspectives on what is going on in their lives.

POWER AND CONTROL CHART

The Center for Nonviolence, in its networking with other programs and especially in its connections with the National Coalition Against Domestic Violence, has implemented a program of monitoring our groups by formerly battered women to alert male co-facilitators to male bonding. We make an audiocassette of 30 to 60 minutes of our batterers groups which is then passed on to a group of formerly battered women. They listen to the tapes and write up a report which they then return to the co-facilitators.

Most of the men co-facilitating groups acknowledged fears when this procedure was introduced in 1988. However, even though our egos are occasionally bruised in the process, we have discovered that we learn a great deal from reading the monitors' reports. Formerly battered women have a perspective on batterers that has proven indispensable to our work. They know batterers as no one else can. After co-facilitators have read a certain number of these reports, we begin to see the patterns in our responses to the men that we need to change. And with time, we begin to develop what John Murphy Beams calls the "inner monitor," a part of us that senses how formerly battered women might react in a given situation with batterers.

Two of the monitors, Paula Wilhauck and Betty Meriweather, told me that listening to the batterers groups has been painful to them. Both had flashbacks to the violence they suffered, especially as they began to do the monitoring. However, Betty explained that as the batterers begin to accept some nonviolent approaches, "the gradual progress sustains me, encourages me that they are changing. I think it's working." Betty and Paula believe that monitoring has contributed to healing from the battery that they experienced.

In 1988, men and women at the Center for Nonviolence went through training conducted by the Duluth Domestic Abuse Intervention Project (DAIP) which has become a central element in our work with survivors of battery and with batterers. Barbara Hart of the Pennsylvania Coalition Against Domestic Violence, Ellen Pence, Michael Paymar and others of the DAIP developed educational materials based on a feminist analysis of male violence and on Paulo Friere's methods of education which focus on learning ways to see and interpret the world from the perspective of the oppressed. These activists asked formerly battered women to describe the tactics of power and control that batterers used against them as well as the strategies that they used to liberate themselves from this abuse.

I believe that the methods they used and their results can serve as a model for any group that wishes to come up with nonviolent alternatives to oppression. They discovered that batterers use their physical violence in conjunction with other forms of verbal, emotional and mental abuse, which they summarize in the following Power and Control Chart:[8]

As Pence and Paymar state in their curriculum guide, "Battering is an intentional act used to gain power and control over another person. Physical abuse in only one part of a whole system of abusive behavior which an abuser uses against his partner. Violence is never an isolated behavior." The educational materials for women describe men's power and control tactics and then provide concrete strategies for women's empowerment. The materials for batterers describe these tactics and then seek to give them practical ways to overcome their abuse. The DAIP curriculum includes videos of men's power and control, well-formulated control logs to help batterers analyze their abusive acts, and videos of formerly battered women who talk about their experience.

Within the structure of the Center for Nonviolence, we seek to recognize women's central role in defining their oppression and in the process of liberating themselves from it. Therefore, our Coordinating Panel, which makes decisions along with the Men's and Women's Collectives, always includes a majority of women. Moreover, since we believe that our work involves confronting oppression of people of color and homosexuals, the Coordinating Panel has always included women and men of color as well as gays and lesbians.

The Women's Collective and the Youth Program have transformed the Center for Nonviolence. Although there continue to be more groups for men each week than for women or youth, the two newer programs are growing steadily. The presence of women and young people is a constant reminder for us in the men's groups that male centered approaches to domestic violence are limiting. For men, an end to power and control over women and children involves, at least on some levels, a loss. For women and children, it is incredibly liberating to overcome male dominance. It can be a joy for men to stop hurting others, but it is an even greater joy to share the process of change with those whom we had been oppressing.

As Abbie Winston, Director of the Youth Program, told me, her program is unique at the Center for Nonviolence in that it is the only one that includes women, men and youths. Even though members of the Men's and Women's Collectives are working to end gender-based oppression, that oppression continues to be so pervasive that we must meet in separate collectives to address men's abuse and to develop strategies for liberation. But since women and men abuse young people and since both are responsible for finding ways to end that abuse, it is appropriate that the Youth Program spearheads the efforts of women, men and youth to work together toward the kind of community that we all long for.

Initially, we men hoped that we would help form a critical mass of nonviolent men within our program who would then contribute to a nonviolent society. However, few men who have completed our program show any interest in continuing to work with us. The Women's Collective and the Youth Program have been more successful in their efforts to interest women and young people from their groups in becoming co-facilitators.

Racial Justice

At the Center for Nonviolence we are pioneers in the area of gender justice. Not only have we done considerable work in our community and Northeast Indiana, but also we have presented papers and workshops at national conferences in the area of domestic violence. However, our work on racial justice has been more recent and less successful. One of our five full-time staff members and an increasing number of co-facilitators are African-American, but we have not yet created a coordinated, comprehensive response to racism in the community or in our own organization.

And yet many participants in our groups are women, men and youth of color. Among women of color, it is primarily African-American women who are reporting domestic violence and taking the risk of turning their partners into a system that they themselves know to be racist. As Betty Meriweather stated, "a lot of times an African American woman is the bread winner, the backbone of the family. On the one hand, there's a man who wants to be the head of the family, but he's not pulling his weight. She's hearing from other African American women that she doesn't need to take this any more. So she says, 'I'll call the Law.'"

Betty explained that a growing number of African American women are coming together in churches, clubs, other social settings and at work. They are talking about the level of domestic violence in their lives and about alternatives, including reporting the violence to the prosecuting attorney, sending their partners to the Center for Nonviolence, and getting counseling themselves at the Center and other agencies. A formerly battered woman herself, Betty said that she hears more African American women state, "We have seen too many homicides against women of all races. It's a reality. If I don't do anything, I'll be on the slab next. I've got to think of my kids."

The Center for Nonviolence has formed a women of color group, which so far includes only African American women, but they have made contacts with Asian and Latina women who have expressed an interest in joining them later on as they formulate more specific goals. They are working on proposals to increase the proportion of people of color in our groups. They see the need for more outreach so that the work at the Center for Nonviolence is more visible in their communities.

The Youth Program has initiated a young women of color group for 13 to 17 year olds which is co-facilitated by African American women. The co-facilitators have told me that the participants in their groups, who are mentally and emotionally girls in women's bodies, have suffered an enormous amount of violence which they often believe to be their responsibility. A key to this group-- and it is the philosophy in most of our groups--is to create an atmosphere where everyone is treated with respect and where the co-facilitators are not seen as authority figures which the young women must obey. Rather, they work together on problems that they all face, or have faced, in their lives. Betty Meriweather and Abbie Winston, who have both co-facilitated this group, have said that young women of color are much more likely to share personal experiences in this group than in a group where they are in a minority.

Economic Justice

Batterers come from all socio-economic groups. However, the men who enter our program--whether through court referrals or on a voluntary basis--are disproportionately from low to middle income brackets. As Earl Hamilton asked rhetorically, "Where are the men in the pinstriped suits?" A smattering of doctors and dentists (but no lawyers) have come into our groups as batterers in the last 11 years, but we know full well that many men from high income brackets batter and that they are generally adept at avoiding the consequences of their actions from the criminal "justice" system. Everyone who comes into our groups--abusers and abused, men, women, and youth--understands this inequity.

And yet it remains and seems to be getting worse. Our efforts toward racial and gender justice give us hope at times that we are making a difference; but the economic divisions in this country seem so deep and intractable that it is easy to believe that we will never be able to approach economic justice.

We have always sought to be just in our fees and in our salaries. Initially, the Men's Collective underwrote the program until the fees we generated exceeded our expenses. As we began to get paid, we divided the pay by the number of hours we worked, leaving a certain amount for additional expenses. In the early years, we were not strict or consistent in demanding fees for services. But with time we learned that the men would not pay unless it was required.

We use a sliding scale of fees according to a man's income, and we remove a man from the program or stipulate that his attendance does not count toward completion of the program if he does not pay for his groups as agreed in his contract. Fees are less for women and youth, and payment schedules are not always strictly enforced. With batterers, we consider timely payment to be an integral part of their accountability; whereas with women and youth, we recognize that their economic status makes it even more difficult for them to pay than it is for the men.

If men do not have sufficient money to pay at all, they can attend our Prosperity Group in lieu of paying in the first phase of the batterers program and they can perform community service in the second phase. The Prosperity Group is unique in the batterers program because it is the only group that focuses on the men as victims of an unjust system and how they can overcome this oppression. John Murphy Beams, who co-facilitates it with Sox Sperry, said that a sense of esprit is often developed because it is easier in this group for the men to be open and honest. John believes that the unemployed men carry over this connection with the co-facilitators into the batterers groups.

A major dilemma for us is that fees are not sufficient to pay for the services we provide. We therefore seek grants from foundations, and we have generally been successful; but they do not fund ongoing programs, only start-up grants, and the combination of fees and grants is not sufficient to provide reasonable salaries for full-time or part-time workers. Until recently, the hourly wage was equally low for all of us, whatever we do--secretarial services or directing programs, full-time or part-time staff. However, the Coordinating Panel decided recently to pay full-time staff $10/hour and the part-time workers $8.50/hour.

Initially, the low wages were not a serious problem. As privileged intelligentsia, we could afford to live frugally or to make up for the low wages with other income. But as we become more a social service agency and less purely a social action group, the need for decent wages becomes more critical. The work is rewarding (though quite taxing at times), but especially family members of Center staff have complained that they should not suffer because we are underpaid, no matter how fulfilling the work may be.

Cliff Files believes that our low wages make it difficult to attract African-Americans into our program because (1) there are not enough professional women and men of color in Ft. Wayne as a result of racism and (2) they can find employment with much higher salaries.

Evaluation and Proposed Improvements in the Future

The Center for Nonviolence is a vibrant organization of practical visionaries who are working hard to create a modicum of justice in an American rustbelt city with deeply ingrained injustices of gender, race and class. Domestic violence, racial bigotry and economic inequality are such powerful social forces that, as agents of social change, we feel at times as if we are a tiny group on a small island about to be engulfed by towering waves of violence and indifference.

The feelings of inadequacy do come in waves. Recently, a man who had completed the program some months ago killed two of his little children and raped a young woman before he killed himself. As we looked back at his participation in our program, we recognized on certain levels how dangerous he was, but we also made mistakes. He should have been referred to a group for sexual abusers, and he may well have been able to hide some of his abuse from us because he was externally so cooperative and because, as one of the few fairly well-to-do men in the program, his social skills and status may have masked some of his abuse while he was in the program. We have changed our procedures for participants with a history of sexual abuse.

The Persian Gulf War was painful as well, for as many other social activists in this country, we worked hard to shed light on governmental lies and media complicity, and we were swept away by the tide of ignorance, anti-Hussein rhetoric and military success. We presented an excellent program on nonviolent civil disobedience which a local television station covered. And then we saw how it was presented to the public! Short clips of us interspersed with violent protesters in other cities, intercutting to calm, reasonable local officials voicing justifiable concern about the dangers and costs that the community would have to face as a result of our lawless, irresponsible agitation.

But as Gandhi stated and demonstrated in his satyagraha campaigns, to be effective, we must focus our attention on our own nonviolence and on what we can do, not on opponents or on what we cannot do. From this perspective, we have made real progress in working for gender, racial, and economic justice. From the beginning, we have dedicated ourselves to ending domestic violence. We have worked with several hundred batterers, and although we have not researched the results of this work, they have been presented with a fuller understanding of their violence and with a number of nonviolent alternatives. Partner contacts, which women at the Center conduct at regular intervals, indicate that many men have reduced and/or stopped battering and other forms of power and control over them.

In the Spring of 1988, I conducted all eight of the batterers groups one week while the other co-facilitators were out of town at a workshop. I asked all the participants what helped them the most in our groups. Every man stated that he had learned the most from the other men in their day-by-day struggle to be nonviolent. In a recent article, John Murphy Beams wrote: "When questioned at an exit interview, it is the moments of intimate sharing and story telling with other men which they tenderly, fondly recall of their 29-week experience."[9]

As Sox Sperry stated, the original vision of Men for Nonviolence, to transform men into nonviolent activists, has proven illusory. Even though the work with men remains central to our long-term goals and even though we have evidence that many men do reduce their violence, the Center for Nonviolence is focusing more and more on providing "safe breathing space for women and children."

Sox believes that the Center is providing a similar function for those of us who are peaceworkers. It is a place for people who believe in nonviolence and who need to be together on a regular basis to work and to live without the oppression of the dominant culture. Other peace and social justice organizations with which we have participated have not given us a consistent breathing space, and many were not able to form the kind of sustaining community that we have at the Center for Nonviolence.

It is particularly rewarding that more young people are coming on staff to work with us. Many have had to face an enormous amount of violence in their homes, at school, and on the streets, and yet they have less power than adults to create safe spaces for themselves. Clay Blackburn, a 17 year-old who entered the Youth Program four years ago as a participant and who has been co-facilitating groups for the last two years, told me that he is laughed at and shunned by many males his age because of his work on nonviolence. In high school, he has a lot of female friends, but it is only at the Center for Nonviolence where he can find a group of men, women and youth his age who respect and understand him.

The Center for Nonviolence is becoming more multi-cultural, especially in the Youth Program and the Women's Collective. Across the racial divide that is defined by our society and that seems to be getting wider, there is "a sense of community," as Abbie Winston stated. "I can trust. My friends here are available when I just need to cry. No one will use things against me. I can bring my children in here."

We are increasing our solidarity with peace workers in other countries.

Many of us from the Center for Nonviolence went to Nicaragua in the eighties to support the revolutionary change there, and the rest of us sent along material aid. We paid staff members their regular salaries while they were in Nicaragua.

We are currently working with Dr. Juan Almendares, a medical doctor and a major figure in the Honduran peace and social justice movement. He has visited us three times in Ft. Wayne, and we are planning to help him build a new medical clinic in Honduras. He has told us that he is learning from our work with domestic violence, and we have learned a great deal from him about poverty, multinational corporate exploitation, environmental degradation, the U.S. military presence, and the death squads in Honduras, which are all interrelated.

One of the most hopeful new programs at the Center for Nonviolence is AHIMSA, a group of men and women who are working to provide information about non-military careers for young people, especially in the high schools where the military are actively seeking new recruits. Begun during the Persian Gulf War, AHIMSA is now working to obtain grants to fund part-time co-coordinators who would help expand its educational efforts.

There are three major areas of improvement that co-facilitators have suggested for the future which I wish to share at this time. I have reported other more specific suggestions directly to the Center for Nonviolence.

(1) We must recruit co-facilitators whose experience is as close as possible to that of the men, women and young people with whom we work, especially in race, economic origin and the experience of battery.

We must talk about and face racism on staff so that we can understand racial oppression as well as we understand gender oppression and so that we can recruit more women and men of color. As Cliff Files stated, the first step is allotting enough time to talk at length about racism and about the incredible accomplishments of women and men of color. As I see it, white staff members are supportive of people of color and eager to create racial justice, but most of us are ignorant of how pervasive racism is in our society and our own psyches, and we do not know the most effective ways to work against racism with participants in our groups.

Rheba Knox conducted a workshop a few years ago on racism, and although I had sought to understand racism in this country over the years, I was shocked to discover how much racial harassment that she and other African-American professionals faced on a daily basis here in Ft. Wayne. I knew that large numbers of women and men of color were oppressed, but I had thought that "the talented tenth" was able to create lives in which racism was no longer a cause of daily discrimination. But in fact, across the board, racism is hurting all people of color in this country every day. And according to Cliff Files, it has grown in the Reagan and Bush years. In the late seventies in Baltimore, he worked with 40 African American professionals who had received good jobs in a large corporation as a result of affirmative action hiring practices. But in the eighties, most had lost those jobs and few could find comparable work.

As Abbie Winston emphasized, we must have "a more diverse staff. . . .

Culturally, people are different. It's a lot more comfortable to connect with someone who looks like them." We have a significant proportion of African-Americans coming through the program, and we will, I believe, have many more Latinos and Asians as women in those communities break free of male dominance. We must reduce the number of white professionals co-facilitating groups and increase the number of people of color in all aspects of our work. The Youth Program is paving the way, and the Women's Collective is making strides, but at present, the Men's Collective is lagging behind, especially in the early phases of the program where we have the highest percentage of men of color.

It is also a challenge for many lower to middle income blue collar workers to believe that their experience and that of a professor or a lawyer are congruent enough for them to learn from us. It is essential in all our groups that participants feel connected with the co-facilitators and that they can feel commonalities more than differences. But much of their experience teaches them that economic class is an unbridgeable barrier to equal human communication.

It is also true that batterers are more likely to learn from former batterers and that battered women are more likely to learn from formerly battered women. The Women's Collective and the Youth Program are increasing the number of survivors of violence, but we have not been successful in recruiting former batterers in our groups. We know full well that it is difficult to accomplish, but I believe we need to redouble our efforts.

(2) Several co-facilitators stated that we need to take our skills and commitment to social justice out into the community. To be sure, we have conducted workshops and given talks in the community from the very beginning, and we are receiving more requests to come into the schools. However, most of our group work has been at the Center for Nonviolence. In his discussion of the problems that young African American males face, Earl Hamilton suggested that they are "trapped in the inner city. You've got to go into their arena. They feel safe there. They find strength in violence. We need blacks who are willing to go to them."

It seems to me that all participants are more likely to hear us if we can co-facilitate groups in their communities, particularly with local leaders. One of our most promising programs is doing just that. We have received a HUD grant to work with women and young people in urban housing projects. Center for Nonviolence staff members have gone into the projects and are helping residents there to organize themselves to make their lives safer and more fulfilling. A gardening project, an onsite store run by young people, and a leadership training session for local "court captains" have been initiated.

(3) Our work at the Center for Nonviolence would be enhanced if we were to get a grant to research the effectiveness of our programs. To what extent have participants changed as a result of working with us? What do they feel to be the most effective aspects of our programs, and what simply did not work for them? Careful research into the past can be crucial as we choose how to shape the future.

Conclusion

The Center for Nonviolence has grown and matured considerably since its inception in 1981. In 1992, we would certainly not accept as co-facilitators that ragtag group of minimally trained, inexperienced idealists for gender justice. The diversity of our current programs as well as the creativity and rich experience of our staff give me hope for the future. However, like most social justice groups, the Center for Nonviolence oscillates between innovation and routinized activity. It has had incredible bursts of creative transformation, and it has then fallen into habits that continue beyond their usefulness. Several co-facilitators feel now that the Center is resting too comfortably on its laurels. Beth Murphy Beams and Rick Ritter, two of our most experienced staff members, believe that significant changes are needed.

Rick stated that as a collective, we talk about changes, but we fail to put them into practice. Beth told me that we are no longer on the cutting edge of nonviolent work in Ft. Wayne: "We are at a place of transition. The rest of the community is catching up with us. We need to look at the next piece, to take new risks, to get out onto the ice."

In Earl Hamilton's words, we will do well if we keep in mind our fundamental purpose, "to practice and teach nonviolence. Yes, we need to talk the talk, but we **have** to walk the walk." That walk means taking risks, putting our jobs on the line, even, as both Gandhi and King said, being willing to die to end oppression. They practiced what they preached. From that perspective, taking risks, even great risks, is the only way we can create gender, racial, and economic justice at the Center for Nonviolence or in any other program for peace and social justice.

ENDNOTES

[1] At the time, we were particularly influenced by Brownmiller's analysis of rape in war. For a more recent discussion of patriarchy and militarism, see Brock-Utne, 1985 and 1988.

[2] See Ginsberg for an excellent discussion of love in nonviolent action, especially 163-164.

[3] I co-directed the Center for Nonviolence from 1981-1986. In 1987, I took a leave of absence from the Center to write a book. Since then, I have been a co-facilitator in batterers groups, a member of the Men's Collective, and an intake officer. I interviewed 13 staff members in 1992: Five (of seven) women, one youth of 17, and seven (of 10) men. The interviewees included six African Americans and seven whites. All references in the body of the text are to staff members. See Schon, Whyte, Katz and Thorson, and Katz for discussions of methodology of primary research. Katz' insight was particularly important to me: "As we understood more how activists thought, felt and behaved, we not only adjusted our appreciation of them and their world, but also became more convinced of the perniciousness of the commonly believed separation of the world of theory and the world of action" (1990, 116). I do find that my fellow activists at the Center for Nonviolence spend time reflecting on what they are doing, and I also believe that my involvement at the Center has enriched my university teaching and research.

[4] 7A. See Kamarck as well for the reference to William Julius Wilson in this paragraph.

[5] See Marable's recent book of essays on race, class and power.

[6] Simone de Beauvoir's The Second Sex was the first book in the second wave of feminism to examine the patriarchal norm of woman as Other.

[7] The literature on domestic violence is extensive and growing. Major books include Gordon, Loseke, Martin, Pleck, Roy, Schechter, Straus (1980, 1990), and Walker. See Warters for an excellent analysis of domestic violence, especially as it relates to men's programs, and Almeida and Bograd, who advocate "the inclusion of non-violent men from the community as part of the intervention plan" (245).

[8] Pence and Paymar, 11, and the quote in the next paragraph of text. The materials in their Educational Curriculum can only be used after receiving training from the DAIP.

[9] 30.

REFERENCES

Almeida, Rhea V. and Michele Bograd. (1990). "Sponsorship: Men Holding Men Accountable for Domestic Violence." Journal of Feminist Family Therapy. Vol. 2, No. 3/4, pp. 243-259.

Beams, John Murphy. (1991). "A Meditation on Men's Spirituality." Changing Men 23, pp. 30-31.

Brock-Utne, Birgit. (1985). Education for Peace: A Feminist Perspective. New York: Pergamon.

----------------. (1988). Feminist Perspectives on Peace and Peace Education. New York: Pergamon.

Brownmiller, Susan. (1975). Against our Will: Men, Women and Rape.

Beauvoir, Simone de. (1953). The Second Sex. New York: Knopf.

Freire, Paulo. (1986). Pedagogy of the Oppressed. New York: Continuum.

Ginsberg, Robert. (1990). "The Paradoxes of Violence, Moral Violence, and Nonviolence." In V.K. Kool (ed.) Perspectives on Nonviolence. New York: Springer-Verlag. pp. 161-167.

Gordon, Linda. (1988). Heroes of their Own Lives. New York: Viking.

Kamarck, Elaine Ciulla. (1992). "Fathers are Key to Stopping Violence." Fort Wayne Journal-Gazette. May 12, p. 7A.

Katz, Neil H. (1990). "Evaluation Research of Nonviolent Action." In V.K. Kool, (ed.) Perspectives on Nonviolence, pp. 109-117. New York: Springer-Verlag.

Katz, Neil H. & S. Thorson. (1988). "Theory and Practice: A Pernicious Separation." Harvard Negotiation Journal. Vol. 4, No. 2, April, pp. 115-118.

Loseke, Donileen. (1992). The Battered Woman and Shelters. Albany: State Univ. of New York Press.

Marable, Manning. (1992). The Crisis of Color and Democracy: Essays on Race, Class and Power. Monroe, ME: Common Courage Press.

Martin, Del. (1976). Battered Wives. New York: Pocket Books.

Pleck, Elizabeth. (1979). Domestic Tyranny. New York: Oxford University Press.

Roy, Maria. (1977). Battered Women. New York: Van Nostrand Reinhold.

Schechter, Susan. (1982). Women and Male Violence. Boston: South End Press.

Schon, Donald A. (1983). The Reflective Practitioner: How Professionals Think in Action. New York: Basic Book Publ.

Straus, Murray. (1980). Behind Closed Doors. Garden City, N.Y.: Anchor.

--------------. (1990). Physical Violence in American Families. New Brunswick, N.J., Transaction.

Walker, Lenore. (1979). The Battered Woman. New York: Harper & Row.

Warters, William. (1991). "The Social Construction of Domestic Violence and the Implications of 'Treatment' for Men Who Batter." Men's Studies Review. Volume 8, No. 2, pp. 7-16.

Whyte, William Foote. (1984). Learning from the Field. Beverly Hills, CA: Sage Publ.

CHAPTER 17

Protective Accompaniment: How Peace Brigades International Secures Political Space and Human Rights Nonviolently

Patrick G. Coy

Conflict between individuals and groups brings forth diverse responses from those involved directly in the conflicts, and from others who are on the sidelines. One such response is that of interpositioning, physically interposing oneself between the conflicted parties in the hope of deterring attack and reducing the level of violence. Interpositioning of this sort is often useful on the interpersonal level, where the parties in conflict are two individuals (O'Gorman & Coy, 1992). Indeed, simply stepping between two hostile individuals, literally pulling them apart, or stepping between them and talking down the emotions of the antagonists is a practice used by children on playgrounds, teachers in classrooms, and parents in the home on nearly a daily basis.

But interpositioning is less often utilized between groups on national or international levels. This has begun to change, however, especially since 1965 when the United Nations established a formal framework for peacekeeping operations. The U.N. has subsequently deployed peacekeeping forces to Lebanon, Cyprus, Cambodia, Namibia, Croatia, and many other places where unarmed observer forces, or lightly-armed buffer forces were deemed expedient. Not surprisingly, there is a growing field of literature examining U.N. peacekeeping operations of this sort (James, 1990; Rikhye, 1984; Wiseman, 1983).

Although U.N. efforts at interpositioning in national and international conflict garner serious attention from the mass media and from the scholarly community, there is also a rich tradition of nonviolent interpositioning in national and international conflict that is outside the efforts of the U.N. This tradition, which includes initiatives from various international nongovernmental organizations, is not nearly as well known. With only a few exceptions it has received far too little study in the professional literature (Hare and Blumberg, 1977; Keyes, 1978; Weber, 1991).

What follows is meant to be a contribution to that literature. This chapter examines the nonviolent interpositioning efforts of Peace Brigades International (PBI). While PBI's main deployments are in Guatemala (beginning in 1983), El Salvador (beginning in 1987) and Sri Lanka (beginning in 1989), due to space limitations I will focus primarily upon the Guatemala program.

I will sketch the developments leading to the founding of the Guatemala project, and proceed to an examination of the various social and political dynamics at play in PBI interpositioning. I argue that Peace Brigades International's use of "first world" nonviolent escorts for endangered "third world" human rights and political activists is a creative, and ultimately helpful use of the privileges that accrue to citizens of first world nation-states. While not supporting the value-laden connotations inherent in "first world" and "third world," I use the terms here for convenience and ease of reading. I further suggest that this sort of transnational citizen peacemaking can be an important first step in breaking the hegemonic grip of the nation-state in international affairs.

But all is not rosy in PBI's experiment in nonviolence. I also examine the potential pitfalls in PBI's attempt to exploit positions of first world privilege in their nonviolent interpositionary work. Most notable here are the issues of promoting first world cultural hegemony and paternalism. And I conclude with some reflections on future trends in the practice of unarmed international peacekeeping, especially as it is practiced by transnational social movement organizations like PBI.

History

Peace Brigades International was founded in September, 1981, in Canada by a group of internationals, many of whom were long involved in independent nonviolent interpositioning efforts. In constituting PBI, its founders relied on the experience of the World Peace Brigade (Walker, 1979), and the Cyprus Resettlement Project (Hare, 1984).

The PBI "Founding Statement" describes an ambitious work load that goes far beyond simple nonviolent interpositioning. It encompasses "nonpartisan missions which may include peacemaking initiatives, peacekeeping under a discipline of nonviolence, and humanitarian service." The document further claims that PBI will have the "capability to mobilize and provide trained units of volunteers. These units may be assigned to areas of high tension to avert violent outbreaks. If hostile clashes occur, a brigade may establish and monitor a cease-fire, offer mediatory services, or carry on works of reconstruction and reconciliation."

By May, 1982, plans were well under way to field the first brigade. A PBI advance delegation toured Central America on an information-gathering mission, visiting major conflict areas, meeting with government and church officials, and with popular and community groups.

In Guatemala, human rights violations, death squad activity, forced relocations of indigenous communities and overall political repression had marked social and political life for some time. But Guatemalan President Rios Montt announced a "political opening" to begin in March, 1983. The opening would relax the severe restrictions on political activity in Guatemala. In January and February, 1983, another PBI exploratory delegation spent four weeks in Mexico, Guatemala, El Salvador and Panama. Honoring a precept of intermediate theory, which calls for extensive information gathering and trust building amongst the conflicted parties by the intervener (Curle, 1986; Young, 1967), the team met with a full range of people working on various Guatemalan human rights, political organizing, and refugee issues. PBI decided to deploy an ongoing team in Guatemala, coinciding with the "political opening."

The team's functions were threefold: (1) develop contacts across the political spectrum of the country; (2) monitor and report human rights abuses (at the time, no human rights group operated openly in the country; (3) and use its international presence as an intermediary or interpositionary element (*PBI Reports*, March, 1983). When PBI evaluated the program and decided in December, 1983 to continue the Guatemalan project, the expanded and revised statement of the project's goals deemphasized human rights reporting. But it also included an increased emphasis on peace education, and on what was to become a central aspect of PBI programs in Guatemala, El Salvador, and Sri Lanka: protective accompaniment for those threatened with physical violence and intimidation. (*PBI Reports*, January, 1984).

Nonviolent Interpositioning

This "escort" work is at the heart of PBI's interpositionary activities. It is the key contribution PBI is making to the field of unarmed peacekeeping. An activist who receives a death threat, a threat of physical violence, or who is in fact attacked, may request accompaniment by PBI. The organization then conducts interviews to determine compatibility between PBI and the activist. One criterion is that the activist or the group can not use, or promote the use of violence.

Unarmed volunteers then accompany those threatened, literally interposing their bodies between the target and the likely source of the threat. For example, when walking down the sidewalk, the PBI member will walk between the activist and the street, from whence most abductions or attacks come. This accompaniment may be 24 hours a day, it may be only while the threatened person is in public, or it may be only while they are in contact with certain people or social elements. The particulars of the accompaniment vary according to the needs of the situation.

Sometimes the "client" is not simply one individual, but a group. Examples include: PBI maintained an around-the-clock presence at the Lunafil textile factory near Guatemala City when striking workers occupied the plant for a year beginning in June 1987; representatives from the Village Communities in Resistance of the Mountains (indigenous villagers resisting service in the government-sponsored "civil patrols") came to the capitol for the first time to argue their case and tried to safeguard their human rights, with PBI providing protective accompaniment; PBI furnished a protective presence at rallies of the Organization of the Parents and Family Members of the Disappeared in Maratuwa, Sri Lanka. These are just three examples drawn from hundreds in the ten years of PBI activity.

PBI escorts are always foreign nationals. The presence of unarmed international escorts functions as a deterrent since violence or freedom restrictions directed toward foreign nationals often brings much higher political costs than the same actions directed at local citizens. This general rule (which is subject to exception) is further exploited by PBI since it primarily uses escorts who are citizens of first world, western nation-states. PBI thus takes advantage of the unequal structural power relations in the world, theoretically granting the escorts and their clients a heightened degree of safety or immunity. In the event a client and their PBI escort is arrested, escorts from first world nation-states have tended to be accorded better treatment than PBI escorts from third world nation-states (Bilski, 1989).

But any immunity enjoyed by PBI team members is far from total; a former member of the team in Guatemala called it "quasi-immunity." A sampling of violent incidents involving PBI demonstrates this point.

In Guatemala on August 15, 1989, the office of GAM (Mutual Support Group), a community organization accompanied by PBI, was bombed. And the PBI residence a mile away was also attacked with hand grenades on the same day. Although both buildings were occupied, the bombings caused no injuries (*Boston Globe*, 1989, August 30, editorial). On December 20, 1989, three PBI team members returning to the PBI residence suffered serious lacerations when they were attacked by men with knives. Since they were not robbed and a pocketbook that was dropped during the attack was not picked up by the attackers, it seems likely that intimidation motivated the attack.

Beyond demonstrating that PBI's immunity is only partial, these attacks are interpreted by some in the organization as proof of the effectiveness of PBI's work. They are said to indicate a desire to intimidate the organization into abandoning it's mission in Guatemala (*Peace Brigades*, April, 1990).

When the U.N. fields unarmed peacekeeping and observer forces, they often gain quick respect simply because of the fact that they represent the U.N. and are a symbol of the entire international community (Galtung, 1976a; Urquhart, 1983, p. 166). But unarmed peacekeeping forces fielded by nongovernmental organizations are far less fortunate. This is another reason why PBI puts primarily first worlders in the field.

First world media outlets dominate and control the dissemination of world news (Chomsky & Herman, 1988). However sad, it remains true that first world social movement organizations can more easily generate international media attention than can third world organizations. To attack a campesina agitating for her land rights in the rural Guatemalan high lands is one thing; indeed, such a scene often seems like the tree that no one heard fall in the forest. But to attack that same campesina and her first world nonviolent escort--who is equipped with a camera and notebook--may be something completely else: now not even the leaves can fall without being heard.

Ed Griffin Nolan was the media coordinator for Witness for Peace in the mid-1980s. In its program in Nicaragua around the contra war, Witness for Peace utilized elements of interpositonary nonviolence. Griffin-Nolan (1991) says that the use of first worlders as "human shields" drew the media "like flies to honey." By using first worlders in this way, PBI exploits the mass media's fixation on first world news, making it work on behalf of those whose voice and struggle is seldom acknowledged.

To compliment the escorting, PBI created an Emergency Response Network (ERN). Similar to the "Urgent Action Appeals" of the human rights organization, Amnesty International (Clark & McCann, 1991), the ERN consists of hundreds of people across the world who have signed on to receive fast-breaking PBI information calling for immediate action on a crisis case. That action takes the form of letters, faxes, telexes or phone calls to key government officials to correct the perceived injustice. One example, from El Salvador, will suffice to demonstrate.

In July, 1991, PBI team member Phil Pardi, a U.S. citizen, was escorting Gloria and Ernesto Zamora. Gloria is with the Association of Women for Dignity and Life; Ernesto is the brother of Ruben Zamora, then Vice President of the National Assembly and the leader of the opposition party. Both Gloria and Ernesto received death threats for several weeks previous to the attack. Along with Pardi, their PBI escort, their vehicle was stopped by uniformed men who searched them. All three were handcuffed and spirited away in a National Police truck. Within hours, PBI's Emergency Response Network members sent 350 telexes to President Cristiani, and made hundreds of phone calls to the U.S. Embassy. By the next morning, the three were released, unharmed, with no charges and no explanations. However, a U.S. embassy officer reportedly told Pardi upon his release, "You have one hell of a lot of friends" (Funding Letter, PBI-USA Development Office, Fall, 1991).

This example demonstrates another creative use by PBI of the privileges that accrue to first worlders in the present world order. The team members cultivate contacts and access to a relatively influential diplomatic corps (E. Kinane, personal interview, September 3, 1991), whose governments can bring diplomatic pressures to bear in the short term, and perhaps even political, economic and trade pressures in the long term. Many third world countries are dependent on economic aid from first world nations and are therefore susceptible to pressures from their benefactors. The October, 1990 European Economic Community aid package to Sri Lanka, for example, called on Sri Lanka to improve human rights conditions and made explicit reference to a PBI accompaniment case.

Richard de Zoysa was a journalist who was abducted in Columbo in February, 1990. His mother, however, recognized the abductors as high-level members of the Columbo police force; she enlisted a lawyer to help her press for prosecution. They both received death threats, so PBI provided accompaniment for her and her lawyer for nearly the whole of 1990. But PBI also put them in touch with sympathetic European diplomatic contacts, including the Swedish and Dutch embassies. This may have contributed to the case being cited in the EEC aid report as an example of why the EEC wanted to see Sri Lanka make more progress in protecting human rights (E. Kinane, personal interview, November 21, 1992).

I have shown that PBI's nonviolent interpositioning is more than simply physically deflecting the attack. It also involves a deterrence based on symbolic and real geopolitical power relations that are exploited by PBI to decrease the likelihood of violence, while increasing the political space within which local activists can work. This concept of political space deserves further exploration.

Political Space

Peacekeeping is often used by the powerful to control the less powerful, by the few to prevail over the many. Such control usually aims to preserve the political and economic status quo. Here peacekeeping may be motivated less by a desire for peace founded on justice, and more by a fear that conflict or violence could lead to significant social change. But the waging of conflict can be an important tool for the oppressed, winning recognition and legitimacy for groups that are traditionally cut out of the political marketplace. Moreover, it can lay bare the reality of structural violence and unleash powerful social forces that upset the status quo.

In vertical conflict situations such as these, where social and political domination is a factor, proponents of peacekeeping must take special care not to simply halt direct violence and thereby safeguard ongoing structural violence. Johan Galtung (1976b) argues that the only form of peacekeeping that is tenable in situations of vertical conflict is third party intervention on the side of the first or oppressed party. Arguing that keeping peace by ending direct violence is not a worthy goal because it serves the status quo, Galtung suggests that peacekeeping in situations of vertical violence must also be concerned with abolishing structural violence.

Galtung's reflections on peacekeeping relate to wars of liberation, but his analysis applies equally well where the oppressed are organizing for change nonviolently. Galtung says that modern wars of liberation involve liberating territories and turning them into models of what the future state shall be once structural violence is abolished. While peacekeeping in a horizontal conflict (between equals) can be likened to a two-way wall separating the parties, Galtung (1976b) suggests that peacekeeping in vertical conflicts (between unequals) should be more like a one-way wall, permitting freedom fighters out to expand the liberated territories, but preventing oppressors from getting in. This conception of peacekeeping is acutely aware of unequal social and political factors, and it puts the tools of peacekeeping to work for the oppressed. Since Peace Brigades International works only with those who do not use violence, Galtung's terminology does not exactly fit, but the basic notions do.

If we exchange "freedom fighter" for "human rights activist," and "liberated territories" for "political space," we are talking about essentially the same phenomenon. The one-way wall that PBI endeavors to build is there to give human rights and political activists political space to use as an organizing base. Somewhat like Galtung's freedom fighters, the goal is to secure more political space so a just society can begin to be prefigured in the structures, processes, and work of the social change organizations themselves.

This dynamic is illustrated by how the PBI house in Guatemala City was used in the mid-1980s. The PBI office and residence became an important meeting space for human rights, labor and indigenous activists, especially those working to end the "disappearances" (Lernoux, 1982) that rocked Guatemala in the 1970s and 1980s. In 1984 the PBI house hosted monthly meetings of relatives of the disappeared. On the night *New York Times* reporter Steven Kinzer attended, over 100 people were at the meeting (Kinzer, 1984).

In 1985, these meetings led to the formation of GAM, the Mutual Support Group of relatives of the disappeared, the first independent human rights group to survive in Guatemala. By September, 1986, GAM membership reached 1,300, most of whom were indigenous women whose villages and families suffered many political disappearances. GAM's bold and vocal organizing gained it increasing attention, both domestic and international. Many of the groups leading activists began receiving violent threats; they asked for and received PBI protective accompaniment. PBI continued to host the GAM meetings during the crucial first three years of the group's existence, a concrete expression of the "one-way wall" advocated by Galtung.

When coupled with the nonviolent escorting of GAM members, this demonstrates the kind of political space PBI strives to create with and for local activists. Knowing that one is not alone in the struggle, but standing with others for basic human rights and a new social and economic order, can enliven people to exploit what Richard Falk (1992, p. 132, 136) calls the "hidden spaces," those social pockets empty of state control that are present in even the most authoritarian and repressive state structures.

Implications

In his search for a more viable world order, Falk (1992, pp. 83-99) argues that the nation-state system itself is a powerful brake on the creation of a more people-centered politics, what he names "humane governance." Falk calls not only for the development of alternative problem-solving frameworks that are not inherently prejudiced toward the political status quo, but for alternative "problem-stating" frameworks.

How an issue is stated, or framed to the larger public, and who frames it, can have far-reaching effects on how the issue is perceived and responded to (Snow, Rochford, Worden, and Benford, 1986; Snow & Benford, 1988). Indeed, how an issue is framed can determine what the issue is since framing has the potential to be defining. Simply by being "on-site" and recording the violent reality of social and political oppression in a manner that increases understanding of the forces undergirding the oppression, PBI takes an important first step in building a viable transnational movement for social and political rights. Moreover, nongovernmental organizations like Peace Brigades International can frame the issues in a way that highlights the extraordinary struggle of ordinary people for control over their own lives. The far-flung appeal of this framing is hard to miss.

By framing the issue in such a way that the threatened third world activist remains the central actor--the main focus of the story and no less than the subject of her history--PBI invites very concrete responses from others, reciprocal actions of resistance and involvement. The focus on the personal--on the human--helps prepare the soil of the soul for the seed of solidarity. I suggest that part of the long-term significance of PBI's work lies herein. For such solidarity builds bridges between peoples, tearing at the interlocking but artificial barriers that define the nation-state system. The information-gathering aspect of PBI's work--striving to be the voice of the voiceless by publicizing human rights violations--and the Emergency Response Network itself, are both examples of the kind of "globalism from below" that is the pathway to a more viable and humane way of conceiving of international relations, and ultimately of the future itself (Falk 1992, p. 124; Kavaloski, 1990). This more viable conception is illustrated by the way PBI volunteers often explain their willingness to take risks on behalf of others suffering persecution. They understand their own liberation to be tied up with the liberation of their third world colleagues (E. Kinane, personal interview, September 3, 1991).

But Peace Brigades International's reliance on first world citizens has both strengths and weaknesses. While this paper has focused on the strengths, the potential drawbacks are many and deserve attention here, in the hope they can be explored more fully in a later study.

The current relationship between the first and third worlds cannot be separated from its history. That history is defined by colonialism and various manifestations of neocolonialism. While neocolonialist patterns are often less visible and appear on the surface to be more hospitable, in fact they are little less exploitive than their predecessors (Amin, 1989; Nandy, 1987; Sklar, 1979). Given that history and current reality, it would behoove first worlders working in the third world to be extraordinarily sensitive to issues of paternalism and the exporting of ideologies and solutions.

Peace Brigades International seems vulnerable here given its reliance on citizens from first world nation-states. Because PBI exploits the fact that the safety and well-being of first worlders is valued more highly in the current world order than is the safety and liberty of third worlders does not put PBI outside of that system of unequal worth. An argument could be made that PBI's use of and reliance upon the system of unequal worth--even though PBI exploits the current system's weaknesses to the advantage of third worlders in the short run--also serves to bolster the current world order in the long run by continuing to grant it credence. Here we must at least acknowledge, if not in fact resolve, a familiar dilemma in social change work: whether to focus on reform or on radical, substantive change. To the degree that PBI is able to focus on the work of local and indigenous social movement organizations to reconstitute community and reclaim social institutions, it is less vulnerable to the danger of simply perpetuating the current world order.

PBI will not offer its services to anyone who has used or promotes the use of violence as a means of social change. This rule raises still more issues. While not exactly a forced imposition of views or tactics, these conditions may, in fact, be perceived or experienced as constraining by third worlders. These conditions can hardly, in any event, be separated from the larger issue of cultural hegemony which so colors relations between the first and third worlds (Hoogvelt, 1982; Roxborough, 1979).

Concluding Reflections

After a decade of increased use and prominence, the United Nations peacekeeping forces received the Nobel Peace Prize in 1988. There are at present many proposals to further expand the work of the U.N. peacekeeping forces to include such tasks as humanitarian relief, drug interdiction, combatting terrorism, and coordinating development projects in conflicted areas. (Rikhye, 1990). Now that the Cold war paralysis that afflicted the U.N. has abated, the agency is moving from ad hoc peacekeeping initiatives to institutionalizing its peacekeeping activity. Hence some of these proposals may eventually be undertaken by U.N. peacekeeping forces.

Likewise peacekeeping endeavors launched outside of the U.N. may also increase. Indeed, the numbers of non-U.N. efforts rose significantly in the 1980s. And as more people become aware of peacekeeping and interpositioning in the 1990s through the increased prominence of the U.N. efforts, it seems likely that increased interest and respect will also accrue to non-U.N. efforts.

Already a network of North American churches and synagogues are active as "companion communities" to Central American political refugees living in Mexico but preparing to return to their home villages. These companion communities befriend the refugee communities, sending delegations to accompany them on their often dangerous journeys to resettle their homelands. The delegations serve as buffers, deterrents, and the eyes of the world community.

In January, 1993, for example, the first negotiated return of Guatemalan refugees will occur under the Central American Peace Accords. Five thousand of the 45,000 refugees currently residing in officially recognized camps in Mexico will be the first to test whether a safe return can be made to their homelands in Guatemala. The refugees successfully negotiated with the Guatemalan government for the right of international accompaniment during their return and resettlement. Among the nongovernmental organizations sending delegations to accompany their return are PBI, Witness for Peace, and Going Home.

Maximally, it is hoped that delegations like these and the ongoing accompaniment of PBI actually deter human rights violations and offer some protection for populations traditionally at risk. If so, that is a significant contribution, especially in the lives of those individuals who have already experienced oppression and the loss of loved ones. Minimally, it is hoped that the availability of protective accompaniment is a factor in helping those at risk decide how to respond to those risks. For past violence, coupled with the threat of future violence and oppression, is frequently enough to make some feel they have few choices other than surrendering their human rights.

But these transnational citizen peacekeeping initiatives also serve as something more, something that reaches beyond this moment in time, and beyond the lives of the individuals receiving nonviolent accompaniment. These initiatives can be likened to a sign, a symbol that points away from the constricting boundaries of the nation-state system, and toward a new globalism, one that arises out of the experience of solidarity in the shared struggle to create a different, more humane future.

REFERENCES

Amin, S. (1989). Eurocentrism. New York: Monthly Review Press.

Bilsky, A. (1989, December 4). Under suspicion: a peace activist's chilling experience. Macleans. p. 52.

Chomsky, N., & Herman, E.S. (1988). Manufacturing Consent: The Political Economy of the Mass Media. New York: Pantheon.

Clark, A.M., & McCann, J.A. (1991). Enforcing International Standards of Justice: Amnesty International's Constructive Conflict Expansion. Peace and Change (4), 379-398.

Curle, A. (1986). Non-Official Mediation in Violent Situations. Leamington Spa, U.K.: Berg Publishers.

Falk, R. (1992). Explorations at the Edge of Time: The Prospects for World Order. Philadelphia: Temple University Press.

Galtung, J. (1976). Three Approaches to Peace: Peacekeeping, Peacemaking, and Peacebuilding. In Peace, War and Defense: Essays in Peace Research (Volume II). Oslo: International Peace Research Institute, 282-304.

_____ (1976). Some Factors Affecting Local Acceptance of a U.N. Force. In Peace, War and Defense: Essays in Peace Research (Volume II). Oslo: International Peace Research Institute, 240-263.

Griffin-Nolan, E. (1991). Witness for Peace: A Story of Resistance. Louisville: Westminster/John Knox Press.

Guatemala's Sad Chapter. (1989, March 30). Boston Globe [editorial].

Hare, P.A. (Ed.) (1984). Cyprus Resettlement Project: An Instance of International Peacekeeping. Beer Sheva, Israel: Ben-Gurion University.

Hare, P.A., & Blumberg, H.H., (Eds.). (1977). Liberation Without Violence. Totowa, NJ: Rowman and Littlefield.

Hoogvelt, A.M. (1982). The Third World in Global Development. London: Macmillan.

James, A. (1990). Peacekeeping in International Politics. New York: St. Martin's Press.

Keyes, G. (1978). Peacekeeping By Unarmed Buffer Forces: Precedents and Proposals. Peace and Change (5), 3-10.

Kinzer, S. (1984, July 21). Guatemalans organize to find missing kin. New York Times.

Lernoux, P. (1982). Cry of the People: The Struggle for Human Rights in Latin America. New York: Penguin.

Mackinlay, J. (1989). The Peacekeepers: An Assessment of Peacekeeping Operations at the Arab-Israeli Interface. London: Unwin Hyman.

Nandy, A. (1987). Traditions, Tyranny, and Utopias: Essays in the Politics of Awareness. New Delhi, India: Oxford University Press.

O'Gorman, A. & Coy, P.G. (1992). Houses of Hospitality: A Pilgrimage Into Nonviolence. In P.G. Coy, (Ed.), A Revolution of the Heart: Essays on the Catholic Worker. (rev. ed.). Philadelphia: New Society Publishers.

Rikhye, I.J. (1984). The Theory and Practice of Peacekeeping. New York: St. Martin's Press, 1984.

Rikhye, I.J. (1990). The Future of Peacekeeping. In I.J. Rikhye, & K. Skjelsbaek, (Eds.), The United Nations and Peacekeeping. London: Macmillan, 1990.

Roxborough, I. (1979). Theories of Underdevelopment. London: Macmillan.

Sklar, H. (Ed) (1979). Trilateralism. Boston: South End Press.

Snow, D.A., Rochford, E.B., Wordemn, S.K., & Benford, R.D. (1986). Frame Alignment Processes, Micromobilization, and Movement Participation. American Sociological Review (51), 464-481.

Snow, D.A., & Benford, R.D. (1988). Ideology, Frame Resonance, and Participant Mobilization. In B. Klandermans, (Ed.). International Social Movement Research, (Vol. 1). Greenwich, CT: JAI Press.

Staff. (1989, August 30). Guatemala's sad chapter. Boston Globe. [editorial].

Staff. (1984, January). PBI Reports. (PBI newsletter, available from: PBI, Box 1233, Harvard Square Station Boston, MA 02238).

Staff. (1990, April). Peace Brigades. (PBI newsletter, available from: PBI, Box 1233, Harvard Square Station Boston, MA 02238).

Urquhart, B.E. (1983). Peacekeeping: A View from the Operational Center. In H. Wiseman, (Ed.). Peacekeeping: Appraisals and Proposals. New York: Pergamon Press.

Walker, C.C. (1979). Nonviolence in Africa. In S.T. Bruyn & P.M. Rayman, (Eds.), Nonviolent Action and Social Change. New York: Irvington Publishers.

Weber, T.A. (1991). "Unarmed Peacekeeping and the Shanti Sena." Unpublished doctoral dissertation, LaTrobe University, Bundoora, Australia.

Wiseman, H. (Ed.). (1983). Peacekeeping: Appraisals and Proposals. New York: Pergamon Press.

Young, O.R. (1967). The Intermediaries: Third Parties in International Crises. Princeton: Princeton University Press.

CHAPTER 18

Hannah Arendt on Nonviolence and Political Action

Gail M. Presbey

In this chapter I hope to first describe the joys of political action as Arendt recounts them. Political action, acting in concert with one's peers according to new ideas generated from the group itself, is for her one of the highest forms of self-expression and self-fulfillment. One of the paradigm examples of political action in this sense is in revolutionary activity. But Arendt insists that what goes on in a revolution is not mainly violence, although some violence is usually present; what is mostly involved is people expressing and acting on their opinion. When people gather together in movements, they become powerful, more powerful than the government, and it is this show of power rather than the show of military strength that is the decisive factor in the success of the revolution. Arendt insists, power is not violence; in fact, it is the opposite of violence, and the really successful revolutions need little or no violence.

If this is so, then what do we make of Fanon's account of the oppressed, who find themselves only in the act of revolutionary violence? With the help of Arendt's analysis I will suggest that self-fulfillment is misplaced when attributed to the violent act; rather, it is the act of self-assertion, and once again in the context of acting in concert with one's peers, that is the really freeing, fulfilling, and healing act.

The Joys of Political Action

One of the main reasons for engaging in political action, according to Arendt, is that people experience joy in expressing themselves in public, in debating, in trying to win over others, and deciding issues of importance. Freedom unfolds its charms; political actors enjoy their activity beyond their "duty," according to Arendt.

It is Arendt's insistence that political action is so enjoyable in itself that lends her to use a model for politics based on widespread participation. Arendt cites Sophocles, who stated that the only thing that makes life bearable is political action. But if this is true, why are so few engaging in political action? Arendt says one reason is that they are shut out of the public, political world, and consequently they don't have a chance to taste political action. (Arendt, 1965, p. 281; Parekh, 1981, p. 14).

According to Arendt, political action makes use of the highest human capacities. Political skills and virtues are many. Political action helps people acquire a public identity; it is the context in which people can reveal themselves and thereby discover themselves; it affirms human dignity; it gives people a chance to shape the political world in which they live; it gives people a chance to develop skills of creative imagination, persuasion, and conciliation. (Parekh, 1981, p. 175).

Power, Violence, and Nonviolence

When people act politically together they experience power. What is power? Arendt defines it as the ability to act in concert. When a group is organized, and all members freely agree to engage in a certain action, they are powerful. Parekh describes Arendt's notion of power as the "ability to secure another's energetic cooperation and support." The relationship between those in the same group is one of trust and approval. (Arendt, 1972, p. 143; Parekh, 1981, p. 161).

Arendt is describing here the concept of "power with" or sometimes called "people's power," which is different than the notions of "power over," measured by one's ability to get someone else to do something they really don't want to do. "Power over" involves coercion and often violence, whereas "power with" does not need violence at all, since it is the voluntary cooperation of people in a group. Whenever Arendt uses the term "power" she means it in the narrower sense of "power with."

Arendt explains that "power and violence are opposites." Power itself is never violence, since violence is a sign of the absence of power. Arendt states that to speak of "nonviolent power" is in fact redundant, since power (in the special sense of "power with") implies nonviolence. (Arendt, 1972, p. 155). Arendt preferred the word "power" to the word "nonviolence," and insisted that the pair of opposite terms should be violence and power instead of violence and nonviolence, because she thought that the term "power" had more active and positive connotations, and was more than just the absence of violence.

In many nonviolent activist circles, and in Gandhi's work, the emphasis on active resistance to violent oppression is implicit for them in the term nonviolence; they would not see nonviolence as a quietism or avoidance of responsibility. Arendt points out the inadequacy of Gandhi's earlier term, "passive resistance," asserting that in fact Gandhi's protests that went by that name were the epitome of action, and not passivity at all. Gandhi himself preferred the term "Satyagraha," or "love force," since it stressed the activity the nonviolent resister. (Arendt, 1958, p. 201; Gandhi, 1961, p. 6).

Arendt uses the example of an armed robber as a person who gains our temporary cooperation through the threat of violence. She asserts that that is not power at all, but mere violence. The robber can't get me to freely consent and follow a certain prescribed activity; as soon as the threat of violence is removed, I revert to my former activities. Power, instead, emerges when the threat of violence is not needed, for all freely consent to a certain action and act of their own volition. (Arendt, 1972, pp. 139-40).

Arendt insists that violence is resorted to in weakness, when power fails. A government uses violence when it doesn't have the consent of the people. Violence forces the people to outwardly comply to its wishes. But violence can't reach into the minds and wills of people, so that they will want to comply. Violence is a poor substitute for power and is a sign of the collapsing of the government. Arendt's theory of power favors the people united, not the government armed. (Arendt, 1972, pp. 152-3).

Dynamics of Power between People and Government

Arendt explains that in any government the power always comes from the people, whether it's a representative democracy, King, or tyrant. In each case the people lend their power and support to the government by agreeing to act according to its rules. The people may not have a self-understanding that in some cases they are aiding the government in ruling over themselves, but that is the case. (Arendt, 1958, pp. 200-1). As Arendt explains, power is a relationship, not a property, of those that belong to a group. Individuals are not powerful. If it ever looks like a particular person is "powerful," that person is being empowered by a group. In other words, the others in the group agree with the person and are willing to act in concert with him or her. (Arendt, 1972, p. 143). Arendt did note, however, that rulers can win cooperation and therefore power from the people by lying to them. Propaganda is a way in which a ruler can become more powerful, since it reaches into people's minds and influences them to act of their own volition. However, she saw lying and propaganda as unstable, since the lies could be found out. (Arendt, 1968, pp. 108, 263-4).

Arendt's insight explains why popular revolts against materially strong rulers are often successful. The power involved in the people's consent and support is made apparent when that consent is withdrawn. Arendt refers to Gandhi's experiments with noncooperation as "enormously powerful" and a "successful strategy." (Arendt, 1972, p. 152). Gandhi explains that withdrawing cooperation from a corrupt State is easily understandable and can be safely practiced by huge numbers of people. It doesn't even necessarily involve going out and marching, etc; it can be as simple as staying home from work in a strike or "hartal," or refusing to send one's children to the government school. When the people of India withdrew their consent from the British government, it became impossible for the British to maintain rule there. (Gandhi, 1961, p. 4).

Gandhi explains the dynamics of noncooperation:

Two kinds of force can back petitions. "We shall hurt you if you do not give this," is one kind of force; it is the force of arms, whose evil results we have already examined. The second kind of force can thus be stated: "If you do not concede our demand, we shall be no longer your petitioners. You can govern us only so long as we remain the governed; we shall no longer have any dealings with you." The force implied in this may be described as love-force, soul-force, or more popularly but less accurately, passive resistance. (Gandhi, 1961, pp. 13-4).

Gandhi points out that rulers are dependent on their followers.

Rulers could and have decided to crush nonviolent resistance with violent means. However, there is a "high cost" involved in using violence. Arendt notes that it is very difficult to rule people purely through violence, since they will need constant supervision or restraint. It is much easier to control large numbers of people if their consent can be won. But to totally control them takes vast amounts of resources. Just as a kidnapped person must be guarded constantly, the person who does not consent to a government needs constant supervision or threat. Arendt notes that the whole "concentration camp" enterprise of the Nazis, if concerned merely for efficiency of work output, would have run much easier as a work camp, where people were given low wages but their lives were protected from violence. But to control them through terror and violence takes many more resources and could never be profitable. In fact the camps were a constant economic loss. (Arendt, 1950, pp. 50-1, 54).

If one chooses to kill people instead of trying to rule them through violence, then the "high cost" is the loss of power. A ruler wants someone to rule over; he becomes powerful if people lend him their support. The more people he kills, the less power he could ever have. Arendt explains that tyrants with lesser populations must be moderate so that they still have people to rule. Totalitarianism needs a dense population, since total domination entails great losses of population; yet the warning is that some rulers are willing to kill many people. Hitler decided he could afford to kill the Jews and Poles, and replace them with "Aryans" who were being especially bred to replace them. Where people are rare and hard to replace, they can be more assured that their life will be preserved. (Arendt, 1951, p. 310).

Power's vulnerability is its material and communicative conditions. Power needs prerequisites: the ability to gather together and speak with others. When those prerequisites are taken away, power is crushed or hindered. It is no use denying that superior weapons of violence can obliterate any group, no matter how righteous and committed it is. A group like this can only hope that those with the violence will see the high costs of their action and desist from the slaughter. For example, Arendt notes that the British government could have chosen to slaughter all Indian resisters, but it chose not to. However, she predicts that other rulers and governments may not make the same decision. (Arendt, 1972, p. 152).

Gandhi rejected violence, because he was certain that any seeming "gains" made by violence or coercion were illusory, since if the people were not converted in their hearts, they would revert back to their former behavior as soon as the violence was removed. That's why Gandhi insisted on nonviolent resistance, aimed at changing the oppressor. Exercises of power were preferable to forcing others through violence. A nonviolent revolution would occur by having the old government voluntarily capitulate; then worries of later counterrevolution would be diminished. (Gandhi, 1961, p. 13).

Power, Nonviolence, and the Revolutionary Situation

Oftentimes, since people aren't allowed to act politically in the context of a repressive government, they experience political action in organizing to overthrow the government. As an example, Arendt refers to the memoirs of Rene Char, the French poet who participated in the Resistance for four years. The overwhelming sense of freedom those in the Resistance experienced did not come merely from fighting tyranny, for soldiers were also engaged in that battle. As Arendt explains, "they had become 'challengers,' had taken the initiative upon themselves and therefore, without knowing or even noticing it, had begun to create that public space between themselves where freedom could appear." They were in the position to begin something new, to use their own minds and initiative to try to change their world. And there was a lot of self-fulfillment that came along with that struggle: Arendt notices that Char had discovered "that he who joined the Resistance, *found himself*,' that he ceased to be 'in quest of [himself] without mastery, in naked un-satisfaction,' that he no longer suspected himself of 'insincerity'." There was the self-satisfaction and confidence of someone who knows that he acted on his convictions. (Arendt, 1968, p. 4).

Now the question is, what is the relationship of revolution and violence? Is it the act of violence that gives one such a thrill while engaging in revolution? Arendt wants to insist that it is not the act of violence per se that gives one the feeling of fulfillment; it is rather the participating in "power," as she understands it.

In the light of her conception of power, Arendt analyzes the phenomena of the "revolutionary situation." How is revolution possible? Arendt explains that revolutions are not so much a "military" phenomenon as they are phenomenon of power. Revolution can only happen when the authority of the body politic is disintegrating, when the armed forces won't obey civil authorities. A "revolutionary situation" occurs when the monopoly of violence breaks down, when the soldiers or police no longer obey orders to use their weapons. (Arendt, 1965, pp. 115-6; Arendt, 1972, pp. 147-8).

Arendt explains:

In a contest of violence against violence the superiority of the government has always been absolute; but this superiority lasts only as long as the power structure of the government is intact--that is, as long as commands are obeyed and the army or police forces are prepared to use their weapons. When this is no longer the case, the situation changes abruptly. Not only is the rebellion not put down, but the arms themselves change hands--sometimes, as in the Hungarian revolution, within a few hours . . . Only after this has happened, when the disintegration of the government in power has permitted the rebels to arm themselves, can one speak of an "armed uprising," which often does not take place at all or occurs when it is no longer necessary. Where commands are no longer obeyed, the means of violence are of no use; and the question of this obedience is not decided by the command-obedience relation but by opinion, and of course, by the number of those who share it. (Arendt, 1972, p. 148).

Sometimes the governmental leaders and the soldiers give up and decide not to pursue a civil war because they feel that they are outnumbered by those who hold a different opinion. The hypocrisy involved in asserting that the government represents the people is exposed when the people, in large numbers, make visible their opposition to the government.

Arendt refers to Tocqueville's observation of the fall of the French monarchy in 1848. Tocqueville notes that the monarchy fell "before rather than beneath the blows of the victors, who were as astonished at their triumph as were the vanquished at their defeat." This is another example of how, if the people have the power, violence is superfluous. The opposing government can crumble without need to actually engage in violence. (Arendt, 1965, p. 260).

This refusal of the soldiers or police to use their weapons, and their going over to the side of "the people" instead of the government, is one of the most curious recurring phenomena in history. There are indeed historical examples of this pattern. For example, in the Paris Commune of 1871: when the soldiers of the Central Versailles government were sent to capture the Paris cannon, and were met by both civilian opposition and the City's National Guard, they sided with the people and disobeyed orders. As historian Stewart Edwards describes,

> Events first took a serious turn at Montmartre, when the troops refused to fire on the crowd and instead arrested their own commander, who was later shot. Elsewhere throughout the city officers found they could no longer rely on their men, and in the early afternoon Thiers decided to abandon the capital. (Edwards, 1973, p. 25).

Why do the soldiers change their allegiance? It partly depends on the numbers of people who show their resistance to the government. If there is a large crowd, the soldiers may feel overwhelmed. They may finally realize that their position is not the popular one. It depends partly too on how closely they identify with those who are disobeying the government orders. In the case of the Paris Commune, Frenchmen were reluctant to fire on their own people. There was still a strong bond between the average Frenchman in the military and the Parisians. Unfortunately, that common sympathy was later eroded, through constant government propaganda that the Parisians were radicals destroying France. The reformed Army battled Parisians in their own streets, killing many, until Paris surrendered.

To understand the different roles of power and violence in a revolution, it might help to picture the two extremes, abstracted cases of power and violence. Arendt explains that power needs numbers, whereas violence doesn't. What violence does need is implements. The two extremes would be like this: power is all against one; violence is one against all. In a situation where the people are very powerful, united around a single opinion, and dedicated to a single action, say, the overthrow of a tyrant, there will be no violence at all. If the people are so powerful that even the army and the police join them, there is no one to protect the tyrant with violence. He realizes the game is up, and he must surrender without a fight. At the other extreme, if the people are isolated, disagreeable, or apathetic, a tyrant with a few heavily armed soldiers can effectively terrorize the entire population. (Arendt, 1972, p. 141).

Of course, the real situations of the world are usually a mixture of the two. Arendt notes that power and violence are almost always found mixed with each other. Most revolutions aren't so organized that they can elicit everyone's cooperation, including the soldiers of the tyrant. Consequently they often must resort to violence. And the tyrants usually have a power base in some of the people of their country. Perhaps the support of the richest 10% of the population is enough to make them powerful. Often the organized solidarity of the "masters" is enough to make rule over the people possible, if the people are unorganized. (Arendt, 1972, pp. 149, 151).

What about cases of "nonviolent revolution," where the foreign occupying forces decide to leave, even though they have not been attacked at all by an army? Let's take for example Great Britain pulling out of India in the face of Gandhi's organization of nonviolent resistance on a large scale. He was able to do such a thing because the people were unified behind him on this one simple issue: home rule instead of British rule. But what were the limits of Gandhi's nonviolent campaign? The problem came immediately after independence. A whole nation that was unified by the idea of home rule was now divided in opinion about who would rule or how. And although Gandhi did his best to convince people to sit down and talk about things, the leaders that he had to deal with would not sit down at the table. And the citizens in the villages were divided. The power of the people was broken in two; and where there is loss of power, there is violence. India was engulfed in a Civil War, which resulted in the splitting of the country down religious lines into India and Pakistan.

Arendt, Sartre, and Fanon on Revolutionary Violence

Let's go back to our resistance fighter, Rene Char, whom Arendt used as an example cited earlier in this paper. Is Rene Char fulfilling himself by participating in the group, the nonviolent "power" aspect of his relationship with his peers? Or is he fulfilling himself in the acts of violence he is perpetrating against the enemy (for surely he is engaging in both)? Although Arendt does not comment directly about Char, her comments on Franz Fanon's book *The Wretched of the Earth* lends some insight on this question.

In his book, in which Fanon calls on his experiences during the Algerian Revolution, Fanon suggests that when the oppressed use violence to win their freedom from their oppressor, they are experiencing freedom and fulfillment. They are healed psychologically and physically. As Fanon describes, "At the level of individuals, violence is a cleansing force. It frees the native from his inferiority complex and from his despair and inaction; it makes him fearless and restores his self-respect." (Fanon, 1968, p. 94). This works not only on the individual level but also the social. "The period of oppression is painful, but the conflict, by reinstating the downtrodden, sets on foot a process of reintegration which is fertile and decisive in the extreme. A people's victorious fight not only consecrates the triumph of its rights; it also gives to that people consistence, coherence, and homogeneity." (Fanon, 1968, p. 293).

And Sartre explains in his preface to Fanon's book that the act of killing leads to a birthing: "...to shoot down a European is to kill two birds with one stone, to destroy an oppressor and the man he oppresses at the same time: there remain a dead man, and a free man..." (Fanon, 1968, p. 22). The old, oppressed self dies, and the new, free self lives for the first time. The "net gain or loss" of life here remains stable or increases: before, the oppressor was living well but the oppressed was walking death, was deprived of life, although biologically existing; after the act of violence, yes, there is the corpse, the oppressor's, but the formerly oppressed is now free. The implied conclusion: violence hasn't really "killed." In fact, violence has increased life, made it more worthwhile.

I think that it cannot be denied that a person who was formerly oppressed begins healing when the oppressor is gone. And if that person has had an active role in the abolishing of the oppressor, then it is his or her own act that heals him or herself. Yes, I agree with all of this; but I would like to ask, was it the *violence* itself that healed? Or was it the fact that the person has *acted*? I suggest that it is the experience of acting with others to free oneself that gives these formerly oppressed peoples a new confidence in themselves, a reconciliation with others who were oppressed (where formerly there was competition for survival), and a reconciliation with the world which is now changing its form to a more human shape. It is action which accomplishes all this, and not the fact that the particular action Fanon describes is violence.

The act of violence may be important for other psychological reasons, such as the release of pent-up hostility. Rage longs for expression, and perhaps there is joy in finally expressing one's rage. This joy can be distinguished from the joy of acting with one's peers. Although the joy of revenge can't be overlooked, it is not my focus here. Fanon himself suggests that the joy of revenge can devour the society, and will not provide a sound basis for a new society, whereas as Arendt notes, the joy of acting with one's peers can serve as a foundation for the creation of a new government. Arendt approvingly quotes Barbara Deming's comment on Fanon:

It is my conviction that he can be quoted as well to plead for nonviolence...Every time you find the word "violence" in his pages, substitute for it the phrase "radical and uncompromising action." I contend that with the exception of a very few passages this substitution can be made, and that the action he calls for could just as well be nonviolent action. (Arendt, 1972, p. 168n).

It is at least imaginable that a "radical and uncompromising" nonviolent action would have the same healing qualities that Fanon gives to the violent action. The feeling of acting together as a group, making history, begins a healing process in the oppressed that is immediate, even before any (strategic) gains have been made. In contrast, the acts of violence people commit, even for a "good cause" during a revolution, can leave psychological scars on the perpetrator. (Fanon's appendix is full of case studies of this sort, as will be shown shortly). Although Fanon doesn't use the terminology of "action" as Arendt does, he seems to be describing the same experience. The native is hemmed in; he or she dreams of action. And yet, from the settler's viewpoint, only the settler acts; the native is on the level of inorganic matter, incapable of action. We see in this quote emphasis that action is both beginning and carrying through something new, that will make history:

> The settler makes history; his life is an epoch, an Odyssey. He is the absolute beginning: "This land was created by us;" he is the unceasing cause: "If we leave, all is lost, and the country will go back to the Middle Ages." Over against him torpid creatures, wasted by fevers, obsessed by ancestral customs, form an almost inorganic background for the innovating dynamism of colonial mercantilism. (Fanon, 1968, p. 51).

Although Fanon may partly mean this as a satire on the settler thinking that he or she is God (known in Thomistic circles as creator and preserver), it also shows that the settler knows that he or she is acting, and that the native is not, caught in what Arendt would consider the realm of laboring where there is no action.

But this situation is changed in the fight for decolonization. "Decolonization...transforms spectators crushed with their inessentiality into privileged actors, with the grandiose glare of history's floodlights upon them." (Fanon, 1968, p. 36). In the revolt, the natives break out of their usual mode of mere laborers and become actors. It is this acting that transforms them.

Fanon insists that revolt and struggle are necessary psychological components for revolution. In a section of *Black Skin, White Masks* on "The Negro and Hegel," Fanon explains that there is something amiss when the colonized are handed freedom by the "white masters," as happened in parts of Africa and the Carribean. Hearing the announcement of freedom and saying "thank you" to the white man is not enough to radically change the formerly colonized person into the new being they need to become. (Fanon, 1967, pp. 220-1). Quoting and then commenting on Hegel, Fanon says: "It is solely by risking life that freedom is obtained; only thus is it tried and proved that the essential nature of self-consciousness is not bare existence, is not the merely immediate form in which it at first makes its appearance, is not its mere absorption in the expanse of life." Thus the human reality in-itself-for-itself can be achieved only through conflict and through the risk that conflict implies." (Fanon, 1967, p. 218). Fanon is insisting that freedom must be won with a struggle, in order for the newly freed persons to change their consciousness. To point out the necessity for struggle is helpful; but, as with Deming's quote, and with Gandhi's practical experiments in nonviolent resistance, in a nonviolent resistance there would equally be struggle and risk.

Fanon had repeated experience with both the perpetrators and victims of violence, especially during his time working with patients in Algeria embroiled in the war of independence from France. As a psychiatrist he knew the effects violence had on the psyche of those who inflict and suffer violence. It certainly could not be described as a healing process. Although he admits that the sufferer is harmed more by the violence than the perpetrator, (Fanon, 1968, p. 252n) it is still true that both suffer. The perpetrator especially suffers if he or she is a thoughtful, sensitive person; but even stubborn and unfeeling people are harmed by acting violently.

Fanon gives the example of an Algerian who set off a bomb in a cafe which killed ten nationals from the colonizing country (France). After the war of liberation this Algerian man met some former nationals and found them to be likeable, and in fact in favor of the revolution that had happened. He began to wonder if some of the people he had killed in the cafe were like his new-found friends. Every year on the same date as the bombing he would suffer attacks of insomnia and suicidal tendencies. But, of course, he could not undo his action. (Fanon, 1968, p. 253).

He gives another example of a nineteen year old suffering from depression, insomnia, and hallucinations. The story came out that he and friends had gone to a settler's house. The settler was known to have killed two Algerians. They came to the house at night, but only his wife was there. The wife was terrified, and begged them not to kill her, for she had children, and she had always implored her husband not to become involved in politics. But the man knifed and killed her. Since then he slept badly, with the woman always haunting him in his dreams. His room became invaded with women, each with an open wound in her stomach. (Fanon, 1968, pp. 262-4).

Fanon is equally troubled by seemingly "guiltless" perpetrators as he is by the cases where neuroses and suffering are obvious. He gives the example of two Algerian children, ages 14 and 13, who murder a European child. Fanon quotes the thirteen-year-old's remarks: "We weren't a bit cross with him. Every Thursday we used to go and play with catapults together, on the hill above the village. He was a good friend of ours...One day we decided to kill him, because the Europeans want to kill all the Arabs..." Fanon's discussion with them brings out the fact that he is very disturbed that they so matter-of-factly disregarded their friendship and sympathy with the murdered boy because of the "grown-up people"'s concerns. Fanon notes that the atmosphere of "total war" in Algeria was responsible for the appearance of mental illness in this case. (Fanon, 1968, pp. 270-2).

I suggest that these examples, and myriads of other examples that Fanon himself gives of native Algerians suffering violence, and colonists inflicting harm, and torturers and the tortured, show that violence in itself is destructive to persons on both the giving and receiving ends. Violence causes harm, both physically and psychologically. Violence itself is not a healing act.

Arendt criticizes Sartre for emphasizing only the parts in Fanon's book that call for revolutionary violence, while neglecting the parts where Fanon suggests that violence alone is not enough. In fact, in his book *Black Skin White Masks* Fanon clarifies:

> These truths do not have to be hurled in men's faces. They are not intended to ignite fervor. I do not trust fervor. Every time it has burst out somewhere, it has brought fire, famine, misery.... And contempt for man. Fervor is the weapon of choice of the impotent. (Fanon, 1967, p. 9).

Here Fanon implies that the consequences of violence are more negative than positive. Although Fanon often speaks of violence as the means of humanity recreating itself, he more often speaks of the role of action and education as creating this new humanity. He says that when spectators turn to actors, they become new people. He explains that the "native," with their traits of laziness, crime, etc, was created by the settler; when the settler, during decolonization, is thrown out, the "new humanity" can come to be. "Decolonization is the veritable creation of new men. But this creation owes nothing of its legitimacy to any supernatural power; the 'thing' which has been colonized becomes man during the same process by which it frees itself." (Fanon, 1968, pp. 36-7).

At least as often as Fanon speaks of violent revolution creating the new humanity, he speaks of education creating the new humanity. He warns, "you won't change human beings if you forget to raise the standard of consciousness of the rank-and-file." There is no mention of violence in the last words of his book: "we must turn over a new leaf, we must work out new concepts, and try to set afoot a new man." He explains: "in the end everything depends on the education of the masses, on the raising of the level of thought... political education means opening their minds, awakening them, and allowing the birth of their intelligence." (Fanon, 1968, p. 197). This would be exactly the same advice Arendt would give modern day society.

In conclusion, it is not so much the act of violence as the act of ridding oneself of the oppressor that brings about the new self. So the emphasis on violence is misplaced. It is acting nonviolently together with one's peers to transform one's self and the world that is fulfilling and freeing.

REFERENCES

Arendt, Hannah. (1950). "Social Science Techniques and the Study of Concentration Camps," Jewish Social Studies, vol. 12, pp. 50-4.

Arendt, Hannah. (1951). The Origins of Totalitarianism. New York: Harcourt Brace Jovanovich, New Edition, 1979.

Arendt, Hannah. (1958). The Human Condition. Chicago: The University of Chicago Press.

Arendt, Hannah. (1965). On Revolution. New York: Viking Compass Edition; reprint, New York: Penguin Books, 1985.

Arendt, Hannah. (1968). Between Past and Future: Eight Exercises in Political Thought, Enlarged Edition. New York: Viking Compass Edition, 1968; reprint, New York: Penguin Books, 1985.

Arendt, Hannah. (1972). Crises of the Republic. New York: Harcourt Brace Jovanovich.

Edwards, Stewart, ed. (1973). The Communards of Paris. Ithaca, NY: Cornell University Press, Cornell Paperbacks.

Fanon, Frantz. (1967). Black Skin, White Masks. New York: Grove Press.

Fanon, Frantz. (1968). The Wretched of the Earth, preface by JeanPaul Sartre, trans. Constance Farrington, Evergreen Black Cat edition. New York: Grove Press, Inc.

Gandhi, Mohandas K. (1961). Nonviolent Resistance. New York: Schocken Books.

Parekh, Bhikhu. (1981) Hannah Arendt and the Search for a New Political Philosophy. Atlantic Highlands, New Jersey: Humanities Press.

CHAPTER 19

Teaching Human Rights in the Social Sciences

Joseph Wronka

When I was young and foolish, I used to speak at schools concerning human rights issues. I spoke to audiences as the Group Coordinator for the Fairbanks Chapter of Amnesty International. In Fairbanks, I also taught psychology at the University of Alaska and had a private practice.

What I would do, for example, was, upon the invitation of a local teacher, talk about human rights to a high school class. I would begin my presentation by arbitrarily singling out one or two individuals for talking out inappropriately in class. I would tell them to come to the front of the class. Then, I would in a rather angry tone, begin to yell at them. I would say, for instance, "Can't you see that we are trying to teach a class concerning human rights issues?"

Very, very soon thereafter, I would, immediately tell them that I merely wanted to prove a point. I told them that they were unfortunately the victims of my occasional megalomaniacal tendency to confirm my own hypothesis. In this case, I wanted to illustrate on a micro-scale, feelings that injustice can arouse. Imagine, I would say, how it would feel to be arbitrarily taken, infinitely more arbitrary, than what I just did, from your home in the middle of night, then interrogated, at times violently, and then tortured.

Then, I would do some experimental exercises with the class, such as telling students to pair up with someone. I would first ask them to choose who will be a kind of "grand inquisitor," or torturer, if you will. Then, I would say: "Imagine that you are a grand inquisitor or a torturer, who has no other motive than to break, if not silence the other person forever through torture or intimidation. What would you say or do to your victim? How would you say it? Really try to relive it and experience how being a kind of torturer might be!"

Then I asked them to trade places. The grand inquisitor would be a victim and the previous victim a grand inquisitor. Then, we reflected together upon the experience. In general, students discussed how easy it was to play the role of a potential torturer, but how terrible it felt to be a victim. When we did the same exercise again, with bags over each others' heads, thereby ensuring, more or less, anonymity, students noticed that it was even easier to be abusive to the other person. These experiences, I would also point out are slightly, but vaguely, similar to Zimbardo's work on roles and Milgram's work on obedience.

But, that was in my younger days when I thought that human rights was something that only human rights groups, like Amnesty International, defined. According to Amnesty International (1991), they have three goals: the release of prisoners of conscience i.e. people detained for their beliefs, color, sex, ethnic origin, language or religion. Recently, they expanded their mandate to also include imprisonment for homosexual orientation (Matas and Wiseberg, 1992). Furthermore, these prisoners of consciousness may not have used or advocated violence. Amnesty International also calls for fair and prompt trials for all political prisoners and an end to the death penalty and torture or other forms of degrading punishment. While I do not in any way want to discount the importance of Amnesty's work, especially since Amnesty "openly acknowledges that it deals with only a small part of the total human rights picture" (Matas and Wiseberg, 1992, p. 30), it is important to point out that their work is extremely limiting.

For a more inclusive definition of what human rights are, it is important to turn to the Universal Declaration of Human Rights, endorsed by the United Nations General Assembly with no dissenting vote on December 10, 1948. An American, Eleanor Roosevelt, chaired the committee which drafted the Declaration. Pope John Paul II (1979) has referred to it as "a milestone in the long and difficult struggle of the human race," the United Nations (1985) called it "the authoritative definition of human rights standards" and, scholars (Humphrey, 1976; Vasak, 1982; Buergenthal, 1988; Rosensweig, 1988; Lillich, 1989, 1990; Reisman, 1990) and federal court cases, such as *Filartiga v. Pena* (1980), have declared it "customary international law."

Human rights scholars Thomas Buergenthal and W. Michael Reisman have asserted, for instance: "Today, few international lawyers would deny that the Declaration is a normative instrument that creates legal obligations for the member states of the U.N." (p. 29) and "The Universal Declaration of Human Rights, a document then describing itself as 'a common standard of achievement'...[is] now accepted as declaratory of customary international law" (p. 867).

In the precedent setting case of *Filartiga v. Pena* (1980), which in the United States ruled against a Paraguayan official Pena-Irala, for the torture and death of a seventeen year-old boy, Joel Filartiga, the judges declared that the United States had jurisdiction to try that case, ruling that the prohibition against torture is a violation of customary international law, "as evidenced and defined by the Universal Declaration of Human Rights" (630 F.2d 884-885). The Declaration, however, is not without its detractors. The U.S. Ambassador to the U.N. Jeane J. Kirkpatrick, for instance, exclaimed that it is "a letter to Santa Claus....Neither nature, experience, nor probability informs these lists of 'entitlements,' which are subject to no constraints except those of the mind and appetite of their authors" (Laqueur and Rubin, 1990, p. 364).

I have taught psychology and sociology, on the college level both full-time and on an adjunct basis, having a masters in psychology and a doctorate in social policy. I would like to share with you now how I use the Universal Declaration in my classes, going beyond more traditional notions of human rights concerns.

The Universal Declaration of Human Rights consists essentially of four basic sets of rights. They are:

1)   the right to human dignity, (Article 1);

2)   the right not to be abused by government, often referred to as civil and political rights, like freedoms of speech, the press, and religion, (Articles 2-21);

3)   the right to be provided for by government, which is to reflect the will of the people, referred to as economic and social rights, like guarantees to health care, shelter, food, employment, and education (Articles 22-27); and

4)   the right to solidarity, that is the right to intergovernmental cooperation to solve such global problems as environmental pollution and war (Articles 28-30).

When I ask students to read the Universal Declaration, they do not appear to seriously entertain notions of economic, social, and solidarity rights. That is, they think that the United States, at least as they have been taught, is exemplary in regards to human rights. I would agree that in regard to civil and political rights, the United States appears outstanding. A government official in this country, for example, would neither torture someone nor make him or her "disappear" in the middle of the night, for his or her political or religious beliefs. There appears much truth to the fact that Americans continue to enjoy, basic rights, like freedoms of speech, the press, religion, and assembly.

However, in regard to economic and social rights, the United States, the richest country in the world, is one of the worst, if not the worst offender in the western industrialized world. Students, on the whole, find it difficult to imagine the existence of these alleged human rights violations.

I merely cite relevant data. On some economic and social indices, like life expectancy, illiteracy, and infant mortality, referred to as the PQLI or Physical Quality of Life Index, the United States does not appear to do very well. For instance, the longevity rate of African-American men in the inner cities and Native American men on reservations is approximately 46. This longevity rate is *below* the average life expectancy of 50 in the *developing* world. Furthermore, "adult 'functional' literacy may not exceed 85%" (*Britannica World Data Annual*, 1991, p. 728). We also rank twenty-third in infant mortality rates. These problems are in addition to estimates of 30 million Americans who lack health insurance, 3 million homeless, and an average of 7.1% Americans unemployed (Harvey, 1989).

And, if solidarity rights mean in reality, international distributive justice, I ask my students if we Americans who consume 40% of the world's resources, yet possess only 4% of the world's population, really care about human rights on the global scale. As Shridath Ramphal (1984), Commonwealth Secretary to the United Nations, eloquently asserted:

It does the cause of human rights no good to inveigh against civil and political rights deviations while helping to perpetuate illiteracy, malnutrition, disease, infant mortality, and a low life expectancy among millions of human beings. All the dictators and all the aggressors throughout history, however, ruthless, have not succeeded in creating as much misery and suffering as the disparities between the world's rich and poor sustain today.

I ask if the arms build up in the so-called Third World (i.e. the poorer nations of the world) is in response to this blatant global injustice.

Much of my students' initial reactions are outrage. "Love it or leave it," I am told. "Why that's socialism, that's communism!" With the fall of the Soviet Union, one should know that communism is dead. To be sure, at a recent *human rights* conference, which dealt in large measure with the changes in the Soviet Union, I applauded the release of all political prisoners in the Soviet's hideous *Gulag*. Yet, when I recounted that with the trend toward a free market in the Soviet Union, there are increasing reports of homelessness, high infant mortality rates, illiteracy, and violence, I did not appear to be taken seriously. I was told that these issues had nothing to do with a human rights conference, that they were issues of social policy and not human rights. A major speaker told me, after I recounted these growing social problems, that "If you say anything else you will make me cry."

Having worked as a clinician in predominantly poverty stricken areas of the United States, the failure of our government to meet basic human needs, does make me cry. Some of you may be familiar with the Rorschach card of the boy sitting, I would say, quietly in front of a house. As one poverty-stricken child remarked, "This is a sad boy cause there's all sort of rats inside the house and bugs and everything 'n cockroaches and he got nobody to talk to. Everyone's fighting and everything." Occasionally, some clients would come to a session with their arms in a cast. I would ask what happened. They would tell me that they "got into a pipe fight and some guys got their heads really bashed in." I also heard of teachers and janitors that were "stabbed in the stomach" by students. When I worked in a Native American village for a couple of years, there were also similar stories of violence. I would always wonder why a lot of the stories that I had heard and seemed credible, were never on the news? Did people really care what was happening in the inner cities or in Native American communities. Because I had worked in such communities, students were eager to hear about my experiences.

Often, I begin my discussion of human rights at the beginning of a course, like Introductory Psychology. There is an article I use, for example, by Mark Rosensweig (1988) called "Psychology and United Nations Human Rights Efforts." But, unfortunately, that article and most of the literature concerns itself primarily with civil and political rights. As Steiner (1991) has commented, Americans do not tend to perceive economic and social rights as human rights.

To make up for this lack, I use some of my own research, which has recently been published as a book, *Human rights and social policy in the 21st century* (1992). In that book, I examine constitutional change, as a primary prevention strategy to deal with many issues that social scientists deal with, such as domestic violence and child abuse. The etymological meaning of the word "Constitution" means choice. Constitutions, therefore, reflect decisions that society makes to solve problems.

David Gil (1973), in *Violence Against Children*, for instance, has noted that lack of a job and/or problems on a job, can displace anger, for example, to the boss, onto the children or spouse. As the Universal Declaration clearly states in Article 23 and in language meant not for a doctorate in jurisprudence, but for the layperson: "Everyone has the right to work, to free choice of employment, to just and favorable conditions of work and to protection against, unemployment and to form and to join trade unions for the protection of his interest." Comparing United States federal and state constitutions with the Universal Declaration, I found, for example, that not one constitution definitively asserted the rights to work, shelter, health care, or the majority of economic and social rights proclaimed in the Universal Declaration of Human Rights. Modification of these constitutions, to assert these rights, should assist in the implementation of these rights for all.

While students initially were resistant to viewing such rights to health care, education, work, food, clothing, and shelter as human rights, they tended, however, as the semester progressed, to become quite enthusiastic to advance the cause of all human rights. They wanted to form, for example, watchgroups that monitor compliance with the Universal Declaration, which meant conformity with all the rights of the Declaration.

Human Rights is a powerful social construct which has the power to transform human needs into legally mandated rights. The human rights movement is growing by leaps and bounds, and notions of economic, social, and solidarity rights are increasingly becoming part of this movement. We, as teachers, must assist in the efforts to create a socially just world, in order that, as the Declaration states: "It is essential that man [humanity] is not compelled to have recourse, as a last resort, to rebellion against tyranny and oppression, that human rights should be protected by the rule of law." Were the riots in the aftermath of the Rodney King decision related to government failure to respond to basic human rights?

The Renaissance philosopher Desiderius Erasmus in his well known *Praise of Folly* attempted to expose the snobbishness, vanity and immorality of many of the so-called leaders of that time. So, too, must we show to all, how the realities of, for instance, unemployment, poverty, lack of health care, and lack of security in old age and disability, which are contrary to the Universal Declaration of Human Rights, stand in marked contrast to the pledge that the nations of the world made in the wake of the horrors of World War II. Today, while I have no control over my age, I do, however, have control over whether I am foolish and hopefully I am now more foolish. In my folly, I hope that I can continue to point out government failure, if not hypocrisy, to provide for human needs.

One caveat, however, is in order. Human rights, can at times, mask, as the contemporary political-philosopher Irving Kristol (1990) exclaimed, "hidden agenda." That is, concern for humanitarian concerns, to stem human rights abuses, may serve as a pretext for war. Was, for example, the American Civil War fought to free the slaves, or to cater to the demands of a growing industrial North, in search of cheap labor? Was Hitler's attack on Poland really to stop the "shameful mistreatment of Germans in the Polish Corridor" as he put it, or to regain lost territories? Was President Bush's military intervention in the Persian Gulf really to stop the human rights abuses of the tyrannical Saddam Hussein or to keep Kuwait in control of its oil fields?

Martin Luther King's statement that "What we learn from history is that we do not learn from history" is undoubtedly true when pertaining to war. War solves nothing. But non-violent measures do. When the Barons in drawing up the Magna Carta, surrounded King John at Runnymede in 1215, they could have easily killed this tyrant and his small entourage. Still today, no one knows for sure why they didn't kill King John because violence was the usual way to deal with tyrants. Instead, they drew up a document, the Magna Carta, and today, many of its clauses which, for instance, called for trial by a jury of peers, prohibited the arbitrary taking of property or arbitrary arrest, detention, or exile and expressed the right to travel have stood the test of time and found their way in many beautiful documents, like the American Bill of Rights, the French Declaration of the Rights of Man and the Citizen, the Universal Declaration of Human Rights and the most recent Declaration of Human Rights and Freedoms, drafted in 1991 by the former Soviet Union, now the Commonwealth of Independent States. It is also noteworthy that that last document states in article 1: "Every person possesses natural, inalienable and inviolable rights and freedoms. *They are sealed in laws that must correspond to the Universal Declaration of Human Rights* (italics added)."

So, we must be prepared when students quickly assert that violence must be met with violence. Waging war with Saddam Hussein for torturing innocent civilians (which appears true), or physically attacking government officials for allowing the inner cities to fester (which appears true) is completely counterproductive. There are certainly more creative non-violent ways, evidenced in part by the Magna Carta, to advance the cause of human rights.

I have only touched upon some issues, like the increasing legal status of the Universal Declaration, the important, but limited scope of human rights groups like Amnesty International, the paucity of understanding of economic, social and solidarity rights, and the problems of hidden agenda. To be sure, there are other issues like the problem of the priority of rights. Is freedom of speech, for example, more important than the right to food? Officially, our government says "yes;" most governments at the U.N. say "no." There is also the notion that every right has a corresponding duty. The right to food, for instance, means the duty not to overconsume; the right to health care means the duty to keep healthy. I did not even mention the long train of covenants, such as the International Covenant on Civil and Political Rights, the International Covenant on Economic, Social, and Cultural Rights and the Convention on the Rights of the Child. I hope, however, that this sharing of my experiences in the classroom and brief examination of human rights issues should wet your appetites enough to consider teaching the important, but at times, risky business of human rights.

REFERENCES

Amnesty International. (1991). Amnesty International Report 1991. New York: Author.

Britannica world data annual. (1991). The nations of the world (pp. 538-739). Chicago: Encyclopedia Britannica.

Buergenthal, T. (1988). International human rights law. St. Paul, MN: West.

Filartiga v. Pena-Irala. 630 F. 2d 876 (1980).

Gil, D. (1973). Violence against children: Physical child abuse in the United States. Cambridge: Harvard University Press.

Harvey, P. (1989). Securing the right to employment. Princeton: Princeton University Press.

Humphrey, J. (1976). The International Bill of Rights: Scope and implementation. William and Mary Law Review, 17, 524-541.

Kristol, I. (1990). Human rights: The hidden agenda. In W. Laqueur and B. Rubin (Eds.), The human rights reader (pp. 391-404). New York: New American library.

Laqueur, W., & Rubin, B. (Eds.). (1990). The human rights reader (rev. ed.). New York: New American Library.

Lillich, R. (1989). The Constitution and international human rights. American Journal of International Law, 83,(4), 855-862.

----------. (1990). The United States Constitution and international human rights law. Harvard Human Rights Journal, 3, 53-82.

Matas, D. & Wiseberg, L.S. (1992, Winter). At 30 something, Amnesty comes of age. Human rights tribune, 1, (1), 29-30.

Pope John Paul II. (1979). U.S.A. The message of justice, peace and love. Boston: Daughters of St. Paul.

Ramphal, S. (1984). For inquiries contact: Shridath Ramphal, Commonwealth Secretary of the United Nations. United Nations Plaza, New York, New York.

Reisman, M. (1990). Sovereignty and human rights in contemporary international law. American Journal of International Law, 84, 866-876.

Rosenzweig, M. (1988). Psychology and United Nations human rights efforts. American Psychologist, 43, 79-86.

Steiner, H. J. (1991). Diverse partners: Non-governmental organizations in the human rights movement. Cambridge: President and Fellows of Harvard College.

United Nations. (1985). Secretary-General sketches U.N. successes, hopes at 40th anniversary celebration in San Francisco (pp. 10-14). United Nations Chronicle (Vol. XXII, #4). New York: Author.

Vasak, K. (1982). Distinguishing criteria of human rights. In K. Vasak and P. Alston (Ed.), The international dimensions of human rights (Vol. 1) (pp. 3-10). Westport, CT: Greenwood.

Wronka, J. (1992). Human rights and social policy in the 21st century: A history of the idea of human rights and comparison of the U.N. Universal Declaration of Human Rights with U.S. federal and state constitutions. Lanham, MD: University Press of America.

THE UNIVERSAL DECLARATION OF HUMAN RIGHTS

Preamble

Whereas recognition of the inherent dignity and of the equal and inalienable rights of all members of the human family is the foundation of freedom, justice and peace in the world,

Whereas disregard and contempt for human rights have resulted in barbarous acts which have outraged the conscience of mankind, and the advent of a world in which human beings shall enjoy freedom of speech and belief and freedom from fear and want has been proclaimed as the highest aspiration of the common people,

Whereas it is essential, if man is not to be compelled to have recourse, as a last resort, to rebellion against tyranny and oppression, that human rights should be protected by the rule of law,

Whereas it is essential to promote the development of friendly relations between nations,

Whereas the peoples of the United Nations have in the Charter reaffirmed their faith in fundamental human rights, in the dignity and worth of human person and in the equal rights of men and women and have determined to promote social progress and better standards of life in larger freedom,

Whereas Member States have pledged themselves to achieve, in cooperation with the United Nations, the promotion of universal respect for the observance of human rights and fundamental freedoms,

Whereas a common understanding of these rights and freedoms is of the greatest importance for the full realization of this pledge,

Now, Therefore, The General Assembly Proclaims
This Universal Declaration of Human Rights

as a common standard of achievement for all peoples and all nations, to the end that every individual and every organ of society, keeping this Declaration constantly in mind, shall strive by teaching and education to promote respect for these rights and freedoms and by progressive measures, national and international, to secure their universal and effective recognition and observance, both among the peoples of Member States themselves and among the peoples of territories under their jurisdiction.

Article 1

All human beings are born free and equal in dignity and rights. They are endowed with reason and conscience and should act towards one another in a spirit of brotherhood.

Article 2

Everyone is entitled to all the rights and freedoms set forth in this Declaration, without distinction of any kind, such as race, color, sex, language, religion, political or other opinion, national or social origin, property, birth or other status. Furthermore, no distinction shall be made on the basis of the political, jurisdictional or international status of the country or territory to which a person belongs, whether it be independent, trust, non-selfgoverning or under any other limitation of sovereignty.

Article 3

Everyone has the right to life, liberty and security of person.

Article 4

No one shall be held in slavery or servitude; slavery and the slave trade shall be prohibited in all their forms.

Article 5

No one shall be subjected to torture or to cruel, inhuman or degrading treatment or punishment.

Article 6

Everyone has the right to recognition everywhere as a person before the law.

Article 7

All are equal before the law and are entitled without any discrimination to equal protection of the law. All are entitled to equal protection against any discrimination in violation of this Declaration and against any incitement to such discrimination.

Article 8

Everyone has the right to an effective remedy by the competent national tribunals for acts violating the fundamental rights granted him by the constitution or by law.

Article 9

No one shall be subjected to arbitrary arrest, detention or exile.

Article 10

Everyone is entitled in full equality to a fair and public hearing by an independent and impartial tribunal, in the determination of his rights and obligations and of any criminal charge against him.

Article 11

(1) Everyone charged with a penal offence has the right to be presumed innocent until proved guilty according to law in a public trial at which he has had all the guarantees necessary for his defence.

(2) No one shall be held guilty of any penal offence on account of any act or omission which did not constitute a penal offence, under national or international law, at the time when it was committed. Nor shall a heavier penalty be imposed than the one that was applicable at the time the penal offence was committed.

Article 12

No one shall be subjected to arbitrary interference with his privacy, family, home or correspondence, nor to attacks upon his honor and reputation. Everyone has the right to the protection of the law against such interference or attacks.

Article 13

(1) Everyone has the right to freedom of movement and residence within the borders of each State.

(2) Everyone has the right to leave any country, including his own, and to return to his country.

Article 14

(1) Everyone has the right to seek and to enjoy in other countries asylum from persecution.

(2) This right may not be invoked in the case of prosecutions genuinely arising from non-political crimes or from acts contrary to the purposes and principles of the United Nations.

Article 15

(1) Everyone has the right to a nationality.

(2) No one shall be arbitrarily deprived of his nationality nor denied the right to change his nationality.

Article 16

(1) Men and women of full age, without any limitation due to race, nationality or religion, have the right to marry and to found a family. They are entitled to equal rights as to marriage, during marriage and at its dissolution.

(2) Marriage shall be entered into only with the free and full consent of the intending spouses.

(3) The family is the natural and fundamental group unit of society and is entitled to protection by society and the State.

Article 17

(1) Everyone has the right to own property alone as well as in association with others.

(2) No one shall be arbitrarily deprived of his property.

Article 18

Everyone has the right to freedom of thought, conscience and religion; this right includes freedom to change his religion or belief, and freedom, either alone or in community with others and in public or private, to manifest his religion or belief in teaching, practice, worship and observance.

Article 19

Everyone has the right to freedom of opinion and expression; this right includes freedom to hold opinions without interference and to seek, receive and impart information and ideas through any media and regardless of frontiers.

Article 20

(1) Everyone has the right to freedom or peaceful assembly and association.

(2) No one may be compelled to belong to an association.

Article 21

(1) Everyone has the right to take part in the government of his country, directly or through freely chosen representatives.

(2) Everyone has the right of equal access to public service in his country.

Article 22

Everyone as a member of society has the right to social security and is entitled to realization, through national effort and international co-operation and in accordance with the organization and resources of each State, of the economic, social and cultural rights indispensable for his dignity and the free development of his personality.

Article 23

(1) Everyone has the right to work, to free choice of employment, to just and favorable conditions of work and to protection against unemployment.

(2) Everyone, without any discrimination, has the right to equal pay for equal work.

(3) Everyone who works has the right to just and favorable remuneration ensuring for himself and his family an existence worthy of human dignity, and supplemented, if necessary, by other means of social protection.

(4) Everyone has the right to form and to join trade unions for the protection of his interests.

Article 24

Everyone has the right to rest and leisure, including reasonable limitation of working hours and periodic holidays with pay.

Article 25

(1) Everyone has the right to a standard of living adequate for the health and well-being of himself and his family, including food, clothing, housing and medical care and necessary social services, and the right to security in the event of unemployment, sickness, disability, widowhood, old age or other lack of livelihood in circumstances beyond his control.

(2) Motherhood and childhood are entitled to special care and assistance. All children, whether born in or out of wedlock, shall enjoy the same social protection.

Article 26

(1) Everyone has the right to education. Education shall be free, at least in the elementary and fundamental stages. Elementary education shall be compulsory. Technical and professional education shall be made generally available and higher education shall be equally accessible to all on the basis of merit.

(2) Education shall be directed to the full development of the human personality and to the strengthening of respect for human rights and fundamental freedoms. It shall promote understanding, tolerance and friendship among all nations, racial or religious groups, and shall further the activities of the United Nations for the maintenance of peace.

(3) Parents have a prior right to choose the kind of education that shall be given to their children.

Article 27

(1) Everyone has the right freely to participate in the cultural life of the community, to enjoy the arts and to share in scientific advancement and its benefits.

(2) Everyone has the right to the protection of the moral and material interests resulting from any scientific, literary or artistic production of which he is the author.

Article 28

Everyone is entitled to a social and international order in which the rights and freedoms set forth in this Declaration can be fully realized.

Article 29

(1) Everyone has duties to the community in which alone the free and full development of his personality is possible.

(2) In the exercise of his rights and freedoms, everyone shall be subject only to such limitations as are determined by law solely for the purpose of securing due recognition and respect for the rights and freedoms of others and of meeting the just requirements of morality, public order and the general welfare in a democratic society.

(3) These rights and freedoms may in no case be exercised contrary to the purposes and principles of the United Nations.

Article 30

Nothing in this Declaration may be interpreted as implying for any State, group or persons any right to engage in any activity or to perform any act aimed at the destruction of any of the rights and freedoms set forth herein.

CHAPTER 20

Exercises in Nonviolent Action

Theodore Herman

The purpose of this chapter is to offer a few exercises for training oneself or other people in nonviolent action. Exercises such as these, whether performed for some specific occasion or reported on after they have occurred, make us aware of how much we can learn from actual experience once we begin looking. And that realization can be the stimulus that many of us need to use nonviolence purposely in our daily lives.

In order to reveal some of the varieties of nonviolence, we offer both a simple and a more extended definition of the word, followed by a conceptual framework that leads to designing specific exercises for designated purposes.

"The word itself has many meanings, even to the same person. This, however, is not unusual, because many words have different meanings and are constantly acquiring new ones. Just as the words 'peace', 'war', 'love', and the like are used to mark different conditions, 'nonviolence' is also used quite broadly, especially in its religious and ethical context." (Herman, 1991). A general definition that expresses the negative connotation of the word would be: Nonviolence is a way to resolve conflicts without the use or threat of physical force.

To give meaning to this definition through action, we can identify four kinds of action that cover most of the ideas in the literature to date. Thus

> Nonviolence is both an attitude and a course of action that leads both an individual and a group of people to resist tyranny and injustice other than by physical force, and to build a community of caring by the reconciliation of adversaries. It also has a positive meaning as people strive to remove the causes of violent conflict, both human and environmental.

Whether the action is confrontational or restorative, the effort is always to devise new ways of thinking and acting in order to achieve a more peaceful relationship. The question of whether the emphasis on action rules out the Daoist teaching of *wu wei*--the action of no action--can be left to those who wish to explore this ancient East Asian teaching (Liu, 1991). A less benign meaning of nonviolence would reveal its use to suppress dissent, a condition all too familiar to people in many parts of the world. In any case, nonviolence provides a rich field for understanding any society's values, institutions, and techniques, while putting it into action becomes a creative option for people everywhere.

In seeking to use that four-part definition given above, I have found the simple conceptual framework set out below quite helpful to generate ideas, identify attitudes, and indicate relationships. The actual exercises will illustrate some of them as shown on the pages that follow.

Ideally the exercises should involve a group of no more than 20 people, as different as possible in physical characteristics and cultural background, and conducted in a room that permits free movement rather than in a lecture hall with fixed chairs in rows. Whether or not the participants are strangers to each other, the exercises selected should fill from six to eight hours, if each of the seven categories is attempted. The time would also include a brief discussion after each exercise, and two or three extended refueling breaks where some sharing of experiences might continue. It is not advisable to do all of the seven categories in one day, and certain parts might be repeated as desired, especially as people offer their own exercises as a creative option.

A further caution--there is no guarantee that such exercises will convert a non-believer to nonviolence with the first encounter. For some, it might be more convincing to carry out some nonviolent action, either alone or with someone already involved, while others might "catch fire" eventually after doing some of the exercises according to the framework below (Herman, 1991):

TABLE I

Framework For the Meanings of Nonviolence

Personal or Individual		*Group*	
1.	Transformation or psycho-spiritual change	4.	Nonviolent struggle and civilian-based defense
2.	Pacifism or non-retaliation in kind	5.	Conflict resolution
3.	Reconciliation	6.	Removing the causes of violent conflict
		7.	Developing a sound relationship with the earth

"It is easy to make connections between most of these forms, although there does not seem to be any necessary numerical order of influence. For example, most people who practice #2 or #3 would have experienced #1, while #5 would probably reflect some aspects of #3. A national or international policy for #7, generally regarded as protection of the earth's environment, would combine #5 and #6. In short, the flows can move in any direction and involve several forms together, leading to a more unified way of life.

"Also, these forms are not walled off in exclusive categories. For example, noncooperation and civil disobedience are just as important under #3 as under #4, even though they might be justified differently. And anyone who experiences a strong change in personal outlook, as in #1, stands a good chance of moving through the other six forms from a personal to a global outlook. Obvious examples are William Penn, Leo Tolstoy, Gandhi, and Martin Luther King, Jr., but many other outstanding people could also be listed". (Herman, 1991) Each began at one point and grew to include all the others.

Exercises for Training in Nonviolent Action

1.   *Personal transformation or psycho-spiritual change*

1.1.   With chairs in a large circle, sit quietly together and relax muscles. Within your own sphere you are in control and can quiet your ego.

1.2.   Stand in a circle for childish touchy-feely exercises alongside people who differ in appearance. Place all jewelry, watches, money, memo books, letters, etc., on the floor under your chair. The circle revolves several places in the same direction so that no one is close to his/her original seat.
        Expresses a sense of common humanity and trust in working and laughing together to overcome negative stereotypes and fears often buttressed by physical possessions and occupational status. (CCRC)

1.3.   Mark with contrasting symbols or colors, five items in the daily newspaper that express Violence, and five for Nonviolence. Explain your choices. (This is best done for several days before these exercises to give people time to explore.)
        Widens one's range of experience in recognizing both of these aspects of human behavior.

1.4.   In your regular life over the next few days, perform some different act of nonviolent intent, write the story briefly, and report to the group at the next meeting. (This could be a regular activity.)

Encourages each person to observe and act. Gives training in organizing and explaining an often-moving experience.

2. *Pacifism or non-retaliation in kind*

2.1.   Who in the group has ever been discriminated against for some reason not connected with actions or behavior? How did you respond?
Reveals the habit of negative stereotyping and the deep hurt to the victim.
Did your own response give you and the other person any lesson for the future? What was the lesson? (see Smith, Note 1).

2.2.   In a sport of body contact or a contest of strong rivalry, salute your opponent's good actions as soon and as often as possible.
Gives respect to both persons in place of avoidance, but without reducing the quality of the contest.

3. *Reconciliation*

3.1.   What did he say? Two people should choose a subject about which they honestly disagree, but which is neither silly or highly inflammatory. Each lists on a slip of paper the points that support his/her position. Then each speaks for about five minutes at normal speed while the other jots down those points in the order given. After both have finished, each listener briefly repeats in turn the points made by the other in the same order, but without first looking at his/her notes. Such listening can also be done with a taped speech, or in a group when two or three speakers offer different views on a common subject.
Reminds us to pay careful attention to another without interruption or silent refutation.

3.2.   Describe an important confrontation that you have had with another person, the outcome, and how it might have been conducted differently to the benefit of BOTH parties. Ask for suggestions from others present.
Shows the importance of good listening and of putting oneself in the other's place. Draws on the helpfulness of other people in the group as they realize the common needs of human beings.

4. *Nonviolent struggle and civilian-based defense*

4.1.   Design a scenario for nonviolent struggle, or base it on some story in literature or in the current news. (See the attached scenario for this exercise enacted at Elizabethtown College, 23 October 1990, page 7) Shows eight steps in organizing and conducting a nonviolent action that united the participants, conducted negotiations, displayed nonviolent power, and settled for a modest gain.

4.2. Additional learning comes from analyzing a real action, such as France halting nuclear weapons tests in the South Pacific in 1992 after open nonviolent struggle by Greenpeace (*New York Times*).

Shows strong commitment at great personal risk. Demonstrates the importance of widespread publicity by the weaker challenger.

5. *Conflict resolution (between groups)*

5.1. Perform a skit or simulation of a group confrontation that includes as many of those present as possible. It should be within people's real experience rather than something far away and long ago. In the evaluation, the contrast with #3. Reconciliation between individuals should show how much harder and uncertain 5.1 is because members of a group usually have different roles, aims, and prejudices. Solving a specific conflict does not necessarily lead to reconciliation between the opposing groups' members.

Resolving conflicts between groups work works best when the individual members are in harmony with each other, both within and across the groups.

6. *Removing the causes of violent conflict*

6.1. Select a serious local conflict known to all present and ask for suggestions on the causes, both systemic and overt, that led to it. (Dividing into small groups for part of the time may be useful to open up the discussion, but the whole process needs good leaders.)

Shows the need to understand the human and social conditions involved. Reveals the participants' own values and outlooks. Should bring a recognition of the need to bring those involved in local conflict into the process of social change.

6.2. Share examples from the humanities--literature, biography, religion, and the arts--that move people to deepen their commitment to peace and justice as individuals committed to nonviolence.

Creates an appreciation for human values common to all people. Encourages the participation of all as a way to build community.

7.   *Developing a sound relationship with the earth*

      7.1.   Promote a spontaneous action to clean up a public space, as the room where the participants are now engaged.

                Makes everyone aware of our hesitation to act upon our professed care for the environment. Shows how group action can be used to support individuals in public caring, and raises questions of each person's motives. (Both Gandhi and King emphasized doing good without seeking praise as part of the non-attachment required for true nonviolence.)

      7.2.   Prepare a campaign against a powerful local polluter and carry it into action as in 4.1. above.

                Requires convincing all parties involved that all of us and our descendants live on the same planet.

In conclusion, it seems to me that the most important of the seven forms of nonviolence shown in Table I is the first, the personal transformation. And the transformation can only take place by putting our nonviolence into action. That is why, I believe, we should be educating our world about the heroes and heroines of peace, those who dare to speak truth to power through their actions.

THE ORANGE EXPERIMENT

Contributed by Amina Smith, Director AFSC Lancaster (Pa.) Peace Education Project, who specializes in prejudice reduction workshops.

*   to recognize how similar human beings are to one another and how differences make each person unique and special

*   to recognize the advantages of getting to know others before judging them

Time: 45 minutes

Materials: An orange for each student (or potatoes or similar leaves from the same tree)

Procedure:

1.   Each student chooses an orange from a bowl that is passed around the circle.
2.   Students take time to get to know their orange, giving it a name, a history, a personality.
3.   Each student introduces his/her orange to the person sitting next to him/her, sharing all the personal information.

4.   Several students introduce their oranges to the class. If time permits, each student can introduce his/her orange.

5.   All the oranges are collected and mixed around in the bowl. A show of hands can be taken to see how many students believe that everyone will be able to identify his/her own orange.

6.   Students are called up in groups of 4-5 to try to pick their orange out of the bowl of oranges.

7.   After everyone (or almost everyone) has been reunited with their orange, the teacher leads a discussion centered around the following questions:

      *   What do you think was the purpose of this experiment?

      *   What is the same about each orange? What is different about each orange?

      *   Let's relate this experiment to human beings. What is the same about every human being? What is different about each human being?

      *   Which differences among people affect us the most strongly?

      *   Are there advantages and disadvantages to having differences?

      *   Have you ever been judged unfairly from the outside?

Note: This experiment works well in a large group of 40 or a smaller group of 15.

SCENARIO ON NONVIOLENCE AT ELIZABETHTOWN COLLEGE,
23 OCTOBER 1990

IDENTIFY THE PROBLEM OF BROAD APPEAL

        Democracy in education

        Specific example: Persuade instructor to try a new method for a new issue. Discuss alternative solutions to the Gulf crisis

RESEARCH THE FACTS (STRATEGY SESSIONS)

        Nature of the group, nature of the adversary and his resources
        Organization of the protest, and possible leader: KIRSTEN CONRAD

BUILDING UNITY

        Group stands up, deep breathing together
        Puts valuables on floor

DISCUSS CHANGE WITH ADVERSARY IN SPIRIT OF TRUST IN HIS/HER GOODNESS

Specific change is put in larger terms to win his/her understanding

ADAMANT ADVERSARY STICKS ON INTERESTS (?) or POSITION (?) or BOTH

Group begins disruptive behavior
> Parade around room shouting "Emancipate E'town", "Conrad for leader"
>
> Sits down anywhere (not in original seats)

Adversary threatens disciplinary action

GROUP SHOWS WILLINGNESS TO SUFFER FOR CAUSE, BUT NOT TO HATE ADVERSARY

Leader reminds group to have faith in the future because cause is right and adversary will recognize this also some day

NEGOTIATION OF CONFLICT

Leader and adversary agree to one-day discussion of Gulf crisis
> All participants must do homework on the events and on the issues:
>> No war because all life is sacred
>>
>> Belief that all people agree that life is sacred
>>
>> Must put self in other's place
>>
>> What are the long-time impacts of a peaceful settlement, incl. justice vs. reconciliation?

RECONCILIATION WITH ADVERSARY

Use of classroom disruption for specific change in program
Hope to broaden E'town College's hierarchical system of education
Extend to American education in general (!)

NOTE

[1] Smith Note, p. 6. This is another example of an innovative exercise to show how to recognize our tendency to stereotype people, whether unfavorably or favorably.

REFERENCES

Herman, T., (1991). A Conceptual Framework of Nonviolence for Peace Research, International Journal of Group Tensions, 21.1, 3-15.

Liu Xiaogan, (1991). Wuwei (Non-Action): From Laozi to Huainanzi, Taoist Resources, 3.1, 41-56.

CCRC. Useful guides to such warm-up exercises for small children and adults alike are given in Sharing Space, bulletin of Children's Creative Response to Conflict, Fellowship of Reconciliation, P.O. Box 271, Nyack, NY 10960-0271, issued 3/year.

New York Times, April 9, 1992.

Contributors

Herbert H. Blumberg
(Goldsmiths' College
University of London)
Department of Psychology
Haverford College
Haverford, PA 19041

Kenneth E. Boulding (Deceased)
Institute of Behavioral Sciences
University of Colorado at Boulder
Campus Box 483
Boulder, CO 80309-0483

Michael Britton
453B South 2nd Avenue
Highland Park, NJ 08904

Patrick Coy
712 Ostram Avenue
Syracuse University
Syracuse, NY 13244-2340

Ian A. Harris
University of Wisconsin
Dept. of Education & Comm. Studies
School of Education
P.O. Box 413
Milwaukee, WI 53201

Theodore Herman
Ex-Professor, Colgate University
2030 Rosewood Drive
P.O. Box 215
Cornwall, PA 17016-0125

Richard Johnson
Peace Studies
Indiana University
Ft. Wayne, IN 46805-1499

Joanne Joseph
Department of Psychology
SUNY Institute of Technology
P.O. Box 3050
Utica, NY 13504-3050

V. K. Kool
Department of Psychology
SUNY Institute of Technology
Utica, NY 13504-3050

Jeff A. Mann
Psychology Department
Wheaton College
Norton, MA 02766

Stephen C. McConnell and co-workers
Wright State University
Ellis Human Development Institute
9 North Edwin C. Moses Blvd.
Dayton, OH 45407
(co-authors, Jill Alexander, Barry
Duncan, and Debra Merrifield)

Donna Nagata
Department of Psychology
University of Michigan
580 Union Drive
Ann Arbor, MI 48109-1346

Gail Presbey
Marist College
Division of Humanities
Poughkeepsie, NY 12601-1387

Milton Schwebel
Graduate School of Applied and
  Professional Psychology
P.O. Box 819
Piscataway, NJ 08855-0819

Manisha Sen
Dept. of Applied Psychology
University of Bombay
Kalina, Bombay
INDIA

Richard V. Wagner
Department of Psychology
Bates College
Lewiston, ME 04240

Michael G. Wessells
Department of Psychology
Randolf-Macon College
Ashland, VA 23005

Lynn W. Woehrle
P.A.R.C.
712 Ostram Avenue
Syracuse, NY 13244-2340

Joseph Wronka
9 Phoenix Road
Auburn, MA 01501